SOVIET POLICY AND THE CHINESE COMMUNISTS 1931–1946

STUDIES OF THE RUSSIAN INSTITUTE
COLUMBIA UNIVERSITY

Soviet Policy and the Chinese Communists

1931–1946

BY CHARLES B. McLANE

1958 • Columbia University Press • NEW YORK

The transliteration system used in this book is based on the Library of Congress system, with some modifications. In the case of Chinese proper names which have been transliterated, or transcribed, directly from Russian and Comintern sources, the normal English transliteration, according to the Library of Congress system, is given in brackets. Many of these names, however, are obscure and it has not always been possible to identify them with certainty.

PUBLISHED IN GREAT BRITAIN, CANADA, INDIA, AND PAKISTAN
BY THE OXFORD UNIVERSITY PRESS
LONDON, TORONTO, BOMBAY, AND KARACHI

Library of Congress Catalog Card Number: 58–11903
MANUFACTURED IN THE UNITED STATES OF AMERICA

THE RUSSIAN INSTITUTE OF COLUMBIA UNIVERSITY

The Russian Institute was established by Columbia University in 1946 to serve two major objectives: the training of a limited number of well-qualified Americans for scholarly and professional careers in the field of Russian studies, and the development of research in the social sciences and the humanities as they relate to Russia and the Soviet Union. The research program of the Russian Institute is conducted through the efforts of its faculty members, of scholars invited to participate as Senior Fellows in its program, and of candidates for the Certificate of the Institute and for the degree of Doctor of Philosophy. Some of the results of the research program are presented in the Studies of the Russian Institute of Columbia University. The faculty of the Institute, without necessarily agreeing with the conclusions reached in the Studies, believe that their publication advances the difficult task of promoting systematic research on Russia and the Soviet Union and public understanding of the problems involved.

The faculty of the Russian Institute are grateful to the Rockefeller Foundation for the financial assistance which it has given to the program of research and publication.

STUDIES OF THE RUSSIAN INSTITUTE

SOVIET NATIONAL INCOME AND PRODUCT IN 1937 — *Abram Bergson*

THROUGH THE GLASS OF SOVIET LITERATURE: VIEWS OF RUSSIAN SOCIETY — *Edited by Ernest J. Simmons*

THE PROLETARIAN EPISODE IN RUSSIAN LITERATURE 1928–1932 — *Edward J. Brown*

MANAGEMENT OF THE INDUSTRIAL FIRM IN THE USSR: A STUDY IN SOVIET ECONOMIC PLANNING — *David Granick*

SOVIET POLICIES IN CHINA, 1917–1924 — *Allen S. Whiting*

UKRAINIAN NATIONALISM, 1939–1945 — *John A. Armstrong*

POLISH POSTWAR ECONOMY — *Thad Paul Alton*

LITERARY POLITICS IN THE SOVIET UKRAINE, 1917–1934 — *George S. N. Luckyj*

THE EMERGENCE OF RUSSIAN PANSLAVISM, 1856–1870 — *Michael Boro Petrovich*

BOLSHEVISM IN TURKESTAN, 1917–1927 — *Alexander G. Park*

THE LAST YEARS OF THE GEORGIAN MONARCHY 1658–1832 — *David Marshall Lang*

LENIN ON TRADE UNIONS AND REVOLUTION 1893–1917 — *Thomas Taylor Hammond*

THE JAPANESE THRUST INTO SIBERIA, 1918 — *James William Morley*

SOVIET MARXISM: A CRITICAL ANALYSIS — *Herbert Marcuse*

THE AGRARIAN FOES OF BOLSHEVISM: PROMISE AND DEFAULT OF THE RUSSIAN SOCIALIST REVOLUTIONARIES FEBRUARY TO OCTOBER, 1917 — *Oliver H. Radkey*

SOVIET POLICY AND THE CHINESE COMMUNISTS, 1931–1946 — *Charles B. McLane*

PREFACE

The present study, begun eight years ago but frequently interrupted, has been in progress during a period when many new works have appeared, both in Communist and in Western countries, on the subject of Soviet-Chinese Communist relations. This has made the writer's task easier in some respects, but has not eliminated a problem facing all students of Soviet revolutionary strategy: the scarcity, or absence, of data revealing the working relations between Moscow and local Communist parties. The difficulty seems to be particularly acute in the case of China, where virtually no materials are available which bear on this problem after the so-called "Kiangsi period" (1931–34). In order, therefore, to discover what Soviet policy toward the Chinese Communists was at any given juncture, it has been necessary, in so far as Russian sources are concerned, to rely largely on materials meant for general public consumption—materials such as monographs on China, both scholarly and popular, and editorial opinion in Soviet and Comintern periodicals. It is through analysis and interpretation of these materials that the general lines of Soviet policy emerge. The writer should note here that no effort has been made in this study to distinguish between a Russian and a Comintern line. Among students of the USSR the identity of the two is so widely taken for granted that a mere acknowledgment of the identity is believed sufficient.

On occasion the writer has felt handicapped by his ignorance of the Chinese language, which has prevented him from inspecting a large volume of material now available to the student of Chinese Communism. However, increasing amounts of this material are becoming available in translation, either in Russian or in English, and where such translations exist they have of course been consulted—both to supplement Russian materials and, in particular, to determine in which respects the Chinese leadership adhered to Soviet policies and in which respects it seems to have departed from these policies. The focus of the present study, it should be noted at the outset, is not the history of Chinese Communism itself, though much of this history is dealt with, but Russian policy vis-à-vis the Chinese Communist movement during a particular period.

No writer engaged in research of this sort works entirely alone. The author owes numerous debts of gratitude: to Robert C. North, a staff member of the Hoover Institute and Library at Stanford University, for assistance in the early stages of research and for generously opening to the author his valuable files on Chinese Communism; to Professor C. Martin Wilbur, for a thorough and thought-provoking reading of the manuscript in its later stages; to Professors Henry L. Roberts, Nathaniel Peffer, and other members of the Columbia University faculty, who also read the manuscript and commented upon it as it approached final form. Above all, the author is indebted to Dr. Philip E. Mosely for his continuing interest, guidance, and encouragement and for three or four detailed readings of the manuscript at various stages. The value of Dr. Mosely's exacting guidance can be fully appreciated only by someone who has benefited from it in a similar way. Finally, any author who is also *pater familias* can hardly be insensitive to the debt he owes his wife for services and solaces too numerous to list; the present author acknowledges such a debt to Carol Evarts McLane.

Financial assistance for this study was made possible by a grant to the author in 1953 of an Area Research Fellowship by the Social Science Research Council and by two grants for clerical help by Swarthmore College. It goes without saying that neither of these institutions, nor the individuals whose assistance has been acknowledged above, bear responsibility for the views expressed in this study.

CHARLES B. MCLANE

Hanover, New Hampshire
April, 1958

CONTENTS

INTRODUCTION

In 1944 and 1945 Stalin and Molotov are reported to have made disparaging remarks about the Chinese Communists on several occasions. These remarks were perplexing at the time and continue to be so. In June, 1944, for instance, Stalin told W. Averell Harriman, the American Ambassador in Moscow, that "the Chinese Communists are not real Communists. They are 'margarine' Communists." [1] In August of the same year Molotov made similar remarks about the Chinese Communists to Patrick Hurley and Donald Nelson, President Roosevelt's two personal representatives to Chungking. Nelson reported Molotov's observations as follows:

> Although he said that the Soviet government had unjustifiably been held responsible for various happenings in China during recent years, Molotov stressed that it would bear no responsibility for internal affairs or developments in China. Molotov then spoke of the very impoverished conditions of the people in parts of China, some of whom called themselves Communists but were related to Communism in no way at all. It was merely a way of expressing dissatisfaction with their economic condition and they would forget this political inclination when their economic condition improved. The Soviet government should not be associated with these "communist elements" nor could it in any way be blamed for this situation.[2]

Eight months later, in April, 1945, Ambassador Hurley, again in Moscow on his way to Chungking, drew from the Soviet leaders further confirmation of the official Russian view that the Communists in China were not real Communists in the Soviet

[1] See the account of Harriman's interview in Feis, *The China Tangle,* p. 140.
[2] *United States Relations with China,* p. 72.

sense.[3] Similar assurances were given to Secretary of State Byrnes at Potsdam in July[4] and to a group of American Congressmen visiting Moscow in September, 1945.[5]

The effect these statements may have had on the determination of American policy in China at the end of the war is not easy to gauge. For a number of years an idea had circulated among some foreign observers in China that the so-called "Communists" under Mao Tse-tung were in reality "agrarian reformers," which implied that their allegiance to Moscow was tenuous.[6] This idea had been especially stimulated by sympathetic reporting of the activities and programs of the Chinese Communists from 1937 on.[7] By the end of the war, therefore, many Americans were quite prepared to believe, on the basis of the incomplete appraisals then available, that Mao's Communism was relatively free of Russian control.

Such a label as "agrarian reformer" also had the effect of ren-

[3] *Ibid.*, pp. 94–95. Harriman was also present at this conference with Stalin and Molotov on April 15, 1945. His impression of the attitude of Soviet leaders, which differs somewhat from Hurley's, may be found in *ibid.*, pp. 97–98 and in *Military Situation in the Far East,* p. 3336.

[4] James F. Byrnes, *Speaking Frankly* (New York, 1947), p. 228.

[5] Feis, *The China Tangle,* p. 171 *n.*

[6] This concept of the Chinese Communists had been advanced as early as 1932; e.g., Nathaniel Peffer, "Chinese Idea of Communism," *Current History,* July, 1932, pp. 400–404, and J. O. P. Bland, *China: The Pity of It* (Garden City, N. Y., 1932), pp. 273–84.

[7] The first visit to Yenan by a foreign observer was made by Edgar Snow in 1936 and was reported in his *Red Star over China* the following year. Within the next four years two dozen or more foreign observers visited the Chinese Communist areas before they were sealed off by the Kuomintang late in 1940: e.g., Agnes Smedley, Nym Wales, James Bertram, Haldore Hanson, Anna Louise Strong, Earl Leaf, Victor Kean, George Hatem, H. Dunham, T. A. Bisson (all correspondents or journalists), Colonel Evans Carlson (a U.S. military observer), Stanton Lautenschlager (a missionary), George Hogg (a cooperative official), Owen Lattimore, and others. During the war years Michael Lindsay and Claire and William Band, British subjects formerly at Peiping University, were more or less continuously in Yenan following their escape from Peiping in 1941. In the summer of 1944 Chungking permitted an American military mission under Colonel David Barrett to visit Yenan; Foreign Service observers were at one time or another attached to this mission—e.g., Raymond Ludden, John S. Service, and John P. Davies. At the same time the blockade was lifted enough to permit a correspondents' team including, among others, Harrison Forman, Gunther Stein, and Israel Epstein to visit the Communist areas for a period of three or four months; other foreign correspondents were also allowed to visit Yenan late in 1944 and in 1945—e.g., Brooks Atkinson, Theodore White, Robert Payne, and others. With few exceptions the reports rendered by these observers were sympathtic to the Chinese Communists; for works by these observers cited in the present study, see Bibliography.

dering Mao's forces less objectionable to Americans than they perhaps would have been as allegedly disciplined Marxists, although it is not likely that more than a few who used the term did so with this design. The result, in any case, was that many Americans, both within and outside the government, came to consider the Communists as acceptable allies in China at a time when efforts were being made to stiffen Chinese resistance against the Japanese. Stalin's and Molotov's disclaimers respecting the Chinese Communists (which seem to have been taken more or less at face value by some American officials)[8] undoubtedly added weight to these views and, in this respect, helped to shape an attitude toward Mao which was more tolerant—at least until the end of the war—than it might otherwise have been.

This then might be said to be one effect of Stalin's and Molotov's much-quoted remarks. But was this the intent in Moscow? Did Soviet leaders seek deliberately to deceive American officials in order to conceal their true objectives in China after the war? Or had Chinese Communism by 1944 and 1945 grown so independent of Moscow, as many believed, that these statements reflected more or less accurately Moscow's attitude toward Mao and his followers? Or were there perhaps other considerations at the end of the war which might have led the Soviet leaders to raise official doubts as to Mao's orthodoxy? The present study seeks answers to such questions.

But it attempts to do more than this. In recent years—since 1949—the Moscow-Peiping alliance has become a crucial factor in world diplomacy. There can be little doubt that the Soviet Union speaks with added authority because of this tie. And there is equally little doubt that the Western nations judge the strength of the Soviet Union and the Communist bloc with the

[8] Hurley, in particular, clung to his belief that the Russians meant what they said. See his review of Soviet-Chinese Communist relations early in July, 1945, in *United States Relations with China*, pp. 99–100. As late as November 28, 1945, Hurley told the National Press Club in Washington that "the only difference between Chinese Communists and Oklahoma Republicans is that the Oklahoma Republicans aren't armed." A week later he testified before the Senate Committee on Foreign Relations that Moscow was not supporting the Chinese Communists; *Military Situation in the Far East*, pp. 2894–95. See also President Roosevelt's reference at Yalta to the "so-called [Chinese] Communists"; *Foreign Relations of the United States: The Conferences at Malta and Yalta, 1945*, p. 771.

Sino-Soviet alliance in mind. The alliance has defied much so-called "expert" opinion on China. In the United States especially many continue to be amazed that this alliance is still evidently firm and to doubt that it will remain so, despite the fact that all signs since 1949 point to the strengthening rather than the weakening of the coalition.[9] This bond was not created after the Communists came to power. Nor was it a mere revival of ties known to have been strong between Moscow and the Chinese Communist movement in the 1920s. Rather, the ties established earlier were somehow preserved through the long lean years of Chinese Communism, between 1931 and 1946, and reappeared—if anything, stronger than before—at the very time when many in the West were minimizing these ties on the basis of wholly negative evidence of their survival. A broader purpose of this study, then, is to discover what political, ideological, or other links there were between Moscow and Chinese Communism during these fifteen crucial years which might explain the emergence of so strong an alliance after 1949.

[9] For a dispassionate study of the Sino-Soviet alliance since 1949, see Howard L. Boorman and others, *Moscow-Peking Axis: Strengths and Strains* (New York, 1957). This study, on the balance, emphasizes the strength rather than the weakness of the alliance.

1

SOVIET POLICIES IN CHINA DURING THE KIANGSI PERIOD, 1931–1934

A new attitude toward China can be seen in Soviet pronouncements and behavior after 1930. During the preceding decade, although its policy shifted several times, Moscow's general view of China was that here, if anywhere, a Communist revolution might succeed. This was important to the Soviet leadership, not only because a successful revolution in China would lend support to the Marxist-Leninist claim that the Communist revolution was world-wide, but also because it would have given the Soviet Union a valuable ally in a period of relative diplomatic isolation. For these reasons, the Soviet government expended great energy in promoting Communism in China during the 1920s, as a rule operating through the organization set up for this purpose, the Third Communist International (Comintern).[1] As time passed, however, the Soviet government, for reasons that will become clear, reduced its efforts to bring about revolution in China. By the early 1930s it was apparent to careful observers of Soviet foreign policy that Moscow was now looking

[1] Of the many studies of Soviet policy in China from 1917 through 1930 the following, in the author's view, are the most useful: Allen S. Whiting, *Soviet Policies in China, 1917–1924* (New York, 1954); Schwartz, *Chinese Communism and the Rise of Mao* (covering the period from 1920 to roughly 1932); Wilbur and How, *Documents on Communism, Nationalism and Soviet Advisers in China, 1918–1927;* Xenia Joukoff Eudin and Robert C. North, *Soviet Russia and the East, 1920–1927* (Stanford, Calif., 1957); North, *Moscow and Chinese Communists,* chaps. I–IX; and Brandt, Schwartz, and Fairbank, *A Documentary History of Chinese Communism,* Secs. I–III. A current project of particular interest, both for the 1920s and for the 1930s (up to 1938), is the compilation of the memoirs of Chang Kuo-t'ao, a leading figure in the Chinese Communist movement from its origins in 1920 to his expulsion from the Party early in 1938; Chang himself is working on this project in collaboration with Robert Burton.

at China through changed eyes, though elements of the earlier view persisted.

A plenary session of the Central Committee of the Chinese Communist Party held early in 1931 is an important landmark in the transformation of Soviet policy and serves as a suitable point of departure for the present study.

THE COMINTERN IN RETREAT

The Fourth Plenum of the Central Committee of the Chinese Communist Party was held in January, 1931, following the Third Plenum by four months. Not much is known about the Fourth Plenum. It probably took place in Shanghai, or in the outskirts of Shanghai. It certainly met secretly. It was evidently attended by most of the leaders then prominent in the Chinese Communist movement: Hsiang Chang-fa, Secretary-General of the Party since 1928; Ho Meng-hsuing and Lo Chang-lung, two labor union leaders who perhaps commanded the greatest support among the rank-and-file Party membership; Ch'ü Ch'iu-pai, formerly head of the Party—following the rout in August, 1927, of the founder and early leader of the Chinese Communist movement, Ch'en Tu-hsiu—and now recently returned from a two-year visit in Moscow; Chou En-lai, a peripatetic Party stalwart, even then, and a member of the Politburo since 1927; and a group of former students at the Sun Yat-sen University in Moscow headed by Wang Ming [Ch'en Shao-yu] and including Lo Fu [Chang Wen-tien], Po Ku [Ch'in Pang-hsien], and others. Li Li-san, *de facto* leader of the Party from early 1928 (after the removal of Ch'ü Ch'iu-pai) until the end of 1930, was evidently not present, having already departed for Moscow to "confess" his errors. Chang Kuo-t'ao, another Party leader of long standing who had had periodic differences with the Comintern leadership, was also not present, though he arrived in China from Moscow shortly after the plenum. Nor were Mao Tse-tung and Chu Teh, the leaders of the soviet movement in South China, present at the plenum, although it is reported that they sent delegates from the soviet areas.[2]

[2] Smedley, *The Great Road,* p. 294.

An official history of the Chinese Communist Party published in 1951 gives this account of the Fourth Plenum and of the circumstances under which it was held:

In September, 1930, Li Li-san's mistakes were corrected by the Third Plenum of the Party's Central Committee. In January, 1931, however, a new "Left" opportunist clique under Wang Ming and Po Ku—a group adhering to dogmatism and masquerading as Marxists—conducted an attack on the decisions of the Third Plenum. This group considered that Li Li-san's principal error and the principal danger to the Chinese Communist Party at that time was Right opportunism rather than "Left" opportunism. It therefore censured the Third Plenum "for not having completely unmasked the unalterably Right opportunist theories and practice of the Li Li-san line." At the Fourth Plenum these "Left" opportunists seized the leading positions in the Central Committee.[3]

This analysis, which, needless to say, was made with the hindsight of twenty years and was obviously intended to discredit the leadership immediately preceding Mao's, gives a distorted picture of the situation within the Chinese Communist Party at this juncture. To judge from accounts of the Chinese Communist movement published in the Comintern press early in 1931, the Third Plenum, held in September, 1930, did not correct Li Li-san's errors but, on the contrary, endorsed his leadership. Allegedly this was due to the fact that Ch'ü Ch'iu-pai, whom the Comintern had dispatched to China to expose Li Li-san, had been unable to consolidate the various opposition factions within the Party against Li.[4] It was apparently not until November, 1930, two and a half months after the Third Plenum, that Li was finally overthrown, following the receipt of a letter addressed to the Chinese Communists by the Executive Committee of the Communist International (ECCI) in which his errors were itemized and sharply attacked.[5] Shortly thereafter Li Li-san de-

[3] Khu Tsiao-mu [Hu Chiao-mu], *Tridtsat' let KPK*, pp. 40–42 (English ed., pp. 36–37).

[4] See Kuchymov, "The Struggle for the Bolshevization of the Communist Party of China," *Communist International*, No. 6, March 15, 1931, pp. 162–67.

[5] For an analysis of this letter, dated November 16, 1930, and of its impact on the situation within the Chinese Communist Party, see Schwartz, *Rise of Mao*, pp. 156 ff. See also North, *Moscow and Chinese Communists*, pp. 140–46.

parted for Moscow to make an appropriate apology (and to commence a period of "political reorientation" that was to last fifteen years), leaving the leadership of the Party momentarily open. The ostensible purpose of the Fourth Plenum, therefore, was to constitute a new leadership. Actually, it was to confirm the leadership of the so-called "returned students' clique" of Wang Ming,[6] which Comintern agents in China had by that time imposed on the Party.

The dominant figure at the Fourth Plenum was beyond any doubt Pavel' Mif, formerly the director of the Sun Yat-sen University in Moscow and since the spring of 1930 the Comintern's principal agent in China. He ensured the leadership of his former students by virtually eliminating all possible opposition within the Party. Ch'ü Ch'iu-pai was accused of having wholly ignored Li Li-san's errors in a recent review of the Third Plenum and of having shown an "inexcusably disrespectful attitude" toward the Comintern representative (Mif) in failing to communicate with him concerning a revision of the Third Plenum's political resolutions during the autumn of 1930.[7] According to one account, Ch'ü was obliged publicly to confess his "cowardly rotten opportunism." [8] Chou En-lai, the only figure of importance left over from the Li Li-san leadership, was also obliged to confess his errors and to condemn his own report on the Third Plenum. He managed, however, to retain his seat on the Politburo.[9] A faction

[6] Also called, somewhat derisively, the "twenty-eight Bolsheviks"; see Schwartz, *Rise of Mao,* p. 152. According to one account, the "twenty-eight model Bolsheviks" did not reach Shanghai until the spring of 1931, when they were sent to China by the Comintern to assist Wang Ming; Wan Yah-Kang, *Rise of Communism in China,* p. 23.

[7] "Resolution of the Enlarged Fourth Plenum of the CC, CPC" (January, 1931); text in Brandt, etc., *Documentary History,* p. 213.

[8] Isaacs, *Tragedy of the Chinese Revolution,* p. 407. Recent Chinese Communist sources state that, following his removal from the Party's central organ at the Fourth Plenum, Ch'ü remained for two years in Shanghai, engaged in cultural work, before proceeding to the soviet areas in 1933. He served in the soviet government until the beginning of the Long March, regaining some of his earlier prestige, but was left behind when the Red Army moved north, apparently due to ill health. He was allegedly arrested by Kuomintang officials in March, 1935, and executed three months later; Mao, *Proizvedeniia,* IV, 400 (English ed., IV, 340). See also the account of Ch'ü Ch'iu-pai's death in North, *Moscow and Chinese Communists,* p. 165.

[9] Chou is apparently the only Chinese Communist to have served continuously on the Politburo since 1927; see North, *Kuomintang . . . Elites,* pp. 111–13.

centering around the two labor union leaders, Ho Meng-hsiung and Lo Chang-lung, was totally routed at the Fourth Plenum. Immediately following the plenum the leaders of this faction formed an "emergency committee" to consider their further course of action and were thereupon expelled from the Party.[10] The "returned students" were left in undisputed control of the Party apparatus.[11]

The Fourth Plenum is primarily significant, not because it marked another change in the Party leadership, but because it is the last identifiable instance of outright Soviet intervention in the internal affairs of the Chinese Communist Party. In this sense the plenum marks the end of a phase in Moscow's relationship to the Chinese Communist movement. From the origins of the movement in 1920 to the Fourth Plenum no major policy was adopted, and no change in the leadership brought about, except on instructions from the Comintern. A formidable succession of Comintern agents had been sent to China during these years to see that these instructions were followed: Grigorii Voitinskii in 1920 and 1921 to guide the preparations for the founding congress; the Dutch agent Maring to supervise Party activities during the first year of its existence; Michael Borodin and later M. N. Roy to supervise Comintern strategy during the revolution of 1925–27; Besso Lominadze in 1927 to overthrow the Ch'en Tu-hsiu leadership; Heinz Neumann in the same year to help organize the uprising at Canton; and many others.[12] Pavel' Mif, in January, 1931, was acting in accordance with this tradition. It is likely, in fact, that he was not the last Comintern representa-

[10] A secret meeting of the "emergency committee" was allegedly discovered by the British police in Shanghai and its members were arrested on January 17, 1931. Ho Meng-hsiung and twenty-four others are said to have been executed by the Kuomintang three weeks later; Isaacs, *Tragedy of the Chinese Revolution*, p. 407. One source—a notably unreliable one, however, in this writer's view—claims that the British police were informed of the committee's whereabouts by Wang Ming; Li Ang, *Red Stage*. See also Wan Yah-Kang, *Rise of Communism in China*, p. 34.

[11] Nominal leadership of the Party was retained by Hsiang Chang-fa until his arrest and execution by the Kuomintang in the late spring of 1931; actual control of the Party's central organs, however, was held by the "returned students' clique" from the Fourth Plenum to the Politburo conference at Tsunyi in January, 1935 (see pp. 52–54 below).

[12] See Schwartz, *Rise of Mao*, p. 81; Isaacs, *Tragedy of the Chinese Revolution* (rev. ed., 1951), p. 220. For a detailed account of the activities of Soviet agents in China through 1927, see Wilbur and How, *Documents on . . . China.*

tive in China, though it is conceded by most students of Chinese Communism that he was the last to exercise any significant influence over the Party leadership.[13] Mao's ascendancy in the Chinese Communist movement, which culminated, we shall see, early in 1935 when he gained control of the Party's central organs, appears to have depended little if at all on the Comintern's explicit approval.

What happened during the years after the Fourth Plenum in 1931 to cause this decline of Comintern influence in Chinese Communist affairs?

We can perhaps dismiss at the outset any notion that the Comintern retreated from China because in its view the prospects of revolution there no longer warranted its efforts. If official estimates have any significance, the period from 1931 to 1934 was one when the revolutionary wave in China was said to be steadily rising, both in the so-called "Kuomintang" sector of China (i.e., where there were no soviets) and in the soviet areas centered in Kiangsi province. In 1932 Comintern sources reported that the number of industrial strikes in Kuomintang China had increased from 730 to 1,215 within a twelve-month period.[14] In 1933 there were said to have been three times as many strikes as in 1932, with more than 300,000 workers participating.[15] Party strength in the Kuomintang areas, a high Comintern official noted in February, 1934, had increased by 200 per cent during the preceding twelve months.[16] In the soviet areas, it will be shown, the gains, as reported by Russian spokesmen, were greater still. An official Comintern source stated as late as 1935 that the revolution in China "is developing in a period when the end of capitalist stabilization is at hand and when we approach a new round of wars and revolution." [17] There is in fact

[13] According to Chiang Kai-shek, Lominadze returned to China in 1932 or 1933 to survey conditions in the soviet areas; Chiang Kai-shek, *Soviet Russia in China*, pp. 64–65. This information, however, is not corroborated in other sources. A German Communist known as Li Teh is believed to have served as military adviser to the Red Army in China from 1933 to 1939 but apparently had little voice in political matters; see Snow, *Red Star over China*, pp. 416 ff.

[14] *Programmnye dokumenty kommunisticheskikh partii Vostoka*, p. v.

[15] *XIII plenum IKKI*, p. 356.

[16] Manuil'skii, *Otchetnyi doklad XVII s"ezdu VKP(b)*, p. 34.

[17] *Programmnye dokumenty kitaiskikh sovetov*, p. 3.

nothing in Soviet estimates of the revolutionary upsurge in China during these years which suggests that the Chinese Communists were less deserving of the Comintern's support than during the 1920s.

These estimates were of course exaggerated, particularly as they applied to the labor movement in the Kuomintang areas.[18] Perhaps this was because the Comintern wished to keep alive a militant spirit in the Chinese proletariat by stimulating it artificially during a period when the real possibilities of revolt were admittedly dim. Possibly Moscow meant to ward off foreign rivals by showing that China was on the brink of revolution and therefore unsafe for their "imperialist" adventures. One can imagine many reasons for overestimating publicly the chances of a Communist revolution in China. But let us suppose that in private Soviet appraisals of the situation in China were more realistic and candidly acknowledged the unpromising prospects for the revolution early in the 1930s. Need we expect that the Comintern would therefore have curtailed its activities in China? There had been no retreat in 1927 when the outlook must have appeared considerably less promising, following the disastrous uprising in Canton in December of that year. It is a reasonable assumption that there would have been no retreat after 1930—if Soviet objectives in China had remained unchanged.

One important reason for the evident decline of Comintern influence in the Chinese Communist movement during the Kiangsi era was the reduced role of the Comintern itself after 1930 as an instrument of Soviet foreign policy. Two circumstances prompted a redefinition in Moscow of the Comintern's proper sphere of activity: the effort at home to establish "socialism in one country" and, abroad, the twin threat to Soviet security posed by the Japanese seizure of Manchuria at the end of 1931 and Hitler's rise to power in Germany a year later. Soviet policies and strategies were geared to these new circumstances. In China, for instance, diplomatic relations were estab-

[18] A recent Chinese Communist source acknowledges this period as "the low ebb of the labor movement in China"; Ch'ang Shao-wen, "Short History of the Labor Movement," *Ta Kung Pao* (Shanghai), November, 1950—February, 1951 (trans. in *Current Background,* No. 108, August 20, 1951, American Consulate, Hong Kong).

lished in 1932 with the Kuomintang government in Nanking. The following year relations were established with the United States. In 1934 the Soviet Union entered the League of Nations. In 1935 defensive alliances were concluded with France and Czechoslovakia. In undertaking these engagements Moscow, of course, had to curtail its earlier program of more or less openly supporting foreign revolutionary movements through the Comintern. This was particularly true in countries like China which were now considered "friendly." [19]

This change of policy did not mean that the Russians abruptly ceased to express interest in the development of the Communist movement in China. The situation in China during the Kiangsi period, it will be seen, evoked many of the same responses and observations among Soviet writers that it had during the 1920s. The "change" was not so much in the content of Soviet policy—that is, in revised appraisals of the revolution itself—as in Moscow's outward behavior with respect to this revolution. It was only the Comintern's operational activities which were affected by the new direction of Soviet foreign policy.

There were, however, other reasons for Moscow's waning influence in the Chinese Communist movement after 1930, reasons connected with the changing character of this movement itself as its principal strength came increasingly to be centered in the scattered soviet districts in South China. In the first place, these areas were relatively inaccessible and communication with them from the outside was, at best, tenuous.[20] The Comintern, we may presume, would have had great difficulty in exercising an effective

[19] The influence of general Soviet foreign policies on Soviet policy toward the Chinese Communists between 1931 and 1935 is discussed more fully at the end of this chapter.

[20] For descriptions of a number of harrowing journeys into the soviet areas during this period, see Wales, *Red Dust.* Edgar Snow states that there was radio communication between the soviet capital at Juichin and "a Comintern-led advisory committee, which for a while functioned in Shanghai"; Snow, *Red Star over China,* p. 417. This presumably was the Far Eastern Bureau (Dal'biuro) of the Comintern, said to have been disbanded in June, 1931, following the arrest of the Noulens, a Belgian couple allegedly in charge of this office; see T'ang Leang-li, *Suppressing Communist-Banditry in China,* p. 71. Chang Kuo-t'ao has stated that there was intermittent radio communication beween Juichin and Moscow until the beginning of the Long March in October, 1934; see North, *Moscow and Chinese Communists,* p. 164. For a variety of reasons that will become apparent, this last evidence seems to the present writer extremely doubtful.

authority in the soviet territories, assuming that it was its intent to do so. Let us imagine for a moment, however, that Comintern agents had found ways of maintaining regular contact with the Chinese soviets early in the 1930s and that there had been no change in the Kremlin's policy of providing guidance to the Chinese Communist movement: can we be sure that the soviet leadership under Mao would have submitted to this supervision? The soviets, it will be seen, were predominantly agrarian in their composition and their early development had necessarily been outside the orbit of the Comintern's influence, which after 1927 had been largely confined to the industrial cities along the coast. More than this, by the early 1930s the soviet movement represented the chief strength of the Communist movement in China and on these grounds its leadership, which owed little to the Comintern, could claim the right to develop its own policies without undue outside interference. The fact that the soviet leadership was essentially orthodox, as will be shown, should not obscure the fact that it was a different leadership, standing somewhat apart from the nominal Party leadership established at the Fourth Plenum. A Comintern authority seeking to control this new leadership as it had controlled the urban leadership in the 1920s might well have encountered resistance.

It is too early in this study, of course, to determine the most likely cause of the Comintern's retreat after 1930—as between objective conditions within the Chinese Communist movement itself and subjective considerations influencing the Soviet leadership at home. For present purposes it is enough to indicate that this change in the Comintern's relationship to Chinese Communism occurred; the reasons for it may be judged more intelligently when further evidence has been presented. As far as the time when the change took place is concerned, no precise date may be attached to it. The Fourth Plenum of the Chinese Communist Party in January, 1931, is taken as a convenient point of departure for this study, not because it coincides with any known decision to curb the Comintern's activities in China, but simply because, as has been noted, it marked the last appearance in China of an important political representative sent by the Comintern.

SOVIET THEORIES ON THE REVOLUTION IN CHINA

That the Comintern's retreat from China did not necessarily mean a slackening of Russian interest in the Chinese revolution is nowhere seen more clearly than in the volume of attention Soviet and Comintern writers on China continued to give to theory. Let us begin by analyzing the prevailing theories on the revolution in China early in the 1930s, as revealed in official and quasiofficial documents.

The Chinese revolution, it was said in Moscow, was passing through an "agrarian" phase. In December, 1926, when the possibility of Chiang Kai-shek's breaking off the Kuomintang-Communist alliance was first being discussed in Moscow, Stalin had said: "Chiang Kai-shek's turn means that the revolution has entered the second stage of its development: the change has been from the revolution of the *national* united front . . . to the *agrarian* revolution." [21] A resolution passed by the ECCI on December 16, 1926, stated that "the development of the national-revolutionary movement in China at the present time depends upon the agrarian revolution." [22]

The Russians attached a special meaning to the term "agrarian." It was associated not so much with peasant uprisings, land reform, and the usual characteristics of a rural, as distinct from urban, revolution, but with the broader struggle against Chinese feudalism in general. It denoted a more popular period of revolution in China, in contrast to the preceding united front period when workers and peasants had allied with a significant part of the "national bourgeoisie" against the worst manifestation of feudalism in the Peiping government. As long as this alliance was in operation, it would have been inappropriate to acclaim an "agrarian" revolution. By the end of 1926, however, the tactical situation was rapidly changing. The basis of the alliance was narrowing and its total collapse was already anticipated in Mos-

[21] Address to the Seventh Plenum of the ECCI, quoted in *Voprosy kitaiskoi revoliutsii,* p. 127 (italics in original).

[22] "Rezoliutsiia po voprosu o polozhenii v Kitae" (Resolution on the Question of the Situation in China), quoted in *ibid.,* p. 22.

cow. Under these new circumstances Stalin argued that the revolution in China was entering a phase when the workers and peasants, with only the most liberal elements of the "national bourgeoisie," would of their own initiative carry on the struggle against Chinese feudalism. This was the "agrarian revolution" of which he spoke.[23]

Stalin also considered the revolution in China to be "anti-imperialist." In May, 1927, he had said:

Of course the revolution in China is directed not only against the remnants of feudalism. It is also directed against imperialism. Why? Because imperialism with all its financial and military power in China is the force which supports, inspires, cultivates and preserves the remnants of feudalism and its bureaucratic-militarist superstructure. Because it is impossible to liquidate the remnants of feudalism in China without at the same time carrying on a revolutionary struggle against imperialism in China.[24]

He concluded:

Thus the present revolution in China is a union of the two currents of the revolutionary movement—the movement against the remnants of feudalism and the movement against imperialism.[25]

It should be noted that the more general "bourgeois-democratic" character of the Chinese revolution was unaffected by its having entered an "agrarian" phase and by being considered also as "anti-imperialist." In September, 1928, the Sixth Comintern Congress had called the revolution in China "bourgeois-democratic" and had described this period broadly as "a stage characterized by preparations for a proletarian directorship and a so-

[23] See also Stalin's fuller description of the "agrarian revolution" in his speech at the tenth session of the ECCI on May 24, 1927; *ibid.*, pp. 134–36. There was of course, disagreement in Moscow at the end of 1926 and early in 1927 concerning the extent to which the united front had already disintegrated. Stalin, though he appears to have acknowledged the need for a new policy as early as December, 1926, did not actually order a change in tactics until the summer of 1927. Trotsky, on the other hand, had been demanding for many months that the Chinese Communists sever their crippling alliance with the Kuomintang and proceed to a massive uprising against the entire "national bourgeoisie." His analysis of the Chinese revolution is given in his *Problems of the Chinese Revolution*.

[24] Speech before the ECCI on May 24, 1927, quoted in *Voprosy kitaiskoi revoliutsii*, p. 135.

[25] *Ibid.*, p. 136.

cialist revolution."[26] Both this congress and the Sixth Congress of the Chinese Communists, held in Moscow a month earlier under Comintern supervision, had considered the content of the bourgeois-democratic revolution to be "agrarian" and "anti-imperialist."

After 1930 there was no immediate change in these descriptive concepts of the revolution in China. The terms "bourgeois-democratic," "agrarian," and "anti-imperialist" continued to appear in Soviet accounts almost interchangeably. As late as 1935 an official Comintern publication described the Chinese revolution in these words: "The bourgeois-democratic revolution in China is anti-imperialist and agrarian in its content, developing under the hegemony of the proletariat and under the leadership of the Communist Party."[27]

By 1935, however—to look ahead for a moment—the tactical situation was again changing in China. Japanese imperialism was replacing domestic feudalism as the most formidable enemy to the revolution and the time was approaching when a new alliance between the masses and the "national bourgeoisie" would be in order. Since Japanese imperialism also threatened the Soviet Union, it is not surprising that Russian and Comintern writers on China increasingly emphasized the "anti-imperialist" character of the revolution there; the term "agrarian," describing a more uncompromising phase of the revolution, was once again becoming inappropriate. Thus Wang Ming could assert early in 1935 that "the primary and fundamental quality" of the Chinese revolution was its "anti-imperialist character."[28] After the Comintern's formal call for a united front in China, in August, 1935, the term "agrarian" disappeared almost entirely from Russian accounts of the Chinese revolution.

[26] "Resolutions of the Sixth Congress on the National Question," quoted in *Programmnye dokumenty kommunisticheskikh partii,* p. v of "Introduction."

[27] *Programmnye dokumenty kitaiskikh sovetov,* p. 3 of "Introduction."

[28] *Vtoroi s"ezd kitaiskikh sovetov,* p. 11 of Wang Ming's "Introduction." From the end of 1931 to the end of 1937 Wang remained in Moscow as the Chinese Communist representative to the Comintern. During this period he was one of the most prolific writers on China in Comintern publications; on all occasions, due to Wang's primary identification with the Comintern, we may presume him to represent the Soviet rather than the Chinese Communist point of view where there is any difference between the two.

In Stalin's view the formation of the soviets in China was directly related to the unfolding of the agrarian revolution. The type of soviet he had in mind, however, was not the rural or peasant—and, in this sense, "agrarian"—soviet that actually flourished in China during the Kiangsi era but the workers' soviet patterned more nearly after those that had sprung up in Moscow and Petrograd in 1917. This is clear from his remarks in May, 1927, to a group of Chinese students at the Sun Yat-sen University in Moscow. Purely peasant soviets, he said, were out of the question inasmuch as China was not a country with "no or almost no proletariat," the only kind of country in Leninist ideology where peasant soviets were possible.[29] Workers' soviets, on the other hand, might someday be feasible, but "only on condition that they become organs for throwing off existing authority."[30] Stalin continued:

Of course workers' soviets can be established; this is not very difficult. The question is not the establishment of workers' soviets but their transformation into organs of revolutionary power. Without this, soviets are empty shells; they are a parody on soviets.[31]

The reason why Stalin did not consider soviets appropriate in the spring of 1927 was that as "organs for throwing off existing authority" they would have been in conflict with the Wuhan government, an uneasy coalition between the Communists and the Left Kuomintang which it was then the Comintern's policy to support. After the collapse of this coalition and the total disruption of the united front during the summer, Stalin viewed the situation in China differently. In his view, the agrarian revolution was by then in full swing and he could acclaim a new revolutionary upsurge throughout the country. Accordingly, on September 27, 1927, he called for the immediate formation of soviets.[32]

[29] "Beseda so studentami universiteta imeni Sun-iat-sena" (Talk with Students at Sun Yat-sen University), quoted in *Voprosy kitaiskoi revoliutsii,* p. 177.

[30] *Ibid.,* p. 178.

[31] *Ibid.,* p. 179.

[32] *Sovety v Kitae,* p. 105. Mao claims to have called for soviets during the Autumn Crop Uprising in Hunan a month earlier, even though he was aware that this policy was opposed at the time by the Comintern and by the Party Central Committee. His action, he has said, led to his expulsion from the Politburo; Snow, *Red Star over China,* pp. 167, 169.

The only soviet ever established in China which appears to have conformed fully to Stalin's specifications, as indicated to the students at the Sun Yat-sen University, was the "workers'" soviet which was set up during the Canton uprising in December, 1927. This lasted only three days.[33] Rural, or peasant, soviets, on the other hand, sprang up rapidly during the winter of 1927–28, evidently in response to the Comintern's new line announced in September. Located in the mountainous districts of Hunan, Kiangsi, and Kwangtung in southern China, these soviets appear at first to have been relatively independent of the Party's central organs, which at this time were carrying on an underground existence in Shanghai. In due course, however, especially after the Sixth Party Congress held in Moscow in August, 1928, a special effort was made to harness the soviet movement to the Comintern's program of urban insurrection directed by the Party center.[34]

It is one of the anomalies of the Chinese revolution that an institution intended to serve the proletariat in its effort to seize power became, in a somewhat different guise, a vehicle for the development and consolidation of predominantly agrarian strength. The soviets, in this sense, competed with the Party's underground urban organization for Moscow's favor. No such competition, of course, could come into the open since Soviet revolutionary theory was founded on a presumption of urban leadership: rural soviets, in theory, could be given no more than a supporting role in the Chinese revolution. There were, moreover, strong voices both in Moscow and in Shanghai which openly opposed the soviets as long as they remained necessarily a rural phenomenon.[35] The Comintern continued to authorize the soviets, we may assume, for two reasons: first, because the offi-

[33] See Isaacs, *Tragedy of the Chinese Revolution* (rev. ed., 1951), pp. 284 ff.

[34] For a discussion of the early phases of the soviet movement, see Schwartz, *Rise of Mao,* pp. 103–5, 135–43 *passim;* North, *Moscow and Chinese Communists,* pp. 125–27; also Yakhontoff, *The Chinese Soviets.* Party-soviet relations during this period are reviewed more fully below (pp. 35–44).

[35] One Chinese faction, for instance, which opposed the soviets was the Labor Union Clique under Ho Meng-hsiung; see Schwartz, *Rise of Mao,* p. 154. In Moscow, opposition to the soviets and to the allegedly swashbuckling adventures of the Red Army under Mao and Chu Teh came from the Indian Communist M. N. Roy, according to his own evidence; Roy, *Revolution and Counter-Revolution in China,* p. 628.

cial expectation between 1928 and 1930 was that an uprising was at hand in China, in which event the reserves of strength represented by the rural soviets and the newly formed Red Army would prove invaluable; second, because the solid successes of the soviets were sufficiently impressive, as compared to the Comintern's other success-starved ventures in China, to justify some modification of the Leninist formula that revolutions must everywhere be urban-based. This was the situation up to the autumn of 1930.

At the time Li Li-san was removed from the leadership of the Chinese Communist Party the status of the soviets was somewhat clarified. The soviet movement had by this time grown to such proportions that it could no longer be effectively controlled by the Party's central organs in Shanghai. The use, moreover, which Li Li-san had made of the soviets and of the Red Army units operating from their areas had come under very critical review following the Changsha episode in July, 1930. On this occasion the Fifth Red Army, on Li's orders (which were in turn determined by directives he had received from the Comintern), occupied Changsha but was forced to withdraw three days later with considerable losses when a scheduled proletarian uprising there failed to materialize.[36] The bankruptcy of Li's policy, the Comintern asserted, ignoring its own role in the Changsha affair, was apparent. It was no longer possible to argue, on the basis of an illusion of imminent revolts in the industrial centers, that the function of the soviets was to hold themselves in readiness at all times to support such uprisings. In its letter to the Chinese Communists dated November 16, 1930, the ECCI called for the immediate establishment of a soviet regime which would not be bound by the Party's urban program.[37] The resolution passed by the Fourth Plenum two months later echoed this view:

> The clumsiest mistake resulting from Comrade Li Li-san's position has taken place within the soviet areas. . . . There was a premature, adventurous and dogmatic instruction to seize big cities when we had no consolidated rear, had not made necessary preparation, and had an

[36] For a discussion of the Changsha uprising, see Schwartz, *Rise of Mao*, pp. 143–45.

[37] *Ibid.*, p. 168.

insufficient base in the masses. The Changsha debacle was a result of these mistakes. . . . Li Li-san's leadership completely neglected the task of establishing a strong soviet base, and completely neglected the establishment of a strong soviet political regime.[38]

The Comintern's new line in China did not mean that the Party was now instructed to transfer its attention solely to building up the soviets. For a year or two after the Fourth Plenum, and possibly longer, the effort in urban areas, as will be seen later, remained the primary task of the Party's central organs. The new line did, however, grant the soviets for the first time a semi-independent stature within the Communist movement in China. After the Fourth Party Plenum, and particularly after the First (Chinese) Soviet Congress, which met in Juichin in November, 1931,[39] the Comintern devoted increasing attention to the soviet movement and in due course came to identify it as the symbol of the Chinese revolutionary movement. In September, 1932, among the principal tasks which the Comintern placed before all its sections was "the mobilization of the masses for active defense of the USSR, China, and the Chinese soviet revolution."[40] In December, 1933, Dmitrii Manuil'skii, the representative from the Russian Communist Party to the Comintern, told the Thirteenth Plenum of the ECCI that "the successes of soviet China not only make the Chinese revolution invincible but they strengthen the position of the working class throughout the world in its struggle against the bourgeoisie and make soviet China an important element in the unfolding of the world revolutionary crisis."[41] An official Comintern view of the Chinese soviets in

[38] "Resolution of the Enlarged Fourth Plenum of the CC, CPC" (January, 1931), quoted in Brandt, etc., *Documentary History*, p. 210.

[39] According to Chu Teh, a preparatory conference of Party delegates in the soviet areas was held in Shantang (Kiangsi) soon after the Fourth Party Plenum to implement the Plenum's decision to call an All-China Soviet Congress on August 1, 1931; Smedley, *The Great Road*, p. 294. This congress was postponed several times, due to a new campaign against the soviet areas by the Nanking government, and opened only on November 7, 1931, the anniversary of the Bolshevik Revolution. (Miss Smedley's account erroneously gives the opening date as December 11, the anniversary of the Canton Commune of 1927).

[40] Resolution passed by the Twelfth Plenum of the ECCI, quoted in *Strategiia i taktika Kominterna v natsional'no-kolonial'noi revoliutsii*, p. 320.

[41] Quoted in Kuchumov, *Ocherki po istorii kitaiskoi revoliutsii*, p. 12.

1935 is indicated in the following excerpts from a study of the movement published on the eve of the Seventh Comintern Congress:

The soviets in China are the basic form of the revolutionary-democratic dictatorship of the proletariat and peasantry. The soviet standard, which was raised by the Canton proletariat in the days of the heroic uprising of December, 1927 [the Canton Commune], has become the standard for the entire succeeding stage of the Chinese revolution. The small, scattered soviet centers which sprang up in the fury of the agrarian and anti-imperialist revolution of 1928–30, have become, in the period of the new revolutionary upsurge, powerful bases for strengthening and expanding the revolution.[42]

The soviet revolution in China is developing under conditions of a new imperialist partition of China, begun by Japanese imperialism with the seizure of Manchuria and Jehol and with the extension of its aggression into northern China and Inner Mongolia. The soviets in China are the symbol of the anti-imperialist struggle, in particular the struggle against Japanese imperialism . . . the soviets are the only force capable of resisting the colonial exploitation of 400,000,000 people, of rallying the masses for the struggle with imperialism and of showing the way to liberation from the imperialist yoke.[43]

[The laws and resolutions of the First and Second Soviet Congresses] have an immensely wider significance than that of mere guides to action in the areas already won by the soviets. *They are the program documents for the entire national-revolutionary war in China and for the development of the agrarian revolution.*[44]

The Soviet and Comintern press also reflected the growing interest in Chinese soviets after 1930. *Revoliutsionnyi vostok,* for instance, the only regular Soviet periodical specializing in Far Eastern problems during the Kiangsi era, gave little attention to the labor movement in its coverage of China yet followed the fortunes of the soviets in some detail. The Comintern periodicals *Communist International* and *International Press Correspondence* also gave most of their space on China to the soviet movement. Of the numerous monographs on China still published in

[42] *Programmnye dokumenty kitaiskikh sovetov,* p. 3 of "Introduction."
[43] *Ibid.,* p. 4.
[44] *Ibid.,* p. 5 (italics in original).

Moscow during the early 1930s the great majority dealt with the soviets, despite the fact that information concerning them was meager and often inaccurate.

Another issue which invariably crops up in Soviet revolutionary theory is that of transition—that is, transition to a more advanced stage of revolution. Under what conditions and at what juncture can a revolution heretofore described as "bourgeois," or "bourgeois-democratic," be expected to proceed to a socialist stage? In the case of China this issue contained certain pitfalls for Soviet and Comintern writers. Li Li-san, for instance, had been deposed ostensibly for having shown too great optimism over the possibilities of an early revolutionary advance in China. A long-standing charge against Trotsky by his Stalinist opponents was that he had sought to sabotage the Chinese revolution by advocating *putschist* tactics. Any who ventured to express opinions on the transition issue, therefore, needed to be aware of the risks they took.

In a resolution dated August 26, 1931, the ECCI limited itself to an enigmatic statement of the conditions necessary for the transition to socialism without risking a prediction as to when these conditions might be fulfilled. The Chinese revolution could advance to the socialist phase, this resolution read, only when the bourgeois-democratic-agrarian-antiimperialist phase had been completed.[45] No more, no less. Wang Ming was hardly more specific when he observed, three and a half years later, that "the development of the Chinese revolution from a bourgeois-democratic to a socialist stage will occur only *when the authority of the soviets has been extended to the industrial centers of the country.*" [46] Nothing could be safer than this.

The word sometimes used to describe the duration of the current phase of the Chinese revolution was "protracted"—a word which seemed to suggest a decent interval before socialism without, however, implying that this interval was interminable. Rationalizing this view in 1934, V. Kuchumov contrasted conditions in China with those in prerevolutionary Russia as follows:

[45] Resolution on China passed by the Eleventh Plenum of the ECCI (August 26, 1931), quoted in *Strategiia i taktika Kominterna*, p. 309.

[46] *Vtoroi s"ezd kitaiskikh sovetov*, p. 25 (italics in original).

Under conditions in Tsarist Russia such bases for the revolutionary army and for revolutionary power could exist for only a comparatively short period of time; a decisive engagement between the revolutionary and the Tsarist forces had to be undertaken very quickly. This is not the situation in China where a revolutionary base under the correct leadership of the Communist Party . . . may exist under conditions of hostile encirclement for years, during which the Party may effect its revolutionary transformation and strengthen and cultivate its revolutionary forces.[47]

There is only one instance known to this writer when it was predicted with any confidence in Moscow that the transition to socialism in China would be a comparatively quick one. The author of this prediction was Manuil'skii and the occasion was the Seventeenth (Russian) Party Congress, held in February, 1934. Reviewing the recent successes in China, Manuil'skii stated:

The soviet government is leading the bourgeois-democratic revolution to its conclusion and in the process is carrying out a number of measures of a socialist character. All this taken together guarantees a quick transition from the bourgeois-democratic to a socialist revolution, on the condition that the authority of the soviets is extended to the industrial centers.[48]

It is not possible to determine whether the Comintern actually held this view early in 1934 or merely advanced it as a tactical maneuver serving some obscure end, or, for that matter, whether Manuil'skii, in an excess of optimism, made the prediction on his own initiative. Within a year, in any event, the prediction was necessarily modified by new developments in China. The soviet areas in Kiangsi had been abandoned, the Red Army was engaged in a complex strategic withdrawal whose outcome was still uncertain, and the long-anticipated upsurge in the cities had come to nothing. Under these circumstances the Comintern, early in 1935, gave a more sober and sobering analysis of the issue of transition.

At the present time the Chinese Soviet Republic is not faced and must not be faced with the immediate task of liquidating capitalism and

[47] Kuchumov, *Ocherki po istorii kitaiskoi revoliutsii,* p. 122.
[48] Manuil'skii, *Otchetnyi doklad XVII s"ezdu VKP(b)*, p. 36.

building socialism. It is not yet a proletarian government, even though it is a soviet government under the hegemony of the proletariat and with the Communist Party having the monopoly of leadership as the only ruling party.[49]

In essence this remained, until after the Second World War, the Soviet view on the question of transition to socialism in the Chinese revolution.

It will be noted that the phrase "hegemony of the proletariat" creeps into Soviet analyses of the revolution in China during the Kiangsi era again and again. This phrase has no exact meaning in the Communist vocabulary. Some students of Chinese Communism believe it to mean simply the hegemony, or leadership, of the Party in a given organization.[50] Others—the present writer among them—understand the phrase more literally, at least as it was used in connection with the soviet movement in the 1930s. That is, it was meant to suggest a preponderance of proletarian over peasant elements in the soviet leadership.[51] This was, of course, an entirely appropriate objective during the Kiangsi period, as a counterpoise to the officially designated, and actual, agrarian character of the revolution at this time. What is curious, however, in view of the known numerical preponderance of peasants in the soviets, is that the hegemony of the proletariat in the soviet areas was said to be not merely a future objective but an actual achievement. In asserting this, spokesmen in Moscow were apparently willing to ignore statistics which were readily available to them and which in fact were sometimes included in Russian sources. A popular account of the soviets published in 1931, for instance, quoted a letter from Hunan province stating that

[49] *Kommunisticheskii internatsional pered VII vsemirnym kongressom,* p. 463.

[50] See, for instance, Schwartz's view that the "hegemony of the proletariat," as applied to the Kuomintang in 1926, meant "control of the Kuomintang by the Communist Party"; Schwartz, *Rise of Mao,* p. 59.

[51] Note the distinction that appears to be made between mere Party control and "proletarian hegemony" in the following statements by Soviet writers: "The bourgeois-democratic revolution in China . . . is developing under the hegemony of the proletariat and under the leadership of the Communist Party"; *Programmnye dokumenty kitaiskikh sovetov,* p. 3 of "Introduction." "[The Chinese Soviet Republic] is a dictatorship conducted under the hegemony of the proletariat and under a monopoly of political leadership by the Communist Party"; Manuil'skii, *Otchetnyi doklad XVII s"ezdu VKP(b),* p. 36.

the social composition of the soviets there was 60–80 per cent peasants and 20–40 per cent rural workers; no purely proletarian elements (i.e., industrial workers) were indicated.[52] The account of the Second (Chinese) Soviet Congress published in Moscow early in 1935 included figures which showed that of 821 delegates to the Congress only eight were described as industrial workers.[53]

Russian writers went to some length to show that, despite all external evidence, the soviet government was still a "government operating under the hegemony of the proletariat." It was asserted, for instance—though there was little obvious connection between the two developments—that industrial strikes led by Communists in Kuomintang China from 1928 to 1930 had greatly facilitated the initial formation of the soviets.[54] An important factor, it was said, in soviet resistance to the Kuomintang's campaigns against them early in the 1930s was the desertion of workers from Chiang Kai-shek's "bandit-extermination" troops. Only the supervision of the soviets by a proletarian-based Party, it was argued, had ensured their success. On this point the editors of *Sovety v Kitae* (the Comintern's most authoritative review of the soviet movement) wrote:

> The Party's principal base, the source of its strength permitting it to lead the soviet movement, is of course the basic proletarian centers of the country. From here, from the underground organization, the party directs the soviets, giving them political directives, recruiting their cadres from among the workers, etc.[55]

Did the concept of "hegemony of the proletariat" imply a dictatorship of the proletariat? It appears that it did not. On this

[52] Vladimirova, *Bor'ba za sovety v Kitae,* p. 35. North refers to an official Chinese Communist document dated March 26, 1930, which shows that the proletarian element in the entire Party at that time was only 8 per cent; North, *Moscow and Chinese Communists,* p. 132.

[53] *Vtoroi s"ezd kitaiskikh sovetov,* p. 55. The complete social breakdown of delegates to the Second Soviet Congress is as follows:

Industrial workers	8	Farm hands	122
Handicraftsmen	244	Poor peasants	303
Coolies	53	Middle peasants	25
Tradesmen's assistants	2	Petty tradesmen, others	64

[54] See *Sovety v Kitae,* "Introduction."

[55] *Ibid.,* p. 109 *n;* see also Erenburg, *Sovetskii Kitai,* p. 122.

point Soviet and Comintern writers were quite explicit. Throughout the Kiangsi period the dictatorship was said to be shared by the proletariat and the peasantry on a more or less equal basis. The "two-class dictatorship" was in fact an important element in Russian theory during the so-called "agrarian" phase of the Chinese revolution. In 1928, speaking on the question of leadership in the soviet movement, Stalin had said:

> When we say that the Communists direct the government there, we must take into consideration that they direct it not under the conditions of the dictatorship of a single class but under the conditions of the dictatorship of two classes. This places their activities within certain limits.[56]

The theory was almost unchanged when Manuil'skii discussed it six years later at the Seventeenth (Russian) Party Congress: "The Chinese Soviet Republic," he said, "is still not a proletarian dictatorship, but it is a particular form of the revolutionary-democratic dictatorship of the proletariat and the peasantry during the general crisis of capitalism." [57]

Other writers spelled out in more detail the significance of the "two-class dictatorship." According to Pavel' Mif, its essence was that the proletariat leads but does not dictate; the proletariat and the peasantry together dictate.[58] Wang Ming called the soviets "a proletarian means and form of struggle, although in their social content they are a form of dual class power." [59] Wang Ming then went on to enumerate, as was customary during these years, various gains in the labor sphere which had aided and were aiding the soviet movement, but reverted strongly to his original thesis before leaving this subject: the fundamental two-class character of the soviet revolution was in no sense altered by the revolutionary upsurge in Kuomintang China.[60]

Why did Wang Ming evidently feel it necessary to deny any threat to the "two-class dictatorship" by the wave of revolution

[56] Stalin, *Voprosy Leninizma* (8th ed.; Moscow, 1933), p. 242.

[57] Manuil'skii, *Otchetnyi doklad XVII s"ezdu VKP(b)*, p. 36.

[58] *Kolonial'nye problemy, sbornik 3–4*, pp. 30–31.

[59] *Vtoroi s"ezd kitaiskikh sovetov*, p. 23 of "Introduction" by Wang Ming (italics in original).

[60] *Ibid.*, p. 24.

which he alleged was rising in nonsoviet China? Presumably because by 1935 the two-class concept had become as completely identified with the current stage of the revolution as the notion of its being "protracted." Wang Ming was simply being cautious. To have implied that conditions were ripe for a dictatorship of the proletariat would have been no different from predicting an imminent transition to socialism, a prediction which, it has been noted, would have left Wang Ming vulnerable to charges of *putschism*, Trotskyism and "Left" opportunism. The time would be ripe for speaking of the next stage of revolution in China when the necessity for a sharing of authority between peasantry and proletariat had ceased to exist.

Let us summarize the substance of Soviet theory on the Chinese revolution between 1930 and 1935—a theory which underwent no appreciable change as a result of the Comintern's withdrawal from China. Seen in its broadest aspects, the revolution was still bourgeois-democratic; its content was still agrarian and antiimperialist. A slight shift was perhaps evident in Moscow's attitude towards the soviets: conceived as urban instruments "for throwing off existing authority" but in fact developing as predominantly peasant organizations, by 1930 the soviets were recognized for what they were and assured a measure of noninterference by the Party's urban-minded leadership. However, their existence was never entirely independent of the workers' movement in the Kuomintang areas, and it is fair to say that, in Soviet theory, Mao's soviets were never more than prototypes of the workers' soviets which would eventually overrun all China. Their true significance would become apparent only when conditions were suitable for the extension of the revolution to the rest of the country—a development not looked for in the immediate, or even the near, future. In the meantime, the fundamental hegemony of the proletariat within the soviet movement was vigorously asserted, both as an objective and as an achievement, but without prejudice to the two-class dictatorship of the workers and peasants upon which soviet leadership was based.

It is worth noting that Mao and his associates in Kiangsi, contrary to a widely held belief, evidently found nothing objectionable in Soviet analyses of the revolution in China. Whatever differences of opinion there may have been in matters of leadership within the Party, there was no observable difference in theory if we are to judge from official records. The agrarian and anti-imperialist character of the bourgeois-democratic revolution was stressed in Juichin as consistently as in Moscow.[61] Of even greater significance is the fact that the Chinese soviet leadership also exhibited its complete orthodoxy in assigning a special role to the proletariat as the class destined to lead the revolution. The first task set for the "democratic dictatorship of the proletariat and the peasantry" in the soviet Constitution of 1931 was "to destroy all feudal remnants, eliminate the influence of the imperialist powers in China [etc.] . . . *in order to effect the transition to the dictatorship of the proletariat.*" [62] After enumerating the various rights and privileges shared equally by workers and peasants in the Soviet Republic, the Constitution went on to state: "Since only the proletariat can lead the broad masses to socialism, the Chinese soviet regime grants special rights to the proletariat in elections to the soviets by allowing it a greater number of deputies." [63] Both of these clauses were retained in the new Constitution adopted by the Second Soviet Congress in 1934.[64] Explaining the electoral weighting in his address to the Second Congress, Mao said:

In order to ensure a proletarian composition of the ruling cadres of the soviet apparatus, it is decreed that one delegate will be elected from every 13 workers and members of their families and one deputy from every 50 peasants.[65]

As far as the soviets themselves were concerned, Mao's notions differed from Moscow's, it may be surmised, only in the degree of

[61] See, for instance, Mao's address at the Second Soviet Congress in *Vtoroi s"ezd kitaiskikh sovetov*, pp. 58–130 *passim.*

[62] Text in Brandt, etc., *Documentary History*, p. 220 (italics added).

[63] *Ibid.*, p. 221.

[64] *Vtoroi s"ezd kitaiskikh sovetov*, pp. 141 and 143.

[65] *Ibid.*, p. 80. Wang Ming indicated a slightly higher weighting of workers in his introduction to this volume. "If out of 200–500 peasants there is one deputy elected," he wrote, "then workers numbering 50–100 have the right to elect one deputy"; *ibid.*, p. 12. Assuming this to be approximately a 5:1 ratio, Wang had, in 1932, indicated a ratio as high as 10:1: "From 200–500–1000 peasants one deputy is elected to a soviet; workers elect one deputy for every 20–50–100 workers"; *XII plenum IKKI*, I, 145.

his conviction that they represented the best hope for the extension of the revolution. In this sense he attached a more literal meaning than observers in Moscow did to Stalin's much-quoted remark in June, 1930, that "only the soviets can save China from eventual disorganization and ruin," a phrase which became the main slogan for the Second Soviet Congress in January, 1934.[66]

SOVIET VIEWS OF MAO TSE-TUNG

Soviet writers, it has been noted, were chiefly preoccupied with theory in their commentaries on China during the early 1930s. This was of course appropriate during a period when the Comintern was cutting back its activities in China and when Moscow would not have wished to call attention to its remaining commitments by expressing too great an interest in the details of the Chinese revolutionary movement. Russian writers, however, could not overlook all political issues. One critical political issue during the Kiangsi period was the attitude Moscow should adopt toward Mao Tse-tung. If Moscow misjudged the strength and character of Mao's leadership and revealed its misjudgment, inadvertently or otherwise—by devoting excessive attention to rival leaders or by slighting Mao—its control of the Chinese Communist movement would become even more doubtful than it already was. The Comintern's finespun theories of proletarian hegemony, of the transition to socialism, of the two-class dictatorship, and so forth, would then have little bearing on the actual course of Chinese Communist policies.

Mao was one of the founders of the Chinese Communist Party and attended its First Congress in Shanghai in July, 1921.[67] According to recent Russian sources, he was first elected to the

[66] The full reference to the Chinese soviets in Stalin's report to the Sixteenth (Russian) Party Congress on June 27, 1930, is as follows: "The Chinese workers and peasants have already responded [to imperialist ventures in China] by creating soviets and a Red Army. It is said [*sic*] that they have already established a soviet government there. If so, I think that there is nothing surprising in the fact. There can be no doubt that only the soviets can save China from evenual disorganization and ruin"; Stalin, *Sochineniia*, XII, 251.

[67] Khu Tsiao-mu [Hu Chiao-mu], *Tridtsat' let KPK*, p. 12 (English ed., p. 8); "Mao Tsze-dun," *Bol'shaia sovetskaia entsiklopediia* (Great Soviet Encyclopedia), XXVI (Moscow, 1954), 244.

Central Committee by the Third Congress in June, 1923.[68] It seems clear, however, to judge from the absence of any reference to his activities in Soviet documents known to this writer which were published at the time of the 1925–27 revolution, that Moscow did not consider him an important leader in the Chinese Communist movement until some time after the launching of the soviet movement in the winter of 1927–28.[69] Even his startling report in March, 1927, on the peasant movement in Hunan seems to have occasioned no public response or rebuke.[70]

One of the earliest references to Mao in Comintern sources seen by the present writer was distinctly uncomplimentary to him. In June, 1929, a letter from the ECCI to the Chinese Cen-

[68] *Ibid.*, pp. 244–45. This source shows Mao's election to the Politburo only in January, 1933. Mao, however, told Edgar Snow that he was first elected to the Politburo in 1924; Snow, *Red Star over China*, p. 166. North does not list Mao as a Politburo member until 1934, although he notes Mao may have been a member in 1927; North, *Kuomintang . . . Elites*, pp. 111–12.

[69] Recent Russian sources give quite a different impression of Mao's role in the 1925–27 revolution. The *Bol'shaia sovetskaia entsiklopediia*, for instance, reports Mao's activities as follows: "During this period [1924–27] Mao Tse-tung, at the direction of the Central Committee, held a number of important positions in the leadership of the revolutionary movement. Following the Third Congress, June, 1923, he headed the organizational section of the Central Committee. In the winter of 1924 he left for Hunan where he directed important work in the organization of the peasant movement; in 1925, he conducted courses in Canton on the peasant movement and simultaneously edited the magazine *Political Weekly*. In the autumn of 1926, after the beginning of the Northern Expedition, Mao returned to Shanghai and headed the Peasant Commission of the Central Committee; later he moved to Wuhan where he was elected chairman of the All-China Peasant Union"; XXVI, 244–45. Kuomintang sources dating from the early 1930s show that Mao's role in the 1925–27 revolution was not insignificant: he was said, for instance, to have been elected a member of the Reserve Central Executive Committee of the Kuomintang in 1924 and to have served in 1926 as deputy to Wang Ching-wei in the Propaganda Department of the Kuomintang and later as Director of the Kuomintang's Peasant Movement Training Center in Canton; Wilbur and How, *Documents on . . . China*, pp. 149 and 217.

[70] This report emphasized strongly the contributions made by the peasants to the revolution to that date and minimized those made by the proletariat. "To give credits where they are due," Mao wrote, "if we allot ten points to the accomplishments of the democratic revolution, then the achievements of the urban dwellers and the military units rate only three points, while the remaining seven points should go to the peasants in their rural revolution"; see the text in Brandt, etc., *Documentary History*, p. 83. A partial translation of this report (omitting the above passage) was included in Bakulin, *Zapiski ob ukhanskom periode kitaiskoi revoliutsii*, pp. 182–86, but it is doubtful if the general substance of the report attracted much attention in Moscow before the publication of this study in 1930. The recent Russian version of the Hunan Report in Mao's *Selected Works* also omits the passage quoted above, although the balance of the work is preserved without appreciable change; Mao, *Proizvedeniia*, I, 33–94 (English ed., I, 31-62).

tral Committee criticized Mao sharply for his attitude toward the kulaks. It drew particular attention to a statement which he had allegedly made several months earlier that "it is necessary to conclude an alliance with the rich peasantry. . . . It would be a mistake if we began deliberately to fan the struggle with the rich peasant-kulaks."

> The Party must not change its general line concerning the kulaks [the ECCI chided]. It must struggle against them for the leadership of the peasant masses, not allowing the kulaks the possibility of using the masses in their own interests.[71]

It would be a mistake to attach too great significance to this criticism. In 1929, we may imagine, Comintern officials probably felt it prudent, in view of the role the kulak issue played in current Soviet politics, to place themselves squarely on record as opposed to any softness toward the kulak. A colonial revolutionary, on the other hand, might err in this matter without necessarily bringing lasting discredit on himself. The criticism, moreover, was no sharper than that administered to many other Chinese Communists during these years of recurrent scoldings and apologies. Of far greater significance than the criticism itself would have been the grace, good or bad, with which Mao accepted it, and there is of course no record of this. The incident in any case is the only one known to this writer when the Comintern officially censured Mao Tse-tung, either directly or indirectly. Needless to say, there is no reference to it in current Soviet and Chinese histories of the Communist movement in China.

By 1930 Mao was gaining a distinctive reputation in Moscow as a peasant leader. One Soviet writer, for instance, described him as "one of the most active Chinese Communists . . . a talented journalist . . . and the representative [within the Party] of the faction demanding the immediate unfolding of the agrarian revolution."[72] In 1930 another writer referred to Mao as the chairman of the Peasant Commission of the Central Committee during the Wuhan period (late 1926 and early 1927), listing him with only four other Chinese leaders as having been partic-

[71] *Strategiia i taktika Kominterna,* p. 242.
[72] Ivin, *Ocherki partizanskogo dvizheniia v Kitae,* p. 91.

ularly active members of the Central Committee at the time.[73] In March, 1930, although its information proved inaccurate, *Inprecor* carried a flattering obituary on the peasant leader "Mau Tze-tung" following his untimely death of consumption! [74]

Mao's election as chairman of the provisional soviet government in Kiangsi in November, 1931, further increased his prestige in Moscow. After this date it was rare for a Soviet writer to fail to mention Mao in discussing the development of the Chinese revolution.[75] Accounts of the soviet movement, which became more and more frequent in Soviet publications after 1931, featured Mao and Chu Teh conspicuously and gave them much credit for the spectacular successes of the soviets. In November, 1933, an article signed by Mao appeared in the Comintern press for the first time.[76]

It is significant, however, that in all the tributes paid to Mao after 1931 he was invariably referred to as a soviet and not as a Party leader. The most authoritative Comintern study of the Chinese soviets, for instance, noted that Mao had been one of the founders of the Soviet movement in 1928–29 and even included a woodcut of Mao as its frontispiece (in the second edition, 1934), yet it ignored him in a discussion of the Party's role in the soviets.[77] Similarly, it may seem odd that in his report on the Comintern to the Seventeenth (Russian) Party Congress in December, 1934, an occasion on which it was traditional to name the Communist leaders in different countries, Manuil'skii conspicuously refrained from naming any Chinese leader.[78]

Where Party rank was not directly concerned, however, Mao was accorded a unique position in the Chinese revolution. The clearest evidence of this is perhaps the attention given to Mao

[73] Bakulin, *Zapiski ob ukhanskom periode kitaiskoi revoliutsii,* p. 283. This reference is of course not necessarily valid as evidence of Mao's prominence during the Wuhan era but does suggest his stature in 1930, the year the study was published.

[74] Tang Shin Sha [Teng Chung-hsia], "Mau Tze-tung," *Inprecor,* No. 14, March 13, 1930, p. 259.

[75] There were of course some exceptions; no reference to Mao, for instance, has been found in Kuchumov's comprehensive survey of the Chinese revolution published in 1934 (*Ocherki po istorii kitaiskoi revoliutsii*).

[76] Mau Dse-Dung [Mao Tse-tung], "Sixth Campaign of the Kuomintang and the Tasks of the Soviet District," *Inprecor,* No. 50, November 17, 1933.

[77] *Sovety v Kitae,* (2d ed., 1933), pp. 103 ff.

[78] Manuil'skii, *Otchetnyi doklad XVII s"ezdu VKP(b)*, pp. 33–36.

in a comprehensive "Who's Who" of the Chinese revolution—including all Chinese political leaders, Communist and Kuomintang alike—published as an appendix to an important collection of documents relating to the Chinese revolution issued by the Comintern in 1934. Here Mao was given more space than any other Chinese leader except Sun Yat-sen and, apart from several purely military leaders like Chu Teh, was in fact the only Chinese Communist listed who was still active at the time the volume was published.[79] If Mao was not at this juncture acknowledged as the leader of the Party, at least no other Party leader, in the minds of the editors of this volume, outranked him.

We touch here upon one of the most critical issues in the entire development of Chinese Communism—the nature of Mao's rise to power during the Kiangsi era and his relationship to the Party hierarchy during those years. After 1935, the Chinese Communist movement bore the stamp of the Kiangsi era rather than that of the presoviet period when the movement had been under the tutelage of the Comintern. In the years since 1949 the leaders in China have for the most part been those who first gained prominence under the Chinese Soviet Republic of 1931–34. It is therefore quite obvious that in a study of this sort the political relationships among Chinese Communist leaders during the Kiangsi period are of paramount importance in understanding later developments in Chinese Communism. This matter will presently be considered, but for the moment our concern is with Moscow's estimate of Mao before he formally took over the leadership of the Party in January, 1935.

Moscow's estimate of Mao prior to 1935 appears on the whole to have been a cautious and somewhat enigmatic one. He was accorded full recognition as the elected chairman of the Chinese soviets and it was occasionally indicated that this might, in fact, be the most important position in the Chinese revolutionary movement. But his position in the Party and his relationship to the existing Party leadership were left obscure, perhaps intentionally so. The way was then open either to acclaim Mao as the undisputed leader of the Chinese Communists, urban and rural alike, or, if it became necessary, to repudiate him as a peasant leader

[79] *Strategiia i taktika Kominterna,* p. 389.

who persistently ignored the primary role of the proletariat in the revolution. It should be noted incidentally that during this period Soviet writers did not always take it for granted that the Chinese soviets would develop, ideologically and politically, in a manner satisfactory to Moscow. They frequently qualified their predictions concerning the spread of the revolution through the growing successes of the soviets with the reservation that this extension would occur only if the soviets developed properly.[80]

Even after Mao's control over the Party was assured, there was no immediate recognition of this in Soviet commentaries. Wang Ming, for instance, gave no specific title to Mao in his references to him at the Seventh Comintern Congress in August, 1935, though he listed him first among the fifty or more heroes of the Chinese revolution.[81] Popular biographies of Mao which appeared in Soviet publications at the end of that year and in 1936 continued to describe him as a soviet rather than a Party leader.[82] Similarly, the entry on Mao in the *Malaia sovetskaia entsiklopediia* in 1937 did not acknowledge his Party position. A year later, however, the article on Mao in the *Bol'shaia sovetskaia entsiklopediia* gave full recognition to his leadership. The first full-length biography of Mao, based largely on Edgar Snow's *Red Star over China,* appeared only in 1939.[83]

[80] Note, for instance, the reservation which Kuchumov inserted parenthetically into a statement in 1934 concerning the issue of transition to socialism: "This transition will be accomplished on the basis and in the form of the soviet authority already won (assuming, of course, the correct development of soviet power and the retaining of a leading role in the soviets by the Communists)"; Kuchumov, *Ocherki po istorii kitaiskoi revoluitsii,* p. 144.

[81] According to one contemporary text of Wang's speech, Mao and Chu Teh were the only Chinese leaders who, when their names were mentioned, were greeted with "prolonged applause"; *Inprecor,* No. 60, November, 1935, p. 1491.

[82] E.g., "Mao Tsze-dun," *Kommunisticheskii internatsional,* Nos. 33–34, December, 1935, p. 90; "Mao Tsze-dun," *Oktiabr',* No. 6, June, 1936, pp. 59–67; Khamadan, *Vozhdi i geroi kitaiskogo naroda.* These accounts were sometimes quite inaccurate. Mao, for instance, was described as of poor peasant origin although he told Edgar Snow in 1936 that his father, once a poor peasant, was rated a kulak before Mao was ten years old; Snow, *Red Star over China,* p. 123. The biographies of Chu Teh were equally inaccurate. One in *Kommunisticheskii internatsional* (Nos. 33-34, December, 1935, p. 91), for instance, asserted that Chu "gave many years of his life to arduous, exhausting work as a coolie." According to Agnes Smedley, Chu Teh was of average peasant stock, received an above-average education—some of it in private schools—and graduated from the Yunnan Military Academy as a second lieutenant in 1911, at the age of twenty-five; Smedley, *The Great Road,* pp. 9–93 *passim.*

[83] *Mao Tsze-dun—biograficheskii ocherk.*

THE UBIQUITOUS PARTY

One reason why the Kiangsi era is obscure to students of Chinese Communism is the absence of precise information concerning the relations of the three principal sources of authority in the Communist movement during this period—the Comintern, the central organs of the Chinese Communist Party, and the soviet government under Mao. Each was distinctive. Each was in its own way important in the revolution during these years: the soviet government, because real power within the Communist movement was centered increasingly in Mao's leadership;[84] the Party's central organs, because they retained the formal authority over the forces of Communism in China; and the Comintern, because of its paternal relationship to Chinese Communism and because of its link with the Russian leadership. What was the pattern of this triangular relationship? This is our problem. Let us begin by considering the relationship, in so far as it can be discovered, between the Party and the Kiangsi soviets.

From early 1928, when the soviet movement in Hunan and Kiangsi registered its first important gains under the leadership of Mao Tse-tung and Chu Teh, it had been under the direction of local party units. As early as the Autumn Crop Uprising of September, 1927, according to the recently published text of a report Mao prepared for the Central Committee on November 25, 1928, a Front Committee had been appointed by the Hunan Provincial Party to serve as the leading Party organ in the soviet areas. Mao was its secretary.[85] This committee was abolished in March, 1928, but in May was replaced by a Special Committee elected by the first "congress" of the Party organization in the soviet region, again with Mao as its secretary. In October, 1928, a second "congress" elected a new Special Committee, and on November 6 this new committee, as well as an Army Committee

[84] Within the Party the group centering around Mao was known as the "real power faction," as distinct from the "returned students' clique"; see Schwartz, *Rise of Mao,* p. 137.

[85] Mao, *Proizvedeniia,* I, 120 (English ed., I, 73).

elected at about the same time,[86] was placed under a reorganized Front Committee consisting of five members "designated by the Party center." Once again Mao was the secretary, according to the recent text of his November, 1928, report.[87]

If this source may be trusted, there would appear to be little doubt of the guiding role played by the local Party organization in the formative years of the soviet movement. By November, 1928, if not earlier, there seems also to have been established a direct link between the Party organization in the Kiangsi-Hunan soviet area and the Central Committee in Shanghai.[88] There is, however, reason to doubt the extent of the Central Committee's authority within the soviet areas during these years. In his report of November 25, 1928, for instance, Mao politely but firmly states certain demands of the soviet center to be met as a *quid pro quo* for demands the Party center has made on the soviets.[89] During 1929, if we may again credit recent texts of documents relating to the early years of the soviet movement, the Front Committee on numerous occasions spoke out unequivocally against certain aspects of the policies of the Central Committee, especially where military tactics were concerned.[90]

During the first half of 1930 the Central Committee continued its efforts to control the soviet movement, apparently with greater success than before. In February, 1930, according to a Chinese

[86] Schwartz believes that the tension between military and civilian leaders (not necessarily between Mao and Chu Teh, however) was as much a source of friction within the soviet areas during the early years of the movement as was the presumed rivalry between the soviet leadership per se and the Party center in Shanghai; Schwartz, *Rise of Mao*, pp. 173–74.

[87] Mao, *Proizvedeniia*, I, 155–56 (English ed., I, 97–98). Mao's report, entitled "The Struggle in the Chingkang Mountains," gives a detailed description of the growth of the Party organization in Kiangsi and Hunan during 1927 and 1928. Not all sources agree on the date when Mao became secretary of the second Front Committee. Mao apparently told Edgar Snow that this occurred in 1929; Snow, *Red Star over China*, p. 177. A Chinese source mentions the "election" of Mao as "chairman" of the Front Committee only at the end of 1930; *Sovety v Kitae*, p. 270.

[88] Chu Teh, on the other hand, told Agnes Smedley in 1937 that the first contact the Chu-Mao forces had with the Central Committee was in the spring of 1929; Smedley, *The Great Road*, p. 252.

[89] Mao, *Proizvedeniia*, I, 159–60 (English ed., I, 100).

[90] See the exchanges between the Front Committee and the Central Committee excerpted in Mao's letter of January, 1930, entitled "A Single Spark Can Start a Prairie Fire"; *ibid.*, I, 190–210 (English ed., I, 116–28).

soviet source, an important conference of Party leaders in the soviet areas, held in southern Kiangsi, was "led by the Central Committee" and guided by recent instructions received from the Comintern and from the Party center.[91] In May the Central Committee is said to have conducted a conference of soviet delegates in Shanghai to coordinate activities in the soviet and nonsoviet areas and to prepare for a full-fledged soviet congress to be held later in the year.[92] And in June the Politburo issued instructions to the Red Army to prepare for direct attacks on urban centers, instructions which were evidently complied with by the soviet leadership in Hunan and Kiangsi. It was these instructions, reflecting the new "Li Li-san line," which led to the Red Army assaults in July and early August, 1930, on Changsha and other cities in Hunan and Kiangsi Provinces.[93]

The ECCI letter of November 16, 1930, and the resolution passed by the Fourth Party Plenum in January, 1931, placed a restriction on the use the Party's central organs might make of the soviets—especially of the armed units in the soviet areas—in supporting urban uprisings. The Party was expected, nonetheless, to continue its supervision of the soviet movement. It was explicitly stated in the Fourth Plenum's resolution that the Central Committee should strengthen its ties with the soviets in order to assist them, where Li Li-san had so spectacularly failed, in the "establishment of a strong soviet political regime." [94] In particular, this resolution set before the Central Committee, as one of its major tasks, the convocation of a soviet congress.[95]

There is some evidence that the new leadership in Shanghai,

[91] *Sovety v Kitae,* pp. 243–44.

[92] *Ibid.,* pp. 255 ff; Vladimirova, *Bor'ba za sovety v Kitae,* p. 40; Schwartz, *Rise of Mao,* pp. 138–41. It is curious that Chu Teh, in his fairly full account of this period to Agnes Smedley in 1937, apparently made no mention of the Shanghai conference. This suggests that the soviet delegates attending the conference (assuming that one was held) may have come from areas other than those controlled by the Mao-Chu leadership.

[93] Chu Teh, in 1937, acknowledged that the Red Army and soviet leadership carried out the Li Li-san line, though with misgivings. The critical shift in their policy, he told Agnes Smedley, occurred on September 13, 1930, when, without consulting the Party center, they withdrew Red Army forces from the vicinity of Changsha and returned to Kiangsi; Smedley, *The Great Road,* pp. 274–79.

[94] "Resolution of the Enlarged Fourth Plenum of the CC, CCP" (January, 1931), quoted in Brandt, etc., *Documentary History,* p. 210.

[95] *Ibid.,* p. 215; see also Smedley, *The Great Road,* p. 294.

presumably in an effort to implement the resolutions of the ECCI and the Fourth Party Plenum, attempted to establish fresh contacts with the soviets during the first part of 1931. Chang Kuo-t'ao, for instance, then recently returned from Moscow and a member of the new Central Committee, has said that he left for a soviet district in Hupeh in April, 1931; that Chou En-lai departed for Juichin in May, to organize the First Soviet Congress; and that other Central Committeemen, including Wang Ming and Po Ku, followed Chou to Juichin in August.[96] There is also evidence that directives from the Central Committee remained influential within the soviet areas at least through 1931. A delegate from the soviet government of southwestern Kiangsi, for instance, stated at a conference of soviet delegates in July, 1931, that the decisions of this conference were correct because they were in accordance with recent instructions received from the Central Committee.[97] A Chinese soviet source dated early in 1932 states that the resolutions on land reform, labor, economic policy, the soviet structure, and the Red Army which were finally adopted by the First Congress in November, 1931, had been worked out in advance by the Party Central Committee and published in draft form as early as March of the latter year.[98]

In 1935 a Russian source made the following assertion respecting Party-soviet relations during the Kiangsi era:

Following the Fourth Plenum the new Politburo revived and strengthened Party leadership in the soviet areas through the creation of a Central Bureau of the Central Committee in the principal soviet area

[96] Chang Kuo-t'ao interview with Lieberman. It is doubtful whether Wang Ming, if he went to Kiangsi at all, stayed through the congress, which did not close until early in December, 1931. A Russian source indicates that Wang reached Moscow in time to address a meeting of the Profintern at the end of 1931; the text of his address is in *Krasnyi internatsional profsoiuzov,* Nos. 1–2, 1932, pp. 67–71. Cf. Wan Yah-Kang, *Rise of Communism in China,* p. 34, in which it is alleged that Wang Ming was detained by Mao in Juichin in the summer of 1932 and was released on petition by Pavel' Mif, on condition that he resign his post as General Secretary of the Party and "be exiled" to Moscow as the Chinese representative to the Comintern.

[97] *Sovety v Kitae,* p. 256.

[98] *Ibid.,* p. 417; this volume contains numerous documents from the soviet areas which refer deferentially to Central Committee resolutions and directives through 1931.

and the appointment of representatives of the Central Committee in all soviet regions.[99]

There may, of course, have existed a Central Bureau in Kiangsi—even in Juichin—which was subordinate to the Central Committee in Shanghai.[100] Chang Kuo-t'ao and Chou En-lai, both of whom are believed to have resided continuously in the soviet areas from 1931 on,[101] and possibly others, may also have served as "representatives of the Central Committee." But it would be a vast overreading of the evidence, in this writer's view, to imagine that the mere establishment of a Central Bureau in Kiangsi and the despatch to the soviet areas of representatives of the Party Central Committee—which probably included, at least nominally, Mao and Chu Teh—assured a lasting revival and strengthening of the Party's urban leadership in the sense which is implied in the Russian source quoted above.

A good deal of confusion concerning Party-soviet relations might be removed if the location of the Central Committee at various stages during the Kiangsi period were known more precisely. Information concerning the movements of the Central Committee, however, is extremely conflicting. Chang Kuo-t'ao, for instance, has stated on several occasions that the decision to transfer the Central Committee from Shanghai to Juichin was

[99] *Kommunisticheskii internatsional pered VII vsemirnym kongressom,* p. 457.

[100] It is possible that the "Resolution on Certain Questions Concerning the History of the Chinese Communist Party," adopted by the Central Committee in April, 1945, was referring to such a Central Bureau in the soviet areas in its criticism of a resolution passed by the "Central Political Bureau of the Central Area" on May 11, 1932; Mao, *Proizvedeniia,* IV, 344 (English ed., IV, 185).

[101] Chang Kuo-t'ao states that he remained in the soviet regions in Hupeh and Szechwan from 1931 to early 1935; interview with Lieberman. Chou En-lai, according to an article by Pavel' Mif in April, 1933, was an important leader in the soviet government and in the Red Army as early as February, 1932. Mif gave this information in the course of denying the authenticity of a letter said to have been written by Chou in February, 1932, in which he allegedly announced his withdrawal from the Party; Pavel' Mif, "Novoe v razvitii revoliutsionnogo krizisa v Kitae" (New Developments in the Progress of the Revolutionary Crisis in China), *Kommunisticheskii internatsional,* No. 10, April 1, 1933, p. 38. Chang Kuo-t'ao, in a recent article, has asserted that Chou En-lai, upon arriving in Kiangsi, wrested political control of the Red Army from Mao Tse-tung; Chang Kuo-t'ao, "Chou En-lai Is a Round Man," New York *Times Magazine,* April 25, 1954, p. 56. A claim of earlier rivalry between Chou and Mao, in 1930, is made in Wan Yah-Kang, *Rise of Communism in China,* pp. 35–36.

made as early as the spring of 1931, because of the increasing restrictions imposed on Communist activities by the Shanghai police and because no Comintern agents remained in China, and that the transfer was actually accomplished in August of that year.[102] This date is also indicated by a Kuomintang source based on Shanghai police reports.[103] On at least one occasion, however, Chang gave the autumn of 1932 as the date of the transfer.[104] This date is supported by another ex-Communist, Li Ang.[105] In 1945 an official Chinese Communist source dated the transfer of the Central Committee to the "southern Kiangsi base area" only in the early part of 1933.[106] Russian sources, it has been noted, continued to speak of the Party's central organs as being located in Kuomintang China even after this date.[107]

[102] Chang Kuo-t'ao interview with Lieberman. In other words, the departure of ranking Central Committeemen from Shanghai to attend the First Soviet Congress would have coincided with the transfer of the entire committee to the soviet areas. Some Chinese Nationalist and Japanese sources, however, indicate that most members of the Central Committee returned to Shanghai after the First Congress and fled only in the fall of 1932; Brandt, etc., *Documentary History*, p. 37.

[103] T'ang Leang-li, *Suppressing Communist-Banditry in China*, pp. 70–71. This source also provides some corroboration of the reasons Chang gives for the withdrawal from Shanghai: it describes in some detail, for instance, the anti-Communist round-up which culminated in the arrest and execution of Hsiang Chang-fa, the Secretary-General of the Party, in June, 1931; it also asserts that the Far Eastern Bureau of the Comintern was broken up with the arrest of the Noulens on June 15, 1931. The Noulens were subsequently tried in Shanghai as agents of the Comintern and sentenced to long terms of imprisonment.

[104] Chang Kuo-t'ao interview with North. Chang stated to North that his memory for dates was poor; the discrepancy here may, therefore, be inadvertent.

[105] Li Ang, *The Red Stage*, p. 205. Li Ang's argument is that Mao, following the consolidation of his position at the First Soviet Congress, virtually compelled the Central Committee to transfer its headquarters to Juichin by threatening to cut off funds. Both North and Schwartz tentatively accept 1932 as the date of the transfer, without necessarily associating themselves with the arguments advanced by, respectively, Chang Kuo-t'ao and Li Ang; see North, *Moscow and Chinese Communists*, pp. 157–59 and Schwartz, *Rise of Mao*, pp. 185–86.

[106] "Resolution on Certain Questions Concerning the History of the Chinese Communist Party" (April, 1945), quoted in Mao, *Proizvedeniia*, IV, 344 (English ed., IV, 185). See also Khu Tsiao-mu [Hu Chiao-mu], *Tridtsat' let KPK*, p. 42 (English ed., p. 36).

[107] E.g., *Sovety v Kitae*, pp. 109–10; Erenburg, *Sovetskii Kitai*, p. 122. A Chinese delegate to the Thirteenth Plenum of the ECCI, in December, 1933, explained the Party's recent growth in the Kuomintang areas by the fact that "the Central Committee of our Party conducts the struggle not in the abstract or formally, but actually, operationally and concretely. In order to exercise concrete leadership, the Central Committee mobilizes its members for the organization of on-the-spot instruction to give assistance to and have control over lower Party echelons"; *XIII plenum IKKI*, p. 363.

Wherever the Party's official headquarters may have been located during the Kiangsi period, there is reason to believe, in this writer's view, that the purely Party leadership and Mao's soviet leadership stood somewhat apart, at least after the First Soviet Congress at the end of 1931. It may be significant, for instance, that in his conversations in 1936 with Edgar Snow, Mao apparently did not once allude to his position in the Party after 1929, although he made frequent reference to his position as Red Army political commissar and chairman of the soviet government.[108] In January, 1934, Mao made none of the principal addresses at the Fifth Plenum of the Central Committee held in southern Kiangsi, and to judge from the fragmentary records of the plenum thus far available, he may not have attended it.[109] A fortnight later, by contrast, he was the dominant figure at the Second Soviet Congress held at Juichin, also in southern Kiangsi. Further indication of the distant relations between the Party and soviet leaderships may be seen in the failure of the soviet congress to elect to active membership on the soviet presidium any of the principal spokesmen at the Fifth Party Plenum (Po Ku, Ch'en Yün and Lo Fu)[110] and in Mao's apparently deliberate rejection of the plenum's directive to the congress concerning treatment of the kulaks. According to this directive, the soviet leadership "must conduct a clear and decisive class line in the matter of liquidating the landlords and the kulaks."[111] Mao, in his address to the soviet congress, said that the kulak should merely be "restrained." "The soviet government," he continued, "must take

[108] Snow, *Red Star over China,* pp. 177–78 *passim.* Agnes Smedley's biography of Chu Teh, which might have been a useful source of information concerning Party-soviet relations during the Kiangsi era, unfortunately has no coverage at all of the period from the First Soviet Congress in December, 1931, to the beginnings of the Long March in the autumn of 1934.

[109] A reference to the Fifth Plenum, including a list of the principal speakers, is given in a footnote in *Vtoroi s"ezd kitaiskikh sovetov,* p. 38. See also the discussion of the Fifth Plenum in Mao, *Proizvedeniia,* IV, 345–46 (English ed., IV, 186).

[110] *Vtoroi s"ezd kitaiskikh sovetov,* p. 49. All members of the Party Politburo, however, were elected as honorary members of the soviet presidium along with Stalin, Molotov, and others; *ibid.,* p. 50.

[111] "Direktiva V plenuma TsK KPK komfraktsii s"ezda" (Instructions of the Fifth Plenum of the CC, CPC to the Party Faction at the [Soviet] Congress), quoted in *ibid.,* p. 41.

severe measures with respect to any tendencies . . . to liquidate the kulak." [112]

Chang Kuo-t'ao has stated that Mao was expelled from the Central Committee following its transfer to the soviet areas.[113] If true, this would of course explain the evidently cool relations between the two leaderships at the beginning of 1934. Whether or not Chang's information is reliable, however, it seems reasonable to conclude that after 1931 or 1932 a Central Committee which did not have Mao's explicit support could not function as the dominant organ of authority among Chinese Communists. Mao drew his support from a far wider basis in the soviet structure and in the Red Army than any rival, or group of rivals, could muster in the purely Party structure either inside or outside the soviet areas. As a consequence, it may be imagined, the Party's central organs, after their transfer to Kiangsi, became mere shells of authority until Mao gained, or perhaps simply assumed, control over them in January, 1935.

A recent official history of the Chinese Communist Party gives the following account of the political situation within the Party during the Kiangsi period. The Wang Ming–Po Ku leadership, this account asserts, had, from the Fourth Plenum on, persistently, "opposed Mao Tse-tung in questions of the tactics and strategy to be used by the Red Army in partisan and mobile warfare." In the Kuomintang areas, in the meantime, the strategy followed by this "perverse" leadership was so disastrous that the Party's urban organizations had been completely destroyed, and the "provisional" Central Committee was obliged in 1933 to transfer its headquarters to the soviet centers. Here, despite the fact that the "provisional" Central Committee was reunited with Mao and with other Central Committee members and the "official central organs" reconstituted, "Mao was still deprived of the leadership, especially the leadership of the Red Army." Eventually, this account continues, a special session of the Politburo at Tsunyi, in January, 1935, "with the majority of the comrades

[112] *Vtoroi s"ezd kitaiskikh sovetov,* p. 96.

[113] Chang Kuo-t'ao interview with Lieberman. Chang states that this was Mao's third expulsion from the Central Committee: the first had occurred in 1924 or 1925 as the result of his having been too close to the Kuomintang and the second in 1927 following the arrival of the Comintern agent Lominadze.

supporting it," removed "these 'Left' opportunist elements from the leading positions in the Party and established a new leadership under Mao Tse-tung." [114]

This account obviously oversimplifies the events of these years, and is almost certainly in error on some critical points—as, for instance, Mao's being "deprived" of leadership over the Red Army.[115] Yet it appears to this writer accurate in its fundamental thesis of a growing conflict between Mao Tse-tung and the "returned students" leadership during the Kiangsi period, a conflict which was resolved only at Tsunyi. What this account does not reveal, in its insistence on the ideological nature of the conflict (which was probably quite unimportant), is the source of Mao's strength. Are we to assume that Mao gravitated to leadership of the Party because of his prestige and influence within the soviet organization and in the Red Army? Or should we imagine, though there is little evidence to prove it, the existence of a Party organization within the soviet areas which was under Mao's control and which in due course elevated him—or through which he elevated himself—to a position of leadership over the old Party center? In this writer's view, the existence of such an organization must be taken for granted. In the first years of the soviet movement, it has been noted, Party units, acting quite independently of the Party center in Shanghai, appear to have guided the activities of the soviets and of the Red Army. Mao was evidently the acknowledged leader of these scattered Party units. There is no reason to doubt that after 1930 or 1931 this Party organization simply continued to function within the soviet regions, as it had before, under Mao's leadership. When the time

[114] Khu Tsiao-mu [Hu Chiao-mu], *Tridtsat' let KPK*, pp. 42–44 (English ed., pp. 36–38). This account follows in most details the "Resolution on Certain Questions Concerning the History of the Chinese Communist Party" (April, 1945) in Mao, *Proizvedeniia*, IV, 339–48 (English ed., pp. 182–88). The only significant difference is that the 1945 resolution, although referring several times to a "provisional Central Committee" (apparently a slighting reference to the Central Committee officially constituted at the Fourth Party Plenum in January, 1931), makes no mention of the re-establishment of the "official central organs" after the transfer of the Party center to Kiangsi.

[115] Chang Kuo-t'ao, however, indicates that Chou En-lai, having gained control of the central Red Army in 1931, held this control until the Tsunyi Conference; Chang Kuo-t'ao, "Chou En-lai Is a Round Man," New York *Times Magazine*, April 25, 1956, p. 58.

was ripe, at Tsunyi, Mao used his control of this Party organization to establish control over a reconstituted Party center, much as Stalin, a decade earlier in Moscow, had come to power through his initial control of the lower echelons within the Russian Communist Party.

It would be instructive at this juncture if we could contrast the relationship between the Kiangsi soviets and the Party center with a parallel relationship between the soviets and the Comintern. But, of course, there is no evidence that such a link existed—and, indeed, there is a reasonable presumption that one did not. When Moscow spoke of the responsible organization in the Chinese Communist movement, whether in the nonsoviet or in the soviet areas, it spoke of the "Party." The Comintern made no official, or at least no public, distinction, as has been made here, between a Party and a soviet leadership. The triangular relationship indicated above between soviets, Party, and Comintern becomes, therefore, a simple bilateral relationship when we consider the Comintern as one of the parties—a relationship between Moscow and the Party center in China, wherever it may be located. Even this theoretically simpler relationship is largely obscured from our scrutiny by the fact that almost no overt ties between the Comintern and the Party center during the Kiangsi period have been discovered (though a presumption that none existed, at least until the transfer of the Party center to Kiangsi, is less certain than a presumption of absence of ties between Moscow and the soviet government at Juichin). If we cannot, then, explore actual links between Moscow and the Party center, we can perhaps discover, in the attitude of the Soviet press toward the Party as a whole, Moscow's evaluation of the current Party leadership.

In general, during the Kiangsi period, Soviet estimates of the Party in China were high. Within a year of the Li Li-san crisis, usually considered the lowest ebb in the fortunes of the Chinese Communists, Manuil'skii called the Party in China "an exemplary Communist Party in a semicolonial country." [116] O. A. Piatnitskii,

[116] D. Manuil'skii, *Konets kapitalisticheskoi stabilizatsii i mirovoi revoliutsionnyi pod"em* (The End of Capitalist Stabilization and the World-wide Revolutionary Surge) (Moscow, 1932), p. 18.

head of the Comintern's Orgburo, told the ECCI late in 1933 that "the successes achieved by the Communist Party of China under conditions of war and revolution should serve as an example to all parties."[117] If this seems routine praise, Manuil'skii's comments a few months later were perhaps less so. Addressing the Seventeenth Congress of the Communist Party of the Soviet Union (CPSU), he said that, with respect to carrying out the goals set by the Comintern for all its sections in 1931, "first place in these achievements, after the CPSU, undoubtedly belongs to the Chinese Communist Party . . . one of the best sections of the Comintern today."[118] Manuil'skii's references to the Chinese Communists on this occasion, according to the official text of his address, were punctuated by more applause than any other parts of his report, excepting only his closing hosannas.

In 1935, on the eve of its Seventh Congress, the Comintern gave this comprehensive appraisal of the Chinese Communist Party, complimenting it on the success it had had in overcoming recent deviations alleged to have arisen in both the soviet and nonsoviet areas:

The Bolshevization of the Communist Party of China did not occur of itself. It developed on the basis of an irreconcilable and tireless struggle on two fronts against every kind of deviation from the general Comintern line. In nonsoviet China the Party conducted a resolute struggle against Right opportunism (the negation of the political struggle of the working class, the liquidation of relations with the revolutionary labor union movement, the reluctance to arm the workers during the defense of Shanghai, etc.) and sectarianism (an unwillingness and inability to work among laborers in the yellow Kuomintang trade unions, an inability to create a united front among the toiling masses, etc.). . . . In the soviet regions the Party, under the Central Committee and with the guiding assistance of the Comintern, maintained its line of struggle against the Kuomintang campaigns, defeating Right opportunists who cried out that the victory of the Red Army was impossible in the face of the superior strength of the enemy and who proposed transforming the regular Red Army into partisan units and abandoning its fortified territorial bases without a fight. At the same time the Party struggled against "Left" adventur-

[117] *XIII plenum IKKI,* p. 174.
[118] Manuil'skii, *Otchetnyi doklad XVII s"ezdu VKP(b),* p. 33.

ists who had long regarded the bourgeois, landowning counterrevolution as a "dead corpse" and declared that the Red Army had no serious opposition.[119]

It is apparent in the foregoing analysis that the Comintern chose not to identify too precisely the "Party" in China of which it spoke. The Party, in Moscow's view, was ubiquitous, dividing its time more or less equally between work in the soviet and the nonsoviet areas. It was seen as the symbol rather than the instrument of revolt. By treating the Chinese Party in this anonymous fashion the Comintern was able to avoid committing itself on a number of troublesome ideological and practical issues. How, for instance, could Communist participation be justified in a revolution which, however proletarian in its origins, was, by 1935, receiving its major impetus from a predominantly agrarian movement? By asserting that the Party in China was conducting a dual effort, and by asserting at the same time, however weak the evidence, that the Party's successes in the urban sector matched those in Kiangsi and that the soviets were in any case operating under "the hegemony of the proletariat," Moscow could claim orthodoxy for the Chinese Communist movement taken as a whole. At the same time the fiction of a ubiquitous Party allowed Moscow to ignore, as a rule, the exact location of the Party center, as between the Kuomintang and soviet sectors of China;[120] a commitment on this point would have destroyed the illusion, which Moscow apparently wished to preserve, that the Party was competent to deal with problems arising anywhere in the country. The Comintern was also able, by considering the Party as a symbolic rather than a functional body, to ignore, at least officially, rivalries in the Party leadership (notably between the Mao and the "returned students" factions, but also, as we shall see, between Mao and other soviet leaders such as Chang

[119] *Kommunisticheskii internatsional pered VII vsemirnym kongressom,* pp. 461–62.

[120] In Soviet documents known to this writer there is no mention, until after the Second World War, of the transfer of the Party center to Kiangsi, either in 1932 or in 1933. On the few occasions when published Soviet sources during the Kiangsi era refer directly to the location of the Party's central organs, they are apt to be placed, as one writer stated in 1934 (presumably with intentional vagueness), "somewhere deep underground in Kuomintang China"; Erenburg, *Sovetskii Kitai,* p. 122.

Kuo-t'ao). The Comintern could equally ignore such mechanics of Party organization as conferences and plenary sessions which perhaps revealed these rivalries.[121]

For these reasons and perhaps also because information regarding the Chinese Communists was even more meager than usual after the withdrawal of the Red Army from Kiangsi (October, 1934), Moscow preferred not to discuss the Party in very specific terms. The Party as an instrument, with its hierarchy of organs, its personalities and its channels of command, replaced the Party as a symbol, in Comintern accounts, only after intra-Party rivalries had been resolved and after Moscow was presumably confident that the new leadership could be trusted.

CHINESE COMMUNISM AND SOVIET OBJECTIVES IN THE FAR EAST

The foregoing detailed analysis of Soviet policy toward the Chinese Communists during the early 1930s should not lead one to imagine that Moscow attached any great significance to the role the Chinese Communists might play in its short-range, or even its long-range, objectives. Moscow's attitude toward Chinese Communism was merely one aspect of Soviet foreign policy and a relatively minor aspect if we may judge from the fact that Stalin, in his published statements from 1931 to 1935, made only one passing reference to the soviets in China and none at all to the Communist movement as such.[122] This must not be overlooked in any attempt to place in reasonable perspective Moscow's policy in the Chinese revolution during these years.

[121] In so far as this writer has been able to discover, notice in Moscow of the Fifth Party Plenum of January, 1934, the only plenary session held by the Chinese Communists between early 1931 and late 1938, was confined to a footnote in a volume devoted to the Second Soviet Congress, held two weeks later; *Vtoroi s"ezd kitaiskikh sovetov,* p. 30. Two earlier Party conferences held in southern Kiangsi in November, 1931, and in August, 1932 (see Mao, *Proizvedeniia,* III, 344; English ed., III, 185), and two subsequent conferences, held in 1935 during the first phase of the Long March, were not specifically mentioned in Soviet accounts until some years later.

[122] This conclusion is based on the author's check of the Soviet press of these years and on the absence of references to the Chinese Communists during the same period in Stalin's *Collected Works,* as indexed by Jack F. Matlock, Jr., *Index to the Collected Works of J. V. Stalin,* External Research Paper No. 118 of the Office of Intelligence Research, Department of State (Washington, D.C., 1955). The single reference to the soviets was made in Stalin's address to the Seventeenth Party Congress in January, 1934; Stalin, *Sochineniia,* XIII, 292–93.

During the greater part of the Kiangsi period Soviet policy in the Far East was determined primarily by the new threat posed by the Japanese invasion of Manchuria in September, 1931. In the first aftermath of the Japanese attack Moscow appears to have recognized no immediate danger to the Soviet Union. Three days after the outset of hostilities, for instance, *Izvestiia* considered that "the threat of anti-Soviet provocation which the attack carries with it" was merely a device on the part of the Japanese "to conceal their aggressive designs" on China. The most caustic remarks of the article were reserved not for the Japanese but for the Kuomintang:

> This new and unheard of degradation imposed on their country will doubtless reveal to the Chinese toilers the full measure of collapse and infirmity to which the country has been brought by the bourgeois-feudal reaction of the Kuomintang, shameful agent of world imperialism.[123]

Early in November the ECCI addressed a letter to the "workers of all countries" in which it declared: "The occupation of Manchuria is not a war against Chiang Kai-shek or the Kuomintang; it is a war against the toiling masses of China and against the Chinese revolution. It is a war against you." [124]

As the war progressed, however, and as it became apparent that the League of Nations was powerless to check the Japanese advance in Manchuria, the Russians began to show some anxiety concerning their own defenses in the Far East. At the end of 1931, reviewing developments in the Manchurian crisis, Molotov said: "All this compels us to strengthen our vigilance as regards happenings in the Far East. We must not forget that our border lies along the Manchurian line." [125] Early in 1932, Voitinskii introduced a volume of Chinese Communist documents relating to anti-Japanese resistance in Manchuria with the thesis that the

[123] N. Pakhomov, "Iaponskaia interventsiia v Manchzhurii" (Japanese Intervention in Manchuria), *Izvestiia,* September 21, 1931, p. 2; see also the leading editorial in *Pravda,* October 3, 1931, p. 1, in which the Kuomintang is accused of a willingness to surrender all China in order to save itself from the Chinese soviets.

[124] *Pravda,* November 6, 1931, p. 1.

[125] *Soviet Union Review* (Washington, D.C.), February, 1932, p. 27, quoted in Moore, *Soviet Far Eastern Policy,* p. 11; chap. II of this volume reviews in some detail Soviet policy during the Manchurian crisis.

Manchurian "incident" was "the prologue to an attack on the USSR."[126] In September, 1932, the Twelfth Plenum of the ECCI considered in some detail the challenge to the Soviet Union arising from Japan's seizure of Manchuria and ruled that it was the duty of all sections to organize resistance to any attack from this area.[127] In a volume published early in 1934, G. B. Erenburg, a specialist on the Chinese soviets, wrote that the goal of the Japanese imperialists was "to strangle the soviet revolution in China, to divide up the country, but, most important, *to transform its separate parts into a Far Eastern springboard for war against the USSR.*"[128]

Officially, the Soviet Union remained neutral in the Sino-Japanese conflict. However, its growing sympathy for China became increasingly apparent, despite continuing reservations respecting the character and intentions of the Kuomintang. During 1932, for instance, Moscow intensified its efforts to reach an agreement with China on the resumption of diplomatic relations, a step which Moscow doubtless felt would strengthen China's resistance.[129] Early in 1933, Litvinov is alleged to have said: "Strictly adhering to a policy of non-interference in the internal affairs of China, we are following its fight for independence and national unity with the greatest sympathy."[130]

It does not fall within the scope of this study to take up in detail the various strategies Moscow devised to meet the threat from Japan—such as the rapid build-up of a special Far Eastern Army, negotiations with Tokyo leading to the sale of the Chinese

[126] *Okkupatsiia Manchzhurii i bor'ba imperialistov*, p. 5.

[127] *XII plenum IKKI*, III, 164.

[128] Erenburg, *Sovetskii Kitai*, p. 115 (italics in original).

[129] According to a recent Soviet source a Chinese representative had arrived in Moscow as early as May, 1930, to negotiate a new treaty on the Chinese Eastern Railway, in accordance with the terms of the Khabarovsk Protocol of December, 1929, and also to discuss a renewal of diplomatic relations between the two countries. Negotiations, however, were slow in getting underway and dragged on with little progress and with frequent interruption through 1930, 1931, and most of 1932. Agreement on the establishment of relations was finally reached only on December 12, 1932; Kapitsa, *Sovetsko-kitaiskie otnosheniia v 1931–1945 gg.*, pp. 17–34 *passim.* See also Beloff, *Foreign Policy of Soviet Russia*, I, 85–87. Soviet efforts to foster an anti-Japanese movement in China after the attack on Manchuria are discussed in the next chapter.

[130] As quoted in an editorial on the Sino-Soviet pact of August, 1937, in *Izvestiia*, August 30, 1937; see text in Moore, *Soviet Far Eastern Policy*, p. 244.

Eastern Railway (a perennial trouble spot in Soviet-Japanese relations), proposals for a pact of neutrality and nonaggression with Japan (in the autumn of 1931 and again in the spring and late autumn of 1933),[131] and vigorous diplomatic exchanges with both Japan and China concerning the protection of Soviet interests in the Far East. But these strategies undoubtedly had precedence in Moscow over any strategies the Comintern may have tried to press upon, or did press upon, the Chinese Communists. It should be kept in mind that while Soviet theories on the Chinese revolution reviewed in this chapter were doubtless genuine —in the sense that they reflected an honest appraisal of the revolutionary prospects in China—any specific policy recommendations for the Communists growing out of these theories were necessarily conditioned by the new Japanese threat to the Soviet Union in Manchuria. The most useful purpose the Chinese Communists could serve, in Moscow's view, lay initially in maintaining an independent position in order to appeal for national unity over the head of the Kuomintang government. In the end, however, we shall see that prudence dictated a policy of alliance between the Communists and the Kuomintang, at least temporarily, for the purpose of uniting China more effectively against a common enemy.

[131] Japan's rejection of these offers was accepted by the International Military Tribunal for the Far East after the war as evidence that Tokyo had aggressive designs against the Soviet Union as early as 1931; see International Military Tribunal for the Far East, *Judgment,* Part B, chap. VI, pp. 779–80. See also Beloff, *Foreign Policy of Soviet Russia,* I, 87 and 170.

2

THE FORMATION OF THE UNITED FRONT

1935–1937

From the time Mao Tse-tung and his followers reached northern Shensi in the autumn of 1935, after the Long March, the attitude of the Chinese Communists toward the political situation in China—and in particular toward the Kuomintang government—began gradually to soften. This was due in large measure to a shift in policy in Moscow toward popular anti-Fascist fronts throughout the world, a policy formally proclaimed at the Seventh Comintern Congress held in Moscow in July and August, 1935. But the consolidation of the Chinese Communist leadership under Mao about this time, after four or five years of an ambiguous situation in the Party's highest councils, was also an important factor in the unfolding of the new policy. It made implementation of the new Comintern line easier in China than it might otherwise have been. In the previous chapter it was shown that during the Kiangsi period two distinct, and probably competing, authorities existed within the Chinese Communist movement: the soviet government, which was dominated by Mao after 1931, and the central organs of the Party (the Central Committee and the Politburo), which had been constituted by the Fourth Party Plenum in January, 1931, and which, so far as is known, remained basically unchanged in composition even after they were transferred from Shanghai to Juichin. So long as these two authorities existed side by side there was always the possibility of a conflict between them, a conflict which would have greatly damaged the prospects for strengthening the Communist movement in China. Risk of conflict was in large part removed when Mao, at a conference of Party and soviet leaders held early in 1935, gained control of the Party. At the same time the central organs were evidently reconstituted to reflect this leadership.

MAO CONSOLIDATES HIS LEADERSHIP, JANUARY, 1935–AUGUST, 1935

The conference which elevated Mao to formal leadership of the Party was held in Tsunyi (Kweichow province) in January, 1935, during the first respite on the Long March. As is usually the case with such meetings, the details of the conference—it was called an Enlarged Conference of the Politburo—are imperfectly known. According to Chang Kuo-t'ao's version, given to Robert North, on this occasion Mao and his supporters raised two charges against the leadership of Po Ku, then the nominal head of the Party: failure to support the Fukien revolt in 1933 [1] and the switch from guerrilla to positional warfare, allegedly the cause of the defeat, or near-defeat, of the Red Army during Chiang's most recent campaign against the Red areas.[2] Similar errors during this period are noted elsewhere, charged variously to a group called the "dogmatists," [3] to Li Teh, the German military adviser allegedly sent to the soviet area by the Comintern,[4]

[1] The Fukien revolt was an uprising of several anti-Chiang military leaders in November, 1933. A "People's Government" was set up in Fukien with an anti-Japanese and semisocialist program, but it fell early in 1934 when the expected support from other anti-Chiang forces—including the Communists—failed to materialize. The official position of the Central Committee, according to a statement in December, 1933, was that, while the Fukien government was doing little more than utter "sweet revolutionary phrases," Communists should nonetheless ally with it to combat the Japanese and the Kuomintang; "The CC of the CP of China on the *Coup de Main* in Fukien" (December 13, 1933), *Inprecor,* No. 11, February 23, 1934, pp. 300–301. Mao's criticism at Tsunyi, therefore, would appear to be directed less against the intentions of the Po Ku leadership (assuming that it was this leadership which issued the above statement) than against the failure to carry out these intentions.

[2] North, *Moscow and Chinese Communists,* p. 166. Chang has stated on another occasion, however, that Mao's chief attack at Tsunyi was directed against Chou En-lai, who since 1931 had allegedly held military control in Kiangsi; Chang Kuo-t'ao, "Chou En-lai Is a Round Man," New York *Times Magazine,* April 25, 1954, p. 58.

[3] Lu Ting-yi, Chief of Information in the Yenan government, to Anna Louise Strong in 1946, as reported in *The Chinese Conquer China,* p. 35.

[4] Various Red Army leaders to Edgar Snow in 1936; Snow, *Red Star over China,* pp. 417–20. It is not clear from Snow's account whether Li Teh personally was held responsible for the failure to act at Fukien, but his alleged responsibility for the switch in military tactics, over the "unanimous opposition of the Red mili-

and to the "Left" opportunists.[5] Recent Chinese sources hold the "Left" opportunist leadership of Wang Ming and the "returned students" exclusively responsible for the errors committed during the Kiangsi period and state that this was the faction which Mao displaced at Tsunyi.[6]

Mao's assumption of Party leadership at Tsunyi, now generally accepted as historical fact, was an important event, but the extent and significance of the debate preceding it should not be exaggerated. Evidence presented in the preceding chapter relating to Mao's ascendancy in the soviet areas as early as 1931 suggests that the conference at Tsunyi may have been no more than a formality. Here, in an hour of crisis, it may be argued, Mao simply received the final certification of an authority he already held.[7]

The Comintern probably knew nothing of the Tsunyi Conference at the time it was held. Nor does there appear to have been any mention of it in Soviet publications until after the war, apart from one oblique reference—not to the conference itself but to an alleged intra-Party dispute arising at about this time—in an article appearing in *Communist International* in July, 1935. Writing of the Long March, the author remarked: "When only the first steps of this great plan had been carried out, the Central Committee of the Chinese Communist Party was compelled to face criticism arising from two sides, namely, from those who

---

tary council," is clearly indicated.

[5] Mao Tse-tung, "Strategic Problems of China's Revolutionary War" (December, 1936), Mao, *Proizvedeniia,* I, 330 (English ed., I, 191).

[6] Khu Tsiao-mu (Hu Chiao-mu), *Tridtsat' let KPK,* p. 43 (English ed., p. 37); see also Mao, *Proizvedeniia,* I, 260 (English ed., I, 153).

[7] It is curious, in view of the attention given to the Tsunyi Conference in recent official sources, both Russian and Chinese, that neither Edgar Snow nor Agnes Smedley make mention of it in their accounts of interviews held with Chinese Communist leaders two years later. In reply to a question recently put to him on this point by the present writer, Snow said that he does not recall hearing of the Tsunyi Conference during either of his visits to the Communist areas in 1936 and 1939; letter to the author dated December 5, 1956. It is quite possible, of course, that the serious intra-Party conflict which arose in Szechwan in August, 1935 (discussed below), largely obscured the Tsunyi Conference and made it seem, by mid-1936 and afterward, a relatively unimportant event. The unpurged state, in any case, in which Snow, in the summer of 1936, found Po Ku, Lo Fu, Chou En-lai, Li Teh, and others who may have been part of the Tsunyi "opposition" suggests that whatever took place there left no permanent scars on the Party high command; see Snow, *Red Star over China,* pp. 399–403.

were prone to underestimate the negative features resulting from the evacuation of the soviet district in Kiangsi and from those who fell into a panic and could see nothing but the retreat, after which, as they visualized it, the Chinese revolution would suffer a big set-back." [8] The opposition, however, is here defined very vaguely and would not appear to be readily identified with the faction which Mao is later said to have displaced at Tsunyi. In fact, it is clear from the text of these remarks that the author acknowledged *no* change in the Chinese leadership at this juncture, evidently assuming that Mao was already in control of the Party's highest organs. In recent years, however, Soviet sources follow Chinese sources in dating Mao's control of the Party only from the conference at Tsunyi, although the precise title he received at that time is uncertain.[9]

Moscow appears also to have been both ignorant and confused concerning the purpose and objective of the Long March, to judge from scattered accounts which appeared in the Soviet press. In one of the earliest reports published in Moscow after the Red Army had broken through the Kuomintang blockade at the end of October, 1934, Wang Ming argued that the decision to evacuate Kiangsi had been based on three considerations: on the need to achieve a more fluid defense to counter Chiang's new strategy; on the need to participate in the anti-Japanese defense in North China; and on the need to replenish the Red Army's reserves from new territories.[10] A Soviet review of Chiang's sixth

[8] M. Fred, "At the Front with the Chinese Red Army," *Communist International,* No. 14, July 20, 1935, p. 876.

[9] One recent Soviet source refers to Mao's election, at Tsunyi, as "Chairman of the Central Committee"; Ermashev, *Svet nad Kitaem,* p. 261. Other current Russian sources speak of Mao at this time as "Secretary of the Central Committee": e.g., *Bol'shaia sovetskaia entsiklopediia,* XXVI (Moscow, 1954), 245 and *New Times,* No. 40, 1956, p. 30. Chinese Communist sources appear to be equally conflicting. A pamphlet by Mao (*China and the Second Imperialist World War*) published in 1939 bears the by-line "General Secretary of the Communist Party of China." Another Chinese Communist pamphlet published the following year, however, gives the same title in reverse ("Secretary-General") to Lo Fu; Wang Chia-Hsiang, Chen Po-ta, and Lo Fu, *Communists and the Three People's Principles,* p. 55. Strong, *The Chinese Conquer China,* p. 38, states that Mao was not formally elected to the Party chairmanship (presumably of the Central Committee) until April, 1945.

[10] Wang Ming, "The New Situation and the New Tactics of Soviet China," *Inprecor,* No. 62, December 8, 1934, pp. 1658–59.

campaign against the Kiangsi soviets published three months later, in March, 1935, and based largely on foreign press dispatches, however, failed to note either the apparent success of the campaign or the decision of the Red Army to vacate the soviet areas.[11] Another Soviet account published early in 1935 admitted that "the loss of a significant part of the central soviet territory is undoubtedly a blow," but added that this circumstance only aided the Red Army by allowing it to maneuver again in open country.[12]

None of these early accounts recognized the evident fact that Kuomintang pressure had compelled the Red Army to withdraw from Kiangsi. Even after this had been frankly admitted by responsible spokesmen—by Manuil'skii, for instance, in September, 1935,[13] and by Mao himself a year later[14]—the great majority of Soviet accounts continued to ignore it. So experienced an observer as Voitinskii blandly asserted several years later: "in the interests of an immediate cessation of the civil war in China, the Communist Party decided, after repulsing the sixth campaign, to transfer its strength to the northwest." [15] Only in recent years have Soviet writers on China conceded that the Communists withdrew involuntarily from Kiangsi. In acknowledging it they

[11] G. Kara-Murza, "Konets 6-ogo pokhoda protiv kitaiskikh sovetov" (End of the Sixth Campaign against the Chinese Soviets), *Tikhii okean,* No. 1, 1935, pp. 74–96. Soviet writers normally count six distinct campaigns against the Communists in Kiangsi, Chinese writers only five; the difference seems to arise from varying interpretations of Chiang Kai-shek's military activities in 1932. See Efimov, *Ocherki po novoi i noveishei istorii Kitaia,* p. 319 *n.*

[12] *Kommunisticheskii internatsional pered VII vsemirnym kongressom,* p. 460.

[13] Addressing a meeting of the Moscow organization of the Russian Communist Party on September 14, 1935, Manuil'skii stated that "the Chinese Red Army, surrounded on all sides by superior enemy forces, was obliged to abandon the Central Soviet Region." Manuil'skii, *The Work of the Seventh Congress of the Communist International,* p. 51.

[14] Mao told Edgar Snow in the summer of 1936 that Kiangsi had been abandoned as a result of the tactical errors discussed above, "combined with the overwhelming numerical and technical superiority of the Kuomintang forces"; Snow, *Red Star over China,* p. 187. Mao wrote essentially the same thing in his "Strategic Problems of China's Revolutionary War" (December, 1936); text in Mao, *Proizvedeniia,* I, 330 (English ed., 191–92).

[15] G. Voitinskii, "Natsional'no-osvoboditel'naia voina kitaiskogo naroda" (War of National Liberation of the Chinese People), in *Trudy* Instituta vostokovedeniia, I (1939), 40. Soviet writers on China normally use the term "northwest" to designate the provinces of Kansu, Shensi, and Shansi, thus distinguishing them from the "northeastern" provinces, i.e., Manchuria.

sometimes quote Mao as their authority: "Not wishing to surrender a part of our territory, as a result we lost it all." [16]

So far as the destination of the Long March was concerned, few Soviet writers appear to have anticipated, while the Long March was in progress, that the Red Army would eventually proceed as far north as Shensi province. In June, 1935, a Soviet writer described the object of the Red Army's movement as "the establishment of a new soviet base in Szechwan." [17] On July 3, a writer in *Pravda* considered the "military-political" tasks as having been accomplished with the recent meeting of the First Army (under Mao and Chu Teh) and the Fourth Army (under Chang Kuo-t'ao and Hsu Hsiang-ch'ien) in southern Szechwan.[18] During the Seventh Congress of the Comintern several speakers —including even Wang Ming, who had earlier suggested an objective closer to the Japanese armies in Manchuria—spoke of a new soviet district "of such size and strength as has previously been unknown" already established in the vicinity of Chengtu in central Szechwan. Printing the text of Wang's address, *Pravda* included a map of this new soviet district.[19]

It would not be difficult to imagine, of course, that the Russian press, in claiming the creation of a new soviet stronghold in Szechwan, was merely trying to cover up any further movement of the Red Army, were it not for the fact that some Comintern accounts frankly asserted that the halt was temporary. One writer in *Communist International,* for instance, claimed in mid-July that the stopover at Chengtu was merely a pause in the march to allow the Red Army time to consolidate and to improve its posi-

[16] Erenburg, *Ocherki natsional'no-osvoboditel'noi bor'by kitaiskogo naroda,* p. 158.

[17] S. Gal'perin, "Novyi etap bor'by kitaiskikh sovetov" (New Stage of the Struggle of the Chinese Soviets), *Vlast' sovetov,* No. 11, June, 1935, p. 44.

[18] Al. Khamadan, *Pravda,* July 3, 1935, p. 5. The exact date of the meeting of the First and Fourth Armies is uncertain. Some accounts place it in the vicinity of Moukung in June; e.g., Wales, *Red Dust,* p. 160, citing information received from Hsu Hsiang-ch'ien. Other accounts date the meeting of the Red forces as late as July 20—which of course would make the *Pravda* article, cited above, several weeks premature; see Snow, *Red Star over China,* p. 189 and Smedley, *The Great Road,* p. 382.

[19] *Pravda,* August 9, 1935, p. 5; the same map is reproduced, together with Wang's address, in *Kommunisticheskii internatsional,* No. 25, September 1, 1935, p. 35.

tion.[20] These discrepancies in Soviet accounts concerning the objective of the Long March suggest that there was some real confusion in Moscow over the intentions of the Chinese Communists throughout the summer of 1935. This confusion is in no way surprising in view of the uncertainty among the Chinese Communists themselves at this time concerning the destination of their forces. Disagreement on this matter led to a bitter struggle within the Party leadership and finally to a temporary division of the Red Army.[21]

The details of the political-military conferences held after the junction of the First and Fourth Armies in southwestern Szechwan are imperfectly known. Chang Kuo-t'ao, then the political commissar of the Fourth Army and a major participant in the discussions, has recently given his account of them to Robert North.[22] The debate, according to Chang, centered on two issues: the suitability of maintaining separate soviet areas in China under existing conditions and the destination of the Red forces. With respect to the second issue, evidently the more pressing of the two,[23] Chang favored a destination somewhere to the west,

[20] M. Fred, "At the Front With the Chinese Red Army," *Communist International,* No. 14, July 20, 1935, p. 876.

[21] On the matter of Moscow's presumed ignorance of the purpose and objective of the Long March, Chang Kuo-t'ao's contrary evidence should be noted. According to his account given to North, the question of evacuating the soviet districts in Kiangsi was referred to the Comintern in the autumn of 1934 and the Communists were advised to seek safety elsewhere—if necessary, as far away as Outer Mongolia; North, *Moscow and Chinese Communists,* p. 164.

[22] North, *Kuomintang . . . Elites,* p. 39; a slightly abbreviated report of North's interview with Chang is given in North, *Moscow and Chinese Communists,* pp. 174–75. Chang gives the impression in his account to North that the principal discussions were held at Maoerhkai in northern Szechwan. According to a recent Chinese Communist source, however, the Red Army did not reach Maoerhkai until September, some weeks after the juncture of the First and Fourth Armies and after the initial discussion near Moukung; Mao, *Proizvedeniia,* I, 299, footnote No. 20 (not given in English ed.). According to another source, the First and Fourth Armies did not meet again after leaving the Moukung area in July or early August—that is, until they reunited in Shensi in the autumn of 1936; Smedley, *The Great Road,* p. 331.

[23] No evidence, other than Chang's, is known to this writer which indicates that the soviet issue was seriously considered by the Chinese Communists until early 1937, when concrete concessions to the Kuomintang were discussed in connection with implementing the united front policy; Chang, however, claims to have raised the issue twice before the Maoerhkai talks: in 1932 and, though he was not present in person, at the Tsunyi Conference of January, 1935.

even as far away as Sinkiang, while Mao and Chou En-lai favored settling in the northwest, where they would be in touch with the soviet district already established in northern Shensi.[24] Contact having been momentarily restablished with Moscow, Chang's account runs, the matter was submitted to the Comintern for review. The Comintern first proposed the creation of two independent bases as a solution to the dispute. This, however, proved unacceptable to the Chinese leaders, and, in a further effort at mediation, the Comintern sent one of the Party elders, Lin Yu-ying (then in Moscow for the Seventh Comintern Congress), with authority to find a solution satisfactory to both factions. When this plan also proved unacceptable, according to Chang, Moscow finally approved the Sinkiang destination. An attack by Kuomintang forces while the Communists were attempting to cross the Yellow River, Chang concludes his account, led to a division of the Red forces, the First Army under Mao continuing northward to Shensi, the Fourth Army under Chang and Hsu Hsiang-ch'ien, and including Chu Teh and his staff, marching westward into Sikang province. The two armies were not reunited until October of the following year.[25]

Chang Kuo-t'ao's account is of particular interest for its claim of Comintern participation in the Party crisis in Szechwan. The authenticity of his testimony is open to doubt, however. Surely

[24] See the map in *Pravda*, August 9, 1935, p. 5.

[25] A very different account of the Szechwan crisis appears in Agnes Smedley's biography of Chu Teh; Smedley, *The Great Road*, pp. 328–31. According to her informant (whom she describes as "a Red Army political worker"), Chang's proposal for a westward march of the combined Red forces into Sikang province was defeated at a Politburo conference held near Moukung at the end of July, 1935. The northern destination was reaffirmed and two columns were formed to resume the march—the more easterly column including the Fourth Army and commanded by Mao, the other including the First Army and various other forces, and commanded by Chu Teh. Mao's forces proceeded to Maoerhkai, but the other column, temporarily blocked by a raging mountain stream out of the Kunglai mountains, was presently diverted by Chang Kuo-t'ao, after his "arrest" of Chu Teh and his staff, and led westward into Sikang. In order to avoid open fighting between Chang's troops and troops remaining loyal to Chu Teh, Miss Smedley's informant allegedly told her, Chu offered no resistance. A year later, after the Second Army under Ho Lung had joined the Fourth Army, Chu Teh led the combined forces northward into Shensi and rejoined Mao Tse-tung. This account parallels in most details recent official Chinese Communist accounts, except that the latter make no reference to Chang's "arrest" of Chu and his staff; e.g., Mao, *Proizvedeniia*, I, 299 (English ed., I, 315).

the spectacle of a beleaguered Chinese Communist Party first requesting and then rejecting the advice of the Comintern strains credulity. It is fair to ask in this connection why, if contact was established with Moscow during the summer of 1935, the Moscow press did not show greater consistency in its reporting of the Red Army's movements in central China; why, if the details of the Chinese dispute were known in Moscow, the Seventh Congress should have given Mao the greater acclaim on the eve of a Comintern decision to support, as Chang claims, Chang's view over Mao's on the issue of the destination of the Chinese Red Army forces;[26] why, in fact, the Comintern, in the process of outlining a comprehensive anti-Japanese front for China, should direct the Red Army to remote Sinkiang where it could have played no role in this endeavor. In the absence of other evidence, the Comintern's role in the Szechwan crisis necessarily remains obscure.[27]

In the Soviet press the only reference to a dispute among the Chinese Communists, after Tsunyi, was to one rumored, not between Mao and Chang Kuo-t'ao, but between Mao and Chu Teh. An article in *Bol'shevik* noted that the split of the Red forces in the autumn of 1935 had "produced no small amount of gossip among Chinese correspondents. Almost all of them agreed that, between Chu Teh and his followers on one side and Mao and his followers on the other, a struggle had broken out as a result of disagreement concerning future plans. The result of this struggle,

[26] Chang's prestige is not comparable to either Mao's or Chu Teh's in the Soviet press during this period. The review of the Long March, for instance, in *Pravda* of July 3 (by Al. Khamadan), makes no mention of Chang Kuo-t'ao, although the alleged junction of his Fourth Army with the Chu-Mao forces is the central theme of the review. It is also of interest, in appraising Chang's claim of support from Moscow at this time, that as late as 1934 he is still criticized, in at least two Soviet accounts, for errors he had committed a decade earlier: e.g., *Programmnye dokumenty kommunisticheskikh partii Vostoka,* p. 1 of "Introduction" by Pavel' Mif, and Kuchumov, *Ocherki po istorii kitaiskoi revoliutsii,* p. 126.

[27] It is not clear to this writer whether Chang, in his forthcoming memoirs, will continue to claim Moscow's support during the Szechwan crisis. According to Robert Burton, who is collaborating with Chang on these memoirs, the latter views his role in the Chinese Communist movement as an entirely independent one and does not now claim Moscow's confidence on any occasion; conversation with the author in Hong Kong in January, 1957. In Chang's testimony given to date, however, this claim is clearly made.

according to these correspondents, was Mao's "separation from the main forces of the Red Army." [28] Needless to say, the author of the article in *Bol'shevik* denied these allegations.

Whatever circumstances or considerations led to Mao's movement northward in the summer of 1935, this action seems greatly to have strengthened his position within the Party—at least as against Chang Kuo-t'ao, Chu Teh, and other Party leaders, who had withdrawn, with what appears to have been the larger part of the Red Army, further into the interior of China. In northern Shensi, Mao apparently succeeded with little difficulty in establishing his authority over the local soviet regime and by 1936 had rebuilt the tattered remnants of his army into a force that commanded Nanking's attention in a new round of "bandit-suppression" campaigns. He was also more strategically located than any of the Party leaders who had remained in the south to implement the united front policy in China which had been decreed at the Seventh Comintern Congress in August, 1935.

The disputes that had arisen in the Party leadership in the summer of 1935 may not have been wholly resolved in Mao's favor during the Szechwan conferences, but his position in Shensi proved to be impregnable by October, 1936, when the leaders who had remained in the south rejoined him. There was apparently no serious challenge from this quarter to his leadership until a year or more later, after the formation of the united anti-Japanese front.[29]

[28] M. Fred, "Kitaiskaia krasnaia armiia-peredovoi otriad antiiaponskogo narodnogo fronta Kitaia" (Chinese Red Army—the Advance Detachment of the Chinese Anti-Japanese People's Front), *Bol'shevik*, No. 9, May 1936, pp. 63–64. In contrast to most later accounts of the Long March—e.g., Edgar Snow's—which indicate that the larger part of the Red Army followed Mao northward, it is interesting that the author of this article speaks of Mao's forces as a "detachment" (*otriad*) at the time of their departure from Szechwan; *ibid.*, p. 67. Smedley, *The Great Road*, pp. 329–30, indicates that the First Army numbered 45,000 when it reached Szechwan, the Fourth Army 50,000. Snow, *Red Star over China*, pp. 192–94, gives the size of Mao's forces as 30,000 at the time of leaving Szechwan and 20,000 upon arrival in northern Shensi.

[29] Nothing is known to date of the conflicts which may have arisen between Mao and the Party leaders who accompanied him to Shensi in the autumn of 1935; according to Edgar Snow, these included Chou En-lai, Peng Teh-huai, Lin Piao, and most of the members of the Central Committee (Snow, *Red Star over China*, p. 192). Chang Kuo-t'ao's memoirs will doubtless shed some light on this matter.

THE SEVENTH COMINTERN CONGRESS AND THE ORIGINS OF THE UNITED FRONT

While the Chinese Communists were struggling northward in Western China and resolving internal political crises in their own fashion, the eyes of the world were focused on the deliberations of the Seventh Congress of the Comintern, held at Moscow in July and August, 1935. Chinese Communist delegates were present in some number at this congress. At least nine speeches by Chinese delegates were reported in the Soviet and Comintern press during and following the congress, and a lengthy report by Wang Ming on the revolutionary movements in colonial and semicolonial countries was one of the dozen principal addresses delivered.[30] The new Executive Committee included as many Chinese as Russians, although all but Wang Ming were elected *in absentia*. Wang was also elected to the Presidium of the Executive Committee and chosen as one of three candidates to the seven-man Secretariat.[31]

Praise of the Communist achievements in China was no less enthusiastic than it had been at plenary sessions of the ECCI during the previous five years (the Twelfth in September, 1932, and the Thirteenth in December, 1933). Wilhelm Pieck, speaking in behalf of the ECCI, declared, with more eagerness than accuracy:

[30] Speeches by Chinese delegates were reported as follows in the Soviet or Comintern press: Wang Ming (August 7), in *Pravda*, August 9, 1935, in *Inprecor*, No. 60, 1935, and elsewhere; Chow Ho-sin [Chou Ho-sheng] and Kon Iuan, in *Revoliutsionnyi vostok*, No. 5, 1935, and in *Inprecor*, No. 51, 1935; Lian-pu, in *Pravda*, August 11, 1935, and in *Inprecor*, No. 62, 1935; Sin I-tin, in *Pravda*, August 20, 1935; Kon Sin [K'ang Sheng], in *Inprecor*, No. 51, 1935; Sin Juan-sin and Wang Yung [Wang Yun-sheng?], in *Inprecor*, No. 67, 1935; and Li Maung, in *Inprecor*, No. 3, 1936. Of these speakers, only Chow Ho-sin and Wang Yung reported primarily on the Chinese soviets.

[31] See *Kommunisticheskii internatsional*, Nos. 23–24, August 20, 1935, pp. 160–61. Other Chinese members of the ECCI, beside Wang Ming, were Mao Tse-tung, Chou En-lai, and Chang Kuo-t'ao; K'ang Sheng and Po Ku were candidate members. Chang Kuo-t'ao's membership on the ECCI, despite implied criticism of his past behavior in recent Soviet publications, suggests that his prestige was still of some significance in Moscow. If Chang's claim is correct that Moscow was aware of the crisis in Szechwan in July—which the present writer does not necessarily believe—it is quite possible, of course, that the Comintern deliberately placed Chang on the ECCI, along with Mao, in order to avoid deciding between the two rival leaders at this juncture.

The Chinese Revolution provides the first model of a colonial revolution in which the ideological and also, in its initial form, the state hegemony of the proletariat is realized. In the Chinese working class the colonial proletariat has proved in practice its ability to solve great historical problems, to maintain the complete economic and political independence of the country, to abolish feudal survivals, to put an end to large landed proprietorship, to cut out the cancer of usury, and to undertake revolutionary changes that clear the way for the victory of socialism.[32]

Georgi Dimitrov, the new General Secretary of the Comintern, also made flattering references to the Chinese soviets when he spoke, and these were greeted with more applause than was any other part of his address except his closing remarks.[33] The only criticism of the Chinese Communist Party, in fact, came from its own delegates, and was directed primarily toward the Party's urban organization, which was better represented at the congress than were the Chinese soviets. In retrospect the charges leveled against the Party appear to have been purely formalistic and fail to reflect in any way the weightier problems confronting the Party's leaders during the Long March. Typical charges were, for instance, "excessive centralism," "excessive organizational complexity with too many sections and subsections," "lack of discipline among the individual members in their political lives," "lack of influence with the masses among lower party units," and so forth.[34]

The main purpose of the congress's deliberations on China, however, was not to uncover actual or imaginary shortcomings in the Party leadership but to launch a united front against Japan and Japan's agents in China. In this respect Wang Ming's address on August 7 had considerably more relevance than those by other Chinese delegates. "The Communist Party," he observed, "has no other means for the general mobilization of the entire Chinese nation for the sacred national revolutionary struggle against imperialism than the tactics of the anti-imperialist United

[32] *VII Congress of the Communist International,* p. 51.

[33] *Ibid.*, p. 173.

[34] See Kon-Iuan, "Geroicheskaia bor'ba Kompartii Kitaia v gomindanovskom podpol'e" (Heroic Struggle of the Chinese Communist Party in the Kuomintang Underground), *Revoliutsionnyi vostok,* No. 5, 1935, p. 41.

People's Front."[35] He praised the Party leadership for having, on the whole, applied these tactics successfully since 1932. In a statement that was quoted widely in the Comintern press during subsequent months, Dimitrov, too, applauded "the initiative taken by our courageous brother Party of China in the creation of a most extensive anti-Japanese united front against Japanese imperialism and its Chinese agents.[36]

These claims of a "most extensive" united front policy allegedly pursued in China by the Communists for some time before the Seventh Congress are not easily supported. While it is true that the Chinese Communists, after September, 1931, had repeatedly condemned the Japanese attack on Manchuria and had called for Chinese resistance to it, as often as not they equated the Japanese aggressor and the Kuomintang as enemies of the Chinese people, and not infrequently insisted that the destruction of the Kuomintang must precede any anti-Japanese united front. Ten days after the Manchurian incident had begun, the Central Committee branded as "amusing, absurd, and false" rumors that Mao and Chu Teh "are ready to fight for 'a united front against the external enemy' and to go over to the side of the Kuomintang." The Chinese Communist Party, the resolution continued, was "the eternal enemy of [both] the imperialists and the Kuomintang."[37] During the defense of Shanghai in February, 1932, a declaration issued by the Central Committee insisted that "for a complete victory in the people's revolutionary war it is necessary

[35] *Inprecor,* No. 60, October, 1935, p. 1489.

[36] *VII Congress of the Communist International,* p. 173. The sections of Dimitrov's speech which refer to China are identical in this 1939 text and in the texts published during the congress; cf. *Inprecor,* No. 37, September, 1935, pp. 971–72. Wang Ming's speech, on the other hand, was significantly abridged in the 1939 text.

[37] *Okkupatsiia Manchzhurii i bor'ba imperialistov,* p. 153. The most important statements by the Chinese Communists between September, 1931, and September, 1935, relating to Japanese aggression in Manchuria are listed, with brief summaries of their contents, in the first section of the Appendix. While every effort has been made to determine the authors or organizations issuing these statements, there is no certainty, of course, that the authors indicated in the sources available to this writer were the actual authors. A declaration ascribed, for instance, to the Central Committee, or even to the soviet government in Juichin, could have been prepared and issued in Moscow. Since, however, such practice is not susceptible of proof, these declarations are discussed below as bona fide statements of the indicated authors.

to destroy the leadership of the Kuomintang militarists." [38] The Chinese Soviet Republic's declaration of war on Japan in April, 1932, stated: "In order to wage war actively against Japanese imperialism, it is necessary first of all to destroy the reactionary rule of the Kuomintang which is assisting the imperialists to strangle the national revolutionary movement." [39]

During most of 1933 the Chinese Communists, while still counting the Kuomintang no less an enemy than the Japanese invader, did not consider its destruction a necessary prerequisite to an anti-Japanese united front. In a declaration issued by the soviet government on January 10, 1933, which called for a common struggle "against the Japanese and other foreign imperialists and also against their traitorous and capitulating agent, the Kuomintang," the Red Army was said to be willing to conclude "a military alliance with any armed forces" on the following three conditions:

1. Immediate cessation of the attack on the soviet regions
2. Immediate granting of democratic rights to the masses (freedom of assembly, press, speech, etc.)
3. Immediate arming of the masses and the formation of armed volunteer units for the defense of China and the struggle for independence, unification, and territorial integrity[40]

This declaration was presumably addressed to the Kuomintang units surrounding the soviet areas in Kiangsi[41] and, it may be

[38] *Sovety v Kitae,* p. 451.
[39] *Programmnye dokumenty kitaiskikh sovetov,* p. 91.
[40] *Programmnye dokumenty kitaiskikh sovetov,* p. 95.
[41] In January, 1934, in his address before the Second Soviet Congress, Mao stated—according to two contemporary translations of this address—that the appeal of January, 1933, was addressed to "all Kuomintang forces engaged in the attack on the soviets and on the Red Army"; *Vtoroi s"ezd kitaiskikh sovetov,* p. 65. See also Mao Tse-tung, *Red China,* p. 5. (The translation of Mao's address in Brandt, etc., *Documentary History,* p. 228, however, does not include this reference to Kuomintang troops, and there is no text of Mao's address at the Second Congress in the current edition of his *Selected Works.*) In Nanking, where the full text of the Communist declaration was evidently not known, some newspapers appear to have understood that the appeal was addressed not only to the Kuomintang but to Chiang Kai-shek himself. Pavel' Mif, reviewing favorable reaction to the Communists' proposal in the non-Communist Chinese press, cited one article entitled "If I Were Chiang Kai-shek," the gist of which, Mif implies, was: "If I were Chiang Kai-shek, I would accept the Communists' offer"; Pavel' Mif, "Novoe v razvitii revoliutsionnogo krizisa v Kitae" (New Develop-

imagined, was prompted more by the Communists' desire to have the blockade eased than by any serious intent to resist Japanese aggression in Manchuria, a thousand miles away. The same three conditions for a military alliance between the Communists and "any armies or military units for a struggle against the Japanese invaders" were repeated in similar declarations later in 1933.[42]

There was evidently little response to the Communists' appeals in 1933 for a united front. In January, 1934, as the situation in Manchuria became more or less stabilized and as Chiang Kai-shek's "bandit suppression" campaigns in the south became, by contrast, more menacing, the Communists again emphasized the need to destroy the Kuomintang. At the Second Soviet Congress in January, 1934, Mao referred to the appeals for an anti-Japanese alliance which had been made during the preceding year, but voiced no new ones—except as applicable in Manchuria proper.[43] He considered, instead, that "it is necessary first of all to gather all our forces for victory over that lackey of imperialism, the Kuomintang, since it is an obstacle to the anti-imperialist struggle

ments in the Progress of the Revolutionary Crisis in China), *Kommunisticheskii internatsional,* No. 10, April 1, 1933, p. 36. It is interesting that some Soviet sources now criticize declarations such as that of January 10, 1933, because they raised the question of a united front with the Kuomintang leadership rather than with the Chinese people as a whole; this, it is said, was because the Communist movement was at that time temporarily under the influence of "Leftist" elements. See, for instance, *Noveishaia istoriia stran zarubezhnogo Vostoka,* II, 51.

[42] *Programmnye dokumenty kitaiskikh sovetov,* pp. 93–94 and 96–100; *Inprecor,* No. 44, October, 1933, pp. 971–72. These declarations were all signed by soviet and Red Army leaders. The present writer has seen only one anti-Japanese declaration by the Central Committee between February, 1932, and August, 1935. This was dated December 13, 1933, and concerned the revolt of the Kuomintang Nineteenth Army in Fukien during that month; *Inprecor,* No. 11, February 23, 1934, pp. 300–301 (see Appendix).

[43] A declaration from the congress to Communist partisans in Manchuria instructed them "to ally with all anti-Japanese volunteer units for a common struggle against Japan and the Kuomintang on the basis of the three conditions published in January, 1933"; *Vtoroi s"ezd kitaiskikh sovetov,* p. 181. Similar instructions allegedly had been sent to Communist partisans in Manchuria a year earlier. A Japanese source, referring some years later to these instructions of January 26, 1933, stated that this "established a strong anti-Japanese movement in Manchukuo . . . two years and a half before the Seventh World Congress of the Comintern adopted a clear-cut policy of forming an international popular front"; Hidaka, *The Comintern's Intrigues in Manchoukuo,* p. 44. These instructions are also mentioned in Soviet and Chinese Communist sources: e.g., Yan Sun [Yang Ching-tzu?], "The Anti-Imperialist United Front in Manchuria," *Communist International,* "Special Issue on China," February, 1936, p. 181, and Struggle for Peace and Democracy in the Northeast, p. 18.

of the soviets and of the Chinese people."[44] A proclamation issued by the same congress announced that "at present, when soviet and Kuomintang power stand so sharply opposed to one another, peaceful coexistence is impossible," and it predicted a "struggle to the death."[45]

This appears to have remained the view of the Chinese Communist leadership on the united front issue during the remainder of the Kiangsi era and during the first phase of the Long March. On June 15, 1935, a declaration signed by six soviet and Red Army leaders showed the Chinese Communist leadership still implacably hostile to the Kuomintang and especially to Chiang Kai-shek. "The Chinese soviet government," this declaration read, "declares that it has sentenced Chiang Kai-shek to death; it calls upon people throughout the country to settle accounts with this watchdog of Japanese imperialism."[46]

On August 1, 1935, a declaration issued jointly by the Chinese soviet government and by the Party Central Committee (now under Mao's control) indicated the first significant shift in the Communist position on the united front. Now, for the first time, the Communists specified the Kuomintang—or at least "the Kuomintang armies"—as their intended ally. Following a review of the allegedly traitorous activities of Chiang Kai-shek and the Kuomintang in the past, which was written in language not greatly different from that of the earlier manifestos on the subject of anti-Japanese resistance, the August Declaration went on to say:

> If the Kuomintang armies will stop their attacks on the soviet districts and if their forces will fight the Japanese invasion, then, regardless of the animosity and differences of opinion on internal problems that have existed between them and the Red Army in the past, the Red Army will not only immediately cease its action against them, but is

[44] *Vtoroi s"ezd kitaiskikh sovetov,* p. 66.

[45] *Ibid.,* pp. 175 and 178.

[46] *Inprecor,* No. 32, August 3, 1935, p. 831. This declaration, which is signed by both First and Fourth Army leaders, is dated prior to the junction of these armies in Szechwan, and thus, if dated correctly, is one of those documents mentioned above whose indicated authorship must be questioned.

ready to join hands with them to carry on a joint fight for the salvation of the country.[47]

Only this declaration, which presumably was issued in remote Szechwan province during the Party conferences discussed earlier,[48] could have supported Dimitrov's claim, made the following day in Moscow, of Chinese Communist "initiative . . . in the creation of a most extensive anti-imperialist united front." Until this time it cannot be shown that the Chinese Communists had displayed either originality or consistency in their efforts to organize serious resistance to Japanese aggression, except, perhaps, in Manchuria proper.[49]

It should not, however, be imagined that the Seventh Congress itself had any clear idea of how a united front might be organized in China. Although the decision to launch a broad united front against Japan was undoubtedly the chief long-range consequence of the congress, as far as the Chinese Communists were concerned, and although this decision in due course was to lead to an alliance between the Communists and the Kuomintang, in August, 1935, no one in Moscow appears to have believed that Nanking should be invited to join the proposed coalition. Dimitrov continued to link "the treason of the Nanking government"

[47] "Appeal to the Whole People to Resist Japan and Save the Country" (August 1, 1935), *Inprecor,* No. 70, December 21, 1935, pp. 1728–29.

[48] Chiang Kai-shek states that the declaration was issued at Maoerhkai; Chiang Kai-shek, *Soviet Russia in China,* p. 66; see also Cheng Tien-fong, *History of Sino-Russian Relations,* p. 201. A Japanese source, however, doubts the Chinese origin of the August Declaration. The author believes it was prepared in Moscow, at the time of the Seventh Congress, and reached China only at the end of 1935; Otsuka, *The Red Influence in China,* p. 89.

[49] One source, however—which the present writer has not, as a rule, found reliable—asserts that the Communists issued an appeal very similar to the August Declaration as early as April, 1934. The appeal, according to this source, was "for the formation of an Anti-Imperialist United Front irrespective of political affiliations"; Wan Yah-Kang, *Rise of Communism in China,* p. 39. The present writer has found no other reference to such an appeal in 1934. It should be noted that Communist statements during this period can be misleading if not inspected with great care. A statement like the one referred to by Wan, for instance, might open with an appeal for a united front "irrespective of political affiliations," but indicate that the Nanking government and the Japanese were to be equal targets of any alliance concluded; such, in essence, was the declaration of January 10, 1933. Whether or not, in any case, the Communists issued the appeal to which Wan refers, their continuing hostility toward the government and toward Chiang personally was clearly revealed a year later in the declaration of June 15, 1935.

with "the predatory attack of Japanese imperialism" as the principal cause of China's predicament.[50] A resolution passed by the congress on August 20, 1935, called on all sections of the Comintern to support the Chinese Red Army in "its struggle against the Japanese and other imperialists and the Kuomintang." [51] Virtually all of the Chinese delegates bracketed foreign imperialism, the Japanese (some delegates failed even to specify the Japanese), and the Kuomintang as the composite enemy of the Chinese people.[52] Even Wang Ming, who did not specifically indicate that the proposed united front was to be directed against the Kuomintang and even suggested that "all honest young people from among the membership of the Kuomintang" might be included in it, was sharply critical of Kuomintang behavior in the past. Of Chiang Kai-shek he said: "The Red Army . . . alone is capable of successfully repelling the unceasing campaigns of Chiang Kai-shek and of conducting a war against this archbetrayer of the Chinese people." [53]

The difficulty facing the Chinese Communists and the Comintern during the 1930s in attempting to bring about a united front in China was, from their point of view, that there existed no middle element in the social and political structure—as in France, for instance—with which Communists could ally. Before the Japanese attack on Manchuria, in September, 1931, the official Comintern line in China had been a "united front from below." As popularized in Comintern pronouncements of this period, the "united front from below" was generally understood to be an alliance of proletarian and semiproletarian elements in any country directed against a local ruling group. The united front proper, however, at least as it developed after 1935, was primarily directed against a foreign aggressor—in fact, against the totalitarian powers which were aligned against the Soviet Union—and was expected to include groups of varying outlook

[50] *VII Congress of the Communist International,* p. 173.
[51] *Ibid.,* p. 593.
[52] See especially the speeches of Wang-Yung [Wang Yun-sheng?] and Sin Juan-sin, *Inprecor,* No. 67, 1935, pp. 1660 and 1668.
[53] *Inprecor,* No. 60, November, 1935, p. 1489. The most critical references to the Kuomintang and to Chiang Kai-shek are deleted from the 1939 text of Wang Ming's speech in *VII Congress of the Communist International,* pp. 285–94.

which lay, politically, between the Communists and the most conservative classes and organizations in a given country. In China, apart from the Communists, there was only one well-defined political organization of consequence, the Kuomintang, in which all politically conscious elements in Chinese society (other than the Communists) were somehow or other assembled.

For a time after the invasion of Manchuria the Chinese Communists, apparently on instructions from the Comintern, continued to apply the tactics of the "united front from below," but directed now against the foreign aggressor as well as against the domestic enemy.[54] As the Japanese in Manchuria grew more menacing, however, both to China and to the Soviet Union, it became apparent that an anti-Japanese united front in China would be meaningless if it failed to include the Kuomintang, or substantial parts of it. This realization, both in Moscow and in China, probably came very haltingly and not without recurrent misgivings, inasmuch as an alliance with the Kuomintang necessarily meant a partial surrender of the Chinese Communists' domestic objectives. These waverings perhaps explain the ambivalence of such documents as the August Declaration, which begins by sharply attacking the Kuomintang and then goes on to propose an alliance between Communist and Kuomintang armies against a common foe. They may also explain the apparent difference, in August, 1935, between the attitude toward the united front in China expressed by the authors of the August Declaration and by Wang Ming, on the one hand, and the narrower view expressed, on the other hand, by the remaining Chinese delegates at the Seventh Comintern Congress and by the authors of the Congress's resolution of August 20.

In the summer of 1935, then, the Comintern did no more than propose a united front. It was nearly a year afterward before the full implications of the united front policy were widely appreciated, either by the Russians or by the Chinese Communists, and

[54] In September, 1932, for instance, the Twelfth Plenum of the ECCI directed the Chinese Communists to continue working toward a "united front from below," which it described as an alliance of toilers directed "against all imperialists and for the overthrow of the lackey of imperialism, the Kuomintang"; *Sovety v Kitae,* p. 110.

more than two years before a united front was formally proclaimed.

AFTER THE SEVENTH CONGRESS, SEPTEMBER, 1935–NOVEMBER, 1936

So long as no military or other group in China was likely to heed the Communists' frequent appeals for unified Chinese resistance to Japan, it had cost nothing to issue them. Such manifestos committed the Communists to no specific program, beyond resistance to the Japanese, and within the limited circle in which the manifestos circulated they probably had some propaganda value. The Seventh Congress, however, charged the Chinese Communists with a new responsibility: not merely to talk of unity in China, but actually to establish a united anti-Japanese front. It was presumably the difficulties arising from this new responsibility that caused Wang Ming to write in 1937, after the united front had been established: "The Chinese Communist Party has accomplished in the last few years a sharp turn in its policy such as no other section of the Comintern has had to face." [55]

Neither in Moscow nor in China does there appear to have been a prompt understanding, after the Seventh Congress, of all that this turn involved. This is evident in the continuing sharp criticism of Chiang Kai-shek in both Soviet and Chinese Communist pronouncements during the months following the congress. In Moscow, for instance, the veteran specialist on Chinese affairs, G. Voitinskii, wrote in December, 1935:

> If I have spoken of Chinese resistance to Japan, I was speaking—I repeat—of the Chinese masses, of the working class under the guidance of the Communist Party, of the soviets and the Red Army, of partisans and volunteers, of the revolutionary students. In no sense was I referring to Wang Ching-wei and Chiang Kai-shek, the leaders of the Chinese counter-revolution.[56]

"The essential question," Voitinskii concluded, "is how to unify the scattered forces of the anti-Japanese movement in China into

[55] *Bor'ba za edinyi natsional'nyi anti-iaponskii front,* p. 3 of "Introduction."

[56] G. Voitinskii, "Soprotivliaetsia-li Kitai?" (Will China Resist?), *Tikhii okean,* No. 4, October–December, 1935, p. 7.

a powerful stream which would be led by the vanguard of the Chinese working class—the Communist Party."[57] In China, a resolution of the Politburo of the Chinese Communist Party dated December 25, 1935, reveals a similar view of Chiang, according to a recent text. He is repeatedly referred to in this resolution as "archtraitor," "enemy of the people" and "jackal of foreign imperialism."[58] In a report to a conference of Party workers two days later Mao specifically excluded Chiang from his list of potential allies in China, mentioning him instead as the leader of the faction which believed that "revolution (any kind of revolution) is invariably worse than imperialism."[59]

Some softening, however, may be seen in the Communists' attitude toward other elements in China which formerly had been dismissed as Chiang Kai-shek's supporters. The resolution of December 25, for instance, read, in part:

The workers and peasants are of course the basic motive force of the Chinese revolution, and the broad masses of the petty bourgeoisie and the revolutionary intelligentsia are their most reliable allies. . . . Part of the national bourgeoisie and a number of warlords, [however,] although they maintain a negative attitude toward the agrarian revolution and toward the Communist regime, will nonetheless aid the cause of the anti-Japanese front if they show sympathy or maintain a friendly neutrality toward the struggle against Japanese imperialism and the traitors to the country or take a direct part in this struggle.[60]

In his report of December 27, Mao Tse-tung expanded on this resolution.

Is there any possibility that under present conditions the position of the national bourgeoisie will change? We consider that there exists this possibility . . . because the national bourgeoisie is not the same thing as the class of landowners and the *comprador* bourgeoisie; there is a difference between them. . . . We speak here of groups within the national bourgeoisie which have no ties with foreign capital and land ownership, or whose ties are comparatively weak. We believe that under present conditions, when the threat of China's being transformed

[57] *Ibid.*, p. 23.
[58] Mao, *Proizvedeniia*, I, 473–74 (English ed., I, 328–30).
[59] *Ibid.*, I, 263 (English ed., I, 155).
[60] *Ibid.*, I, 475 (English ed., I, 329).

into a colony hangs over the country, there will be a change in the position of these groups.[61]

Mao's conclusion, after a review of the recent anti-Japanese activities of various Kuomintang units, was that "at the moment of national crisis divisions will inevitably occur within the Kuomintang camp." [62]

The first attempt, either in Moscow or in China, to spell out in concrete terms the steps necessary to implement the united front policy appears to have been made by Wang Ming in a series of articles published in the Comintern press at the end of 1935 and early in 1936. In one of the first of these articles he wrote:

The chief weakness and shortcoming of our Party remain the same; that is, first, we have not understood that the policy of the anti-imperialist united front is the principal and only tactical weapon we can use to put into practice our slogan for a national-revolutionary war; second, we have not yet succeeded in linking up our anti-imperialist united front tactics with our activities in other spheres.[63]

The united front, according to Wang, was to take precedence over all other policies; at the given stage it presented the only opportunity for the further development of the revolution. The specific measures that should be taken, Wang said, were: milder confiscation policies with respect to kulaks, craftsmen, and even landowners who might be sympathetic to the anti-Japanese movement; encouragement of private capital in commerce and industry; giving up the idea of workers' control of industrial enterprises; admission of non-Communists into the Red Army and extension of the franchise in the soviet areas to non-Communists; making a distinction between the various imperialist powers, "not excluding the possibility, under certain conditions, of fighting together with [several of] them against the common enemy." [64]

[61] *Ibid.*, I, 264 (English ed., I, 155–56).
[62] *Ibid.*, I, 268 (English ed., I, 158).
[63] Van Min [Wang Ming], "Bor'ba za anti-imperialisticheskii edinyi front; ocherednye zadachi kompartii Kitaia" (Struggle for the Anti-Imperialist United Front; Immediate Problems for the Chinese Communist Party), *Kommunisticheskii internatsional,* Nos. 33–34, December, 1935, p. 21.
[64] Wang Ming, "For a Change in All Spheres of Our Work," *Inprecor,* No. 8, February 8, 1936, pp. 223–24; see also Van Min [Wang Ming], "Bor'ba za anti-

Wang Ming did not, however, suggest that the Chinese Communists needed to abandon their most cherished domestic objectives in order to pursue a united front policy. In discussing the question of Communist participation in a national defense government, which had been proposed as a corollary to the united military front, both by the Chinese Communists (in their August Declaration) and by Wang Ming (in his speech at the Seventh Comintern Congress),[65] Wang wrote:

It must be clearly pointed out that the [Chinese] Soviet Government . . . cannot be limited in its actions only to the programs of the government of national defense. For example, on the question of developing the agrarian revolution, the Soviet Government will carry out the demands in the programs of the government of national defense regarding the confiscation of the land of traitors to the people. . . . But at the same time it will not only refuse to abandon its principles requiring the utter liquidation of feudal landlord landownership in China, but will fight to carry such principles into practice, in accordance with the given objective conditions of struggle.[66]

The tactics which Wang Ming prescribed for the Chinese Communists might be described as "cooperation with independence" —cooperation in defense measures against Japan, implying some adjustment of policies in preparation for Communist participation in a coalition government, but with full independence of political action. In essence, Wang's recommendations (which presumably had the authority of the Comintern behind them) sought to rationalize the participation of a strong and independent Party in a coalition that by force of circumstances must

---

imperialisticheskii," *Kommunisticheskii internatsional,* Nos. 33–34, December, 1935, pp. 22 ff; Wang Ming, "The New Policy of the Communist Party of China," *Inprecor,* No. 70, December 21, 1935, pp. 1728–29; Wang Ming, "The Basis of Our New Policy," *Inprecor,* No. 71, December 25, 1935, pp. 1751–53; Wang Ming, "The Relations between the Chinese Soviet Government and the People's Government of National Defense," *Inprecor,* No. 6, January 25, 1936, pp. 148–49.

[65] See *Inprecor,* No. 60, November, 1935, p. 1489 (Wang Ming's address), and *Inprecor,* No. 70, December 21, 1935, p. 1728 (August Declaration). The demand for a government of national defense—in essence, a coalition government of all anti-Japanese elements—remained a feature of Russian and, particularly, of Chinese Communist statements on Japanese aggression until the end of 1936.

[66] Wang Ming, "The Relations between the Soviet Government," *Inprecor,* No. 6, January 25, 1936, p. 149.

ultimately include the Kuomintang if it was to have nationwide significance.

From March, 1936, on there were indications that both the Chinese Communists and the Comintern were gradually shifting their position on the critical question of whether or not Chiang Kai-shek should be included in the united anti-Japanese front. In an interview held early in March (or possibly late in February) Mao continued to speak of Chiang as a "traitor to the nation" but said that the Communists would nonetheless ally with him if he began to resist the Japanese.[67] At about the same time Wang Ming wrote that Chiang would be given a chance "to expiate his guilt" by participating in a program of national resistance to Japan.[68] Early in May the Communists, for the first time, addressed an appeal directly to the Nanking government calling for an end to the civil war and for the immediate formation of a united anti-Japanese front of all armies and other groups in China. Several references to Chiang in this appeal indicated that he was not necessarily to be excluded from the proposed alliance.[69]

A further shift in Moscow's attitude toward the united front and toward Nanking's inclusion in it was indicated in the Soviet reaction to an uprising of Kuomintang officers which took place at Canton early in June. This revolt, conducted under anti-Japanese slogans, was directed against the Nanking government, allegedly to compel Chiang Kai-shek to turn his efforts against the Japanese in Manchuria. A writer in *Izvestiia* considered the uprising a Japanese attempt to provoke a civil war in China in order to camouflage new aggression in the north. The rebels' anti-Japa-

[67] "Interview given by Comrades Mao Tsze-dun [Mao Tse-tung] and Wang Dye chan [Wang Chia-hsiang] to Correspondents of the Red China News Agency," *Inprecor,* No. 14, March 14, 1936, p. 377. Wan Yah-Kang believes that the Communist line on Chiang shifted in February, 1936, following the disaster that befell a Red Army contingent that month in Shansi, allegedly while raiding local food stockpiles to ease the food shortage in the Communist areas; *Rise of Communism in China,* p. 40.

[68] Wang Ming, "The Struggle for the Anti-Japanese People's Front in China," *Communist International,* No. 6, June, 1936, pp. 741–51; this is the translation of an article which appeared in the Russian edition of *Communist International* in March, 1936.

[69] The text of this telegram, dated May 5, 1936, is in Mao, *Proizvedeniia,* I, 476–78 (English ed., I, 330–31).

nese slogans, this writer suggested, were merely a mask to conceal their struggle for control of the national government.[70] A fortnight later *Pravda* carried a Tass dispatch from Shanghai which read in part: "In Chinese circles here no one doubts that the movement initiated by the generals in the southwest [actually, the southeast], whatever their personal inclinations, has rolled over their heads and is hindering the anti-Japanese movement which has been growing in central and northern China." [71] To judge from these press reactions to the Canton episode, Moscow was apparently seeking to preserve the integrity of Chiang's government, preferring—for purposes of the united front—a unified, if still reactionary, Kuomintang to one hopelessly split over extraneous issues.[72]

During July and August, Soviet and Comintern spokesmen, in articles commemorating the fifteenth anniversary of the Chinese Communist Party, clarified still further Moscow's attitude toward developments in China. Pavel' Mif wrote: "Under the influence of Japanese aggression a significant portion of the Chinese national bourgeoisie is changing its position and is trying more and more energetically to find a way to resist Japanese imperialism." [73] Wang Ming wrote in August:

> Communists must not place the Kuomintang and Chiang Kai-shek on the same footing with the Japanese aggressors. . . . Moreover the entire Kuomintang and its forces must not be considered as the allies and supporters of Japanese imperialism. It is clear that serious armed resistance to Japanese aggression requires participation by Kuomintang troops, or by a decisive majority of them.[74]

[70] A. Kantorovich, "Dymovaia zanavesa ili provokatsiia?" (Smoke Screen or Provocation?), *Izvestiia*, June 10, 1936, p. 2.

[71] "Napriazhennye otnosheniia mezhdu Nankinom i iugo-zapadom" (Tense Relations between Nanking and the Southwest), *Pravda*, June 24, 1936, p. 5.

[72] Mao apparently accepted the sincerity of the anti-Japanese slogans and, according to his own testimony several months later, offered to ally with the Canton generals against the Japanese, without reference to their struggle against Nanking; see his "Letter to the Leaders of the All-China Association for the Salvation of the Country" (August 10, 1936), *Bor'ba za edinyi natsional'nyi antiiaponskii front*, p. 34.

[73] Mif, *15 let geroicheskoi bor'by*, p. 103.

[74] Van Min [Wang Ming], "15 let bor'by za nezavisimost' i svobodu kitaiskogo naroda" (15 Years of Struggle for the Independence and Freedom of the Chinese People), *Kommunisticheskii internatsional*, No. 14, August, 1936, pp. 88–89.

Both Wang Ming and Dimitrov cautioned against "sectarian" elements in the Party which might sabotage the united front by failing to see it as a union of all Chinese willing to resist Japan.[75] In September, Voitinskii, who nine months earlier had dismissed Chiang as an unreconstructed "leader of the Chinese counter-revolution," found him quite acceptable and even claimed that the Communists had been willing to join with him in an anti-Japanese alliance as early as 1934.[76]

During this same period, the Party Leadership in China was also making clearer its changed attitude toward Nanking and defining more precisely the relationship of the soviet government and the Red Army to the new organs of national authority that would be established were the united front to materialize. On July 16, 1936, in an official interview with Edgar Snow, Mao said that the Red Army would "wholeheartedly" submit to the decisions of a supreme military command and would keep out of areas occupied by other anti-Japanese forces.[77] On August 25, the Central Committee of the Chinese Communist Party addressed an "open letter" to the Kuomintang which read in part:

We declare that, when a united democratic Chinese republic is formed, the soviet regions will become a component part of this republic, delegates from the soviet regions will take part in a national assembly and in the soviet regions there will be established the same type of democratic system that is introduced in other parts of China.[78]

In September, Mao indicated unofficially that the Red Army, and even the soviets, might be renamed in order to facilitate cooperation between the Communists and the Kuomintang.[79] There is

[75] *Ibid.*, p. 86; G. Dimitrov, "K piatnadsatiletiiu kompartii Kitaia" (Toward the Fifteenth Anniversary of the Chinese Communist Party), *Kommunisticheskii internatsional,* No. 14, August, 1936, p. 80.

[76] G. Voitinskii, "K konferentsii Instituta tikhookeanskikh otnoshenii Iosemiti" (Toward the Conference of the Institute of Pacific Relations at Yosemite), *Tikhii okean,* No. 3, July–September, 1936, p. 13.

[77] The text of this interview is in *Bor'ba za edinyi natsional'nyi anti-iaponskii front,* p. 37.

[78] "Otkrytoe pis'mo TsK Kommunisticheskoi partii Kitaia gomindanu" (Open Letter from the CC of the Chinese Communist Party to the Kuomintang), *Kommunisticheskii internatsional,* No. 18, December, 1936, p. 79.

[79] Snow, *Red Star over China,* p. 426. In a note appended to one text of his interview with Mao in September, Snow wrote: "In conversation with various soviet functionaries I was assured that the soviet government might agree to

some evidence that negotiations between Communist and Kuomintang representatives may have begun about this time,[80] although the absence of any reference to such negotiations in the world press suggests that, if there were any in fact, they were of a restricted nature—possibly between local commanders both of Red Army units and of Kuomintang troops blockading the soviet areas.

The Chinese Communists, however, were not prepared to give way on vital issues affecting their independence. On the question of leadership, for instance, while he acknowledged that of the two principal forces in China "the most important, of course, is the Kuomintang," [81] Mao gave no indication that the Kuomintang should therefore lead the united front. In August, 1936, he wrote: "Some say that our solitary struggle against Japan destroys the 'over-all anti-Japanese strategy.' We don't know what this 'over-all anti-Japanese strategy' means; all we ask is that those who lag move faster and march abreast of us." [82] Concerning the soviets, Mao wrote (magnanimously): "We would even agree to put up to a democratic decison by the people of the whole country the question of whether or not the soviet system should be accepted throughout China." [83] When asked, however, whether his statement that "the laws of a democratic republic would have full effect in the soviet areas" meant that the Communists' land laws

---

change the name of the soviets, as well as that of the Red Army. On the latter's banners already the inscription has been altered from 'Workers' and Peasants' Red Army' to 'Chinese People's Anti-Japanese Vanguard Red Army.' . . . Generally there seems to be a willingness among the Communists to make such changes in nomenclature as might facilitate agreement, but not fundamentally affect the independent role of the Communist Party and the Red Army"; *China: The March Toward Unity,* p. 49.

[80] Both Communist and Kuomintang sources, of later date, refer to discussions held in August, 1936; e.g., Mao Tse-tung, "The Tasks of the Chinese Revolution Since the Formation of the United Front between the Kuomintang and the Communist Party" (September 29, 1937), *Communist International,* No. 2, February, 1938, p. 167, and *China Handbook, 1937–1945* (rev. ed., 1947), p. 66. Chiang Kai-shek has stated that there were discussions held in Shanghai as early as May and that an understanding had been reached "on practically all issues" before the Sian episode of December, 1936; Chiang Kai-shek, *Soviet Russia in China,* p. 73.

[81] An interview with Edgar Snow on September 23, 1936; text in *Bor'ba za edinyi natsional'nyi anti-iaponskii front,* p. 50.

[82] "Letter to the Leaders of the All-China Association," text in *ibid.,* p. 36.

[83] *Ibid.,* p. 41.

would be annulled, Mao evaded a direct answer. "The Chinese people," he said, "will welcome this program and—we are sure—will struggle for its fulfillment.[84] Mao's united front was one in which the logic of the Communist program and the superiority of Communist leadership would, he was convinced, prevail. No less than the Comintern's version, it was to be "cooperation with independence."

It is not easy to estimate how much coordination there was between Moscow and the Chinese Communists during this gradual evolution of the united front policy.[85] In December, 1935, to judge from the Politburo's resolution on the political situation at that time—a resolution, be it noted, which was probably designed for the guidance of top Party leaders and which is therefore not comparable to most of the other sources cited above—the Chinese Communists may have been somewhat ahead of Moscow in anticipating the eventual inclusion in the united front of elements of the "national bourgeosie." It was Wang Ming, on the other hand, writing in Moscow and presumably supported by Soviet and Comintern leaders, who seems first to have indicated the concessions the Chinese Communists would have to make in order to achieve unity in China. In June, 1936, it was Moscow, once again, which during the generals' uprising in Canton first gave more or less open support to Chiang's government.

Lacking precise information on the ties that may have been established between Moscow and the Mao leadership following the conclusion of the Long March in the autumn of 1935, we can, I think, assume only a parallel and not a closely coordinated working out of the united front policy in Moscow and in China. By the autumn of 1936 in any case, both the Comintern and the Chinese Communists appear fully to have accepted the idea that the Nanking government and the majority of the Kuomintang should be included in the proposed anti-Japanese alliance. The

[84] *Ibid.*, p. 51.

[85] The only "evidence" seen by this writer of a direct liaison between the Chinese Communists and Moscow during this period is Chiang Kai-shek's assertion that during the negotiations between the Communists and the government, allegedly begun in May, 1936, one of the Communist participants, Pan Han-nien, was discovered to be in possession of a secret code for communicating with the Comintern; Chiang Kai-shek, *Soviet Russia in China*, p. 73.

old "united front from below," which had prevailed in Comintern and Chinese Communist thinking on anti-Japanese resistance since 1931, was now definitely a concept of the past; the united front proper was taking on a character of its own.[86]

THE SIAN CRISIS, DECEMBER, 1936

Soviet and Chinese Communist policy concerning the united front reached full maturity during the crisis at Sian in December, 1936, when Chiang Kai-shek was arrested and held for a fortnight by several of his subordinate officers. Many of the details of this famous and crucial episode in Chinese history are still obscure but from a variety of sources the essentials of the story can be pieced together.[87] The crisis centered chiefly on Manchurian opposition to Chiang's policy of eliminating Communism in China before coping with the threat of renewed Japanese aggression in the north.

Early in December, 1936, Chiang Kai-shek arrived in Sian—it was his second visit to this city in two months—to supervise personally preparations for what was to have been the final assault

[86] It should be noted, however, that the Russians—and probably the Chinese Communists too—reverted on occasions to their earlier sharp attacks on the Nanking government. As late as November, 1936, for instance, a senior Soviet specialist on China wrote: "the Generalissimo and his government have not only refrained from an official declaration of war on militaristic Japan—which we may perhaps understand—but have done everything in their power *to paralyze armed resistance to the Japanese aggressors* by other armed groups"; A. Ivin, "K sobytiiam v Kitae" (Toward the Events in China), *Mirovoe khoziaistvo i mirovaia politika,* No. 11, November, 1936, p. 54 (italics in original).

[87] There is to date no account of the Sian episode which may be considered authentic. The only full-length study of the incident is James Bertram's *First Act in China;* the information for this account was gathered by Bertram during a visit to Sian immediately after Chiang's release and comes chiefly from Miao Chien-ch'iu, an aide of Chang Hsüeh-liang. On January 23, 1957, the present writer was able, through the good offices of Allen S. Whiting, to obtain an interview with Miao in Tokyo, during which the latter added some information not included in Bertram's account. Agnes Smedley, the only foreign correspondent in Sian at the time of the uprising, has left her interpretation of the episode in *Battle Hymn of China,* pp. 133–50. Edgar Snow included an analysis of the events at Sian in his *Red Star over China.* W. H. Donald, an Australian adviser to Chiang and the only foreigner directly involved in the crisis, gave his version of the affair to his biographer shortly before his death after the war; see Selle, *Donald of China,* chap. XXIII. The Generalissimo and Madame Chiang have given their separate accounts in *Sian: A Coup d'Etat;* see also Chiang Kai-shek's most recent work, *Soviet Russia in China,* pp. 72–79.

on the Red Army. Ignoring the arguments of officers of the predominantly Manchurian Northeast (Tungpei) Army, who understandably wished to end the long-drawn out attack on the Communists and transfer their attention to the Japanese invaders in their homeland, Chiang went ahead with his plans and in due course announced the date for launching the new campaign—December 12. This was also the date of his scheduled departure from Sian. In order to put more zest into the campaign, Chiang removed Chang Hsüeh-liang, Commander of the Northeast Army and an outspoken critic of his anti-Communist policy, as chief of the Bandit Suppression Commission which was to coordinate the attack.[88]

The plot to arrest Chiang and his staff was evidently spelled out at an evening meeting on December 11 with Chang Hsüeh-liang and the local commander, Yang Hu-ch'eng, assuming full responsibility.[89] The coup was successfully carried out with minimum bloodshed at dawn the next day. Chiang himself was ap-

[88] Chang Hsüeh-liang (known to most Chinese as the "Young Marshal" to distinguish him from his father, the "Old Marshal," the former Manchurian warlord Chang Tso-lin) had been named head of the Bandit (i.e., Communist) Suppression Commission, with headquarters in Sian, at the end of 1935. During the course of 1936 Chang's attacks on the Communists steadily decreased in intensity and a virtual truce existed between the two forces from the early summer on. According to Chiang Kai-shek's recent version of the Sian episode, contact between Chang Hsüeh-liang and the Communists was made as early as June, 1936, and intermittent negotiations between representatives of the two factions were carried on in Yenan, then under Chang's control, during the summer and fall; Chiang Kai-shek, *Soviet Russia in China,* pp. 73–75. Miao Chien-ch'iu also argues that there was contact between the Young Marshal and the Communists several months before the Sian incident. On August 10, he states, Chang flew secretly into the Communist areas and conferred with Chou En-lai, Peng Teh-huai, and Ho Lung on the need for a program of unified resistance to Japan. It is Miao's view that this secret visit helped to "persuade" the Communists to give up their rebellion against the Nanking government; interview with the author, January 23, 1957.

[89] There is some question as to how long the idea of "kidnaping" Chiang had been actively discussed among the Manchurian officers. Miao Chien-ch'iu told the present writer that he had discussed this possibility with Chang Hsüeh-liang and a few close advisors as early as September, 1936. Donald, on the other hand, who had formerly been an advisor to Chang and who saw him frequently during the fortnight that the Generalissimo was under arrest, believed that the plot was hatched spontaneously, as a result of Chiang Kai-shek's intransigence on the question of the new anti-Communist campaign, and that Chang Hsüeh-liang's chief object in sponsoring it was to protect his Commander-in-Chief from almost certain violence at the hands of the intensely anti-Japanese junior officers of the Northeast Army; Selle, *Donald of China,* pp. 325 ff.

prehended on the mountainside behind his temporary headquarters after a short flight. Martial law was proclaimed in Sian and a telegram was dispatched to Nanking assuring the government of Chiang's personal safety and listing eight demands. These included, among others, a reorganization of the government to provide for the representation of all political parties, release of political prisoners, immediate cessation of the civil war, and the convocation of a National Salvation Conference.[90] On December 14, W. H. Donald, Chiang's political adviser, was permitted to fly to Sian to visit the Generalissimo and to report to the government on conditions there. On December 19, T. V. Soong, Chiang's brother-in-law, also reached Sian, after overcoming strong objections in Nanking toward any dealings with the rebels by members of the government. And on December 22, Madame Chiang joined her husband in Sian, accompanied by Donald and T. V. Soong who had returned from the insurgent city the day before. All three remained with the Generalissimo until his release on December 25.

Two factors seem to have prevailed in Chiang's sudden release by the Manchurian rebels: an apparent change of heart on the part of Chang Hsüeh-liang, and the unexpected attitude taken by the Chinese Communists toward the crisis. As Chiang's detainment continued into its second week, his chief captor evidently concluded—perhaps after listening to arguments advanced by Donald—that it served no good purpose and only added to the general political confusion in China by removing from the scene the one person capable of restoring order. Since neither Chiang nor the Nanking government would negotiate, the Generalissimo's release at the earliest possible date seemed advisable. Chang Hsüeh-liang, moreover, was willing to accompany Chiang from Sian as an earnest of the good intentions of the insurgents and, if necessary, to stand trial for his actions.[91]

It was one thing, however, for Chang to decide to free the Generalissimo and quite another to arrange his safe departure

[90] The text of this telegram may be found in Bertram, *First Act in China*, pp. 126–27.

[91] See the letter from Chang Hsüeh-liang to the China correspondent of the London *Times*, dated December 19; *ibid*, pp. 135–37.

from Sian. Yang and most of the Manchurian officers involved in the uprising remained adamant in their insistence that Chiang should not leave Sian until some commitment had been made, either by Nanking or by Chiang himself, on the "eight demands."

It was the Chinese Communists who proved to be Chang Hsüeh-liang's best allies in the final phase of the episode. Adopting from the outset the position that Chiang's release was essential to Chinese unity, Communist negotiators in Sian, flown in a few days after the coup, persistently pressed their—and Chiang's—case with the insurgents. Nearly all sources agree that it was the Communists' influence with the younger Manchurian officers which eventually removed objections to the Generalissimo's departure. Some years later Donald described Chou En-lai, the chief Communist representative in Sian, as "actually the one man who enabled General Chiang to depart unharmed." [92]

When only the barest details of the kidnaping were known to the world, the Moscow press reacted sharply. In a lead editorial on December 14, *Pravda* accused Wang Ching-wei[93] of instigating the plot, on behalf of the Japanese militarists, and considered Chang Hsüeh-liang, who was allegedly sympathetic to Japan despite the anti-Japanese sentiments of his troops, a willing accomplice.[94] On the same day Vigilis, pseudonym of the chief editorial writer for *Izvestiia*, considered Chang's anti-Japanese demands "probably" a mask.[95] On the following day another writer noted in *Izvestiia* that, whether this were the case or not, the effect of Chang's uprising was to injure the united front

[92] New York *Times*, February 18, 1945, p. 4. Chang Hsüeh-liang, after accompanying the Generalissimo from Sian, was presently placed under arrest and is still in the custody of the Nationalist government on Formosa. His version of the incident has never been made public. Yang Hu-ch'eng was relieved of his military command in April, 1937, and subsequently arrested by the government. According to a Chinese Communist source, he remained in prison until September, 1949, when he was allegedly killed by Kuomintang officials as Red Army troops approached Chungking; Mao, *Proizvedeniia,* I, 501 (English ed., I, 335).

[93] Wang Ching-wei, long a political opponent of Chiang Kai-shek and subsequently a defector to the Japanese in 1939, was in Berlin at the time of the Sian crisis, recuperating from an assassination attempt earlier in the year; he returned to Nanking early in 1937.

[94] "Sobytiia v Kitae" (The Events in China), *Pravda,* December 14, 1936, p. 1.

[95] Vigilis, "Vosstanie Chzhan Siue-liana" (The Uprising of Chang Hsüeh-liang), *Izvestiia,* December 14, 1936, p. 1.

movement at a time when it was just gaining momentum.[96] All three articles, plus a fourth in *Pravda* on the day following its keynote editorial, urged a speedy and peaceful solution of the crisis.[97]

The most arresting feature of the Soviet position was not the charge of Japanese complicity in the uprising, but the attitude taken toward the Nanking government. *Pravda* observed on December 14:

The Japanese military clique . . . correctly considers that the process of unification in China around Chiang Kai-shek's government, which has been moving forward strongly, constitutes a mortal danger to its plans.[98]

On the same day Vigilis declared:

During the last year there has been a significant rallying around the Nanking government by all social forces in China; the Nanking government, despite all its [previous] waverings and retreats . . . its indecisions and its campaign against the united front movement, has nevertheless shown its readiness and its ability to lead the defense [against Japan].[99]

And on December 27, in praising the peaceful resolution of the crisis, Vigilis made these observations, comparing the Sian episode to the generals' uprising at Canton six months earlier:

The success of the Nanking government as the central organizing force in China was based in both cases precisely on those tendencies to be noted in its policies during the last year; that is, the tendency to move in the direction of making peace with public opinion in China, readiness to take more decisive steps to oppose the external enemy, and the ability—although only in prospect and with many hesitations and failures—to be included in the powerful movement, now inspiring that country, demanding the unification of all forces for defense against Japanese imperialism.[100]

[96] A. Kantorovich, "Iaponskii imperializm i Kitai" (Japanese Imperialism in China), *Izvestiia*, December 15, 1936, p. 2.

[97] Khamadan, "Antiiaponskoe dvizhenie v Kitae" (Anti-Japanese Movement in China), *Pravda*, December 15, 1936, p. 4.

[98] "Sobytiia v Kitae," *Pravda*, December 14, 1936, p. 1.

[99] Vigilis, "Vosstanie Chzhan Siue-liana," *Izvestiia*, December 14, 1936, p. 1.

[100] Vigilis, "Posle osvobozheniia Chan Kai-shi" (After the Release of Chiang

For ten years the Soviet press had not carried such conciliatory remarks about Chiang Kai-shek's government.

Some Comintern writers, probably because of insufficient instructions from their editors, were caught off-balance by what appeared to be a sudden reversal in Soviet policy in China. While the principal point of the Soviet position—the solution of the crisis by peaceful means—was fully grasped, there was confusion on a number of other issues relating to the crisis. On the question of Chang Hsüeh-liang's guilt, for instance, *Inprecor* tended to support the charges raised in *Pravda* on December 14,[101] but a writer in *Communist International,* on December 20, quoted approvingly the view of a Chinese periodical some weeks before that Chang "is primarily interested only in a real anti-Japanese movement and sincerely hopes to influence Chiang Kai-shek to lead active resistance."[102]

Inprecor, meanwhile, appears to have overlooked the more respectful attitude toward Chiang Kai-shek which was reflected in the *Pravda* and *Izvestiia* articles. As late as January 2, ten days after the crisis had ended, *Inprecor* still considered Chiang's role no better than Chang Hsüeh-liang's: "There is one point that

---

Kai-shek), *Izvestiia,* December 27, 1936, p. 1; quoted from translation in Moore, *Soviet Far Eastern Policy,* pp. 235–36. Comparison between the Canton and Sian episodes was frequently made in the Soviet press, both during and after the latter crisis: e.g., Khamadan, "Antiiaponskoe dvizhenie," *Pravda,* December 15, 1936, p. 4; G. Voitinskii, "Dvizhenie narodnogo fronta v Kitae i iaponskii imperializm" (The Movement of the People's Front in China and Japanese Imperialism), *Tikhii okean,* No. 1, January–March, 1937, p. 12.

[101] E.g., Michael Hollay, "The Events in China," *Inprecor,* No. 57, December 19, 1936, p. 1496; "Foreign Political Review of the Week," *Inprecor,* No. 1, January 2, 1937, p. 4.

[102] I. Dzhek [Jack], "O sobytiiakh v Siani" (Concerning the Events in Sian), *Kommunisticheskii internatsional,* No. 18, December 20, 1936, p. 77; the quotation is from *China Weekly Review* (Shanghai), October 24, 1936. This was also the view of the Chinese Communists during the Sian incident. In recent years most Soviet writers have accepted this view; e.g., Efimov, *Ocherki po novoi i noveishei istorii Kitaia,* p. 335; *Novaia i noveishaia istoriia Kitaia,* p. 143 (footnote by the Russian editor). One later Soviet explanation of the Sian episode which squares with no other known to this author was Molotov's to Donald Nelson in 1944, as reported by Nelson to the State Department: "He [Molotov] said that the Soviet government had turned its back on the Chinese revolutionary groups led by Chang Hsüeh-liang and Wang Ching-wei [*sic*] which included many Communists and which looked to the Soviet Union for sympathy and aid and had issued a statement to the effect that Japanese provocation had been the cause of the uprising in Sian." *United States Relations with China,* p. 72.

should be stressed: both rascals have agreed to simulate penitence for their acts: one because he was given a huge sum by the Bank of China [Chang] . . . the other because he wants to retain power [Chiang]." [103]

There was also confusion in the Comintern press over the merits of the punitive campaign against the Sian rebels which was organized by Nanking shortly after the kidnaping. *Inprecor* implied that the campaign was a praiseworthy development and on December 24 charged Chiang Kai-shek with having "done his best to stop this punitive expediton. His wife and brother-in-law, T. V. Saong [*sic*], president of the Bank of China, have made every effort to help him in this. They have even appealed to the traitor Wang Ching-wei." [104] Ten days later *Inprecor* still viewed the campaign favorably and considered it the decisive factor in Chiang's release:

> The rebellion of the traitor Chang Hsüeh-liang in Shensi has come to a miserable end. This is a real defeat of the Japanese intrigues directed against the unity of the Chinese people. Nanking was not impressed and sent troops against the rebel marshal, who was compelled to release Chiang Kai-shek.[105]

A writer in *Communist International*, meanwhile, expressed a directly opposite view. "The Japanese imperialists," he stated in the Russian edition of December 20, "have set in motion all their connections with the Nanking government in order to bring about an armed struggle between Nanking and Chang Hsüeh-liang and thus make maximum use of the Sian events." [106]

[103] "Foreign Political Review of the Week," *Inprecor,* No. 1, January 2, 1937, p. 4.

[104] "Foreign Political Review of the Week," *Inprecor,* No. 58, December 24, 1936, p. 1514. According to Donald's account, only Madame Chiang and T. V. Soong tried to call off the expedition; see Selle, *Donald of China,* pp. 325 ff. The Generalissimo, by his own admission, was "very glad" when he learned of the punitive action; Chiang Mayling Soong, *Sian: A Coup d'Etat,* p. 87.

[105] "Foreign Political Review of the Week," *Inprecor,* No. 1, January 2, 1937, p. 4.

[106] I. Dzhek [Jack], "O sobytiiakh v Siani," *Kommunisticheskii internatsional,* No. 18, December 20, 1936, p. 77. This later became the generally accepted view of Nanking's action in Comintern accounts of Sian. E.g., D. Manuil'skii, "Japan's Attack on China," *Inprecor,* No. 54, December 15, 1937, p. 1310; Chen Tsin, "The Anti-Japanese National United Front in China," *Communist International,* No. 7, July, 1938, p. 649.

Despite these discrepancies in the Comintern and Soviet press and despite a widespread belief abroad that the Sian crisis had produced a dramatic and thoroughgoing reversal of Soviet policy in China, the offical Soviet position, as enunciated in *Pravda* and *Izvestiia,* was in fact only the first open expression of a policy that had been under consideration for at least six months, since the officers' uprising at Canton in June, 1936. When the Sino-Soviet nonaggression pact was concluded in August, 1937, an editorial in *Izvestiia* noted that the negotiations leading to it had been in progress "for more than a year." [107] If this was so, Moscow and Nanking must have been engaged in these talks before the Sian episode, a circumstance that might further explain the moderate Soviet position at this time. There is also the evidence of the Soviet Ambassador to China during this period, D. V. Bogomolov, as reported by an American correspondent who interviewed him in April, 1937:

> The outline of our [i.e., Russia's] new policy toward China was adopted just before the Sian coup last year. That is why we were able immediately to convince Nanking that the Soviet was guilty of no complicity in the kidnaping of the Generalissimo.[108]

Japanese charges of Russian complicity in the revolt, abetted by the awkward similarity between Chang's telegram to Nanking on December 12 (containing the "eight demands") and earlier Chinese Communist statements, may well account for the speed with which the Moscow press reacted.[109] A disclaimer was urgently needed. *Pravda* and *Izvestiia,* departing from their normal habit of giving only delayed editorial comment, countercharged immediately that the Japanese were behind the plot in conjunction with Wang Ching-wei and—for good measure—Chang Hsüeh-liang. The compliments paid Nanking, on the other hand,

[107] "Sovetsko-kitaiskii dogovor o nenapadenii" (Sino-Soviet Nonaggression Pact), *Izvestiia,* August 30, 1937, p. 1. According to Chiang Kai-shek, informal talks had been held in Nanking early in the spring of 1936 and were resumed in Moscow in the autumn; Chiang Kai-shek, *Soviet Russia in China,* pp. 69 and 71. Dallin, *Soviet Russia and The Far East,* p. 67, speaks of Sino-Soviet discussions having taken a "favorable turn" at the time of Sian, but gives no source for his statement.

[108] Abend, *My Life in China,* p. 239.

[109] See Moore, *Soviet Far Eastern Policy,* p. 77.

as well as the recommendation that the crisis be resolved peacefully, were merely manifestations of a more fundamental policy change which had already been mapped out. Were it not for the serious consequences which might arise from unanswered Japanese charges of Soviet complicity in the plot, Moscow would doubtless have delayed any indication of this policy change until the crisis had passed or at least until its course could be more clearly predicted.

The position taken by the Chinese Communists during the Sian crisis was identical with Moscow's, in insisting on a solution reached through peaceful means. On December 19, the Communists sent a telegram to both the Nanking and the Sian authorities calling for an immediate truce and proposing a peace conference in Nanking to determine the future of Chiang Kai-shek. The Communists offered to participate in this conference together with delegates from the national government and from insurgent headquarters. Above all, the telegram concluded, unity must be preserved.[110] Chou En-lai's role as mediator in the final phase of the crisis, to which W. H. Donald and others have testified, illustrates the tactics the Communists used to implement their stated policy and shows to what extent Communist behavior in Sian matched Soviet policy in Moscow.

This similarity has caused some writers to argue that Moscow directed the Chinese Communists' hand at Sian.[111] While this is

[110] "Telegram to the Nanking and Sian Authorities" (December 19, 1936); text in *China: The March toward Unity,* pp. 122–23. One recent account of the Sian episode argues that initially broadcasts from the Communist radio at Paoan demanded a trial and the death penalty for the Generalissimo; Cheng Tien-fong, *History of Sino-Russian Relations,* p. 204. The present writer knows of no corroboration of this evidence.

[111] E.g., Cheng Tien-fong, *History of Sino-Russian Relations,* p. 205; Dallin, *Soviet Russia and the Far East,* pp. 68–70; Wan Yah-Kang, *Rise of Communism in China,* pp. 42–43; Hu Shih, "China in Stalin's Grand Strategy," *Foreign Affairs,* October, 1950, pp. 30–32. Hu Shih offers in support of his claim an interesting quotation from what he calls a "secret pamphlet" issued by the Communists after the Sian incident: "In the Sian affair, Chang Hsüeh-liang and Yang Hu-ch'eng and the other militarists were really more interested in opposition to Chiang than in resistance to Japan. The Communist Party saw this clearly. . . . Therefore our tactical line was 'Peaceful settlement of the Sian affair!' and 'End all civil wars!' *Because the Chinese Communist Party is an International Party and the directives we received from the Third International also said that a peaceful settlement would be right and profitable, it was decided that for the greater benefits of the future we must have peace*" (italics in Hu Shih's

of course a possibility, it would appear to be an unlikely one in view of several discrepancies between the initial Soviet and Chinese Communist positions. *Pravda*'s and *Izvestiia*'s praise of the Nanking government, for instance, has no counterpart in the Communists' telegram of December 19. This telegram, moreover, directly contradicts *Pravda* and *Izvestiia* on the question of the motives of the rebels, asserting that "the Sian leaders acted with patriotic sincerity and zeal." [112] Why, if the Comintern advised the Chinese Communists what line to take at Sian, did it not at the same time indicate the official Russian position with respect to Chang Hsüeh-liang? This was a matter of some interest to the Communists in their efforts to mediate the crisis. It was also not a position which the Chinese Communists could have foreseen, inasmuch as it corresponded so little to the known circumstances of the uprising. The Chinese Communists were well aware—and presumably would have informed Comintern leaders in Moscow, had communication between them in fact existed—that the revolt was not Japanese-inspired but, on the contrary, had come about largely as the result of their own anti-Japanese propaganda among Chang Hsüeh-liang's troops.[113]

article); from Chang Hao [Lin Yu-ying], "The Tactical Line of the Chinese Communist Party" (1937?), p. 48. The authenticity of this document, in the present writer's opinion, is open to much doubt both because of its unorthodox phrasing, as a statement asserted to have been written by the Communists, and because Chang Hsüeh-liang and Yang Hu-ch'eng are considered militarists here, a view that Yenan—as distinct from Moscow—did not hold, so far as is known.

[112] "Telegram to the Nanking and Sian Authorities," in *China: The March Toward Unity*, p. 122.

[113] Communist influence on the troops of the Northwest Army as a factor in the Sian uprising has been widely commented upon in foreign accounts of the incident; e.g., Selle, *Donald of China*, pp. 319 ff.; Snow, *Red Star over China*, pp. 431 ff.; Bertram, *First Act in China*, pp. 105 ff. An article published in the Soviet press immediately after the incident also stressed this point; M. Aleksandrov, "Iaponiia—ochag voiny na Dal'nem Vostoke" (Japan—Hearth of War in the Far East) *Vlast' sovetov*, No. 1, January 1, 1937, p. 35. A recent Chinese Communist source freely admits that "the Sian uprising occurred as the result of strong Red Army influence on the Northwest Army . . . located in its immediate vicinity"; Mao, *Proizvedeniia*, I, 500 (English ed., I, 335). No reliable source known to this writer, however, suggests that the Communists were privy to the plot or directly involved in any way in the kidnaping. Miao Chien-ch'iu, who claims that there was discussion of the plot in the Young Marshal's immediate entourage early in the autumn of 1936, insists that the Communists had no knowledge of these discussions until after the Sian incident; interview with the author on January 23, 1957. Cf. Wan Yah-Kang, *Rise of Communism in China*, p. 42.

There is in any case no reason to assume that the Chinese Communists needed prompting from Moscow to adopt the position they did at Sian. As noted above, the development of the Communists' view of the united front had closely paralleled Moscow's, and by the end of 1936 the necessity of allying themselves with the Kuomintang, or a large portion of it, was taken for granted. Steps to avoid war between rival groups within the Kuomintang was as much in accordance with their anti-Japanese slogans as steps to avoid war between the Kuomintang and themselves. Releasing Chiang Kai-shek could do no worse than restore the *status quo ante,* and their efforts in his behalf, meanwhile, served as an excellent defense against widespread rumors that the Communists themselves had been implicated in the uprising. In short, nothing in the Communists' behavior at Sian was alien to their own best interests, and there was nothing in their position which was inconsistent with their announced policy at this time.

It may be presumed that, as a price for their mediation, the Communist delegates at Sian sought assurances from Chiang that the attacks on the soviet areas would not be resumed. Mao subsequently claimed that such assurances had been given. "The plenipotentiaries of the Chinese Communist Party," he wrote in September, 1937, "finally obtained, with the chief of the Kuomintang at the end of 1936, an agreement important in the political scene of the time, namely, the cessation of the civil war by both parties and both armies, and the peaceful settlement of the Sian incident."[114] If there was in fact such an agreement—Chiang, in his account of the Sian incident, repeatedly denies making any agreement[115]—it was probably not in writing. A few days after Chiang's release Mao acknowledged that the General-

[114] Mao Tse-tung, "Urgent Tasks of the Chinese Revolution since the Formation of the KMT-CCP United Front" (September 29, 1937), quoted in Brandt, etc., *Documentary History,* p. 248; this translation was made from the Chinese edition of Mao's *Selected Works* published in 1944. The translation in *Kommunisticheskii internatsional,* No. 1, January, 1938, p. 69, however, made directly from the text published in *Emancipation* (organ of the Central Committee of the Chinese Communist Party), refers to an agreement only with "representatives of the Kuomintang."

[115] Chiang Mayling Soong, *Sian: A Coup d'Etat,* pp. 54 ff; see also Chiang Kaishek, *Soviet Russia in China,* pp. 72–79 *passim.*

issimo had not signed Chang Hsüeh-liang's "eight demands" and, on this occasion, made no mention of any separate agreement between Chiang and the Communists.[116] Donald, moreover, has stated that Chou En-lai, the only Communist to visit Chiang's quarters in Sian during his arrest, did not even speak with the Generalissimo.[117] The Communist-Kuomintang truce, therefore, probably came about as a result of the changed general climate of opinion in China following the Sian episode, which favored the truce, rather than as a result of any decision or "agreement" reached during the crisis itself.

Much remains obscure about Soviet and Chinese Communist policy during the Sian crisis: the extent to which a general reorientation toward Nanking had been worked out prior to the uprising, the extent to which policy was coordinated between Moscow and Yenan,[118] the reason for the discrepancy (if there was coordination) between Soviet and Chinese Communist views of Chang Hsüeh-liang's role in the uprising, the effect that Japanese charges of Russian complicity in the kidnaping may have had on the attitude Moscow adopted toward the crisis. It is also unclear what assurance the Communist delegates received (if any) that the "bandit-suppression" campaign would cease. Nevertheless, the success of Soviet and Chinese Communist policy, in its broadest outlines, cannot be denied. Chiang Kai-shek might well have been released in due course and civil war averted even if the Communists had not intervened. Yet, as matters developed, Yenan could always claim with some accuracy that its efforts had played no small part in the peaceful resolution of the crisis. "This was an epic event in the history of China,"

[116] Mao Tse-tung, "Statement Apropos of Chiang Kai-shek's [post-Sian] Declaration" (December 28, 1936); text in Mao, *Proizvedeniia,* I, 434 (English ed., I, 254).

[117] Selle, *Donald of China,* p. 330. According to Donald, Chou came to the Generalissimo's quarters once, on the eve of Chiang's release, and on this occasion spoke only with Madame Chiang and Donald himself. Some accounts, however, claim that Chou and Chiang Kai-shek did meet and even describe this meeting in detail; e.g., Snow, *Red Star over China,* p. 475; Bertram, *First Act in China,* p. 133; Elegant, *China's Red Masters,* p. 216. Miao Chien-ch'iu also states that Chou and Chiang met.

[118] According to Chu Teh, the Chinese Communists moved their headquarters from Paoan to Yenan during the crisis, while Red Army troops advanced to within a few miles of Sian; Smedley, *The Great Road,* p. 352.

wrote Mao nine months later. "Henceforth was established the indispensable premise for the formation of a united front."[119]

THE UNITED FRONT ACHIEVED, JANUARY, 1937–SEPTEMBER, 1937

The Sian settlement did not lead immediately to the creation of a united front between the Communists and the Kuomintang. As Mao suggests in the statement quoted above, the Sian settlement was only the premise for unity. It did no more than bring about a truce between Communist and Kuomintang armies. Unity, it will be seen, was not fully achieved until some weeks after the Japanese attack at Lukouch'iao (Marco Polo Bridge) on July 7, 1937.

In the first weeks following the Sian incident the Chinese Communists appear to have been somewhat concerned over the course of events in Nanking. On December 28, for instance, Mao was bluntly critical of Chiang's first declaration following his release. This declaration, according to Mao, was premised on the Confucian maxim "Fidelity to promises; determination in deeds," which Mao understood to signify Chiang's intent to observe the promises he had made at Sian even though these had not been put in writing. Mao did not, however, find that the substance of Chiang's remarks reflected any such intent. He called the statement "cloudy and confused . . . one of the curious political documents in all Chinese history." He denied that the Sian leaders were "reactionaries," as Chiang had claimed. On the contrary, he said, they were "revolutionaries." He sternly cautioned Chiang that he could demonstrate his fitness for leadership only by fulfilling the "eight demands" set forth by Chang Hsüeh-liang, whether or not he had formally acceded to them.[120] On January 6, 1937, a Communist statement addressed to the Kuomintang, the national government, Chiang Kai-shek, and others expressed frank alarm at the resurgence of allegedly pro-Japanese elements

[119] Mao Tse-tung, "Urgent Tasks of the Chinese Revolution," quoted in Brandt, etc., *Documentary History*, p. 248.

[120] Mao, *Proizvedeniia*, I, 434–37 (English ed., I, 254–57). Chiang's declaration was said to have been made at Loyang on December 26, 1936, the day after his release; the author has not discovered the text of this statement in sources relating to this period.

in Nanking. "The present situation," this statement read, "applies an acid test to General Chiang's political integrity and to his expression 'Fidelity to promises; determination in deeds.'"[121] These doubts did not, however, prevent Yenan's sending Chou En-lai to Nanking early in 1937 to discuss the terms of an alliance with government officials.[122]

In February, 1937, the Central Executive Committee of the Kuomintang held a plenary session, the third since the Fifth Congress in 1935, during which the question of an alliance with the Communists was reviewed in some detail. Both in Moscow and in Yenan the preparations for the Third Plenum were watched with interest. On February 10, a week before the plenum convened, the Chinese Communists sent a telegram to the Kuomintang requesting a definite termination of the civil war, a guarantee of civil rights, convocation of a "national salvation" conference, immediate preparations for active resistance to Japan, and efforts to improve the standard of living in China. In return the Communists offered:

1. To stop our program of conducting armed uprisings throughout the country for the overthrow of the National Government in Nanking
2. To change the [Chinese] Soviet Government into the Government of the Special Region of the Republic of China and the Red Army into the National Revolutionary Army under the direct leadership of the Military Affairs Commission in Nanking
3. To enforce the thorough democratic system of universal suffrage within the special regions under the regime of the Government of the Special Region
4. To put an end to the policy of expropriating the land of landlords and to execute persistently the common program of the anti-Japanese united front[123]

[121] "Telegram to the Kuomintang, the Chinese Government, the Military Affairs Commission, Chiang Kai-shek, . . . [and others]" (January 6, 1937); text in *China: The March Toward Unity,* pp. 124–25.

[122] No details of these discussions are available, but Chou En-lai's visit (or visits) to Nanking are referred to in a number of sources: e.g., Bisson, *Japan in China,* p. 180; Rosinger, *China's Wartime Politics,* p. 24; *Foreign Relations of the United States, 1937,* III, 25, 70, and 79; and Smedley, *The Great Road,* p. 354.

[123] "Telegram to the Third Plenary Session of the Fifth Central Executive Committee of the Kuomintang" (February 10, 1937); text in *United States Relations*

This statement was notably more conciliatory in tone than any the Communists had made previously. There was no longer any mention of the establishment of a democratic republic, or of a government of national defense, as a minimum prerequisite for cooperation (subsequently this demand was to reappear in Communist declarations, but only as an objective, not as a condition for the united front).[124] Also, the changes the Communists indicated might be made in the soviet areas went considerably further than any concessions offered before. If carried out, they might in fact have established a firmer basis for Kuomintang-Communist collaboration.

In Moscow, meanwhile, the favorable predisposition of the Soviet press toward the Third Plenum, even before it opened, was reflected in *Izvestiia*'s carrying, on February 17, a Tass dispatch from Nanking under the heading "Draft Resolutions [of the Third Plenum] Defend the Popular Front Policy." On February 22, while the plenum was in session but before the final text of its resolution on the Communist question had been received in Moscow, Vigilis of *Izvestiia* appeared willing to overlook, in advance, any awkward statements the plenum might make. He wrote:

> The political results of this plenum will become apparent in deeds rather than in resolutions, which, according to Chinese tradition generally—and under present circumstances particularly—require diligent reading between the lines. Whatever these decisions, they cannot alter the historical tendency toward unity and the struggle for the liberation of the country, so clearly manifested in recent months.[125]

The plenum's resolution, passed on February 21 and published

---

with China, p. 522. This translation is from the text in the periodical *New China* (Yenan), March 15, 1937. The translation in Mao's *Selected Works* is similar to that quoted above except that "Workers' and Peasants' Democratic Government" is used for "Chinese Soviet Government"; Mao, *Proizvedeniia,* I, 481–82 (English ed., I, 332–33).

[124] E.g., "Declaration of the Central Committee of the Chinese Communist Party" (July 23, 1937), text in *Kommunisticheskii internatsional,* No. 8, August, 1937, pp. 59–61; "The Ten Great Policies of the Chinese Communist Party for Anti-Japanese Resistance and National Salvation" (August 15, 1937), text in Brandt, etc., *Documentary History,* p. 243.

[125] Vigilis, "Gomindanovskii plenum v Nankine" (The Kuomintang Plenum in Nanking), *Izvestiia,* February 22, 1937, p. 4.

in Moscow on February 27, was doubtless a disappointment to the Russians. Although the resolution asserted that "the achievement of internal unity by peaceful means continues to be our guiding principle" and approved, in principle, an alliance with the Communists on four specific conditions,[126] it also placed on the Communists full responsibility for having obstructed Chinese resistance through their terrorist activities since 1927. "In connection with the Communist elements in China," the manifesto read, "the cardinal policy of the central authorities should be their eradication." [127]

In Moscow there was a mixed reaction to the Third Plenum's resolution. *Pravda*'s chief editorial writer on the Far East, A. Khamadan, making a distinction between the Kuomintang and the Nanking government which it was always theoretically possible to make but which Soviet writers rarely made,[128] observed on February 27 (the day the Moscow press published the text of the resolution):

These pro-Japanese policies, deservedly, are held in such universal contempt and distaste that, despite the support they gained both in the plenum and from outside, many of them can hardly gain support in the government proper; Chiang Kai-shek will undoubtedly have to pass them by.[129]

[126] These conditions were: "(*a*) abolition of the separate army and its incorporation into the united command of the nation's armed forces; (*b*) dissolution of the so-called 'Chinese Soviet Republic' and similar organizations and unification of the government power in the hands of the National Government; (*c*) absolute cessation of Communist propaganda and acceptance of the Three People's Principles; (*d*) stoppage of class struggle." These conditions, but not the remainder of the resolution, are given in *China Handbook, 1937–1945,* (rev. ed., 1947), p. 66; see also *Pravda,* February 27, 1937, p. 5. Although no reference was made in the Kuomintang resolution to the Communists' telegram of February 10, it should be noted that the first two conditions closely parallel the concessions offered by the Communists in point two of their telegram, cited above.

[127] *Pravda,* February 27, 1937, p. 5; see also *United States Relations with China,* pp. 48–49, and Chiang Kai-shek, *Soviet Russia in China,* p. 80.

[128] According to Sun Yat-sen's theories of the revolution in China, the military phase of the revolution (the Northern Expedition) was to be followed by a "period of tutelage" during which the Kuomintang was to assume the role of tutelary party until the country was ready for constitutional democracy. This phase began in October, 1928, and lasted, formally, until December, 1946.

[129] Al. Khamadan, "III plenum Tsik gomindana" (Third Plenum of the Kuomintang CEC), *Pravda,* February 27, 1937, p. 5. This is the only comment in the Soviet press of this period, seen by this writer, which suggests Moscow's view of Chiang's position during the Third Plenum. Subsequently, after the Japanese

Vigilis, on the other hand, while clearly disappointed in the manifesto, tended to view the Third Plenum more charitably. The text of the resolution, he suggested, may have been garbled in transmission (it was not). Whatever the plenum's views of the Communists, he continued, the Kuomintang had adopted a position on Japanese aggression which would give little satisfaction in Tokyo. Finally, the plenum had taken place in an atmosphere of "a return to the policies of Sun Yat-sen," in itself a favorable omen for the development of the united front. Vigilis again noted that in China resolutions were not as important as deeds.[130] Actually, neither Khamadan nor Vigilis appears to have felt that the Third Plenum caused more than a temporary setback, if that, to the steady progress in China toward a united anti-Japanese front. Their comparatively mild reaction to the plenum's resolution, despite the Kuomintang's apparent intention eventually to "eradicate" Communism in China, may perhaps be explained by the receipt in Moscow—through diplomatic or other channels—of assurances that the government's policy toward the Communists was not as irreconcilable as the Third Plenum seemed to indicate.

Ten days after the plenum had closed, another Soviet specialist on the Far East observed in *Izvestiia* that the Chinese language was obscure and that probably the Kuomintang's real intent with respect to the Communists was concealed.[131] Wang Ming, writing in the March issue of *Kommunisticheskii internatsional,* displayed a cautious but not unfriendly attitude toward the Kuomintang and suggested that the four conditions proposed by the Third Plenum might serve as the basis for more concrete negotiations between Nanking and Yenan.[132] On March 21,

attack at Lukouch'iao, it was asserted in Moscow that Chiang was "among the more far-sighted leaders of the Kuomintang . . . who [during the Third Plenum] came out in favor of cooperation with the Chinese Communists"; M. Zakarov, "Iaponskaia agressia v Kitae" (Japanese Aggression in China), *Partiinoe stroitel'stvo,* No. 16, August 15, 1937, p. 43.

[130] Vigilis, "Manifest gomindana" (The Kuomintang Manifesto), *Izvestiia,* February 27, 1937, p. 1.

[131] A. Kantorovich, "Na kitaiskie temy" (On Chinese Topics), *Izvestiia,* March 9, 1937, p. 2.

[132] Van Min [Wang Ming], "Kliuch spaseniia kitaiskogo naroda" (Key to the Salvation of the Chinese People), *Kommunisticheskii internatsional,* No. 3, March, 1937, pp. 48 ff.; the same article, with a few changes, appeared also in *Bol'she-*

Pravda indicated Moscow's continuing official confidence in the Nanking government by reviewing favorably a recent statement by a high Chinese official urging an immediate end to Sino-Japanese trade.

The Chinese Communists do not appear to have issued any official statement on the Kuomintang resolution of February 21, 1937, despite the accusations it leveled against them. An American correspondent who was in Yenan late in February, while the Third Plenum was in session at Nanking, reported that "while the Kuomintang proposals are not entirely acceptable to the Red leaders, they seem confident that an eventual agreement will be reached after prolonged discussion." [133] No evidence of the Communists' attitude toward the course of negotiations with Nanking during March and April has been discovered by this writer, but on May 3, 1937, Mao reviewed the situation at that time in an address to a Party conference at Yenan. Commenting on the Third Kuomintang Plenum, Mao said (according to a recent text of his report) that, while it "neither made a definite and complete change in policy nor solved any problems concretely," it nonetheless "took the first clear step in the direction of accepting the policy of the united anti-Japanese front." [134] In a second speech to the same conference Mao said, in answer to those in the Party who were allegedly critical of the current advances to Chiang:

> We must understand that neither the Communists nor Chiang Kai-shek are sainted or detached individuals but members of their respective parties and class. . . . Chiang Kai-shek and the Kuomintang have begun to change their policies, but without a still greater effort on the part of the entire people they cannot of course cleanse themselves in one day of the filth that has been accumulating for ten years.[135]

vik, No. 8, April 15, 1937. Concerning the soviets, Wang Ming pointed out that the Communists themselves, in the telegram of February 10, 1937, had proposed their "reorganization"; their "complete abolition," however, which he understood to be the sense of the Kuomintang's resolution, was out of the question. "The readiness of the Communists to make concessions in politics has definite limits," Wang wrote. "To go beyond these limits would be harmful to the liberation struggle of the Chinese people."

[133] Dispatch by H. Dunham; New York *Times*, March 1, 1937, p. 8.

[134] Mao, *Proizvedeniia*, I, 454 (English ed., I, 261).

[135] *Ibid.*, I, 490 (English ed., I, 275); the second speech was made on May 7, 1937.

Mao's phrasing, of course, is hardly flattering to Chiang, but the sense of his remarks was perhaps more conciliatory than that of any which had been made by a Chinese Communist since 1927.

Yenan, in the meantime, appears to have been taking concrete steps in the spring of 1937 to prepare the way for an alliance with Nanking. The soviets, for instance, were reportedly in the process of formal dissolution by early May. On May 3, in his first address to the Party conference in Yenan, Mao observed: "The slogan of a workers' and peasants' republic [i.e., a soviet republic] was correctly advanced in the past, and it is correctly withdrawn at the present time." [136] A Kuomintang observer in the Communist areas some weeks later reported that a temporary Assembly of People's Representatives met in Yenan in June, replacing the soviet government, and that preparations were in progress for electing a permanent assembly.[137] Direct negotiations between Communist and Kuomintang military leaders also appear to have been intensified in May and June, 1937, but evidently they did not lead to a definite political and military agreement before the launching of the Japanese assault on China proper on July 7, 1937.[138]

[136] *Ibid.*, I, 464 (English ed., I, 268). It should be remarked that while Mao, in his two addresses to the May conference, spoke of the dissolution of the soviets and of other policies (e.g., ending land confiscation by force) which were designed to facilitate an agreement with the Kuomintang, he also asserted the independence of the Communists within the proposed alliance. On May 3, for instance, Mao said: "The Communist Party will continue its leadership of the Special Region and the Red Army and, in its relations with the Kuomintang, will maintain its independence and freedom of criticism. Such are the limits to our concessions. It is inadmissible to go beyond them"; *ibid.*, I, 460 (English ed., I, 265). On May 7, Mao reminded the delegates to the Party conference that the ultimate goal of the Party remained unchanged: "We are struggling for socialism. This distinguishes us from the ordinary supporter of Sun Yat-sen's 'Three People's Principles.' Our present efforts must be directed toward the achievement of this great future goal. To lose sight of it is to cease being a Communist"; *ibid.*, I, 495 (English ed., I, 278).

[137] Hsu Yung-ying, *A Survey of Shensi-Kansu-Ninghsia Border Region*, p. 4; the Kuomintang source cited here is Chen Yun, *Factual Account of a Shensi Trip* (Hankow, 1938; in Chinese).

[138] According to Agnes Smedley, a Kuomintang military delegation visited the Communist areas in the spring of 1937 to inspect the Red Army and to negotiate with Communist leaders in Yenan; Smedley, *The Great Road*, p. 355. See also a telegram from the American Embassy in China to the Secretary of State, dated June 2, 1937, in *Foreign Relations of the United States, 1937*, III, 107–8. T. A.

The formal announcement of the united front in China was undoubtedly related to the conclusion of the Sino-Soviet pact in August, 1937. Discussions leading to this pact were said in Moscow to have been in progress for "more than a year" prior to its conclusion,[139] that is, at least as long as the talks between the Kuomintang and the Communists had been going on. Early in the spring of 1937 the Moscow-Nanking talks were reported to have taken an especially favorable turn. On March 26, Ambassador Davies in Moscow recorded his impression that some agreements had been reached, involving principally a Soviet commitment to refrain from giving further support to the Chinese Communists.[140] In April, the Soviet Ambassador to China, D. V. Bogomolov, was reported to have told an American correspondent in Nanking that the Sino-Soviet talks were progressing satisfactorily and that the Soviet government hoped the following points would be covered in the final agreement: supplies for China on long-term credit, restoration of Sinkiang to Chinese sovereignty, joint ownership of a projected railway from Urumchi to Lanchow and of an airline connecting several principal cities in northwestern China, a commercial treaty, Chinese sovereignty over Outer Mongolia but with Nanking's recognition of the status quo there in view of Japan's position in Manchuria, a nonaggression pact to be proposed jointly by China and the Soviet Union to all Pacific powers, and—perhaps most important—a commit-

---

Bisson, an American correspondent who was in Yenan on the eve of Lukouch'iao, found that no agreement had yet been reached but that Communist leaders felt one was imminent; Bisson, *Japan in China,* p. 181. Some accounts, however, argue that a Communist-Kuomintang agreement had been reached before Lukouch'iao; e.g., Motylev, *Tikhookeanskii uzel vtoroi imperialisticheskoi voiny,* p. 13, and Taylor, *The Struggle for North China,* p. 19.

[139] *Izvestiia,* August 30, 1937, p. 1.

[140] Davies, *Mission to Moscow,* p. 134. The entry in Ambassador Davies's journal on March 26, 1937, following a conversation with the Chinese Ambassador, is as follows: "My impression is that relations between China and the Soviet Union have improved immeasurably within the past few days; that a definite understanding has been arrived at; that there is an agreement that the Soviet Union will refrain from communistic activity in China which was antagonistic to the present Chinese government; that this specifically involved that the U.S.S.R. would lend no support to any independent communistic Chinese military forces or local government; that this means a very great deal to China and gives much promise for the strengthening of the situation in China; that on their part the Chinese government will make provision to take care of those people in China who were thereby deprived of a means of support." Used by permission of the publisher, Simon and Schuster, Inc.

ment on Moscow's part to "give no assistance of any kind to the Chinese Communists" in return for China's commitment "to conclude no agreement with any power to grant [i.e., accept] assistance for the suppression of communism in China." [141]

One need not inquire closely whether Moscow was sincere in making these proposals or even whether they were actually on the agenda in the Sino-Soviet talks. What is important is that mere discussion of them by a high Russian official indicates Moscow's intent at this time to conclude a strong alliance with China, an alliance which was meant to be directed primarily against Japan.

Why then Sino-Soviet negotiations, reported on good authority to have been so promising in March and April, failed to produce a pact until the end of August is not clear. Since the initiative in these discussions seems to have come from the Russians and since there appears to have been no change in the Soviet attitude toward China during the spring and early summer of 1937, the delay was probably due to some lingering uncertainty in Nanking about the wisdom of the pact.[142] By the same token, the delay in the conclusion of the united anti-Japanese alliance between Nanking and Yenan, the negotiations toward which appear also to have been well advanced in the spring of 1937, was due perhaps to a similar uncertainty concerning the wisdom of an alliance with the Communists. The Japanese attack at Lukouch'iao apparently dispelled this uncertainty, especially when it became clear that the incident was developing into a full-scale war. This was the catalyst needed to precipitate a final accord between Nanking and Moscow and between Nanking and Yenan. While nothing, evidently, had assured this accord before Lukouch'iao, nothing blocked it once the magnitude of the new aggression was acknowledged.

On August 21, following an unprecedentedly favorable Soviet

[141] Abend, *My Life in China,* pp. 237–38. See also the account of Anthony Billingham's interview with Bogomolov in April, 1937; *Foreign Relations of the United States, 1937,* III, 69–70. Chinese officials, some time later, also reported that discussions leading to a Sino-Soviet pact were in progress during the months before Lukouch'iao; see Beloff, *Foreign Policy of Soviet Russia,* II, 175 *n.*

[142] Bogomolov was reported to have said, after the conclusion of the Sino-Soviet pact, that he had had some difficulty in persuading the Chinese to sign it; *Foreign Relations of the United States, 1938,* III, 180.

press reaction to Chinese resistance,[143] the Sino-Soviet Treaty of Nonaggression was signed in Nanking.[144] A month later, after Kuomintang-Communist military collaboration had been progressing satisfactorily for some weeks,[145] the united front was formally announced through the publication in Nanking of parallel statements by the Chinese Communists and Chiang Kai-shek. On September 22, in their statement on unity, the Communists pledged themselves to support Sun Yat-sen's "Three People's Principles," renounced their former policies of sovietization and forcible land confiscation, formally abolished the soviet government, and announced the reorganization of the Red Army under the control of the Military Affairs Commission of the national government.[146] On the following day Chiang publicly approved the Communists' statement, calling it "an outstanding instance of the triumph of national sentiment over every other consideration." [147]

[143] E.g., Ia. Viktorov, "Iaponiia i Kitai" (Japan and China), *Pravda*, July 22, 1937, p. 2; A. A., "Severnyi Kitai" (North China), *Izvestiia*, July 29, 1937, p. 2; E. Zhukov, "Iaponskaia avantiura v severnom Kitae" (Japanese Adventure in North China), *Bol'shevik*, No. 15, August 1, 1937, pp. 79–92.

[144] The text of the pact was released in Nanking and Moscow on August 30, 1937; an English text may be found, *inter alia*, in *China Handbook, 1937–1943*, pp. 169–70.

[145] As early as August 9, 1937, Chu Teh and Chou En-lai reportedly flew to Nanking for a conference of the National Military Defense Council; Smedley, *The Great Road*, p. 357. (American diplomatic sources indicate that Mao also visited Nanking early in August and met with Chiang Kai-shek; *Foreign Relations of the United States, 1937*, III, 377 and 447. The present writer, however, has found no corroboration of this report). The Red Army underwent extensive reorganization during August, and was designated the National Revolutionary Eighth Route Army early in September. On August 22, Chu Teh and Peng Teh-huai were named, respectively, its commander and deputy commander; Chiang Kai-shek, *Soviet Russia in China*, p. 83, and *China Handbook, 1937–1945* (rev. ed., 1947), pp. 66–67. An American correspondent in North China reported that Communist troops were already wearing Nationalist insignia before the end of August; Wales, *Inside Red China*, p. 211.

[146] The full text may be found in Rosinger, *China's Wartime Politics*, pp. 96–97. On September 29, 1937, Mao said that the statement on unity had been sent to Nanking on July 15; see his speech (or article) "Urgent Tasks after the Announcement of Kuomintang-Communist Co-operation" in Mao, *Proizvedeniia*, II, 49–50 (English ed., II, 79). Another translation of this speech indicates that the Communists' statement, in addition to being delivered to Nanking by mid-July, was drafted as early as July 4—that is, before Lukouch'iao; Brandt, etc., *Documentary History*, p. 248.

[147] Rosinger, *China's Wartime Politics*, p. 99.

3

THE UNITED FRONT IN ACTION

1937–1941

With the establishment of the united front in China in the autumn of 1937, Russian writers ceased to express interest in the Chinese revolution per se. Moscow's total effort in China, to judge from all evidence, was directed at nothing more devious than the stiffening of Chinese resistance, in order to ease Japanese pressure on Russia's eastern frontier. Questions of ideology were for the most part set aside. Even the Communists' short-range political objectives were ignored.

The Chinese Communists, on the other hand, were neither willing nor able to end all discussion of their revolutionary objectives. They had already been obliged, as a gesture of unity, to drop from their program a number of features which seemed inimical to collaboration with the Kuomintang—the soviets, land reform, and the confiscation of large estates, for instance. Much of their support in China had depended, and continued to depend, however, on such objectives as these. It is understandable, therefore, that the Communists were anxious not to appear to be forsaking their entire revolutionary program in the interests of the united front. To have done so would have cost them the support of elements in China, especially those among the peasantry, which were genuinely dissatisfied with Kuomintang rule and which had been attracted by the Communists' slogans. These were the reasons the Chinese Communists and the Comintern did not always respond similarly to developments in China after 1937.

MOSCOW AND THE UNITED FRONT: THE FIRST TWO YEARS SEPTEMBER, 1937–SEPTEMBER, 1939

The announcement of the Communist-Kuomintang alliance in September, 1937, produced fresh indications of confidence in Moscow concerning China's ability and determination to resist Japan. On October 3, for instance, *Pravda* sharply criticized Voitinskii, editor of *Tikhii okean* and dean of Soviet Far Eastern specialists at the time, for doubting China's will to fight.[1] It made little difference that the articles in which Voitinskii had made these "improper" judgments had been wrtten and published from six months to a year earlier; *Pravda* now praised retroactively China's resolution to resist.[2] On November 1, Litvinov confidently predicted to Ambassador Davies that China would not consider any peace involving the loss of its northern provinces and that, if these areas were lost despite its determination, China would "carry on" with guerrilla warfare. He implied that supplies sufficient to support such guerrilla activity would be sent from the Soviet Union.[3] According to Chiang Kai-shek, Stalin at about this time called in the Counselor of the Chinese Embassy in Moscow and after expressing his satisfaction with Chinese resistance declared that if the situation should become unfavorable to China, the Soviet Union might declare war on Japan.[4]

Coverage of events in China by the Soviet and Comintern press, meanwhile, increased appreciably after the formation of the united front. By the end of 1937, *Pravda* and *Izvestiia* were devoting an average of a column a day to China battle dispatches, in addition to occasional feature articles on various aspects of

[1] According to Freda Utley, who then was working in the Pacific Ocean Cabinet of the Institute of World Economy and Politics in Moscow, Voitinskii was head of this division as well as of the Russian branch of the Institute of Pacific Relations; *Institute of Pacific Relations, Hearings,* pp. 738–39.

[2] L. M., "Vrednaia orientatsiia" (A Harmful Orientation), *Pravda,* October 3, 1937, p. 4. Voitinskii was dropped as editor of *Tikhii okean* following this attack, and editorial responsibility was lodged in a three-man board, including Voitinskii, Pavel' Mif, and E. Varga. This journal, which *Pravda* called the "only periodical in the USSR covering current Pacific problems," ceased publication in June, 1938.

[3] Letter from Ambassador Davies to the Secretary of State, November 9, 1937; quoted in Davies, *Mission to Moscow,* pp. 241–42.

[4] Chiang Kai-shek, *Soviet Russia in China,* p. 86.

China's political and economic development. *Inprecor* increased its China coverage from a dozen or so items in 1936 to more than thirty-five in 1937—all dated after the Lukouch'iao incident—and to approximately twice this number in 1938. Throughout the Soviet and Comintern press China ranked second only to Spain in the coverage given to international affairs during this period.

The Kuomintang, not the Communists, received the lion's share of Moscow's praise of China, however. Recent Chinese history was conveniently rewritten to show the Kuomintang in a new light. Here, for instance, is a revised version of the so-called "civil war" of 1927–37, written early in 1938:

> Until very recently the Chinese Republic had no central authority. Each province had its own authority, centered in the generals of local armies who gave only formal allegiance to the central government organized by the party of national unity—the Kuomintang. These generals fought among themselves as much as against the central government. . . . As a result, continuous civil war tore China apart.[5]

No reference was made in this account to any past conflict between the Kuomintang and the Communists. The next year V. Motylev, a leading Soviet historian, reviewed the era since 1930 as follows: the seizure of Manchuria had caused many Chinese leaders from among the intelligentsia and the national bourgeoisie, previously disillusioned with the Kuomintang after its "betrayal" in 1927, to rejoin its ranks; this in turn had led the Kuomintang to accomplish "fundamental improvements" within the government even before 1935; as a result of these developments resistance was possible in 1937 where there had been none in 1931. Motylev attributed the "abrupt switch" in Chinese Communist policy after 1935—that is, a switch to collaboration with the Nanking government—to "the growth of the national spirit throughout the country and the widening of the social base of the Kuomintang." [6]

[5] "Iaponskaia interventsiia v Kitae" (Japanese Intervention in China), *Vlast' sovetov*, No. 8, April, 1938, p. 24.

[6] Motylev, *Tikhookeanskii uzel vtoroi imperialisticheskoi voiny*, pp. 9–10; see also Liakhov, *Kitaiskii narod v bor'be za svoiu nezavisimost'*, pp. 9 ff.

This was what Moscow now said of the Kuomintang's past. As to its present, the Soviet press found the party successfully ridding itself of elements which had once hindered its progress and which had kept the Nanking government from exercising an effective leadership in the anti-Japanese movement. In February, 1939, for instance, when Wang Ching-wei was expelled from the Kuomintang, a writer hailed this event in *Pravda* as further evidence that "the Kuomintang more and more firmly follows the course of liberation from internal reactionary forces and enters a new stage of the struggle for liberation." [7]

Chiang Kai-shek was, of course, singled out for special praise. As the head of the Kuomintang he was now pictured as the personification of Chinese resistance. His public statements and interviews with foreign correspondents were reviewed prominently in the Soviet press.[8] When the Japanese made peace overtures to the Kuomintang at the end of 1937 and again late in 1938, Chiang was credited with having rejected them.[9] Although charges of defeatism were later raised against certain elements in the Kuomintang, the Soviet press did not suggest until after the war that Chiang had been identified with them.

The Communists were not overlooked in this sudden new interest in China expressed in the Moscow press. For eight or ten months prior to the formation of the united front the Soviet press had largely ignored the Chinese Communists[10]—perhaps to allay

[7] M. Tikhomirov, "Rastet novyi Kitai" (A New China is Growing), *Pravda,* February 6, 1939, p. 5. Shortly after his expulsion from the Kuomintang, Wang Ching-wei deserted the Chinese cause entirely and in March, 1940, established a puppet government in Nanking under Japanese control.

[8] Some twenty-five statements by Chiang were summarized in *Pravda* between September, 1937, and September, 1939.

[9] See *Pravda,* January 5, April 20, July 27–28, 1939; Tass dispatches from Chunking. As late as 1943, in an article generally critical of the Kuomintang's conduct of the war, Chiang was still considered to have "decisively rejected" the 1937 Japanese peace offers; Vladimir Rogov, "Polozhenie v Kitae" (The Situation in China), *Voina i rabochii klass,* No. 5, August 1, 1943, p. 20.

[10] The Communists' role in the Sian incident, for instance, was ignored in the *Pravda* and *Izvestiia* commentaries at the time. On February 18, 1937, *Pravda* printed the text of the Communists' telegram to the Third Kuomintang Plenum but thereafter made virtually no further reference to the Communists until the autumn of that year. The important Party conference in May, 1937, received no notice in the Soviet and Comintern press until the text of Mao's first address on this occasion was printed in *Kommunisticheskii internatsional* in September (No. 9, 1937, pp. 68–74). *Inprecor* carried no full-length articles on the Chinese

suspicions in Nanking, on the eve of its alliance with Yenan, that the Communists were mere puppets of the Comintern. The political amnesty in China in September, 1937, however, again made the Communists a proper topic of discussion in the Soviet press. During the two years after the united front was established, Mao's major public statements were also given some prominence in Moscow—not in *Pravda,* to be sure, but in *Communist International.*[11] *Pravda,* however, carried its first pictures of Mao and Chu Teh in its issue of July 6, 1938, the anniversary of Lukouch'iao. The Sixth Party Plenum in November, 1938, in contrast to the important Party conference in May, 1937, which had passed unnoticed in the Soviet press, was widely commented upon.[12] The first full-length biography of Mao, it has been noted, appeared in 1939. For the first time since the commemoration of the Party's fifteenth anniversary in the summer of 1936 the Soviet press again carried articles in which, as their titles suggest, the focus was mainly on the Communist effort.[13]

But these commentaries were perfunctory. As a rule, they gave

Communists from December, 1936, to August, 1937. During the same period *Kommunisticheskii internatsional* carried only three articles which dealt with the Chinese Communist movement, as contrasted with more than a dozen during the preceding eight-month period: one by V. Chen, on the strike movement in China, in the issue for May, 1937, and two by Wang Ming, on the general political situation, in the issues for March and August, 1937.

[11] See *Kommunisticheskii internatsional,* No. 9, 1937, pp. 68–74; No. 1, 1938, pp. 69–74; No. 2, 1938, pp. 106–15; No. 6, 1938, pp. 116–19; No. 10, 1938, pp. 98–102; No. 4, 1939, pp. 110–14. Only three of these six statements by Mao appear in the current edition of his *Selected Works.*

[12] See San-Bo, "Important Session of the Central Committee of the CP of China," *World News and Views* (formerly *Inprecor*), No. 9, March 4, 1939, p. 185; A. Kolan, "Bor'ba kitaiskogo naroda za natsional'nuiu nezavisimost' " (Struggle of the Chinese People for National Independence), *Kommunisticheskii internatsional,* No. 1, January, 1939, pp. 96–97; Wang Tsia Siang [Wang Chia-hsiang], "Some Questions of the Anti-Japanese War," *World News and Views,* No. 33, June 24, 1939, pp. 727–28; Chzhen-lin, *Dva goda geroicheskoi bor'by kitaiskogo naroda,* pp. 43–44.

[13] E.g., Chen Hsing Feng, "The Communist Party of China and the Anti-Japanese National United Front" *Inprecor,* No. 54, December 15, 1937, pp. 1328–29; N. Shvertsov and K. Chirkov, "Kompartiia Kitaia v bor'be za natsional'nuiu nezavisimost' " (The Chinese Communist Party in the Struggle for National Independence), *Propagandist i agitator,* No. 4, February, 1939, pp. 18–24; Chzhen-lin, "Kompartiia Kitaia v natsional'no-osvoboditel'noi bor'be" (The Chinese Communist Party in the National-Liberation Struggle), *Pravda,* March 4, 1939, p. 3; Li-piu [Li Pai-chao?], "The Communist Party of China and the Anti-Japanese War of Emancipation," *World News and Views,* No. 36, July 15, 1939, pp. 793–94.

the Communists some credit for having initiated the united front and for now faithfully adhering to it, but rarely was there comment on future objectives or on any independent programs within the framework of the alliance. A "protracted" collaboration with the Kuomintang was now Moscow's line in China. "This is no temporary maneuver or game," Wang Ming asserted early in 1938; "it is a serious turn in the policy and tactics of the Communist Party of China." [14]

Alliance with the Kuomintang did not, however, mean that the Communist Party was to sacrifice its identity. It was a narrow and hazardous line, as always, to which the Communists had to hew, avoiding, on one hand, a "Leftist" tendency to deny the need of any alliance with the Kuomintang and, on the other, a Rightist inclination to surrender the Party's independence. Early in 1938 Wang Ming warned that there was a "small number of Party members who do not clearly grasp the main question of collaboration between the two parties"—that is, a lasting collaboration, but one in which the identity of the Communists was to be preserved.[15] A year later the dangers were said to be still present, as indicated in this typical Comintern analysis of the Party's problems during the first years of the united front:

All Communists must wage a decisive struggle against the danger from the so-called "Left." These "Leftists" do not understand that the only

[14] Wang Ming, "For the Consolidation and Extension of the Anti-Japanese National United Front," *Communist International,* No. 5, May, 1938, p. 463. This article first appeared in a Chinese periodical in Hankow in January, 1938, shortly after Wang's return from Moscow; the translation in *Communist International* bears Wang Ming's Chinese name, Ch'en Shao-yü, its first appearance in the Soviet or Comintern press for many years. For other expressions of the view that the alliance with the Kuomintang was a serious turn in Communist policy and not simply a "temporary maneuver," see "Render All Aid to the Chinese People," *Communist International,* No. 7, July, 1938, p. 692; G. Mordvinov, "The Protracted War in China," *World News and Views,* No. 33, June 24, 1939, p. 724. The sincerity of the view expressed in these articles is of course open to some doubt, as indicated, for instance, in this recent Soviet appraisal of the united front: "The program of the united national anti-Japanese front, established on the *temporary* political basis of resisting Japanese aggression and on the union not only of the toilers but also of the exploiting classes, could not pose the question of the basic reorganization of Chinese society"; *Krizis kolonial'noi sistemy,* p. 49 (italics added).

[15] Wang Ming, "For the Consolidation and Extension," *Communist International,* No. 5, May, 1938, p. 462.

way to free the Chinese people is to strengthen and widen the united anti-Japanese national front and, in particular, to realize a protracted collaboration between the Kuomintang and the Communist Party. On the other hand . . . an unrelenting struggle must be waged against the danger from the Right, because the Right opportunists, hiding behind the slogan of the united front, actually endanger its realization by demanding the liquidation of the organizational independence of the Communist Party and by attempting to relegate the Party and the proletariat to the role of supernumeraries. . . . The Communist Party knows that to a significant degree the stability of Kuomintang-Communist collaboration and the final victory of the united front depends on the maintenance of iron unity in the Party's ranks.[16]

This showed, it is true, that some attention was given by Moscow to the question of Communist independence during the united front era, but the focus of the article is clearly the development and strengthening, not of the Party, but of the united front itself. In the eyes of the Comintern, at the given stage the united front presented the only line of development both for China and for the Communists. No considerations not directly linked with the strengthening of this effort were likely to be given space in the Soviet press.

One should not, in any case, be deceived by the way in which Soviet and Comintern writers now commented openly on the Communist movement in China. These comments were few in number, as compared to the number of comments which made only casual or no reference to the Communists,[17] and appear simply to have reflected Moscow's official interest, after a decade, in China as a whole. The Communists, ostensibly, were just one part of the total Chinese polity now deserving attention. On occasion the Chinese Communist Party was still called "one of the best sections of the Comintern,"[18] but it is undoubtedly significant that in Manuil'skii's report to the Eighteenth (Russian)

[16] A. Kolan, "Bor'ba kitaiskogo naroda," *Kommunisticheskii internatsional*, No. 1, January, 1939, p. 97.

[17] See, for instance, the "Special China Supplement" of *World News and Views*, No. 33, June 24, 1939, in which the Chinese Communists are mentioned only half a dozen times.

[18] E.g., M. Fred, "Formy i methody khoziainichaniia imperialistov v Kitae" (Forms and Methods of Imperialist Housekeeping in China), *Bol'shevik*, No. 7 (April), 1938, p. 63.

Party Congress in March, 1939, he gave more attention to Chungking's efforts than to Yenan's.[19]

Moscow's enthusiasm over the course of the united front in China was not without cause. According to most accounts, Communist-Kuomintang collaboration was more successful during 1937 and 1938 than anyone had anticipated. In the former soviet areas, it has been noted, ex-Red Army men were already wearing Nationalist insignia in August, 1937, that is, before the united front had been announced.[20] In September, Chiang's picture was reportedly displayed in the Communists' Eighth Army Headquarters at Sian, along with those of Lenin, Stalin, Mao Tsetung, Chu Teh, and Sun Yat-sen.[21] The Kuomintang representative in the Hopei Border government is reported to have said in the summer of 1938 that Communists in this government were "definitely in the minority" and that voting in any case was "rarely" along party lines within the various government councils and agencies.[22]

The Kuomintang government, meanwhile, authorized publication of a Communist newspaper at Hankow early in 1938, and reportedly gave it financial assistance.[23] The Communists were either allowed their own press in Chungking or were given access

[19] Manuil'skii, *Doklad delegatsii VKP(b) v IKKI na XVIII s"ezde VKP(b)*, pp. 31–32. It is clear from Manuil'skii's report that the Spanish Communist Party had by this time replaced the Chinese Communist Party as the second most important section of the Comintern—after the CPSU.

[20] Wales, *Inside Red China*, p. 211.

[21] Bertram, *Unconquered*, p. 80. Colonel Evans Carlson, a U.S. military observer who visited the Eighth Army Headquarters in December, 1937, noted the same group of pictures—except that he found Marx instead of Lenin and Stalin; Carlson, *Twin Stars of China*, p. 54.

[22] Taylor, *The Struggle for North China*, p. 38. The Communist "minority" probably reflects the "three-thirds" policy allegedly in effect in the Border government during most of the war—i.e., a limitation on Party members in any elective organ to one third of the total membership; see North, *Moscow and Chinese Communists*, p. 192 and Compton, *Mao's China*, p. 168. It is rarely argued, however, that the "three-thirds" system seriously restricted Communist control over the Border government. Taylor remarks that since the Communists were a numerical minority in the government they relied on persuasion rather than force and therefore observed a "scrupulous adherence" to the new collaboration policy; *Struggle for North China*, pp. 97 ff.

[23] Rosinger, *China's Wartime Politics*, p. 29; see also *Foreign Relations of the United States, 1938*, III, 388. This paper, *Hsin Hua Jih Pao* (New China Daily), was subsequently moved to Chungking and was listed in Kuomintang sources as still in publication in July, 1945; *China Handbook, 1937–1945* (rev. ed., 1947), p. 507.

to other printing facilities, for a dozen or more Communist pamphlets were issued in Chungking between 1938 and 1940.[24] A People's Political Council was formed early in 1938 and held its first meeting in July with Kuomintang, Communist, and other representatives attending.[25] Shortly thereafter Chou En-lai was named vice minister of the Political Training Board of the National Military Council, a position that made him virtually a member of the national government.[26]

As far as military cooperation was concerned—the crux of the united front effort—diplomatic observers in China reported that despite Japanese victories Communist and Kuomintang troops collaborated successfully during the first eighteen or twenty months of the alliance.[27] In fact, the accomplishments during this period so far exceeded expectations that reports of friction dating from mid-1939 did not cause American diplomats seriously to doubt the continued collaboration of the Communists and the Kuomintang as long as the war lasted until a year and a half later.[28] In Moscow acknowledgment of a serious split in the united front was delayed even longer.[29]

[24] These pamphlets—several of them in 1939 and 1940 highly critical of the national government—were written by leading Communist spokesmen in Yenan. The English language editions were published as *Bulletins* of the New China Information Committee.

[25] *China Handbook, 1937–1945* (rev. ed., 1947), p. 112; the Communists attended the five plenary sessions of the first PPC, through April, 1940, but thereafter attended only irregularly.

[26] *Ibid.*, p. 648.

[27] See *Foreign Relations of the United States, 1938,* III, 165 and 387–88; *Foreign Relations of the United States, 1939,* III, 144 and 190.

[28] In a review of events during 1939, for instance, the American Embassy in Chungking, while noting "serious friction" between the Communists and the Kuomintang, opined that the united front would be maintained, "so far as the continuance of hostilities against Japan was concerned"; *Foreign Relations of the United States, 1940,* IV, 287. Ambassador Johnson reiterated this view throughout 1940, although he acknowledged in November the virtually irreconcilable cleavage between the two groups on domestic policies; *ibid.*, IV, 453.

[29] The end of 1938 is now accepted by virtually all sources as the termination date of any serious collaboration between the Communists and the Kuomintang. A recent Soviet account, for instance—directly contradicting views expressed at the time—reads: "When the Japanese generals, halting the offensive on the Kuomintang sector of the front in October, 1938, once again attempted to come to agreement with Chiang Kai-shek on peace terms, he quickly responded. From this time to the end of the war, the Kuomintang in fact conducted no further military activity at all against the Japanese armies"; V. N. Nikiforov, "Predatel'skaia politika kliki Chan Kai-shi na pervom etape anti-iaponskoi voiny" (The Traitorous Policies of the Chiang Kai-shek Clique during the First Stage of the Anti-

THE UNITED FRONT AND YENAN: THE SAME TWO YEARS SEPTEMBER, 1937–SEPTEMBER, 1939

In their initial pronouncements on the united front, the Chinese Communists praised and promised no less than the Russians. Mao's first public statement on the united front, for instance, cautioned Party members not to consider this "a temporary measure," but to regard it as a fundamental change in Party policy.[30] A Politburo conference, in March, 1938, spelled out in some detail for the benefit of Party members the full significance of the change:

> [The elimination of the soviets] brings about a theoretical controversy among our comrades. Some say this is a tactical change, others say this is a strategic change. How do we comprehend this problem correctly? . . . At the stage of struggle for the national united front against Japan and for a democratic republic, the target of our revolution is to overthrow the Japanese imperialists. . . . In this respect the Chinese Communist Party [has] made a strategic change, a basic change of the plan of arrangement of the broad revolutionary forces, not a separate or partial change of struggle-form or organization-form. Since the strategy has been changed, the tactics will also change to serve the strategy.[31]

The Sixth Party Plenum, in November, 1938, the first plenary

Japanese War), in *Uchenye zapiski* Instituta vostokovedeniia, III (1951), 61. See also *Krizis kolonial'noi sistemy*, p. 43; Khu Tsiao-mu [Hu Chiao-mu], *Tridtsat' let KPK*, p. 60 (English ed., p. 54); *United States Relations with China*, pp. 52–53.

[30] Mao Tse-tung, "The Tasks of the Chinese Revolution after the Formation of the UF between the Kuomintang and the Communist Party" (September 29, 1937), *Communist International*, No. 2, February, 1938, p. 169. A statement later in the Comintern text which directly contradicts this one is probably a mistranslation. It reads (p. 171): "We have unambiguously explained our viewpoint concerning the objective causes which have caused us to change our policy *temporarily*" (italics added). A recent and probably more accurate translation of this passage, made directly from the Chinese original, reads as follows: "We have already clearly explained our point of view concerning the objective reasons and *time factors* involved in this change of policy." Brandt, etc., *Documentary History*, p. 254; see also the translation in Mao, *Proizvedeniia*, II, 59 (English ed., II, 85). Another discrepancy between versions of this statement published at the time and recent texts is the omission in the former (or, conceivably, addition in the latter) of Mao's criticism of Chiang for his "inherent Kuomintang arrogance" and his "lack of self-criticism"; Mao, *Proizvedeniia*, II, 50 (English ed., II, 79).

[31] Ch'en Shao-yü [Wang Ming], Summary of the Conference of the Politburo.

session of the Central Committee since January, 1934, was largely taken up with oratory commending the successes of the united front under Chiang Kai-shek's leadership and pledging even greater Communist cooperation in the future. The plenum's principal resolution, subsequently published in Hong Kong, read: "Cooperation in the war of resistance serves as the foundation for cooperation after the war is won." [32] Thus both internal Chinese Communist documents, designed for the guidance of Party leaders, and official pronouncements acknowledged a general shift in policy.

To judge from these documents, there was no explicit contradiction between the Russians and the Chinese Communists on issues relating to the united front. In so far as their respective pronouncements dealt with the united front as such they were virtually identical. But the Chinese went further than Moscow. They looked beyond the immediate requirements of the united front toward objectives which the Comintern appears largely to have ignored. One of these, for instance, was the establishment of a democratic republic.

Following the Sian episode, the formation of a democratic republic, it will be recalled, had been dropped as one of the Communists' conditions for unity, although it had been retained as an objective to be achieved during the united front era. After the conclusion of the agreement with the Kuomintang in September, 1937, the Communists, both in public statements and in closed Party sessions, continued to argue for a democratic republic as an essential corollary to military collaboration. In January, 1938, for instance, a speaker at a Party conference in Fuping said: "The Communist Party is determined to support the formation of a democratic republic and to execute the duties laid upon it by this new political power." [33] The Politburo declared in March that "the direct aim of the revolution is to establish a Chinese democratic republic of a national united front of all strata and political parties." [34] Mao Tse-tung in an interview during the

[32] *Resolutions and Telegrams of the Sixth Plenum,* p. 6.

[33] Quoted in Taylor, *Struggle for North China,* p. 97.

[34] Ch'en Shao-yü [Wang Ming], Summary of the Conference of the Politburo, p. 39.

same month emphasized the readiness of the Communists to participate in a National Assembly which might be called to elect a new government.[35] A pamphlet issued by the Central Committee in June considered it a "primary task of the CCP . . . to establish a democratic republic based on national independence, democratic liberty and the people's welfare." [36] The Sixth Party Plenum in November, 1938, inserted into its general approval of the Kuomintang's conduct of the war this guarded warning against one-party rule in China:

Both the international and internal situation of China clearly show that in this historical stage no dictatorship of a single party is possible. Also the socialist soviet system cannot arise at this stage, but only the setting-up of a democratic regime, a new republic based on the Three Principles of the People.[37]

It should perhaps be pointed out that the "democratic republic" for which the Chinese Communists called so persistently during the first years of the united front was never spelled out in any detail. There is little reason to doubt that the Communists would have genuinely welcomed the establishment of such a republic if it could have been established on their terms, but what further concessions they were ready to make to achieve it were never indicated. Would they, for instance, have surrendered their autonomy within the so-called Border areas in exchange for a centralized government for all China? Would they have allowed their armed forces to be fully integrated into the Chinese National Army? It is a reasonable assumption that Chinese Communist leaders never seriously imagined that a workable "democratic republic" could be established at this time and so felt free to propose one as a means of attracting liberal elements in China to their cause.

[35] Mao Tsze-dun, "Interv'iu s korrespondentom amerikanskoi gazety 'Assoshieted press' g-dom Van Gun-ta" (Interview with Mr. John Gunther, Correspondent for the American Newspaper [*sic*] "Associated Press"), *Kommunisticheskii internatsional*, No. 6, June, 1938, p. 119.

[36] "Propaganda Outline Issued by the CC [CCP] on the Seventeenth Anniversary of the CCP" (June 24, 1938); text in Brandt, etc., *Documentary History*, pp. 258–59.

[37] Quoted in San-Bo, "Important Session of the Central Committee of the CP of China," *World News and Views*, No. 9, March 4, 1939, p. 185.

The Chinese Communists appear to have been undecided, during the early stages of the united front period, whether or not participation in the existing national government might be considered a suitable substitute for the alleged objective of a democratic republic. In December, 1937, Wang Ming, who had evidently conferred with Stalin just prior to his departure from the Soviet Union,[38] explained to an American correspondent in China that he had returned expressly for discussions with Chiang Kai-shek. He implied that closer Kuomintang-Communist collaboration—including, perhaps, token Communist representation in the Nanking government—would be the subject of these discussions.[39] If this was so, Wang had no immediate success. It does not appear that his intended discussions with Chiang ever took place, and in March, 1938, in any case, Mao made clear the Communists' firm intention not to enter the government, even if asked. He did, however, pledge Communist support of the government in view of its anti-Japanese program.[40] By July, 1938, Wang Ming was speaking in similar vein.[41]

A few months later there appears to have been a temporary shift in Yenan's policy of nonparticipation in the national govern-

[38] Reference to this meeting between Stalin and Wang Ming may be found in Chang Kuo-t'ao, "Mao—A New Portrait by an Old Colleague," New York *Times Magazine*, August 2, 1953, p. 47. Chang gives a curious account of Stalin's remarks on this occasion. The gist of them, according to Chang, was that while Comintern directives had been binding on the Chinese Communists formerly, now, after the formation of the united front, they need no longer be so regarded.

[39] Van Min [Wang Ming], "Interv'iu s amerikanskim korrespondentom B" (Interview with the American Correspondent B), *Kommunisticheskii internatsional,* No. 5, May, 1938, p. 71; the transcript of the interview appeared first in the Chinese Communist organ *Hsin Hua Jih Pao* on December 25, 1937.

[40] Mao Tsze-dun, "Interv'iu s korrespondentom amerikanskoi gazety," *Kommunisticheskii internatsional,* No. 6, June, 1938, p. 116. This was the first public statement since the formation of the united front concerning Communist nonparticipation in the existing government. The decision to refrain from entering the government, if invited, was apparently made in September, 1937, several days after the official announcement of the united front in Nanking; see the text of the Central Committee's "Draft Resolution on the Question of Communist Participation in Organs of Authority" (September 25, 1937), in Mao, *Proizvedeniia,* II, 113–15 (English ed., II, 285–86).

[41] See the text of Wang's address before the opening session of the People's Political Council on July 6, 1938; Van Min [Wang Ming], "Rastet i krepnet sotrudnichestvo mezhdu gomindandom i kompartiei" (Cooperation between the Kuomintang and the Communist Party Is Growing and Strengthening), *Kommunisticheskii internatsional,* No. 10, October, 1938, p. 97.

ment. At the end of the summer, as noted above, Chou En-lai entered the Chungking government—at least nominally. In November, the Sixth Party Plenum resolved that Communists should join the Kuomintang, a step which may be considered as a preliminary to wider participation in all organs of authority. The plenum described this as "the best form of cooperation" at the present stage.[42] The new line, however, was not of long duration. By the end of 1938 joining the Kuomintang had ceased to be one of the Communists' slogans—possibly due to the Kuomintang's intransigence on this point[43]—and no other Communist, so far as is known, joined Chou En-lai in the Chungking government.[44] There was in the meantime no interruption in Yenan's policy of calling for a wholly new democratic republic.

Another matter on which Yenan expressed itself with some candor (especially in internal Party documents), and which was understandably ignored in current Soviet commentaries, was the ultimate Communist objective of the revolution. The "Propaganda Outline" of June, 1938, considered it a primary task of the Party "to direct the Chinese revolution along the road to Communism. Only a Communist society will completely realize the final liberation of the Chinese nation and the Chinese people." [45] At the Sixth Plenum later in the year Mao reconciled the nationalism of the united front with the internationalism of Communism as follows:

The Communist Party obliges its members in a most decisive manner to struggle for the defense of the fatherland against Japanese aggression. Such patriotism on the part of the Communists exists together with manifestations of internationalism in China in certain specific

[42] *Resolutions and Telegrams of the Sixth Plenum,* p. 7.

[43] According to Chiang Kai-shek, after the Sixth Party Plenum Chou En-lai proposed that Communists be permitted to join the Kuomintang at the same time retaining their membership in the Chinese Communist Party. The proposal, Chiang says, was rejected; Chiang Kai-shek, *Soviet Russia in China,* p. 88.

[44] Chou En-lai remained a member of the National Military Council until 1940. Thereafter he served as the representative of the Chinese Communist Party in Chungking until the end of the war; *China Handbook, 1937–1945* (rev. ed., 1947), p. 648.

[45] Cited from text in Brandt, etc., *Documentary History,* p. 259.

respects. There is no infringement here on the principle of [Communist] internationalism.[46]

The author of a Party pamphlet issued in May of the following year headed a section devoted to qualifications for membership: "CP Members Must Not Only Participate Actively in the Struggle Against Japan, But Must Also Struggle for Communism." The text under this heading reads in part:

Not every person who engages actively in the anti-Japanese war can become a Party member. In order to request admission into the CP, he must subscribe to the Party program and be willing to dedicate himself to the Communist cause of the liberation of the proletarian class and the whole of mankind.[47]

A later section in the same pamphlet, entitled "The Interests of the Revolution Above All," includes the following statement: "Our Party is a political party aiming at the complete liberation of the proletariat of China, the entire Chinese nation and people, and the establishment of a Communist society." [48]

The method by which the goal of a Communist society was to be achieved was entirely orthodox, in Marxist terms. The Chinese Communists appear never to have doubted that, in the final analysis, the proletariat must lead the revolution. But they claimed no support where none existed. "In the past few years," the Chinese Politburo declared in March, 1938, "owing to the special historical environment and various other reasons, the majority of our Party are peasants, hired peasants and handicraftsmen. The proportion of industrial workers in the cities is not adequate." [49] A Party pamphlet issued in May, 1939, stated, under the heading "We Must, First of All, Strengthen the Repre-

[46] Mao Tsze-dun, "Novyi etap razvitiia anti-iaponskoi natsional'noi voiny i zadachi kompartii Kitaia" (New Stage in the Development of the Anti-Japanese National War and the Tasks of the Chinese Communist Party), *Kommunisticheskii internatsional,* No. 4, April, 1939, p. 110.

[47] Ch'en Yün, "How to Be a Communist Party Member" (May 30, 1939); cited from text in Brandt, etc., *Documentary History,* p. 324.

[48] *Ibid.,* p. 330. See also Liu Shao-ch'i, "On the Training of a Communist Party Member" (August 7, 1939); *ibid.,* pp. 336–44.

[49] Ch'en Shao-yü [Wang Ming], Summary of the Conference of the Politburo, p. 33.

sentation of Superior Elements of the Working Class in the Party":

The comparative weakness of Party work in the urban workers' movement, the unprecedented suppression of the working class in the past, and the occupation of large industrial cities [by Japan] during the war, have further aggravated the suffering and hardships of the Chinese working class. The increasing unemployment of huge numbers of the workers and their dispersion throughout the country further increase the Party's tasks in absorbing workers into the Party. . . . [We must] broaden the proletarian base of the Party, activate the workers to play a central role in the war of resistance, and strengthen the leadership of the workers over the vast masses of peasants and urban petty bourgeoisie.[50]

Before this goal could be achieved, however—that is, before the broadening of the Party's proletarian base could be accomplished—the revolution might succeed in the rural areas. Mao had perhaps already been thinking in these terms when, at the Sixth Plenum in November, 1938, in defending his thesis that guerrilla warfare should and could be continued even though the principal cities fell, he said:

The large city . . . cannot exercise complete control over the villages and their surrounding country because the city is small in comparison with the expanse of countryside with its numerous villages. By far the greater amount of manpower and material strength lies in the vast countryside, not in the cities.[51]

A year later Mao made his view entirely clear on the relationship of city to country and of worker to peasant:

Because of the unbalanced condition of the Chinese economic development . . . and [because] of the vastness of China's territories and of the disunity and conflicts existing in the Chinese anti-revolutionary camp and because of the fact that the main force of the Chinese revolution, the Chinese peasantry, is under the leadership of the Communist Party . . . there is a great possibility for the Chinese revolution to succeed first and foremost in the countryside. Thus it

[50] Ch'en Yün, "How to Be a Communist," in Brandt, etc., *Documentary History*, pp. 324–25.

[51] Quoted in Wang Tsia Siang [Wang Chia-hsiang], "Some Questions of the Anti-Japanese War," *World News and Views*, No. 33, June 24, 1939, p. 728.

plunges the revolution into an unbalanced state and prolongs its total success as well as increasing its difficulties. . . .

But we must not overlook the other form which revolutionary struggle must take . . . we do not mean to give up the work in the cities and towns or in other rural districts which have not yet become bases, for without these the revolutionary strongholds would become isolated and the revolution would be a failure.[52]

These remarks by Mao late in 1939 were less unorthodox than may at first appear. In stressing the central place of the peasant problem, Mao was merely acknowledging a basic characteristic of the Chinese revolution, one which had never before been stated so candidly. In doing this he was not deviating from the standard concept of the "bourgeois-democratic" phase of the Chinese revolution. His reference to the peasantry as "the main force of the Chinese revolution" must also be compared with a reference to the proletariat in this same study. "The proletariat," Mao wrote, "is ultimately the fundamental force of the Chinese revolution. Without the participation and leadership of the proletariat, the Chinese revolution can never succeed." [53]

It seems clear, in contrasting Soviet and Chinese Communist pronouncements during the first years of the Sino-Japanese war, that initiative in questions of theory was passing to Yenan. In the early 1930s the Kremlin had taken the initiative in this regard and the Chinese Communists, whether in the soviet areas or in Kuomintang China, had simply parroted Soviet formulas and theorems. Now at the end of the 1930s, Moscow was normally silent on these matters, and Mao and his associates in Yenan were beginning to evolve concepts of their own. This was an important factor in the emergence during succeeding years of a body of more or less indigenous Chinese Communist thought known as "Maoism." For the present, however—that is, up to the era of the Nazi-Soviet pact—Chinese Communist formulations were in the main orthodox and, as we look back on

[52] Mao Tse-tung, *The Chinese Revolution and the Communist Party of China*, pp. 9–10. This important treatise was written at the end of 1939 but was not made generally available, even in China, until Mao's *Selected Works* were published in 1948.

[53] Mao Tse-tung, *The Chinese Revolution and the Communist Party of China*, p. 16.

them, give no reason to suspect any growing coolness between Moscow and Yenan.

Mao's leadership of the Party was challenged twice in the first years of the Sino-Japanese war, both times unsuccessfully. The two episodes deserve attention here because they cast some light on the attitudes taken toward the united front in Yenan and on the nature of Soviet-Chinese Communist relations during this period.

The initial test came from Chang Kuo-t'ao at a Party conference in the late summer or early autumn of 1937.[54] On this occasion, according to Chang's testimony, he proposed the slogan "Victory for all!" By this he meant a victory for both the Communists and the Kuomintang over the Japanese. He makes it clear that he favored a sincere alliance with the Kuomintang in the hope that through such an alliance the Communists might influence Nanking to pursue more liberal policies than in the past. Mao opposed this policy, according to Chang, with the slogan "Defeat for all!" By this he allegedly meant a victory first over the Japanese and subsequently over the Kuomintang. Chang claims that there was a majority in support of his proposal, including even Chou En-lai, and that, realizing this, Mao called off further debate and closed the conference.[55]

[54] Chang states that this was the Lochuan Conference which he dates October, 1937; North, *Moscow and Chinese Communists,* p. 180. Recent Chinese Communist sources, however, date the Lochuan Conference as August, 1937; e.g., Khu Tsiao-mu [Hu Chiao-mu], *Tridtsat' let KPK,* p. 58 (English ed., p. 52). Inasmuch as there were other Party conferences held in October and early November, Chang may be confused as to which one gave rise to the crisis which he describes.

[55] North, *Moscow and Chinese Communists,* p. 180. The only corroboration of Chang's version of this dispute seen by the author is in Li Ang, *The Red Stage,* chap. XV. A Right opportunist element opposed to Mao at a Party conference in November is mentioned, however, in an editor's note in Mao, *Proizvedeniia,* II, 93 (English ed., II, 105), but Mao's address on this occasion contains no reference to the slogans or the issues Chang describes; *ibid.,* II, 95–110 (English ed., II, 105–15). See, however, the alleged text of a Politburo resolution passed in October, entitled "The Future of the War of Resistance and the Chinese Communists' Line of Action," in Chiang Kai-shek, *Soviet Russia in China,* p. 86; see also Cheng Tien-fong, *History of Sino-Russian Relations,* pp. 225–26. It should be understood, of course, that any debate on Communist strategy such as the one to which Chang Kuo-t'ao refers would have been held in strictest secrecy and could have applied only to the more concealed aspects of the Party's behavior; the policy publicly announced at this time was one of full cooperation with the Kuomintang.

The second challenge to Mao's leadership came from Wang Ming following his return from Moscow at the end of 1937. Although it was generally assumed abroad that Wang had had some falling-out with the Party leadership in 1938 or 1939 because of his eclipse during the war years, the specific charges raised against him after his return from Moscow have only recently been revealed. An official history of the Party published in 1951 explains Wang's "deviation" of 1938 as follows:

Some comrades under Wang Ming's leadership, the same who had committed serious "Left" opportunist errors during the second revolutionary war (1927–37), now opposed and criticized the Party line from a Right opportunist standpoint. . . . Seeing the temporary weakness of the Communists and exaggerating the strength of the Kuomintang, they erroneously concluded that victory in the war against Japan must depend upon the Kuomintang and that inevitably this would be a Kuomintang victory rather than a popular one; they asserted that leadership in the war should be exercised by the Kuomintang rather than by the Communist Party.[56]

The accuracy of these charges is difficult to demonstrate, if one measures Wang's outlook by his articles as published in the Comintern press of this period. Wang may have returned to China, it has been noted, in order to promote closer collaboration between the Communists and the Kuomintang, but there is no indication that he sought in this effort to submerge the interests and independence of the Party. His published views were identical with Mao's on the issue of the role the Party should play in the united front.[57] At the opening session of the People's Political Council, held in July, 1938, Wang cautioned that in supporting the national government the Communist Party "frankly announces that it does not reject its unique struggle for Communism."[58] Justification of charges, however, is not normally a feature of intra-Party disputes, in China or elsewhere, and it is

[56] Khu Tsiao-mu (Hu Chiao-mu), *Tridtsat' let KPK,* p. 59 (English ed., p. 53).

[57] E.g., Wang Ming, "The New Stage of Japanese Aggression and the New Period of the Struggle of the Chinese People," *Communist International,* No. 10, October, 1937, pp. 719–36; "For the Consolidation and Extension," *Communist International,* No. 5, May, 1938, pp. 461–65.

[58] Van Min [Wang Ming], "Rastet i krepnet sotrudnichestvo," *Kommunisticheskii internatsional,* No. 10, October, 1938, p. 97.

of course entirely possible that, with or without justification, the charges noted above were in fact raised against Wang as early as 1938.

Assuming this to be so, the case against Wang would have resembled that against Chang Kuo-t'ao in one significant respect: both were charged with seeking an alliance with the Kuomintang that would have submerged the independence of the Communists and precluded any possibility of their following an independent policy. This was not an illogical charge for Mao to have raised at this juncture, whether or not there was any basis for it. Prior to the formation of the united front, a deviation to the Right was not a shortcoming that appears to have attracted much notice in Yenan. According to all evidence, the emphasis at that time had been on the need to make concessions in the interests of national unity. Once the united front was assured, however, Yenan appears immediately to have focused its attention on the risk of conceding too much. In November, within seven weeks of the formal announcement of the united front, Mao noted: "The principal dangerous deviation within the Party lies not [as formerly] in 'Left' opportunism, but in Right opportunism—that is, in capitulationism." [59] The charges against Chang and Wang Ming are doubtless related to this reorientation of Mao's views on the issue of "Left" and Right deviation.

It would be naïve, of course, to conclude that only ideological considerations were involved in the action taken against Chang Kuo-t'ao and Wang Ming. Both could be counted Mao's rivals. Each, in a different way, posed an obstacle to Mao's undisputed leadership of the Party. As far as Chang was concerned, his decision, for whatever reasons, to remain in the southwest in 1935 and most of 1936 had removed him from the center of Party activity. Following this decision, he appears never to have recovered his former stature in the Party, although he apparently retained his seat on the Politburo at least through July, 1937.[60]

[59] Mao Tse-tung, "The Situation and Tasks of the Anti-Japanese War after the Fall of Shanghai and Taiyuan" (November 12, 1937); text in Mao, *Proizvedeniia*, II, 101 (English ed., II, 109).

[60] North, *Kuomintang . . . Elites*, p. 112. Cheng Tien-fong, *History of Sino-Russian Relations*, p. 206, states that Chang was named chairman of the Shensi-Kansu-Ninghsia "Soviet Government" established in March, 1937.

Nearly a year before his reported clash with Mao in the autumn of 1937, the latter had attacked him at a Party conference for his "Right opportunism" and for "disrupting discipline in the Party and in the Red Army." [61] It may be presumed that the final showdown, when it came, was a one-sided affair. On April 17, 1938, Chang was expelled from the Party by a Central Committee resolution charging him with Trotskyist activity.[62] Two months later the Comintern, breaking a long official silence with respect to the Chinese Communists, confirmed the Party's action and made it public.[63]

Wang Ming could not be dismissed so summarily. Whether or not he had returned to China late in 1937 as the Comintern's official emissary, he returned in any case with a unique prestige. As a member of the Presidium of the ECCI since 1935 and as the Comintern's foremost authority on colonial affairs and one of the most regular contributors to Comintern publications, Wang was undoubtedly far better known in Moscow than any other Chinese Communist leader. There is no indication that he lost this prestige following his return. A Comintern account of the opening session of the People's Political Council in July, 1938, for instance, lists Wang Ming at the head of the seven-man Chinese Communist delegation, despite the fact that Mao, according to this account, was one of its members.[64] Wang's articles continued

[61] Mao Tse-tung, "Strategic Problems of the Revolutionary War in China" (December, 1936); text in Mao, *Proizvedeniia*, I, 330 (English ed., I, 191). This article, according to an introductory note attributed to Mao in one text, was not made generally available in China until February, 1941; Steiner, *Maoism: A Sourcebook*, p. 13.

[62] See V. N. Nikiforov, "Predatel'skaia politika Chan Kai-shi v 1937–38 godakh" (Traitorous Policy of Chiang Kai-shek in 1937–38), *Uchenye zapiski* Instituta vostokovedeniia, III (1951), 58.

[63] "Decision of the Presidium of the ECCI," *Communist International*, No. 7, July, 1938, pp. 688–89. It must be imagined that the dispute between Mao and Chang was considerably more complex than is indicated in these fragmentary Chinese Communist and Soviet sources; the forthcoming memoirs of Chang himself will doubtless help to clarify the conflict between these two Chinese leaders, which apparently was carried on intermittently from 1931 on. In his interview with Robert North in Hong Kong in November, 1950, Chang stated that he had escaped from Yenan to Kuomintang China before his formal expulsion from the Party; see also Cheng Tien-fong, *History of Sino-Russian Relations*, p. 234.

[64] See the editor's note preceding the text of Wang's address on this occasion in *Kommunisticheskii internatsional*, No. 10, October, 1938, p. 95. Mao did not, evidently, attend; see Cheng Tien-fong, *History of Sino-Russian Relations*, pp. 226–27.

to appear regularly in the Comintern press until June, 1939.[65]

Wang's prestige in Moscow, however, did not assure his prestige in China. On the contrary, it may have been precisely because of his prestige in Moscow and because of an imprudent assertion of the Comintern's authority, vested in himself, that his fortunes in China suffered. The official Party history of 1951, referred to above, further accuses Wang of having "arbitrarily published a number of declarations, decisions and articles without the consent of the Central Committee." [66] This is not improbable. There was certainly some arrogance in Wang's statement that the purpose of his return to China at the end of 1937 was to conduct discussions with Chiang Kai-shek, as though he, of all Chinese Communist spokesmen, had unique qualifications for this task. There was also arrogance, or at the very least indiscretion, in his professing repeatedly, in his address before the People's Political Council in July, 1938, to speak "in the name of the Communist Party of China" despite the fact that other important Party leaders were present on this occasion.[67] Chang Kuo-t'ao lends some support to this view in describing Wang Ming, on his return from Moscow, as bent on asserting his leadership of the Party.[68] Wang may further have offended Party leaders in January, 1939, when, in the course of a speech delivered in Yenan, he repeatedly quoted Chiang Kai-shek and quoted Mao only once.[69]

So far as is known, Wang Ming was not publicly reprimanded for his alleged deviations and indiscretions. In December, 1939, he was mentioned in a Chinese Communist source as the Party's representative in Chungking.[70] As late as February, 1940, he was signing a telegram addressed to the Secretariat of the People's

[65] The last article by Wang Ming appeared in *Kommunisticheskii internatsional,* No. 6, June, 1939. The last mention of Wang in *Pravda* was on October 21, 1939, reporting an address he had made in Chungking the day before.

[66] Khu Tsiao-mu [Hu Chiao-mu], *Tridtsat' let KPK,* p. 60 (English ed., p. 54).

[67] Van Min [Wang Ming], "Rastet i krepnet sotrudnichestvo," *Kommunisticheskii internatsional,* No. 10, October, 1938, pp. 95–97.

[68] Chang Kuo-t'ao interview with Lieberman.

[69] Ch'en Shao-yü [Wang Ming], *Old Intrigues in New Clothing,* pp. 1–19 *passim.*

[70] *Friction Aids Japan, Documents Covering Instances of Friction, 1939–1940,* p. 19. Since Chou En-lai was in Moscow at this time, it is probable that Wang Ming was replacing him temporarily as the Communist representative in Chungking.

Political Council along with Mao and other Communist members of this council.[71] Thereafter, however, Wang appears to have been largely eclipsed, and there is no mention of him in either Russian or Chinese sources known to this writer until after the war.[72]

Whether ideological considerations or intra-Party rivalry was the major factor in these two cases it is not now possible to say with any assurance. Both factors were present. If Right opportunism had not been a convenient label to pin on Wang Ming and Chang Kuo-t'ao, another would have been found. On the other hand, Right opportunism was perhaps a sufficient danger in itself to have warranted searching out other scapegoats if Wang and Chang had not conveniently presented themselves at this juncture.

SOVIET FAR EASTERN POLICY AND AID TO CHINA, 1937–1941 [73]

The united front policy was of course linked with Moscow's attempts in the 1930s to achieve protection from Germany and Japan through collective security. Both policies aimed at the defense of the Soviet Union, the first through domestic alliance between Communists and non-Communists in countries likely to be friendly with the USSR, the second through a system of diplomatic alliances to be concluded with these countries by the Soviet Foreign Office. While they were complementary, these two aspects of Soviet foreign policy proceeded along different lines and had different fortunes. The united front, for instance, had some success in France and Spain and, as has been shown, a good deal of success in China. Collective security, on the other

[71] *Ibid.*, p. 45.

[72] According to North, Wang Ming was on the Central Committee in 1945, and in 1951 ranked thirty-ninth out of the forty-three members of this body as the result of the balloting which allegedly determined its composition; North, *Kuomintang . . . Elites,* pp. 113–15.

[73] Soviet Far Eastern policy in the years preceding the Second World War has been treated by a number of writers; the most useful surveys are Beloff, *Foreign Policy of Soviet Russia,* Vol. II, chap. VIII, and Moore, *Soviet Far Eastern Policy,* chaps. IV and V. The present study concerns only those aspects of Soviet policy in the Far East which relate to the China aid program between 1937 and 1941.

hand, as the Russians conceived it, had by 1939 failed entirely.

In the Far East collective security was considered by Soviet spokesmen to have become impracticable almost two years before it was abandoned in Europe. No great effort was made to achieve it—at least in the broad sense of a regional pact such as Ambassador Bogomolov had described in April, 1937 [74]—after the Brussels Conference of November, 1937. Litvinov described this conference as follows:

Its activity was very neatly hit off in a cartoon which I saw in a foreign newspaper. This shows the honorable delegates of eighteen states, not without great effort and strain, dragging a letter to the post-box for Japan. In this letter, as you know, they again demand Japan's confirmation whether she is deliberately committing her aggression in China and request her to stop and accept mediation. Confirmation is not long in coming. Japan, even with an inflection of resentment, replies that there is no need to bother her; she has repeatedly stated that she is attacking China quite deliberately and for quite definite aims. She does not need anybody's mediation; she is ready to negotiate only with China—about capitulation, of course—and the only thing the Conference can do is to make China agree to this capitulation. This reply disarmed the Brussels Conference . . . and the Conference was closed.[75]

The Soviet Union henceforth relied on bilateral nonaggression pacts for its security in the Far East. *Pravda* had in fact anticipated this trend in calling the Sino-Soviet Pact of August 21, 1937, "a new instrument of peace and collective security . . . a graphic example of the practical application of this principle in the Pacific basin." [76]

Before considering the course of Chinese-Russian relations during the first years after the Sino-Soviet Pact of 1937, it is interesting to consider whether Moscow perhaps gave thought to

[74] See p. 98 above for Ambassador Bogomolov's remarks; Abend, *My Life in China*, pp. 237–39. During the first half of 1937 the Soviet press frequently discussed the possibility of a regional pact in the Pacific; see, for instance, "Security in the Pacific," an editorial by Vigilis (*Izvestiia*, May 21, 1937), quoted in Moore, *Soviet Far Eastern Policy, pp.* 237–39.

[75] From a pre-election speech in Leningrad on November 29, 1937, quoted in M. Litvinov, *Against Aggression* (New York, 1939), p. 106.

[76] "Sovetsko-kitaiskii dogovor o nenapadenii" (Sino-Soviet Non-Aggression Pact), *Pravda,* August 30, 1937, p. 1.

a similar pact with Japan, in an effort to round out Soviet security in the Far East. Such a possibility suggests itself, of course, when one recalls that two years later the Soviet Union allied with Germany under somewhat similar circumstances—that is, at a moment when, from the Soviet point of view, the last opportunity for a security alliance against Hitler had passed. It should also be recalled that during the period between the Japanese seizure of Manchuria in 1931 and the Seventh Comintern Congress in 1935 the Russians had on numerous occasions proposed to the Japanese a nonaggression pact which, had it been concluded, would have resembled in outward form the pact concluded with China in 1937.[77]

If Moscow was still tempted by the possibility of concluding a nonaggression pact with Japan, the end of 1937 was not the time to make its intentions known. Not only had there been Moscow's private assurances of support to China in its struggle against Japanese aggression, but since Lukouch'iao Soviet officials had been increasingly outspoken in their denunciation of Japan. In September, for instance, addressing the League of Nations, Litvinov had argued strongly against any association with the Japanese aggressor;[78] in November, at the Brussels Conference, he raised the argument to the level of a warning to all peace-loving nations.[79] To behave in a manner directly contrary to the sense of this warning would have greatly undermined Soviet prestige abroad. This would have been particularly true in China, where after more than two years of effort Moscow had finally succeeded in establishing, or in seeing established, a broad anti-Japanese front. The Chinese Communists might with confidence have been counted upon to defend Soviet policy whatever direction it took, but Nanking's determination, it was perhaps felt in Moscow, would not have survived a Soviet rapprochement with Tokyo. In a sense, then, the Russians were blocked from

[77] According to the American Embassy in Tokyo, a Soviet offer of a nonaggression pact with Japan was made as late as June, 1936, by the Soviet Ambassador in Tokyo to Japanese Premier Hirota; *Foreign Relations of the United States, 1936,* IV, 216. See also Beloff, *Foreign Policy of Soviet Russia,* II, 169.

[78] Speech delivered September 21, 1937; text in Degras (ed.), *Soviet Documents on Foreign Policy,* III, 257.

[79] Speech delivered November 3, 1937; *ibid.,* III, 264.

seeking one logical alternative to that part of their policy which had failed in the Far East (collective security) because in so doing they would place in some jeopardy the part which was succeeding (the united front).

There is another and perhaps more obvious reason in any case why no Soviet-Japanese rapproachement was feasible in 1937 or in the two years following. This concerned not so much the difference in ideology, which, though considerable, might have been swept aside—as a similar difference between Moscow and Berlin was conveniently swept aside in the summer of 1939—but rather the accumulation of specific small grievances between the two nations. These grievances had to do with Japanese fishing rights along the Soviet coastline above Vladivostok, lumber and oil concessions in North Sakhalin, alleged border violations along the Amur River and along the Mongolian-Manchukuan frontier, payments to the Soviet Union for the Chinese Eastern Railway, and various other matters. Taken together, these conflicts constituted a formidable barrier to any easy resolution of the crisis in Soviet-Japanese relations. They could be expected to remain separate sources of friction, irrespective of any general treaty, until the relative military strength of Soviet and Japanese forces in the Far East had more nearly approached equilibrium.

In 1937, the Japanese seemed to have the upper hand militarily. Max Beloff has expressed the opinion that during the Amur incident in June and July, 1937 (an armed skirmish between Soviet and Japanese troops over two disputed islands in the Amur River) "the Soviet Union appears to have acted in an extremely conciliatory fashion." [80] A year later Soviet troops were conceded by most observers to have given a better account of themselves in the Changkufeng incident (another skirmish, lasting a fortnight, over a disputed hill in the Lake Hasan region north of the Yalu River).[81] In the summer of 1939 a more prolonged encounter on the Mongolian-Manchukuan frontier (the Nomonhan

[80] Beloff, *Foreign Policy of Soviet Russia, II,* 180. Ambassador Davies reports, on the other hand, that "a high Japanese official" told him in 1938 that the incident had been deliberately provoked by the Japanese and that they had been impressed with the showing of Soviet troops; Davies, *Mission to Moscow,* p. 166.

[81] Beloff, *Foreign Policy of Soviet Russia,* II, 193; Moore, *Soviet Far Eastern Policy,* pp. 98–101; *Foreign Relations of the United States, 1938,* III, 467 ff.

incident) showed the Soviet forces to be equal, if not superior, to the Japanese.[82]

There is some evidence that both the Changkufeng and Nomonhan incidents were deliberately provoked by the Japanese, presumably as part of a plan to launch an all-out attack on the Soviet Far East. After the war the International Military Tribunal for the Far East accepted testimony to this effect and noted that this evidence was not disputed by the defendants.[83] The judgment handed down by the Tribunal reads in part:

> The Tribunal is of the opinion that a war of aggression against the U.S.S.R. was contemplated and planned . . . that it was one of the principal elements of Japan's national policy and that its objective was the seizure of territories of the U.S.S.R. in the Far East.[84]

If this conclusion was correct and if it is true that a relative equilibrium between Soviet and Japanese troops along the frontiers of Manchukuo did not exist until after the Nomonhan incident in 1939, it is not surprising, of course, that no serious rapprochement occurred between Moscow and Tokyo until the era

[82] See *Foreign Relations of the United States, 1939,* III, 243 and 287; Moore, *Soviet Far Eastern Policy,* p. 113; Cheng Tien-fong, *History of Sino-Russian Relations,* p. 217.

[83] International Military Tribunal for the Far East, *Judgment,* Part B, chap. VI, pp. 827 ff. As far as the Changkufeng incident is concerned, it is interesting to note that, at the time, the American Military Attaché in Tokyo felt that the Russians had instigated this crisis intentionally to test Japanese strength, much as the Japanese are believed to have provoked the Amur crisis a year before for the same purpose; *Foreign Relations of the United States, 1938,* III, 457–58.

[84] International Military Tribunal for the Far East, *Judgment,* Part B, chap. VI, p. 803. This conclusion was based on a variety of documents introduced as evidence by the prosecution, including, for instance, a secret telegram from General Tojo to military headquarters in Tokyo on June 9, 1937. This reads in part: "Judging the present situation in China from the point of view of military preparation against Soviet Russia, I am convinced that if our military power permits it, we should deliver a blow first of all upon the Nanking regime to get rid of the menace at our back"; *ibid.,* p. 807. Another defendant, Muto, according to the *Judgment,* admitted that while he was Chief of the First Section of the General Staff in 1938 "the plan for 1939 was based upon a concentration of Japan's main forces in Eastern Manchuria to take the offensive. The Kwantung Army was to occupy the Soviet cities of Voroshilov, Vladivostok, Iman . . . etc."; *ibid.,* p. 808. According to one report of the Tribunal's proceedings, evidence was submitted which showed that the Emperor himself had approved a plan of attack against the Soviet Union as late as March, 1940; "Tokyo War Guilt Trial," London *Times,* March 10, 1947, p. 5. This evidence does not, however, appear to have been accepted by the Tribunal.

of the Nazi-Soviet pact.[85] By this time the Sino-Soviet pact had been in force for more than two years and had proved to be one of the cornerstones of Soviet Far Eastern policy.

The real significance of the Sino-Soviet pact is poorly expressed in its published text, which pledged the signatories merely to refrain from attacking each other and from rendering aid to third parties attacking either contracting party. In fact, the agreement provided the basis for better than average relations between the two governments until 1941 and for correct relations until the end of the war. Through secret codicils or supplementary agreements,[86] it also paved the way for an active program of Soviet aid which was put into effect even before the end of 1937. In many respects Soviet policy in the Far East from 1937 to 1941 is more accurately reflected in this program than in any official pronouncements or editorial comment, whether with respect to Tokyo, Chungking, or the Chinese Communists.

The total volume of Russian aid to China during the Sino-Japanese war has never been clearly established. It may be presumed, of course, that at the time neither Chungking nor Moscow cared to call Japan's attention to this traffic.[87] Subsequently, for

[85] There were numerous indications after Lukouch'iao, as there had been after the Japanese seizure of Manchuria in 1931, that Moscow was concerned over Tokyo's intentions vis à vis the USSR. See, for instance, an editorial in *Izvestiia,* shortly after the Japanese attack, which stated that "North China enters Japanese strategy as a jumping-off point for an attack on the Mongolian People's Republic and the USSR"; A. A. "Severnyi Kitai" (North China), *Izvestiia,* July 23, 1937, p. 2. See also A. Bederov, "Novyi etap iaponskoi interventsii v Kitae" (A New Stage of Japanese Intervention in China), *Mirovoe khoziaistvo i mirovaia politika,* No. 9, September, 1937, pp. 6–7; E. Aleksandrov, "Voina v Kitae i mezhdunarodnye protivorechiia" (The War in China and International Contradictions), *Bol'shevik,* No. 2, January 15, 1938, pp. 74–87; P. Grebnev, "Voina v Kitae" (The War in China), *Bol'shevik,* No. 5, March 15, 1938, pp. 74–81; B. Perlin, "Iaponiia i Kitai" (Japan and China), *Znamia,* No. 8, August, 1938, pp. 214–58. In the autumn of 1939, however, a possible rapprochement between Moscow and Tokyo, growing out of the negotiations leading to the settlement of the Nomonhan dispute, was discussed in foreign diplomatic circles in the two capitals; *Foreign Relations of the United States, 1939,* III, 78–88, *passim.*

[86] No secret provisions of the Sino-Soviet pact of 1937, so far as this writer is aware, have yet been revealed; the possibility that some existed, however, has been suggested by a number of sources. See Beloff, *Foreign Policy of Soviet Russia,* II, 182; *Foreign Relations of the United States, 1937,* III, 827–28.

[87] Soviet sources, for instance, place the volume of exports to China in 1938—by most accounts one of the most active years in the aid program—only slightly higher than the volume during the preceding year. In 1938, moreover, shipments

political reasons, those sympathetic to Moscow undoubtedly exaggerated the amount of Soviet aid and those sympathetic to Chungking underestimated it.

According to official Chinese sources, at least three formal loans were made during the first two years after the signing of the Sino-Soviet pact in August, 1937: $50,000,000 (U.S.) in March, 1938; another $50,000,000 (U.S.) in July; and $150,000,000 (U.S.) in June, 1939.[88] Reliable but nonofficial sources claim an additional loan of $50,000,000 (U.S.) at the end of 1940, making a total of $300,000,000 (U.S.).[89] This figure can perhaps be accepted as the minimum sum of Soviet credits. The actual figure may be larger. It is doubtful, for instance, whether a $30,000,000 (U.S.) credit which was reported to Ambassador Davies by a Chinese diplomat in Moscow as having been extended to China as early as August, 1937, is included in the above total.[90] Beloff notes a credit of an unspecified amount on June 16, 1940, which

---

to China, according to the published figures on Soviet exports for this year, totaled only one half of those to Germany, two thirds of those to the Mongolian People's Republic, etc.; China, in short, was not indicated as one of the principal recipients of Soviet exports. *Statistika vneshnei torgovli SSSR* (Moscow), No. 12, December, 1937, p. 7, and No. 12, December, 1938, p. 6.

[88] *China Handbook, 1937–1945* (rev. ed., 1947), p. 209. These credits for the 1938–39 period are accepted by most sources, including one recent Soviet account: Erenburg, *Ocherki natsional'no-osvoboditel'noi bor'by kitaiskogo naroda v noveishee vremia*, p. 180. See also Cheng Tien-fong, *History of Sino-Russian Relations*, pp. 213–14.

[89] See *Contemporary China*, No. 1, May 25, 1941, quoted in *The Chinese Communist Movement*, II, 87. This American Military Intelligence report states that prior to Pearl Harbor, Soviet aid to China "vastly surpassed that of any other country." The same report refers also to the first "all-Soviet Russian" air raid (i.e., with Soviet planes and volunteer Soviet pilots), on Japanese installations in Nanking on January 26, 1938; *ibid.*, II, 87–88.

[90] *Foreign Relations of the United States, 1937*, III, 616–18. Davies's informant further reported that Soviet deliveries of military supplies to China had far exceeded the amount of this loan by early November; that these included 400 Soviet-made bombers and pursuit planes accompanied by 40 Soviet instructors; that 200 trucks were engaged in transporting other lighter supplies from the Soviet Union to China; that a Chinese military mission had been in Moscow for six weeks arranging for further purchases; and that the Soviet Ambassador to China, Bogomolov, and his military attaché were in Moscow, or en route, to discuss a better overland supply route. A month and a half later, however, on November 23, 1937, Davies reported from Moscow that the same Chinese informant had given him a very pessimistic account of the amount of assistance actually delivered to China. In particular he expressed resentment that Soviet aid had been substantially less than Bogomolov had led Nanking to believe it would be; *ibid.*, III, 711–12.

also does not appear to be included above.[91] The highest figure seen by the present writer in a Communist source (after it became permissible to discuss Soviet aid in specific terms) was $450,000,000 (U.S.), as of November, 1940.[92] In addition to these varying estimates of the dollar value of Soviet aid to China, there are also numerous eyewitness accounts of a formidable traffic of Soviet convoys along the Northwestern Highway from Sinkiang during 1939 and early 1940.[93]

It has sometimes been argued that Moscow used its aid program to secure changes in China favorable to the Communists. An American Military Intelligence report on the Chinese Communists, for instance, reads in part:

> The correctness of this interpretation [i.e., the thesis that the Russians were making political use of their aid] was confirmed in October, 1938, after the first rift in the united front. At that time the Soviet ambassador presented Chiang Kai-shek with five demands, of which one was that the Communist Party in China should be placed on an equal footing with the Kuomintang.[94]

The accuracy of this information—for which no source is cited—may be challenged. The Communists were not subsequently given status equal to that of the Kuomintang, and yet the largest Soviet credits were extended after the date of this alleged de-

[91] Beloff, *Foreign Policy of Soviet Russia,* II, 317; no source is indicated for this information.

[92] Richard Goodman, "The Soviet Union, Japan and China," *World News and Views,* No. 44, November 2, 1940, p. 621. The American Ambassador in Moscow reported as early as September, 1939, that according to a Chinese diplomatic informant the total sum of Soviet credits at that time amounted to $500,000,000 (U.S.), a sum much larger than credits obtained from all other countries combined. This same informant also said that 1,000 Russian-made planes had been delivered to China and that approximately 2,000 Soviet pilots had served in China in rotation since the outbreak of the Sino-Japanese war; *Foreign Relations of the United States, 1939,* III, 261.

[93] E.g., Edgar Snow, "Will Stalin Sell Out China?" *Foreign Affairs* (New York), No. 3, April, 1940, p. 459; George A. Fitch, "China's Northwestern Lifeline," *Amerasia* (New York), No. 7, September, 1940, pp. 301–6; Owen Lattimore, "Chinese Turkestan-Siberian Supply Road," *Pacific Affairs* (Camden, N.J.), December, 1940; Carlson, *Twin Stars of China,* p. 56. Cheng Tien-fong states that until the autumn of 1938 most Soviet supplies were routed by sea, from Odessa to Canton via the Suez Canal. After the fall of Canton in October, 1938, the Sinkiang route had to be used exclusively; *History of Sino-Russian Relations,* p. 214.

[94] *The Chinese Communist Movement,* II, 88.

mand. Similarly, it is difficult to find any substantiation of Edgar Snow's report a year later that increased Soviet aid awaited political progress within the Chungking government.[95] No such charges, in any case, were raised by Chungking. On the contrary, the Chinese Ambassador in London is reported to have said in July, 1940: "China's great neighbor [Russia] . . . has given us great material assistance by barter agreements *without any political conditions whatever.*"[96] Nor was the charge ever raised that Soviet war materials were sent directly to the Communists, despite the fact that the eastern terminus of the Soviet supply line at Lanchow was close to the Border area. In April, 1941, T. V. Soong gave his opinion, in an interview with an American correspondent, that the Communists had received no supplies from the Soviet Union.[97] Had there subsequently been any suspicion that the Communists did receive such supplies, it may be presumed that Nationalist spokesmen would have made appropriate charges. No such charges, as far as is known, have ever been raised.[98]

The logic of Soviet policy in the Far East, if it has been correctly interpreted above, argues in any case against the thesis that military aid to Chungking had strings attached to it. The primary purpose of Soviet policy was to encourage and sustain Chinese resistance. To have doled out aid in accordance with secondary political principles, or to have risked losing Chungking's good will by surreptitiously supplying the Communists, would have frustrated this purpose. Soviet aid to China, in this writer's view, must be regarded more as a premium on a valuable insurance policy against the danger of a Japanese attack on So-

[95] Snow, "Will Stalin Sell Out China?", *Foreign Affairs,* No. 3, April, 1940, p. 460; Snow's report was based on interviews with Soviet representatives in China in the autumn of 1939.

[96] *Anglo-Russian News Bulletin* (London), July 25, 1940, quoted in Moore, *Soviet Far Eastern Policy,* p. 118 (italics added).

[97] Interview with E. A. Mowrer, *China Weekly Review* (Shanghai), April 19, 1941, quoted in Rosinger, *China's Crisis,* p. 228.

[98] It is the view of most foreign writers on China that the Communists received no pay or military supplies even from Chungking after 1939; e.g., Rosinger, *China's Crisis,* p. 142; *United States Relations with China,* p. 51. Cf. Chiang Kai-shek, *Soviet Russia in China,* p. 120.

viet territory than as a lever to gain incidental advantages for Yenan.

The Nazi-Soviet pact of August, 1939, which marked a total reorientation of Soviet policy in Europe, did not immediately affect Moscow's relations with China. Chungking appears to have been largely undisturbed by the turn of events in Europe. The Chinese press was generally favorable to the Nazi-Soviet pact, considering it a blow to the anti-Comintern pact and therefore a factor promoting the further isolation of Japan in the Far East.[99] On August 29, Chiang Kai-shek argued, without stating precisely why, that the Nazi-Soviet pact and the threat of war in Europe "will benefit even more our national cause."[100] The Communists, as might have been expected, gave the pact their immediate endorsement. In an interview on September 1, Mao stated that it not only isolated Japan in the Far East but also thwarted Anglo-French efforts to provoke a Soviet-German clash in Europe.[101]

Later in September, in an interview given to Edgar Snow, Mao acknowledged that a nonaggression pact with Japan, similar to

[99] See "Chinese Reaction to the Nazi-Soviet Pact," *China Weekly Review*, September 2, 1939, pp. 20–22. It should be noted that the editors of this periodical were themselves critical of the pact; see the editorial in the issue for August 26, 1939, pp. 401–3. Excerpts from the Kuomintang press favorable to the Nazi-Soviet pact were printed in *Pravda*, August 26, 1939, p. 5.

[100] Interview on August 29, 1939; text in Chiang Kai-shek, *Collected Wartime Messages*, I, 323.

[101] Mao Tsze-dun, "O mezhdunarodnom polozhenii i osvoboditel'noi bor'be v Kitae" (Concerning the International Situation and the Struggle for Liberation in China), *Kommunisticheskii internatsional*, No. 8–9, September, 1939, p. 95. In making this defense of the pact, Mao went considerably further than official Soviet spokesmen, who at this time were defending the pact principally on the grounds that Anglo-French-Soviet military negotiations had broken down over Poland's refusal to authorize the passage of Soviet troops through its territories; see Voroshilov's interview in *Izvestiia*, August 27, and Molotov's address before the Supreme Soviet (August 31) in *Pravda*, September 1. See also Beloff, *Foreign Policy of Soviet Russia*, II, 272 ff. Some years later Po Ku (long since absolved of his errors during the Kiangsi era and reinstated in the Party's ruling circle) argued that Mao's prompt denunciation of Anglo-French policy in his September 1 interview was evidence of his initiative and independence of Moscow. This was the first such statement by a Communist leader anywhere in the world, Po Ku asserted; if it was made on Comintern instructions as some allege, why, he argued, was it that Party leaders more concerned—e.g., those in England and France—were not instructed first? Stein, *The Challenge of Red China*, p. 445.

the Nazi-Soviet pact, was a "Leninist possibility" on condition that "it does not interfere with Soviet support for China." [102] On September 28, Mao discussed this possibility in greater detail (according to a text in his recently published *Selected Works*):

As far as a non-aggression pact between the Soviet Union and Japan is concerned, the Soviet Union has been seeking Japan's signature on it for many years, but Japan has continued to reject the pact. Whether the Soviet Union will still be willing to conclude this pact, now that a faction in Japan's ruling class is beginning to express interest in it, depends upon one very basic principle: will this pact correspond to Soviet interests and to those of the depressed majority of mankind? To be specific, will it conflict with the interests of the national-liberation war in China? . . . Should a Soviet-Japanese non-aggression pact be concluded, the Soviet Union will under no circumstances allow this pact to interfere with Soviet aid to China. . . . I consider this absolutely beyond doubt.[103]

Mao's evident conviction that Soviet aid to China would continue despite Moscow's full retreat from collective security and its new orientation toward the Fascist powers may perhaps be explained by assurances he had received that in this respect no change in Soviet policy was anticipated. By the same token, Chiang's rather mild reaction to the Nazi-Soviet pact and to the threat of war in Europe may be explained by similar assurances given Chungking.[104]

Soviet aid to China does not, in fact, appear to have fallen off greatly during the period of the Nazi-Soviet pact. During the last months of 1939 some diplomatic sources in China actually reported an increase in the volume of Russian assistance to Nan-

[102] Snow, "Will Stalin Sell Out China?", *Foreign Affairs*, No. 3, April, 1940, p. 458.

[103] Mao, *Proizvedeniia*, III, 92–93 (English ed., III, 51). Wang Ming also is reported to have defended the possibility of a Soviet-Japanese nonaggression pact at a meeting of the People's Political Council in September, 1939; R. Page Arnot, "Critical Days for China's Revolution," *World News and Views*, No. 13, March 29, 1941, p. 205.

[104] On July 9, 1939, for instance, Stalin replied cordially and reassuringly to Chiang's letter delivered to him at the time of the signing of the Sino-Soviet commercial pact (June 16) and again complimented China on its war effort; see the partial text of this letter in Chiang Kai-shek, *Soviet Russia in China*, p. 90. Now, of course, Chiang views this letter as a typical instance of Stalin's deception.

king.[105] There appears to have been a substantial falling-off in Soviet aid during the summer and autumn of 1940, especially in the delivery of planes,[106] but by December Chinese officials were confident that additional supplies from Russia would be received soon.[107] Diplomatic reports from Moscow and Chungking early in 1941 seemed to justify these expectations.[108]

In the meantime, apparently no longer enjoined to silence on Russian aid to China, the Soviet press frankly acknowledged it and pledged its continuance. A Comintern writer declared in November, 1940:

> Improved Soviet-Japanese relations do not conflict with continued Soviet aid to China. On the contrary, it is clear that a relaxation in the tension between Japan and the U.S.S.R. will actively benefit China, for it will enable the U.S.S.R. more easily to supply China with those materials she needs to continue her war of independence. Moreover, these materials are supplied to China by the U.S.S.R. under a *purely commercial agreement* which is beyond the scope of any diplomatic discussion Japan may attempt to initiate.[109]

[105] *Foreign Relations of the United States, 1939,* III, 283, 289, 718, and 764.

[106] *Foreign Relations of the United States, 1940,* IV, 685–88.

[107] On October 18, 1940, Chiang Kai-shek had informed American Ambassador Johnson that no supplies at all were being received via Sinkiang; *ibid.,* IV, 672. The State Department appears to have been surprised at this information, noting that other sources had indicated continuing Soviet aid at approximately the same rate as previously, and on December 4 asked the Chinese Ambassador in Washington for further information on the matter; *ibid.,* IV, 680 and 705. On December 11, the Chinese reply stated that the Russians had recently assured Chungking of their intent to continue shipments but had not yet indicated the quantity of supplies and the dates of delivery; *ibid.,* IV, 709–10. It is quite apparent from official Chinese statements during this period that Chungking wished very much to increase the amount of American aid to China. To this end Chinese spokesmen perhaps exaggerated to American officials the decline in Soviet aid, thereby calling attention to their greater need of U.S. support.

[108] *Foreign Relations of the United States, 1941,* IV, 3, 112, 281, and 954. See also Beloff, *Foreign Policy of Soviet Russia,* II, 370. According to a recent Soviet source, early in 1941 Russia made a new shipment to China of 200 bomber and fighter planes; Kapitsa, *Sovetsko-kitaiskie otnosheniia v 1931–1945 gg.,* p. 84.

[109] Richard Goodman, "The Soviet Union, Japan and China," *World News and Views,* No. 44, November 2, 1940, p. 621 (italics in original). The reference to Japanese initiation of discussions was probably gratuitous inasmuch as Stalin had indicated to Von Ribbentrop as early as August, 1939, that the Soviet Union would welcome any German efforts to seek an improvement in Soviet-Japanese relations. He cautioned Von Ribbentrop on this occasion, however, that Tokyo should not gain the impression that the initiative in this matter had come from Moscow; *Nazi-Soviet Relations,* pp. 72–73. The Soviet press preserved the fiction of Japanese initiative up to the conclusion of the nonaggression pact in April,

The "Leninist possibility" of which Mao had spoken as early as September, 1939, became a reality nineteen months later. The provisions of the Soviet-Japanese pact, signed on April 13, 1941, were essentially the same as those of the Sino-Soviet pact of 1937: each signatory agreed to respect the territorial integrity of the other and to remain neutral in any conflict in which the other might become involved. There was no reference to China either in the text of the pact or in Soviet editorial comment which welcomed the pact as "a historic reversal of Soviet-Japanese relations" and "a new peace-loving step . . . which the Soviet people warmly supported." [110]

In China reaction to the pact was mixed. Chungking protested immediately against a declaration which accompanied the pact and which implied Soviet recognition of Manchukuo as being under Japan's protection. Molotov is reported to have assured the Chinese Ambassador in Moscow that "Manchukuo" was used in the text for want of a better word and that Soviet relations with China were in any case not affected by the pact.[111] Most of the Chungking press was sharply critical of the pact.[112] Chiang Kai-shek, however, in a telegram sent to his army commanders on April 24, appears not to have been greatly disturbed by the new turn of events: Soviet supplies were continuing to reach China, he said, and Soviet officials had assured Chungking that this aid would continue.[113] The Communists gave the pact their

---

1941. *Pravda,* for instance, claimed on April 19, 1941, that the Soviet Foreign Office had rejected a pact with Japan six months earlier. Subsequent revelations, however, indicate strongly that Moscow in fact accepted an offer to ally itself with Japan in the autumn of 1940, in a Four-Power Pact including Italy and Germany, but was prevented from doing so by a change of attitude in Berlin concerning the inclusion of Russia in this pact; *Nazi-Soviet Relations,* pp. 207 ff., pp. 258–59.

[110] See editorials in *Pravda,* April 14 and 19 and in *Izvestiia,* April 15, 1941.

[111] See Beloff, *Foreign Policy of Soviet Russia,* II, 376; Moore, *Soviet Far Eastern Policy,* p. 124; and *Foreign Relations of the United States, 1941,* IV, 955 and 970.

[112] See the reviews of Chinese editorial opinion on the pact in *Oriental Affairs,* No. 5, May, 1941, pp. 242–43 and pp. 250 ff. Comment favorable to the pact was reviewed in *Pravda,* April 15, 1941, p. 4.

[113] See the summary of this telegram in *Foreign Relations of the United States, 1941,* IV, 182–83. See also the dispassionate account of the background of the Soviet-Japanese pact in the official Chinese government publication, *China at War* (Chungking), No. 6, June, 1941, pp. 5–6.

unqualified endorsement, finding its chief significance "in the fact that it strengthens peace on the eastern frontiers of the U.S.S.R." Aid to China, meanwhile, would be unaffected by the pact, Yenan argued:

The Soviet-Japanese pact has not restricted the aid which the U.S.S.R. renders an independent and just resistance. . . . The hope of the Chinese people for aid from abroad rests, above all, on the U.S.S.R. . . . by this treaty the U.S.S.R. has not disappointed and will never disappoint China.[114]

There was not, however, time to test this thesis. Within two and a half months the Soviet Union was engaged in war in Europe, and military aid to China was terminated shortly thereafter.[115] What restraint, if any, the Soviet-Japanese pact might otherwise have placed on Moscow's China-aid program, it is impossible now to say.

Soviet aid to Kuomintang China, viewed in retrospect, emerges as one of the constant features of Soviet Far Eastern policy between 1937 and 1941. It began strongly, we have noted, soon after the Japanese attack at Lukouch'iao. It appears to have reached its peak during the months when Russia was abandoning its policy of seeking collective security in Europe and was embarking on a program of open collaboration with Germany. Following a decline in 1940, Russian aid was resumed during the months preceding the signing of the Soviet-Japanese pact in April, 1941, and continued, apparently without let-up, during the weeks following this event. It ceased only when Soviet commitments in Europe, after June, 1941, required all available resources. The fact that Soviet aid continued to go to Chungking for two years or more after Communist-Kuomintang relations had

[114] "China and the Soviet-Japanese Treaty," *World News and Views,* No. 19, May 10, 1941, p. 301; this was an official statement by the Chinese Communist Party dated April 21, 1941.

[115] According to diplomatic sources in China, Soviet supplies continued to reach China as late as August, 1941, but no contracts for further shipments were made; *Foreign Relations of the United States, 1941,* IV, 1015 and 1017. One source notes that some Soviet supplies were trickling into China as late as February, 1942, despite the fact that the Soviet Embassy in Chungking had formally notified the government in October, 1941, that owing to the war in Europe no further military materials could be spared; *Foreign Policy Bulletin* (New York), No. 22, 1942, p. 3.

begun to deteriorate and that no aid, in so far as is known, was ever given directly to the Communists emphasizes the extent to which Moscow had retreated from its earlier policies in China. For the present the Communists were of use to Moscow, it may be surmised, only to the extent that they continued to be allied with Chungking, which remained in Moscow's view the focal point of resistance to Japan.

CRACKS IN THE UNITED FRONT, SEPTEMBER, 1939–JUNE, 1941

The tendency of the Chinese Communists to look more critically than their Russian comrades at the situation in China became more accentuated in the third and fourth years of the anti-Japanese united front. In Moscow the signing of the Nazi-Soviet nonaggression pact in August, 1939, brought about no immediate change in the Soviet attitude toward the Sino-Japanese war. It was still considered a just war of national liberation on the part of the Chinese, and Soviet supplies were still made available to Chungking for its war effort. The government at Chungking continued to receive praise in the Soviet press and was stated, officially, to be steadily advancing toward internal democracy. In November, 1939, for instance, Tass dispatches from Chungking emphasized that the decisions of the recent Sixth Kuomintang Plenum had been hailed by "all circles of Chinese society . . . as proof of the strengthening of internal unity and a further step toward the development of Chinese democracy." [116] In May, 1940, *Pravda* applauded a recent Kuomintang decision to call a popular all-Chinese "parliament" and expressed confidence that this "parliament" would meet in the near future.[117] A textbook on China published in June observed that "in the course of the war of national liberation China's internal policies move increasingly toward democracy." [118] An extensive analysis of the war in China by V. Motylev, published in the autumn of 1940, gave a general endorsement of the Kuo-

[116] *Pravda,* November 22, 1939, p. 5.
[117] A. Bederov, "Bor'ba Kitaia za nezavisimost'" (China's Struggle for Independence), *Pravda,* May 3, 1940, p. 5.
[118] Glushakov, *Kitai,* p. 44.

mintang and discussed at some length the steps the national government had taken recently to strengthen Communist-Kuomintang collaboration.[119] Most reviews published at the end of 1940 and in early 1941 continued to praise this collaboration and noted no flaws in the united front to that date.[120]

This was the normal character of Soviet commentaries on China until early 1941. There were exceptions. Manifestations of anti-Communism were not wholly overlooked. Comintern journals, for instance, tacitly acknowledged the existence of Communist-Kuomintang rivalry by publishing articles by Mao and other Chinese leaders which made specific reference to it. In March, 1940, *World News and Views* carried an interview given by Mao to Chinese correspondents in September, 1939, in which he replied as follows to questions concerning friction between the two parties: "You are perfectly right in displaying interest in these questions. A certain improvement is to be recorded lately, but nothing has been changed fundamentally." [121] In April, 1940, an article by Chou En-lai in *Communist International* identified and linked "capitulation" and "division" as the twin evils in China. Capitulation, Chou wrote, was momentarily the "gravest danger in China," as the result of Wang Ching-wei's efforts early in 1940 to form a puppet government in Nanking. It was the capitulators, moreover, according to Chou, who were causing the rifts in the united front, "by insisting on the abolition of the Border regions . . . and by seeking to provoke armed conflicts with the Fourth and Eighth [Communist] Armies." [122]

As a rule the Soviet press emphasized the isolated character of such conflicts and fully exonerated the national government of any responsibility for them. One of *Pravda*'s political commentators observed in May, 1940, that "the efforts of certain generals to provoke civil war in China have been frustrated by the

[119] Motylev, *Tikhookeanskii uzel vtoroi imperialisticheskoi voiny*, p. 29.

[120] E.g., "China's United Front," *World News and Views*, No. 44, November 2, 1940, pp. 622–23; P. Krainov, "Voennye deistviia v Kitae v 1940 godu" (Military Operations in China in 1940), *Propagandist*, No. 2, January, 1941, pp. 23–26.

[121] "Interview with Mao Tse-tung," *World News and Views*, No. 9, March 2, 1940, p. 139.

[122] Chou En-lai, "Against Capitulation and Division in China," *Communist International* (New York), No. 4, April, 1940, p. 258.

government and by Chiang Kai-shek."[123] Fresh outbreaks in northern China, reported early in the summer, were laid wholly to "reactionary generals of the Northwest [Kuomintang] Army who on the pretext of 'fighting the Communists' are actually pursuing a policy of capitulation."[124] On the comparatively rare occasions when these conflicts were noted in the Soviet press they were normally viewed as a symptom of Wang Ching-wei's lingering influence in Chinese politics. As Wang's influence declined, or was said to decline, the possibilities of collaboration between the Communists and the Kuomintang improved. Thus, in December, 1940, a writer in *World News and Views* argued, on the basis of evidence that the threat of capitulation had been removed once and for all, that the united front was entering a new and more successful stage. It would no longer be jeopardized by the efforts of Wang's sympathizers to disrupt it.[125]

Infrequently Soviet writers noted another cause of Communist-Kuomintang rivalry. In September, 1940, a Comintern writer considered that "the actual political and economic administration of the guerrilla war areas has much to do with, and is even the primary cause of, the friction between the Kuomintang and the Chinese Communist Party." Eighth Army officials, this writer continued, had undertaken a number of reforms "which they hold appropriate to the conditions in the guerrilla regions. They quite naturally view the opposition [principally older Kuomintang Army officers] as being retrogressive and conservative. . . . The root of the trouble seems to be the intrigues [of these officers] and open encouragement for supporting the undesirable, to make

[123] Bederov, "Bor'ba Kitaia," *Pravda,* May 3, 1940, p. 5.

[124] Liu Biao [Lin Piao], "Tri goda natsional'no-osvoboditel'noi voiny kitaiskogo naroda" (Three Years of the Chinese People's War of National Liberation), *Kommunisticheskii internatsional,* No. 7, July, 1940, p. 61.

[125] Chen I-wan [Ch'en yi?], "China Defeats Its Fifth Column," *World News and Views,* No. 49, December 7, 1940, pp. 703–4. Chiang Kai-shek holds an entirely different view of the Soviet attitude toward Wang Ching-wei. He claims that Moscow secretly supported Wang's government and promised it early recognition in return for a Japanese agreement to allow Russia a free hand in Sinkiang, Tibet, Outer Mongolia, and parts of Inner Mongolia. Chiang alleges that the Chinese Communists knew of this secret agreement, reached in 1939, and gauged their strategy accordingly; Chiang Kai-shek, *Soviet Russia in China,* pp. 112–14. The present writer knows of no evidence that would support these claims.

something out of nothing and to exaggerate what is trivial in order to enlarge the trouble."[126]

Whether Soviet writers considered civil strife in China a purely isolated phenomenon, caused by a clash of opposing concepts of local government and administration, or a manifestation of Wang's influence in certain reactionary military circles, they did not attribute it, at least outwardly, to any fundamental difference of opinion between Chungking and Yenan. The united front in this respect was considered to be entirely sound. The Kuomintang as a whole continued to play a responsible role in the war effort and Chiang Kai-shek was still the symbol of Chinese resistance. This was the conclusion of Soviet commentators through the third year of the Kuomintang-Communist alliance.

The Chinese Communists approached the problem of civil conflict more directly than the Russians did or could. After Mao's public acknowledgement of conflicts between the Communists and the Kuomintang, in his interview of September 11, 1939,[127] Yenan began to protest in earnest against alleged violations of the united front agreement. On December 22, 1939, Chu Teh and several other Communist generals addressed a personal telegram to Chiang Kai-shek, demanding the immediate cessation of armed attacks on the Fourth and Eighth Route Armies. A similar telegram was sent to the national government on January 23, 1940. On February 13, Mao and other Party leaders, in a telegram addressed to the People's Political Council, protested sharply against the assignment of an investigatory commission to North China, allegedly to discover "materials which will prove the guilt of the Communist Party, the Eighth Route Army and the Shensi-Kansu-Ninghsia Border Region with regard to various

[126] "The Guerrilla Areas in North China," *World News and Views,* No. 39, September 28, 1940, p. 547. A similar conclusion was reached by George E. Taylor. He observed that, while there was some conflict between the Kuomintang and the Communists in 1940, this was not serious. "The most important conflict is between the old China and the new, categories which are not identical with the Kuomintang and the Eighth Route Army"; Taylor, *The Struggle for North China,* p. 167.

[127] A fuller record of the interview than that cited above (*World News and Views,* No. 9, 1940, pp. 138–40) was published in Chungking in October, 1939. This account indicated a number of specific clashes between Communist and Kuomintang troops dating from June, 1939; Mao Tse-tung, *China and the Second Imperialist World War,* pp. 24–28.

incidents of internal conflict." All of these documents, plus some others, were released by the Communists in April, 1940, in a pamphlet entitled *Friction Aids Japan, Documents Covering Instances of Friction, 1939–1940.* Other Communist pamphlets issued later in the year continued to emphasize violations of the Communist-Kuomintang truce and urged the national government to take steps to correct this situation.[128]

The Communists did not limit themselves to a recitation of complaints. As the gaps in the united front became more and more apparent and the likelihood of renewed collaboration more and more remote—whatever the intent of either party to preserve unity—the Communists looked for an alternative course of action. In short, they seem to have been preparing for the worst possible contingency from their point of view: a total collapse of the united front and a Japanese victory in China by means of a negotiated peace with Chungking.

In October, 1939, Mao wrote an introduction to a new journal for Party members, *The Communist,* the need for which he considered particularly pressing at that juncture because of "the daily growing danger of capitulation, division and retrogression in the anti-Japanese national united front." [129] Discussing the danger of defection on the part of the bourgeoisie, Mao wrote:

> An important element in the political line of the Chinese Communist Party is the alliance with, and also the struggle against, the bourgeoisie. An important element in the program to strengthen the Chinese Communist Party is the fact that it develops under conditions of this alliance with, and simultaneous struggle against, the bourgeoisie. By alliance, we mean the united front with the bourgeoisie; by struggle, we mean the "peaceful" and "bloodless" struggle, ideologically, politically and organizationally, during the period of the alliance. This becomes an armed struggle during the period of our inevitable break with the bourgeoisie.[130]

In December, 1939, in his pamphlet entitled *The Chinese Revolution and the Communist Party of China,* Mao elaborated on

[128] E.g., P'eng Teh-huai, *Unity and the Defense of North China,* and Wang Chia-hsiang, *Communists and the Three People's Principles.*

[129] Mao, *Proizvedeniia,* III, 99 (English ed., III, 53).

[130] *Ibid.,* III, 108–9 (English ed., III, 59).

the theme of the inevitable armed struggle with the bourgeoisie:

> The principal strategy and pattern of the Chinese revolution cannot be a peaceful struggle but must necessarily be an armed struggle. Our enemies do not allow the Chinese people the possibility of acting peacefully; the Chinese people possess no political rights and liberties. Stalin has said: "In China the armed revolution opposed the armed counter-revolution; this is one of the characteristics and one of the advantages of the Chinese revolution." This is entirely correct. We must therefore not underestimate the armed struggle, the revolutionary war, the partisan war and our [political] work in the armed forces.[131]

These two statements require little comment. Nothing remotely resembling them had appeared in the Soviet press since before the Seventh Comintern Congress in 1935; nothing like them was to appear until some years after the end of the Second World War.

The second of the two articles quoted above was followed within a month by Mao's first major theoretical work, *On the New Democracy*. This study was intended for a wider audience and perhaps because of this contained no references to the inevitable "armed struggle" with the bourgeoisie. *On the New Democracy* was in fact entirely orthodox in its basic formulations. The revolution in China was in a bourgeois-democratic phase; it could pass to the succeeding socialist phase only when "the tasks of the present revolution, the tasks of anti-imperialism and anti-feudalism, are fulfilled." [132] While the peasant question, Mao wrote, "is the fundamental question of the Chinese revolution and the force of the peasantry is the main force of the Chinese revolution . . . without the workers the revolution will not be able to succeed, for it is they who are the leaders of the revolution and have the highest revolutionary spirit." [133] The "new

[131] Mao, *Proizvedeniia*, III, 155 (English ed., III, 84–85); the quotation from Stalin is from an article written in 1928, "O perspektivakh revoliutsii v Kitae" (Concerning the Prospects for the Revolution in China), *Sochineniia*, VIII, 363.

[132] Quoted from text in Brandt, etc., *Documentary History*, p. 269.

[133] *Ibid.*, p. 270–71. The novelty of this view of the relationship between peasant and worker was noted above, pp. 115–17. Mao's stress on the centrality of the peasant issue was merely a change in emphasis, a recognition of one objective characteristic of the revolution in China; it was not a basic departure from earlier formulations. Mao in fact quoted Stalin as having said, in an address in 1925

democracy" itself was nothing more than the earlier two-class dictatorship of the workers and peasants, now expanded, at least semantically, into a "joint dictatorship of several revolutionary classes." [134]

At first glance, *On the New Democracy* appears to have been a rationale for the united front and it was undoubtedly accepted as such. But it must be judged in the context of the political situation in China early in 1940, or at least in terms of Mao's estimate of this situation. The ominous phrases with which he opens his treatise suggest that it could equally serve as a reserve program in the event that the united front should fail:

> When the war against the Japanese aggressor began our people took heart; everyone believed that a way out had been found; gloomy faces disappeared. But recently an atmosphere of compromise has again emerged. A campaign of anti-Communism has again arisen. The Chinese people are once again frustrated and at an impasse. . . . And once more it becomes unclear what we are doing and where China is going.[135]

Throughout this period the Party was steeling itself against all contingencies. A resolution passed by the Central Committee on November 1, 1939, warned that "it is only by the penetration of CP activities among the masses . . . that we shall be able to forestall unexpected losses to the Party and to the war of resistance, in case any act of capitulation or move against the Communists or other unexpected incident should take place." [136] The same resolution stressed the need "to differentiate strictly between the public and secret work of the Party . . . ; there should be adequate coordination between the two in order to avoid repetition of the failure of work in the white [Kuomintang]

---

before the Yugoslav Commission of the ECCI, that "the national question is *virtually* a question of the peasantry." "This means," Mao wrote, "that the Chinese revolution is virtually a peasant revolution, that the struggle against the Japanese invaders is virtually a peasant war"; *ibid.*, p. 246.

[134] *Ibid.*, p. 267.

[135] Translated from text in Mao, *Proizvedeniia*, III, 202 (English ed., III, 106). For an excellent analysis of *On the New Democracy* see the commentary in Brandt, etc., *Documentary History*, pp. 260–63.

[136] "Decision of the CC on the Work of Penetrating the Masses" (November 1, 1939), quoted in Brandt, etc., *Documentary History*, p. 346.

areas during the civil war days [before 1937]."[137] An official statement by the Party on July 7, 1940, did not deny that secret Communist cells had been organized among Kuomintang troops, in direct contravention of a pledge (given at the Sixth Party Plenum in November, 1938), to refrain from such activity. The Party on this occasion merely apologized for the actions of its lower units, explaining that they had failed to understand the Party line on this point![138]

It is interesting to speculate on the Comintern's probable reaction to Chinese Communist attitudes and behavior in 1939 and 1940. There is little doubt that Soviet leaders knew of developments in Yenan. If they had no other way of learning of them, Chou En-lai—one of the few Chinese who traveled freely back and forth between Chungking and Yenan—would certainly have rendered a full report to the Comintern when he visited Moscow early in 1940, allegedly for treatment of a broken arm.[139] The Comintern staff would certainly have discussed with him Mao's theses presented in *The Communist* and in *The Chinese Revolution and the Chinese Communist Party.* If these theses caused some concern in Comintern circles, as views inimical to the united front policy, Moscow gave no overt indication of it. No official censure of these attitudes appeared in the Soviet or the Comintern press, nor is there any evidence that Mao's views were privately repudiated in Moscow at the time or subsequently. On the other hand, neither of the two works mentioned was made available in Russian until after the war.[140] Even the comparatively mild *On the New Democracy,* now considered Mao's most valuable contribution to Marxist-Leninist theory, was nowhere acknowledged in the Soviet press, so far as is known,

[137] *Ibid.,* p. 347.

[138] Reference to this statement is made in "China's United Front," *World News and Views,* No. 44, November 2, 1940, p. 623.

[139] Chou's return to Chungking after a visit of "several months" in Moscow was noted in the New York *Times,* March 26, 1940, p. 2.

[140] The full texts of these two works appeared in Russian for the first time in Vol. III of Mao's *Selected Works,* published in Moscow in 1953. Only occasional references to the texts in an earlier Chinese edition of Mao's writings, said to have been published in Harbin in 1948, appeared in Soviet monographs prior to 1953.

until after the war.[141] The Russian press, in fact, gave little attention to the Chinese Communists during the years of the Nazi-Soviet pact. The present writer has discovered only two statements by Mao which were reported in the Soviet press of this period, both printed within six months of the signing of the pact, although his *Selected Works* includes nearly twice as many items for these two years as for the preceding two.[142] Coverage of guerrilla activities in North China, once comparable to coverage given the regular Chinese forces, dwindled gradually during 1940 and ceased altogether by the end of the year. While official statements from Yenan appeared infrequently in the Comintern press as late as May, 1941,[143] no articles appeared after 1939 which were wholly devoted to the Communists in China, such as those that had appeared irregularly during the first two years of the alliance with the Kuomintang.

Some of these omissions are readily understandable. Mao's article in the first issue of *The Communist*, for instance, as well as his pamphlet *The Chinese Revolution and the Chinese Communist Party*, were probably not intended for circulation outside Party circles. Their appearance in Comintern publications in 1939 or 1940 would have been quite inappropriate. At the same time the dwindling number of military reports from the guerrilla areas may have reflected the severity of Chungking's new censor-

[141] Anna Louise Strong has claimed that *On the New Democracy* was published in both Russian and English in Moscow in 1940 and hailed as "a new Marxist classic" during the war; *The Chinese Conquer China*, p. 53. No record of these editions has been found. Excerpts from *On the New Democracy*, however, appeared in the American journal *Communist* in March, 1941 (pp. 238–56), translated from the text published in the *Yenan Liberation* early in 1940. A full English text of Mao's treatise was published only in 1944, in Bombay, under the title *China's New Democracy*.

[142] Mao's *Selected Works* includes twenty-seven items for the two-year period beginning in September, 1939, as against fourteen for the preceding two years. The two statements by Mao discovered in the Soviet—rather the Comintern—press during the Nazi-Soviet era are an interview with three Chinese correspondents on September 11, 1939, published in *World News and Views*, No. 9, March 2, 1940, pp. 138–40, and an address at a mass rally in Yenan on February 1, 1940, published under the title "Mao Tse-tung Denounces Wang Ching-wei's Treachery," *World News and Views*, No. 21, May 25, 1940, p. 302; both are included in the *Selected Works*.

[143] E.g., the statement on the Anhwei incident in *World News and Views*, No. 11, March 15, 1941, and the statement on the Soviet-Japanese non-aggression pact in *World News and Views*, No. 19, May 10, 1941.

ship regulations and the restrictions on visits by foreign observers to the Border regions.[144] To some extent, too, what appears to have been a growing inattention to the Chinese Communists in the Soviet press merely reflected a general decline in Soviet interest in China as a whole as relations with Tokyo improved and as the threat of a Far Eastern war involving the Soviet Union receded.[145] Whether or not there was a real decline in Moscow's interest in the Chinese Communists between 1939 and 1941, the Soviet and the Comintern press certainly conveyed the impression of Moscow's lack of interest. Chinese Communism had never been so little in the news in Moscow—apart, perhaps, from the nine months preceding the announcement of the united front in September, 1937—since the beginning of the movement two decades earlier. To judge from Soviet and Comintern publications, by 1941 the Russians were concerned in China only with Chungking and the Kuomintang.[146]

Were it possible to determine more precisely the character of Soviet thinking on China during this period, it would perhaps be found that Moscow's confidence in the continuing solidarity of the united front was a great deal weaker than its official state-

[144] The ban on visits to Yenan after 1939 and the growing censorship in Chungking of any discussion of the Chinese Communists not only meant that Moscow was denied firsthand accounts of the situation in North China, which the Soviet press had quoted widely in earlier years; it also meant that both Soviet and Chinese Communist policies were denied a good deal of gratuitous support from such sympathetic reporters as Edgar Snow, Colonel Evans Carlson, Anna Louise Strong, Nym Wales, James Bertram, and others.

[145] Battle dispatches from China averaged approximately one third of a column daily in *Pravda* and *Izvestiia* at the outset of the Second World War in September, 1939; in the spring of 1941, prior to Russia's entry into the war, this coverage had been cut in half. The decrease in feature coverage of China during this same period was even more noticeable: during the first six months of 1941 the Soviet press carried fewer than a quarter of the number of articles on China it had carried during any comparable period in 1938 and 1939. A. Bederov's article, "Bor'ba Kitaia za nezavisimost'," in *Pravda* of May 3, 1940, was the last political commentary on China to appear in the daily Moscow press until 1945.

[146] No important Communist gatherings, for instance, were reported in the Soviet press after 1939—although there were a number that might have been—yet regular coverage was given the plenary sessions of the Kuomintang and the Kuomintang-controlled People's Political Council; see *Pravda*, September 22, and November 14 and 22, 1939, and April 2 and 10, July 13, and October, *passim*, 1940. In contrast to the omission from the Soviet press of all but two of Mao's public statements during the Nazi-Soviet era, Chiang's were normally, if briefly, noted; see, for instance, *Pravda*, September 20 and 22, October 10–13, and November 14, 1939, and April 4, October 11, and December 5, 1940.

ments implied. Unofficially, the Chinese Communists may not have been blamed by Moscow for seeking an alternative to the 1937 alliance with the Kuomintang, an alliance which, admittedly, imposed some restrictions on the pursuit of their domestic objectives. They may even have received some private encouragement from Moscow to explore alternative courses of action. But, while engaged in any such effort, the Chinese Communists could not, of course, be of use to the Russians. The years 1939 and 1940, it has been observed above, were years when Moscow could ill afford to indulge purely ideological preferences. In China military preponderance lay not with the Communists but with the Kuomintang. The symbol of Chinese resistance, partly as a direct consequence of propaganda that had originated in Moscow, was not Mao but Chiang Kai-shek. If it had come to an absolute choice between Chungking and Yenan in 1940, it is not unlikely that the Russians—at least in their official pronouncements—would have been obliged to choose Chungking. Since it did not come to that, the Soviet press continued to paint a picture of unity in China that was virtually nonexistent and to argue that the future of China depended on continued collaboration even after the war.

It is equally interesting, looking at the other side of the coin, to speculate on the reasons why Mao chose the end of 1939 to express himself, probably without consulting Moscow, on the future course of the revolution. Undoubtedly one reason was the alleged danger of a Nationalist capitulation to Japan and a resumption of the civil war. Whether or not this was a real possibility in 1939, the persistent references to it in Chinese Communist sources suggest that Mao was weighing the danger in all seriousness. It is also likely that Mao's search for an alternative to the united front was directly stimulated by the abrupt turn which Soviet foreign policy took in August, 1939. It would have required little imagination on Mao's part to realize that the Nazi-Soviet pact, despite any assurances he may have received from the Russians, signaled a change in Soviet policy that could, with no ill-will on Moscow's part, work to China's disadvantage. Publicly Mao applauded the pact. Privately he was doubtless aware of the grave consequences it might eventually have for Chinese resistance and for the fortunes of the Communists. Similarly, his bland assertion to Edgar Snow that a parallel Soviet rapprochement with Japan was a "Leninist possibility" need not be accepted as evidence that Mao did not fear that contingency. Mao, it may be presumed, was orthodox enough to value the preservation of the Soviet Union and sophisticated enough to appreciate the complex maneuvers of Soviet foreign policy which this required. He could not, however, ignore his own responsibilities in China. "The Party," Mao wrote in *The Communist* on October 4, 1939, "must prepare itself fully for any sudden emergencies so that, should these occur, neither the Party nor the revolution will suffer unexpected losses."[147] From the autumn of 1939 Mao's efforts were increasingly dedicated to this end.

It is not possible to relate precisely these simultaneous developments in China and in the Soviet Union. The most that can be said with certainty is that shifts in Soviet foreign policy coincided, or nearly coincided, with changes in Mao's attitude on the prospects of the revolution, and that these changes in Mao's attitude in turn coincided, or nearly coincided, with a gradual decline in Moscow's observable interest in the activities of the Chinese Communists. All of these developments occurred at a time when the united front in China was suffering great internal strains. One can do no more than point to the coincidence of these developments without indicating, on the basis of evidence now available, which were causal and which derivative.

The sharpest clash between Communist and Kuomintang troops during the entire existence of the united front was the South Anhwei, or New Fourth Army, incident in January, 1941. This was a major crisis. In several days of heavy fighting some 6,000 Communist soldiers, according to Yenan's estimate, were killed.[148] The Fourth Army was officially disbanded on orders from

[147] Mao, *Proizvedeniia,* III, 99 (English ed., III, 53). See also the resolution passed by the Central Committee on October 10, 1939, entitled "The Current Situation and the Tasks of the Party," *ibid.,* III, 121–25 (English ed., III, 66–68).

[148] See the Communists' declaration on the incident dated February 26, 1941; text in Rosinger, *China's Wartime Politics,* pp. 111–14.

Chungking and its commander, Yeh Ting, arrested.[149] Abroad, the incident was widely reported and caused much concern in circles sympathetic to continued Chinese resistance to Japan.[150]

In view of the seriousness of this incident Moscow's outward reaction was extremely mild. *Pravda* and *Izvestiia* waited ten days after the end of the fighting before carrying a Tass dispatch on the incident and refrained altogether from editorial comment, at the time or subsequently.[151] In the Comintern press some concern was shown and a timid effort was made to determine the causes of the conflict. One writer, for instance, laid it to "the narrow-minded aspirations of certain Kuomintang generals directed against patriotic Communist elements in the ranks of the Fourth Army." [152] Another considered Japanese as well as Anglo-American intrigues in Chungking indirectly responsible for the incident, the former seeking to remove the Fourth Army, and

[149] Current Chinese Communist sources consider the deputy commander of the New Fourth Army, Hsiang Ying, chiefly responsible for the rout although he himself was killed in the course of it. He is accused of having disregarded earlier directives to take suitable precautionary measures against just such an attack as that which occurred in southern Anhwei. See editor's note in Mao, *Proizvedeniia,* III, 369–70 (English ed., III, 204). The New Fourth Army, though officially disbanded in January, 1941, was reconstituted almost immediately by Yenan and remained one of the Communists' major units throughout the balance of the Sino-Japanese war; Rosinger, *China's Wartime Politics,* p. 114.

[150] Accounts of the Anhwei incident vary. Chungking maintained that the New Fourth Army had ignored an order from the War Ministry, issued in October, 1940, to withdraw north of the Yangtze and instead was planning an attack on Nationalist troops south of the river. The Communists, on the other hand, claimed that they were in the process of carrying out Chungking's directive and had in fact transferred 90,000 of their troops across the Yangtze when, early in January, 1941, a vastly superior government force fell upon the remaining 10,000. A Nationalist view of the incident may be found, *inter alia,* in Chiang Kai-shek, *Soviet Russia in China,* pp. 94–95, and in Cheng Tien-fong, *History of Sino-Russian Relations,* p. 230; for a pro-Communist view, see Smedley, *The Great Road,* pp. 378–79. The texts of statements by the Communists and by Chiang Kai-shek following the incident are in Rosinger, *China's Wartime Politics,* pp. 111–21. Most neutral observers conclude that the long antagonism between Communist and Nationalist troops was severe enough by 1941 to cause an outbreak of these proportions on one pretext or another. See North, *Moscow and Chinese Communists,* p. 191; *United States Relations with China,* p. 53.

[151] *Pravda,* January 27, 1941, p. 5; *Izvestiia,* January 28, 1941, p. 2. The New York *Times* first reported the Anhwei incident on January 18, 1941.

[152] "Vokrug mezhdunarodnogo konflikta v Kitae" (Around the International Conflict in China), *Kommunisticheskii internatsional,* No. 2, February, 1941, p. 83.

subsequently the Eighth, as obstacles to a peaceful settlement with the Chungking government, the latter seeking "the destruction of the progressive national revolutionary character of the war and its subjection to the imperialist and counter-revolutionary interests of Britain and America."[153] This writer tended to minimize the seriousness of the clash, arguing that in the end it would, like the Sian crisis, serve to unify the Chinese people even more strongly.

Nowhere in the Comintern press was it suggested that the Kuomintang as a whole, or Chiang Kai-shek personally, should be held responsible for the attack on the Fourth Army. One account, in fact, conspicuously quoted from *Ta Kung Pao* (which was called, erroneously, "the leading organ of the Kuomintang") to show the Kuomintang's generally conciliatory attitude toward the Anhwei incident.[154] As far as moralizing on the disastrous consequences of disunity in China was concerned, this was left largely to liberal opinion abroad, which was widely quoted in the Soviet and the Comintern press during the weeks following the incident.[155]

The reaction in Yenan to the South Anhwei incident was in sharp contrast to that in Moscow. On January 22, 1941, a few days after the fighting had ended, the Communists charged "leaders of the pro-Japanese faction in China, long active in the Kuomintang's party, government and military organizations," with having planned the attack on the Fourth Army as much as four or five months earlier. Yenan made twelve demands covering

[153] Richard Goodman, "What is Happening in China?", *World News and Views,* No. 7, February 15, 1941, p. 108.

[154] Vokrug mezhdunarodnogo konflikta v Kitae," *Kommunisticheskii internatsional,* No. 2, February, 1941, pp. 85–86. The passage quoted, while conciliatory, did not exonerate the Fourth Army from some measure of guilt in the affair. "We do not consider it necessary to inquire into the general circumstances of the Fourth Army incident," the *Ta Kung Pao* comment read, "but we hope that the high command will manifest caution in its settlement of the incident and we hope that apart from the wish to strengthen military discipline, no other sentiments will be displayed."

[155] E.g., *ibid.,* pp. 83–86, *passim; Pravda,* February 3, 1941, p. 5; "O mezhdunarodnom konflikte v Kitae—po stranitsam zarubezhnoi pechati," (Concerning the International Conflict in China—As Reported in the Foreign Press), *Kommunisticheskii internatsional,* No. 4, April, 1941, pp. 92–95. A contrary view on the reaction in Moscow to the South Anhwei incident may be found in Cheng Tien-fong, *History of Sino-Russian Relations,* p. 230.

a wide range of past and present grievances: an official apology for the attack and the immediate release of Yeh Ting; punishment of the generals directly responsible for the outrage; a countermanding of the order dissolving the Fourth Army; release of all political prisoners and patriots; termination of the blockade around the Border areas; abolition of the one-party dictatorship; and so forth. The Communist statement, prepared by Mao, continued:

> If these twelve conditions are fulfilled then the situation will straighten itself out of its own accord and we Communists, and the entire Chinese people with us, will of course do nothing to complicate matters further. But if these conditions are not fulfilled, then we can do nothing in our power to help. . . . We value unity but they too must value it. To speak quite frankly, there is a limit to our concessions and the period of making them is now ended.[156]

On February 26, 1941, the Communists, having received no reply to their demands, made them again in another official statement concerning the Anhwei incident. On this occasion Chang Hsüeh-liang and Yang Hu-ch'eng, Chiang's captors at Sian, were added to the list of political prisoners to be released.[157]

On March 18, in an internal Party directive, Mao directly implicated Chiang himself by holding him responsible for the order disbanding the New Fourth Army and by calling his recent "anti-Communist speech delivered on March 6 before the People's Political Council . . . the rear-guard action in the reactionaries' campaign against the Communists."[158] As for the Kuomintang as a whole, Mao considered that it had "in no respect ceased its policy of suppressing Communists and other progres-

[156] "Statement of the Chairman of the Military Revolutionary Committee of the Chinese Communist Party [Mao Tse-tung] to the Correspondent from the *Sinhua* News Agency" (January 22, 1941); quoted in Mao, *Proizvedeniia*, III, 418–19 (English ed., III, 230–31). The Communist demands, without any accompanying statement by Mao, were noted in *World News and Views*, No. 11, March 15, 1941, p. 166; see also the text of this statement (or one very similar to it) in Strong, *China's New Crisis*, pp. 33 ff.

[157] The text of this statement is in Rosinger, *China's Wartime Politics*, pp. 111–14; excerpts may also be found in *World News and Views*, No. 18, May 3, 1941, p. 286.

[158] Mao, *Proizvedeniia*, III, 425 (English ed., III, 233).

sive groups within its areas . . . and will undoubtedly attack our forces again."[159]

It is of no particular consequence, for the purposes of this study, that the Communist demands were rejected in 1941 although formal unity was preserved.[160] What is significant about the South Anhwei incident is the striking discrepancy between the Russian and Chinese Communist reactions to the crisis. On an issue which clearly affected the fortunes, and perhaps even the legal existence, of the Communists, Moscow could do no more than suggest, rather apathetically, that a few reactionary generals, or even a few foreign agents in Chungking, were responsible for the affair. Comment on the more troublesome political aspects of the incident as it affected the united front was left to the foreign press. The Soviet response, in any case, should surprise no one. It was entirely consistent with policies that had been followed in China for four or five years; in 1941, it would have been more surprising had Moscow reacted otherwise.

One should inquire periodically in a study of this sort whether direct links between Moscow and the Chinese Communists, not easily detected in open sources, might nonetheless have existed during any given period. While the Communists were in the south, the possibilities of direct liaison with Moscow were very meager. Apart from the Comintern military adviser Li Teh, it is believed no other emissary from Moscow reached Juichin during these years, although there were doubtless agents, at least for a time, in Shanghai and other cities. With the transfer of soviet strength to North China in 1935 the opportunities for contact undoubtedly improved, but there is still very sparse evidence of the presence of Comintern agents at the new Communist bases in Shensi[161] and fragmentary evidence at best of anything re-

[159] *Ibid.*, III, 427 (English ed., III, 234).

[160] Chiang dealt with the Communist demands in his March 6 speech to the People's Political Council, professing astonishment at their "resemblance . . . to demands made by the Japanese before the Lukouch'iao Incident"; quoted in Rosinger, *China's Wartime Politics*, p. 116.

[161] According to Chiang Kai-shek, Stalin admitted after the war that there had once been a resident representative from Moscow in Yenan, but Stalin said he "had since been recalled"; Chiang Kai-shek, *Soviet Russia in China*, p. 150. In the present writer's view, it is unlikely that Stalin would have acknowledged the

sembling a courier service, or other liaison, between the Chinese Communists and Moscow.[162] Edgar Snow, who spent two months with the Communists in 1936, found no agents from Moscow—other than Li Teh—and concluded that there had been none for half a dozen years.[163]

During the first two years after the establishment of the united front, access to the Communist areas was easier than it had been for many years and there is some evidence that the Russians made use of it. Anna Louise Strong has reported, for instance, that two Tass correspondents were covering the activities of Chu Teh's forces when she visited his headquarters in 1938.[164] There were also several hundred Russian pilots and transport personnel in Sian and Lanchow in 1938 and 1939,[165] some of whom perhaps made the short trip into the Border areas. It does not appear, however, from available evidence, that any of these Russians were agents in the usual sense. Wang Ming, reaching China at the end of 1937 after six years in the Soviet capital, probably comes closest to qualifying as a Comintern agent of those persons known to have come to China from Moscow, but, as has been shown, his star quickly faded. Chou En-lai, visiting Moscow for a brief period two years later, must be regarded more as an emissary from the Chinese Communists to the Comintern than vice versa. A high-ranking Japanese Communist who went from Moscow to Yenan in 1940, his trip evidently authorized by the

---

presence of a Comintern agent with the Chinese Communists—assuming there was such an agent—as late as 1937, when Yenan had become the Communist capital. He might, on the other hand, have admitted to the activities of a Comintern agent some years earlier, say, in the twenties. Chiang may therefore be confused here as to dates.

[162] Chiang Kai-shek has claimed that Pan Han-nien, a Communist negotiator in Shanghai in the spring of 1936, was in contact with the Comintern; *Soviet Russia in China,* p. 73. According to Miao Chien-ch'iu, former aide to Chang Hsüeh-liang, Pan Han-nien was intercepted in Sian on January 8, 1937, bearing Comintern instructions to Communist headquarters in Yenan. These instructions, allegedly relayed from a Communist organization in Nanking, directed Mao to use the truce following the Sian incident to strengthen his armed forces; interview with the author in Tokyo, January 27, 1957.

[163] Snow, *Red Star over China,* pp. 410–22.

[164] Strong, *The Chinese Conquer China,* p. 60.

[165] See Carlson, *Twin Stars of China,* p. 56; *Foreign Relations of the United States, 1939,* III, 142; George A. Fitch, "China's Northwestern Lifeline," *Amerasia,* No. 7, September, 1940, p. 301.

Comintern,[166] appears to have played a negligible role in Chinese Communist affairs. By 1940 the Border areas had again been sealed off by a Nationalist blockade and the trip to Yenan was hazardous. This same Japanese Communist states that though he was everywhere accepted as a Chinese citizen he reached Yenan only after the greatest difficulties. What short-wave radio communication there may have been between the Comintern and the Chinese Communists during these years is not known, though it is reasonable to imagine that such contact existed.

It is quite possible, of course, that Moscow deliberately refrained from giving detailed guidance to Yenan during the early years of the united front. This would have been entirely consistent with Moscow's policy of preserving the united front in China as its first line of defense against Japan. Any large-scale endeavor to maintain contact with the Communists, especially after the reimposition of the Kuomintang blockade of the Communist areas, would certainly have been detected by Chungking and would have aggravated its suspicions concerning Soviet intentions. Under such circumstances, Russian leaders perhaps reasoned, Chungking might become more receptive to Japanese peace offers, and the quality of Chinese resistance would in consequence be seriously impaired. In weighing these probabilities Soviet leaders may have concluded that where the Chinese Communists were concerned it was more prudent to adopt a distant and somewhat noncommittal attitude than to seek to reestablish, if they could, the sort of relationship that had been maintained during the 1920s.

A closer tie between Moscow and Yenan after 1937 might not in any case have greatly changed the pattern of Comintern-Chinese Communist relations. If we judge correctly that there was an identity, or near-identity, of interests between the two respecting Chinese resistance to Japan, any directions which Moscow would have been likely to send to the Chinese Communists would probably not have conflicted with their prevailing

[166] Rodger Swearingen and Paul Langer, *Red Flag in Japan* (Cambridge, Mass., 1952), p. 74. This Japanese Communist was Nozaka Sanzo (then known by the alias Nakano Susumu), who later became the leader of the postwar Communist Party of Japan.

policies. It is a reasonable assumption, in this writer's view—in the absence of indications of a closer tie between Moscow and Yenan—that the Comintern, appreciating the sacrifice which the Communists had already made to achieve unity in China and anxious not to give rise to undue suspicions in Chungking, was content to let Mao pursue his own course within certain broad limits already well defined and accepted in Yenan.

4

SOVIET POLICY DURING THE WAR, 1941–1945

For several years after Russia's entry into the European war in June, 1941, China appeared to recede still further from the sphere of Soviet attention. This is not surprising when one considers that at least until early 1943 the Soviet Union was engaged in a desperate struggle for survival on battle fronts far removed from China. Had Japan continued to pose a serious threat to the Soviet Union, doubtless Moscow would have displayed greater interest in China, as its first line of defense against Japan. But the Russians appear not to have been greatly concerned about Japan after the spring of 1941. The Soviet-Japanese pact gave Russia protection in the Far East at the outset of its involvement in the European war;[1] Japan's attack on Pearl Harbor six months later and its subsequent commitment to war in the Pacific virtually removed all threat from this quarter for the balance of the war. So long as the Chungking government did not capitulate—and after Pearl Harbor the Soviet Union could rely on the United States and England to avert this—China was not of great consequence in Moscow's war strategies. It was only after the course of the war in Europe turned more in Russia's favor that Moscow again directed its attention to China and gradually worked out a new policy both toward the Chungking government and toward the Chinese Communists.

[1] The "protection" provided by the Soviet-Japanese pact may have been less real than was imagined at the time. It is now known that immediately after the German attack on the Soviet Union in June, 1941, Japan gave serious consideration to a plan to reverse the current direction of its foreign policy, which envisaged expansion in China and Southeast Asia, and to launch an attack on the Soviet Union from Manchuria. See Herbert Feis, *The Road to Pearl Harbor: The Coming of the War between the United States and Japan* (Princeton, N.J., 1950), pp. 209–18.

SOVIET VIEWS OF CHINA DURING THE FIRST TWO YEARS OF THE WAR: CHINA UNCHANGED, JULY, 1941–JULY, 1943

From the summer of 1941, after Hitler's attack on Russia, to the summer of 1943, battle dispatches from Chungking carried in *Pravda* dwindled from an average of about three a week to three a month, or less.[2] During this period neither *Pravda* nor *Izvestiia* carried comment of an editorial character on China, although each in the normal course of its foreign coverage had something to say editorially at one time or another concerning nearly every other country in the world, whether ally, enemy, or neutral. *Bol'shevik* had no articles on China between 1940 and 1944. Even *Communist International,* which before 1939 had sometimes devoted entire issues to China and as late as 1940 had given China almost as much coverage as any other foreign power (fourteen feature articles during the course of that year), carried no items on China or on the Sino-Japanese war between June, 1941, and its final issue in June, 1943.

Such comment on China as did appear in the Soviet and Comintern press during the first two years after the German attack on the Soviet Union differed little from that of the two preceding years. The situation in China, as Soviet and Comintern writers reported it, was essentially unchanged. The war against Japan was still a just war; the united front between the Communists and the Kuomintang, although admittedly under some strain from "reactionary local groups," [3] was still the basis of China's resistance. The united front, officially, was not considered in serious peril. A writer in *World News and Views,* for instance, applauded a Kuomintang resolution in the autumn of 1942 in favor of continued tolerance of the Communists. "This resolution," he observed, "is definitely encouraging and shows that unity continues to be strengthened." [4] Where shortcomings were noted in

[2] To some extent, of course, this decline in the number of battle reports from China reflected the stabilization of the battle lines in China, relative to earlier years, and does not in itself indicate Moscow's intentional disregard of the China theater.

[3] See "China's Victories," *World News and Views,* No. 37, September 12, 1942, p. 375.

[4] "Unity in China," *World News and Views,* No. 51, December 19, 1942, p. 486.

the united front they were sometimes laid to events entirely outside Chungking's control. Another writer in *World News and Views,* for instance, wrote in December, 1942:

> One of the main reasons why the progressive forces in China and in the Chinese government have not achieved more success in placing Chinese unity on a sure, democratic basis has been because of the discouraging effects of the loss of Burma and the failure of Britain to heed Chiang's appeal for the freedom of India.[5]

Chiang Kai-shek's status was unchanged, according to Soviet and Comintern observers. V. K. Krishna Menon, writing in *World News and Views* in March, 1942, considered Chiang "the leader of the Chinese people . . . and the symbol of Chinese unity."[6] Chiang's visit to India, in February, 1942, was given some prominence in the Soviet press,[7] and his major public statements were reported as regularly in the two years after June, 1941, as they had been previously.[8] On the diplomatic front, Stalin reiterated, on occasion, his confidence in continuing good relations between China and Russia.[9]

China's international position, in the meantime, was considered greatly improved by the extension of the war in the Far East following the Japanese attack on Pearl Harbor in December, 1941. Chungking would now receive military aid from the United States; China would share more fully in postwar decisions in the Pacific area; above all, China could now abrogate its unequal treaties. The national government was urged to make the most of these advantages.[10] In January, 1943, a Tass dispatch in

[5] Arthur Clegg, "A Year of War in the Pacific," *World News and Views,* No. 49, December 5, 1942, p. 468.

[6] V. K. Krishna Menon, "India and China," *World News and Views,* No. 10, March 7, 1942, p. 149; see also Clegg, "A Year of War," *World News and Views,* No. 49, December 5, 1942, p. 467.

[7] *Pravda,* February 14–24, 1942, *passim.*

[8] E.g., *Pravda,* November 17, 21, 27, and December 13, 22, 1941; January 23, February 24, November 5, 15, and December 3, 1942; January 20 and February 23, 1943.

[9] See Chiang's reference to Stalin's letter dated December 11, 1942, delivered to him by the Soviet Ambassador Paniushkin; Chiang Kai-shek, *Soviet Russia in China,* pp. 97–98.

[10] G. Astafev, "Kitai vo vtoroi polovine 1941 goda" (China in the Second Half of 1941), *Mirovoe khoziaistvo i mirovaia politika,* Nos. 1–2, January-February, 1942, pp. 71–81.

Pravda reported in some detail Chiang Kai-shek's announcement of new treaties with England and the United States, treaties which ended the ancient practice of extraterritoriality.[11]

As far as the Chinese Communists were concerned, there was still little disposition among Soviet and Comintern writers to consider their problems apart from the general problems of China's resistance. Where reference was made to the Communists—and this was rare—Comintern observers confined themselves to the hope that the Eighth Route Army would again receive pay and supplies (which it was claimed it had not received since 1940)[12] and to assurances that postwar collaboration remained a cardinal policy in Yenan.[13] The focus of attention in a survey of recent Chinese history published by the State Encyclopedic Institute in 1942 was the Kuomintang; Communist activity after 1935 received only the most casual treatment.[14] At the end of 1942 an article in *World News and Views* asserted blandly that Yenan and Chungking "share the same point of view on all important questions relating to home and foreign policy." [15]

The Soviet press could overlook the virtual collapse of the united front which followed the Anhwei incident of January, 1941, presumably because after Pearl Harbor there was no longer a pressing need for it in Soviet Far Eastern policy. In short, Japan had ceased to be a serious threat. Had things been otherwise, the Soviet press would have been more attentive to developments in China that threatened the war effort and would have reissued appeals for unity. At the same time the Comintern would perhaps have tried to strengthen its influence among the Communists in North China in order to establish a base there as a last

[11] *Pravda*, January 15, 1943, p. 4.

[12] "Unity in China," *World News and Views*, No. 51, December 19, 1942, p. 486; see also "China's Victories," *World News and Views*, No. 37, September 12, 1942, pp. 75 ff.

[13] Astafev, "Kitai vo vtoroi polovine 1941," *Mirovoe khoziaistvo i mirovaia politika*, Nos. 1–2, January-February, 1942, pp. 75 ff.

[14] *Strany Tikhogo okeana*, pp. 205 ff. Beloff's statement, however, in *Foreign Policy of Soviet Russia*, I, 70, that this volume makes no reference either to the Chinese soviets or to the Long March is incorrect; see *Strany Tikhogo okeana*, p. 218.

[15] "Unity in China," *World News and Views*, No. 51, December 19, 1942, p. 486.

line of defense in the event that Chungking concluded a separate peace with Japan. But these policies were never needed.

In dissolving the Comintern in May, 1943, Moscow severed the last formal ties it had, or was presumed to have, with Yenan.[16] The Chinese Communists, in acknowledging the ECCI's resolution, paid homage to the "great assistance" received from the Comintern in the past but noted that they had "long since been able to determine their political line independently and to carry it out in accordance with the concrete situation and the specific circumstances in their country." [17] Mao observed that revolutions could not be imported or exported. Although there had been help from the Comintern, the Chinese working class itself had created its Communist Party. "The disbandment of the Comintern," he wrote, "does not weaken the Communist Parties of the various countries, but on the other hand strengthens them, making them more national and more suited to the necessities of the war against Fascism." [18]

[16] The official reason given for the dissolution of the Comintern was that the various Communist Parties throughout the world had matured sufficiently to justify the withdrawal of central supervision. "Communists were never supporters of superfluous organizational forms," the ECCI resolution declared; "Postanovlenie Prezidiuma IKKI" (Resolution of the Presidium of the ECCI), *Izvestiia,* May 23, 1943, p. 1. On May 28, 1943, Stalin added that the disbandment of the Comintern gave the lie to Fascist claims that the Soviet Union interfered in the internal affairs of foreign nations and directed foreign labor movements. It also, Stalin said, made it easier for progressive forces to unite against Fascism, irrespective of political and religious affiliations, and to continue this cooperation after the war; "Otvet tov. I.V. Stalina na vopros glavnogo korrespondenta angliiskogo agenstva Reiter" (Comrade I.V. Stalin's Reply to the Head Correspondent of the British Agency, Reuters), *Kommunisticheskii internatsional,* No. 5–6, May-June, 1943, p. 11. In 1947, on the other hand, A. Zhdanov made no reference to these political advantages and considered the disbandment of the Comintern due solely to the fact that it had outlived its usefulness: ". . . Once the young Communist Parties had become mass labor parties, the direction of these parties from one center became impossible and inexpedient. As a result, the Comintern, from a factor promoting the development of the Communist Parties, began to turn into a factor hindering their development. . . . It was these considerations that made it necessary to dissolve the Comintern and to devise new forms of connection between the parties." A. Zhdanov, "The International Situation," *For a Lasting Peace, For a People's Democracy,* No. 1, November 10, 1947, p. 4.

[17] "Resheniia kompartii" (Decisions of the Communist Parties), *Kommunisticheskii internatsional,* Nos. 5–6, May-June, 1943, p. 23.

[18] Mao Tse-tung, "On the Disbandment of the Communist International" (May 26, 1943), quoted in Gelder, *The Chinese Communists,* p. 170. This article is not included in Mao's *Selected Works.*

The dissolution of the Comintern in any case appears to have had little practical effect on relations between Moscow and Yenan. There were no Comintern agents in Yenan or Chinese representatives in Moscow to be recalled, as far as is known, and no standing orders to be countermanded. Soviet-Chinese Communist ties, nominal for a number of years before the Comintern's dissolution, remained unchanged until the end of the war.

THE REFORM MOVEMENT IN CHINESE COMMUNISM, 1941–1944

The first years of the Second World War, during which Soviet attention was diverted still further from China and the Chinese revolution, were apparently years of extraordinary growth for the Chinese Communists. In 1937, Mao estimated a total party membership of 40,000; five years later Chou En-lai placed the membership at 800,000.[19] This did not, of course, include millions throughout China who sympathized in varying degree with the Communists' goals.

A new Party membership, however, which included many nonproletarian elements presented fresh problems to the Party leaders. In July, 1941, a resolution by the Central Committee underscored these problems:

> It must be pointed out . . . that the specific gravity of small producers and the intelligentsia in the Party is very high and that it is consequently easy for certain Party members to develop "individualism," "heroism," antiorganizational tendencies, "independence," "anticentralism" and other tendencies counter to the Party spirit. If allowed to develop, these tendencies can destroy the Party's united will, united action and unified discipline, can produce clique activities, sectarian struggles, eventual open rebellion against the Party, and can cause great damage to the Party and the revolution.[20]

The Party leadership sought to overcome these dangers in a widespread reform movement launched early in 1942; this was known as the *cheng-feng* movement.[21]

[19] See Compton, *Mao's China,* p. xxviii.

[20] "Central Committee Resolution on Strengthening the Party Spirit" (July 1, 1941); text in Compton, *Mao's China,* p. 157.

[21] *Cheng-feng,* according to one translator, is a contraction of *cheng-tun* (to

Although the *cheng-feng* movement was concerned primarily with the problem of moral reform within the Party and administrative reform within the so-called "Border areas"[22]—and perhaps to a lesser degree with alleged ideological deviation in the Party cadres[23]—there were certain aspects of the movement which raise a question as to the orthodoxy of Chinese Communism during the war and as to its continuing orientation toward Moscow. One of the ideas which runs persistently through the documents used in the *cheng-feng* movement is that Chinese Communists must—to use Mao's phrase—"make Marxism Chinese." Mao first used this expression in his address to the Sixth Party Plenum in November, 1938:

Chinese Communists are Marxian internationalists, but Marxism must be expressed in a national form for practical realization. There is no such thing as abstract Marxism, only concrete Marxism. What we call concrete Marxism is Marxism expressed in a national form. It means utilizing Marxism in the concrete struggle taking place in the concrete Chinese environment, and not utilizing it abstractly. . . . It has become a problem which the entire country must thoroughly un-

---

correct) and *tso-feng* (style of work; spirit); Compton, *Mao's China*, p. xvi. Another translation of *cheng-feng* is "correction of (unorthodox) tendencies"; Brandt, etc., *Documentary History*, p. 517. Both volumes cited include excellent commentaries on the *cheng-feng* movement. Compton's study, in addition to the commentary, consists of twenty-one translations from a Chinese volume published after the war in which many of the *cheng-feng* papers were assembled for the first time.

[22] The dominant mood of the *cheng-feng* movement appears to be well expressed in these homely phrases attributed to Mao in 1943: "We are surrounded tightly by Japanese imperialism and by the looseness [*sic*] character of the petit-bourgeoisie class, and the dirt of bureaucracy is constantly blown upon our faces, therefore we must not feel oversatisfied as soon as we see some achievements. We must suppress such ideas, always criticize ourselves, as if we daily clean our faces or sweep our ground to get rid of the dirt." See Lin Tsu-han, *Annual Report of the Shensi-Kangsu-Ninghsia Border Region Government for the Year 1943*, p. 40.

[23] One of the documents widely used in the *cheng-feng* movement, for instance, was Liu Shao-ch'i's "Liquidation of Menshevik Thought in the Party"; text in Compton, *Mao's China*, pp. 255–68. Compton argues that this article (dated July 1, 1943) and Mao's "In Opposition to Party Formalism" (February 8, 1942) were directed primarily against Wang Ming and his followers and that in this sense the *cheng-feng* movement resembled a purge; *ibid.*, pp. xxxvii-xxxix. Inasmuch as Wang had dropped out of sight several years before the reform movement was under way, this argument appears to the present writer to be of doubtful validity. For another view of the *cheng-feng* movement as fundamentally a purge, see Wan Yah-Kang, *Rise of Communism in China*, pp. 67 ff.

derstand and resolve, *to make Marxism Chinese,* to see to it that in every manifestation it bears a Chinese character, that is to say, that it is applied according to China's special characteristics.[24]

While the effort "to make Marxism Chinese" need not in itself suggest any disrespect for Moscow on the part of the Chinese Communists, it appears, in the case of some writers in Yenan, to have inspired a claim that Chinese Communist experience was unique and had no peer in the world revolutionary movement. Thus, Liu Shao-ch'i, for instance, who was at this time emerging as the chief ideological writer in the Mao leadership, asserted in 1943 that "the Chinese Communist Party has in its twenty-two years passed through many more great events than any other Party in the world and has had richer experience in the revolutionary struggle." [25] Liu also wrote:

If we cast aside the rich experience of the revolutionary struggle of China, if we despise the experience of the struggle of our Party in the great historical events in these twenty-two years, if we do not study such experiences carefully and learn from them, but merely confine our study to the experience of foreign revolutions farther away from us, then we shall be reversing the true order of things and we will have to traverse a much more tortuous road and suffer more setbacks.[26]

Since in 1943 no revolutions other than the Bolshevik Revolution had taken place which would be likely to attract the Chinese Communists, Liu's reference here cannot be mistaken. After the war one ranking Chinese Communist, according to an American observer, declared quite candidly that the aim of *cheng-feng* was to teach the Party that it "must have its own principles; it was not necessary that we travel the same road as the Soviet Union." [27]

It may be imagined that these and other expressions of independence on the part of the Chinese Communists and similar

[24] Mao's address to the Sixth Party Plenum, November 6, 1938, quoted in Compton, *Mao's China,* pp. 253–54 (italics added).

[25] Quoted from an official translation of Liu's article released in Peking in 1951: Liu Shao-ch'i, *Liquidate the Menshevist Ideology within the Party,* p. 2.

[26] *Ibid.,* pp. 3–4.

[27] Belden, *China Shakes the World,* p. 67; Belden's informant was Po I-po, a member of the Central Committee.

efforts to minimize the significance of earlier Bolshevik experience attracted some attention in Moscow (assuming, of course, that the Russians had ways of remaining abreast of developments in Yenan and were familiar with the content of these documents). After the war, in any case, the Russians took a firm position in asserting the unique value and priority of Bolshevik experience for revolutionary movements elsewhere. In all countries, without exception, as a leading historian of the Soviet Party observed in 1948, "the general laws for the transition from capitalism to socialism, which were first revealed by Marx and Engels and were verified, solidified and advanced by Lenin and Stalin on the basis of the experience of the Bolshevik Party and the Soviet state, . . . are mandatory."[28] The possibility must not therefore be overlooked that the Soviet leaders were somewhat apprehensive about the course of Chinese Communism during the war, as this was revealed to them in the *cheng-feng* documents.

At the same time—to be quite frankly equivocal on this point—it would be a mistake to attach too great significance to the *cheng-feng* movement as a possible source of strained relations between Moscow and Yenan. It may be argued, for instance, that during a period when the Comintern was in the process of dissolution it was quite appropriate, in so far as Moscow was concerned, for foreign Marxists to assert the national character of their revolutionary efforts. Liu Shao-chi's insistence on the unique experience of Chinese Communism, therefore, was perhaps less objectionable to the Russians in 1943 than it would have been a few year earlier or a few years later, when Moscow's leadership of the world Communist movement was being more strongly asserted. It should also be noted that any unorthodoxy in Liu's claim was more than matched by the complete orthodoxy of the *cheng-feng* movement in other respects. In asserting the priority of their own experience, the Chinese Communists did not scorn Bolshevik experience as such but merely the undiscerning

[28] E. Burdzhalov, "O mezhdunarodnom znachenii istoricheskogo opyta partii bol'shevikov" (Concerning the International Significance of the Historical Experience of the Bolshevik Party), *Bol'shevik,* No. 17, September 15, 1948, p. 51. This view was altered, officially, only during the Twentieth (Russian) Party Congress in 1956.

imitation of it by Party members in China. It was in part this attitude, the Party leaders argued, which had caused the shortcomings in Chinese Communism that the *cheng-feng* movement was now seeking to correct. Marxism and Leninism per se were held in high regard and played a part in the reform movement that is poorly measured by the comparatively meager percentage of purely Russian materials found among the *cheng-feng* documents.[29] The classics of Marxism were referred to repeatedly in these documents, and the Leninist concept of Party organization and discipline was everywhere reasserted. Liu Shao-ch'i, for instance, in the article quoted above, noted that, while the Party's experience had been rich, it had not been adequately summarized "in the light of the universal doctrine of Marxism-Leninism. . . . A Marxist-Leninist summary of these experiences is the most important condition for the consolidation, education and elevation of our entire Party in its struggle for victory in the Chinese revolution."[30] Mao asked that Stalin's *History of the Communist Party of the Soviet Union, Short Course* be used as the principal document in the cadres' study of Marxism-Leninism and called this

> the best synthesis and summary of the century-old world Communist movement and the most perfect model in the world of a blending of theory and practice. Only by observing how Lenin and Stalin united the general theoretical truths of Marxism with the concrete practice of the Soviet revolution and on this basis developed Marxism, can we learn how to carry out our work here in China.[31]

In short, it was not Bolshevik tactics in 1917 (and subsequently) which provided a formula for the Chinese revolution,

[29] According to the Party report on the *cheng-feng* movement in April, 1942, the original twenty-two documents selected for examination by the cadres included seventeen Chinese items and only five Russian; "Report of the Propaganda Bureau of the Central Committee on the *Cheng-feng* Movement" (April 3, 1942); text in Compton, *Mao's China,* pp. 6–7. The final collection of *cheng-feng* documents after the war, according to Compton, included twenty Chinese and seven Russian items; *ibid.,* pp. x–xi, xii–xiv.

[30] Liu Shao-ch'i, *Liquidate the Menshevist Ideology within the Party,* p. 3.

[31] Mao Tse-tung, "Let Us Reconstruct Our Studies" (May 5, 1941); text in Mao, *Proizvedeniia,* IV, 34–35 (English ed., IV, 19–20). This address to a cadre meeting in Yenan was reworked slightly for inclusion among the first *cheng-feng* papers published in February, 1942; see Mao's preface to this item in Compton, *Mao's China,* p. 59.

but something more valuable—the Bolshevik method, that is, the way in which the Soviet leaders had succeeded in blending theory and practice some years earlier. It was this, above all, which the *cheng-feng* movement sought to teach the new Party cadres.

The *cheng-feng* movement can do no more than raise a very slight question concerning Chinese Communist orthodoxy during the war. If some of its formulations disturbed the Russian leaders, they gave no outward indication of it. As far as can be ascertained, no reference was made to the reform movement in materials published in the Soviet Union while the war lasted, either to praise or to condemn it. In histories of Chinese Communism published in Russia after the war the *cheng-feng* movement, if discussed at all, is dismissed in a few meager sentences.[32] The Chinese Communists themselves became more circumspect after the war in duly acknowledging their full debt to Bolshevism and to the Russian Revolution. The effort "to make Marxism Chinese," intensely urged as it was during the wartime *cheng-feng* period, appears to have been a passing phenomenon in the development of Chinese Communism.

SOVIET VIEWS OF CHINA DURING THE LAST TWO YEARS OF THE WAR: THE REAPPRAISAL, AUGUST, 1943–AUGUST, 1945

In the middle of 1943 there were indications that the Soviet leadership was taking a closer look at the internal situation in China. On July 14, for instance, the Counselor of the Soviet Embassy in Chungking called at the American Embassy to express his concern over current Kuomintang-Communist relations. He cited ten recent instances when Kuomintang troops had fired on Communist positions. According to American diplomats, this was the first time during the war that a Soviet official had "shown concern so unequivocally over what happened to the Chinese Communists." [33] On August 11, the Soviet Military Attaché in

[32] In one standard Soviet account of the Chinese Communists published in 1951, for instance, the only reference to the *cheng-feng* movement is a notation of Mao's appraisal of the *Short History* as the best synthesis of Marxist experience; Efimov, *Ocherki po novoi i noveishei istorii Kitaia,* p. 383.

[33] *The Chinese Communist Movement,* II, 204.

Chungking also called at the American Embassy to express similar views and to inquire what the attitude of the United States would be if civil war broke out in China.[34]

At about this time criticism of the Kuomintang appeared in a much-quoted article, published in *Voina i rabochii klass* on August 1, by Vladimir Rogov, the Soviet Union's veteran correspondent in China. Rogov wrote:

> Capitulators and defeatists who occupy important positions in the Kuomintang are weakening China by their inactivity and by their dangerous political intrigue. . . . Things have gone so far that on all kinds of provocative excuses the Chinese Command has transferred new divisions and enormous quantities of ammunition and food to the [New] Fourth and Eighth [Route] Army areas . . . clearly with a view to their liquidation even at the price of starting a civil war.[35]

Rogov reiterated these charges in his reply (also published in *Voina i rabochii klass*) to a criticism of his article which appeared in a Chinese newspaper early in September.[36]

One reason for Moscow's sudden concern with internal political rivalry in China, after having virtually ignored it for four years, was that tension between the Communists and the Kuomintang was again mounting. During the summer of 1943 this tension appears to have been more critical than at any time since the New Fourth Army incident of January, 1941. In July, 1943, for instance, Chu Teh is reported to have said that as a result of Kuomintang troop movements, following a secret meeting at Chungking in June to determine anti-Communist strategy, "a state of war [now] exists around the Border regions." [37] This

[34] Feis, *The China Tangle,* p. 86.

[35] Vladimir Rogov, "Polozhenie v Kitae" (The Situation in China), *Voina i rabochii klass,* No. 5, August 1, 1943, p. 20. Rogov's article was translated in numerous Communist publications abroad; e.g., *The Soviet Worker Looks at the War,* pp. 67–76, and *Who Threatens China's Unity?*

[36] Rogov, "Otvet kitaiskoi gazete *Shanyzhibaö*" (Answer to the Chinese Newspaper *Shang Wu Jih Pao* [Commercial Daily News]), *Voina i rabochii klass,* No. 8, September 15, 1943, pp. 26–27. The passage in the *Commercial Daily News* criticism which Rogov selected for his sharpest attack was this: "We do not consider that large military forces should be sent by the central government for the liquidation of the Chinese Communist Party. But we do consider that the government should change its policy of excessive magnanimity with respect to the Communists. We call on the government to take decisive measures."

[37] Band, *Two Years with the Chinese Communists,* p. 223. See also Smedley, *The Great Road,* pp. 398–99.

threat of civil war in China was reported by foreign observers in their dispatches home.[38] It was also reflected in the deliberations of the Eleventh Kuomintang Plenum in September, which devoted a large share of its attention to the Communist issue.[39]

Another reason for the sharper attitude toward Nanking reflected in the Rogov article was perhaps the troubled course of Sino-Soviet relations in Sinkiang, which had reached a climax in the first half of 1943.[40] At the same time Soviet successes at Stalingrad early in 1943 had eased the pressure from the West and now allowed Soviet leaders for the first time since the outbreak of the war to give some attention to events in Asia. The Rogov article may have been a feeler in this direction.[41]

[38] See, for instance, the articles by L. K. Rosinger in *Foreign Policy Bulletin,* August 13 and September 3, 1943.

[39] In September, 1943, the Secretariat of the Kuomintang Central Executive Committee presented the Eleventh Plenum with a lengthy and strongly worded indictment of the Chinese Communists, charging them with having conducted attacks on the Kuomintang rear from January, 1938, on. In this document Mao was quoted as having said in October, 1937, a month after the united front had been formed, that the Communists should devote 70 per cent of their energies to expansion, 20 per cent to fighting the Kuomintang, and 10 per cent to resisting Japan. Mao's plan to carry out this program, according to the Secretariat's data, was to fall into three phases: (*a*) a period of outward obedience to Chungking but internal preparation for civil war; (*b*) a contending stage during which the Kuomintang would be matched in strength and kept below the Yellow River and during which the Japanese would receive concessions in North China; (*c*) the final phase of taking over Central China and dispersing the Kuomintang. *Documents on the Problem of the Chinese Communist Party,* pp. 18 ff.; see also Chiang Kai-shek, *Soviet Russia in China,* p. 85; Cheng Tien-fong, *History of Sino-Russian Relations,* p. 226; and Wan Yah-Kang, *Rise of Communism in China,* p. 48. Despite this attack on the Communists, which presumably reflected high official opinion in the Kuomintang, Chiang's remarks at the Eleventh Plenum were comparatively conciliatory in tone: "We should clearly recognize that the Chinese Communist problem is a purely political problem and should be solved by political means. Such ought to be the guiding principle for the Plenary session in its efforts to settle this matter"; text in *China Handbook, 1937–1945* (rev. ed., 1947), p. 67.

[40] Conflicting accounts of developments in Sinkiang during 1942–43 may be found in Dallin, *Soviet Russia and the Far East,* pp. 361 ff.; Moore, *Soviet Far Eastern Policy,* pp. 131–33; Cheng Tien-fong, *History of Sino-Russian Relations,* pp. 177–79; Owen Lattimore, *Pivot of Asia* (Boston, 1950), pp. 76 ff; Rosinger, *China's Wartime Politics,* pp. 55–56; M. R. Norins, *Gateway to Asia: Sinkiang* (New York, 1944), pp. 124 ff; and elsewhere. All sources agree, however, that as the result of Sinkiang's new orientation toward Chungking, following a decade of orientation toward Russia, all Soviet installations were withdrawn from the province by mid-1943.

[41] Postwar accounts of China published in Moscow claim that Russian victories at Stalingrad frustrated Chiang Kai-shek's plans to launch a major attack against

It is a mistake, however, in this writer's view, to consider Rogov's article—as some writers have considered it—the beginning of a clear-cut policy of hostility toward Chungking.[42] As far as is known, the unofficial visits by Soviet diplomats to the American Embassy in July and August were not followed up with official representations to Chiang's government, representations which might have been expected had Soviet policy in China been clearly defined. At the same time the editors of *Voina i rabochii klass* appeared to dissociate themselves somewhat from Rogov's attack on the Kuomintang by giving his first article in August, 1943, the rare by-line "according to personal impressions" and by carrying his reply to the *Commercial Daily News* in September merely as a letter to the editor. *Pravda,* meanwhile, gave normal, if noncommittal, Tass coverage of the proceedings of the Eleventh Kuomintang Plenum in September, including Chiang's conciliatory remarks on the Communist issue.[43] An article in *Mirovoe khoziaistvo i mirovaia politika* in November, 1943, discussed China's wartime economy, including its commercial relations with the USSR, without once referring to the political situation in China.[44] The travel notes of a Soviet official in China, published in *Voina i rabochii klass* in January, 1944, also avoided any comment of a political character and were, in fact, generally complimentary concerning Chungking's war effort.[45] In short, nothing published in the Soviet press, other than Rogov's article and rejoinder, and nothing in official Soviet behavior reflected the low opinion of China, especially of China's fighting capacity, which Stalin expressed privately to Roosevelt at Teheran at the end of 1943.[46]

---

the Communists in the summer of 1943. Because of the pressure of Allied public opinion after Stalingrad, Chungking, it is now argued, could not afford to conclude the treaty with Japan that was a prerequisite for the anti-Communist campaign. See Efimov, *Ocherki po novoi i noveishei istoriia Kitaia,* pp. 387–88, and *Novaia i noveishaia istoriia Kitaia,* p. 243 *n.*

[42] E.g., Chiang Kai-shek, *Soviet Russia in China,* pp. 111–12; Cheng Tien-fong, *History of Sino-Russian Relations,* p. 241.

[43] *Pravda,* September 9, 15, and 16, 1943, p. 4. See footnote 39 above, p. 168.

[44] V. Avarin, "Voprosy voennoi ekonomiki Natsional'nogo Kitaia" (Questions of the Military Economy of Nationalist China), *Mirovoe khoziaistvo i mirovaia politika,* Nos. 10–11, October-November, 1943, pp. 50–61.

[45] A. Bedniakov, "Chyntsin-Guilin', putevye zametki" (Chungking-Yulin, Travel Notes), *Voina i rabochii klass,* No. 1, January, 1944, pp. 28–32.

[46] See Robert E. Sherwood, *Roosevelt and Hopkins* (New York, 1948), p. 777.

It was only in the spring of 1944, eight or nine months after the Rogov article had appeared, that the trend of Soviet press opinion concerning China began clearly to change. Praise of Chungking's leadership ended. Henceforth Soviet writers stressed the internal divisions in China as regularly as they had formerly ignored them. Reactionary elements in the Kuomintang, once ignored altogether or considered to be held in check by progressive forces centering around Chiang Kai-shek, were now seen as ascendant.

Early in May, 1944, *Pravda* indicated the new line by carrying, without comment, an extremely critical article by the Chungking correspondent of the *London News Chronicle.* This article was markedly sharper than Rogov's of the previous summer.[47] In June an article in *Voina i rabochii klass,* now without editorial disclaimer, blamed recent Japanese gains in China, at a time when Japan's over-all military position was greatly weakened by Allied successes, on the Kuomintang's anti-Communist blockade.[48] In October, *Pravda* carried a long summary of an article by Agnes Smedley which was even more critical of the Nationalists than the *News Chronicle* article summarized in May.[49] In November, a writer in *Mirovoe khoziaistvo i mirovaia politika* compared the regime in China to "Fascist totalitarianism" in Europe, citing in support of his views foreign comment in organs such as the New York *Times* and the Washington *Post.*[50] In December, 1944, one of the foremost Soviet authorities on the Far East, V. Avarin, wrote as follows of the situation in China:

Judging from all the evidence coming from China and from the events occurring in that country, the influence of reactionary land-owners, speculators, and war profiteers has noticeably increased in recent

[47] *Pravda,* May 6, 1944, p. 4.

[48] I. Aleksandrov, "K polozheniiu v Kitae" (Toward the Situation in China), *Voina i rabochii klass,* No. 14, June 15, 1944, pp. 9–14.

[49] *Pravda,* October 26, 1944, p. 4. Miss Smedley's article appeared in *PM* (New York), October 21, 1944.

[50] V. Maslennikov, "Kitai na vos'mom godu osvoboditel'noi voiny" (China in the Eighth Year of the War of Liberation), *Mirovoe khoziaistvo i mirovaia politika,* Nos. 10–11, October-November, 1944, pp. 36–48. Maslennikov gave some prominence to a remark by Nathaniel Peffer in the New York *Times Magazine,* May 14, 1944, p. 37: "If a plebiscite of foreigners were taken in Chungking today, it is quite possible that a majority would favor our shifting our support from Chungking to the Communists."

years within the leadership of the Kuomintang. The final word in the determination of military strategy is often left to generals who hide their pro-Japanese sentiments under a mask of patriotism just as the "father of treason," Wang Ching-wei, did in his time.[51]

The attacks on the Chungking government continued during early 1945. In February, *Izvestiia* carried a signed article by one of its staff writers for the first time directly attacking the Nationalist government—on this occasion, for its failure to carry out political and social reforms promised since the outbreak of the Sino-Japanese war in 1937.[52] The travel notes of two Soviet visitors in China, published in *Voina i rabochii klass* in March, in contrast to similar travel notes carried in the same periodical fourteen months earlier, amounted to a frank indictment of Nationalist policies.[53]

In April, 1945, writing in *Voina i rabochii klass,* Avarin made the sharpest attack on the Kuomintang that had appeared in the Soviet press during the entire war. Special significance perhaps attaches to this article in view of the fact that, contrary to Soviet custom, the author made no effort to support his opinions with extensive quotations from foreign publications. "All who love and respect the Chinese people," Avarin declared, "are obliged to acknowledge with the bitterest of feelings that recent events cannot dispel a growing anxiety concerning the political outlook in China." [54] The Chinese people, he continued, were suffering "not only from foreign invasion but from a significant part of their own government. . . . There is not a single member even of a district administration in regions under Chungking's authority who could be popularly elected!" [55]

Despite this mounting criticism of the Chungking government, Chiang Kai-shek continued to escape censure in Soviet commentaries. In the course of quoting foreign opinion the Soviet press

[51] V. Avarin, "Kitai na nyneshnem etape voiny" (China at the Present Stage of the War), *Voina i rabochii klass,* No. 23, December 1, 1944, p. 10.

[52] P. Krainov, "Nekotorye fakty o polozhenii v Kitae" (Some Facts Concerning the Situation in China), *Izvestiia,* February 18, 1945, p. 4.

[53] M. Moskvin i V. Petrenko, "Budni Kitaia" (Everyday Life in China), *Voina i rabochii klass,* No. 5, March 1, 1945, pp. 26–28.

[54] V. Avarin, "Kuda idet Kitai?" (Where Is China Going?), *Voina i rabochii klass,* No. 8, April 15, 1945, p. 15.

[55] *Ibid.,* p. 18.

sometimes carried remarks which were unfavorable to Chiang—the *News Chronicle* item, for instance, cited by *Pravda* in May, 1944, attacked Chiang for having waged a battle at great sacrifice in November, 1943, simply in order to enhance his prestige at Cairo—but Soviet writers themselves scrupulously excluded Chiang from any general criticism of the Chungking government. Avarin, for instance, in his sharp attack on the Kuomintang in April 1945, noted approvingly that in two recent statements Chiang had promised democratic reforms within his government before the end of the war and had announced the convocation of a National Assembly on November 12, 1945, with representation from all political parties.[56] In June, a writer in *Bol'shevik* also called attention to Chiang's apparently genuine efforts to check disunity in China through democratic reform.[57] *Pravda,* meanwhile, continued to give résumés of Chiang's principal statements throughout 1944 [58] and carried his congratulatory telegram to Kalinin on the occasion of the Soviet anniversary celebration in November, 1944, as well as an exchange of telegrams between Chiang and Stalin following the end of the war in Europe in May, 1945.[59]

On the few occasions when the Soviet press or high Soviet officials made a direct, public evaluation of Chiang it was not unfavorable. In November, 1944, for instance, one Russian commentator argued that "the Chinese intelligentsia still respects Chiang Kai-shek . . . but does not like his associates." [60] According to Ambassador Hurley's report of his interview with Stalin on April 15, 1945, "he [Stalin] spoke favorably of Chiang Kai-shek and said that while there had been corruption among certain officials of the National Government in China, he knew that Chiang Kai-shek was 'selfless,' 'a patriot.' " [61] Harry Hopkins,

[56] *Ibid.,* p. 17; the two statements by Chiang to which Avarin referred were made on January 1 and March 1, 1945.

[57] Kon. Evgenev, "O polozhenii v Kitae" (Concerning the Situation in China), *Bol'shevik,* Nos. 11–12, June, 1945, p. 65.

[58] *Pravda,* September 16, 1943; May 31, June 25, July 10, and September 8, 1944.

[59] *Ibid.,* November 7, 1944, p. 4, and May 12, 1945, p. 1.

[60] Maslennikov, "Kitai na vos'mom godu," *Mirovoe khoziaistvo i mirovaia politika,* Nos. 10–11, October-November, 1944, p. 47.

[61] *United States Relations with China,* p. 95.

reporting on an interview with the Soviet leader six weeks later, said that, while Stalin had some reservations about Chiang Kai-shek, he would continue to promote unification in China under Chiang's leadership.[62] The official Soviet position on Chiang during the last phase of the war seems therefore to have been quite clear. Although he was perhaps praised less often for his virtues than during the early years of the united front, he was judged blameless in so far as corruption in Chungking was concerned and was still regarded as the only political figure in China capable of uniting the country.

The Chinese Communists, during the last year or two of the war, were notably less charitable than the Russians where Chiang Kai-shek was concerned. Officially, they continued to acknowledge his leadership. The Border region government, for instance, asserted in January, 1944, that it was "as usual seeking the recognition of the National Government not only in fact but also in law . . . [so that] the strategic counter-offensive against Japan can be carried on more efficiently under the leadership of Chairman Chiang."[63] In June, 1944, in an interview with various Chinese and foreign correspondents who had recently arrived from Chungking, Mao said: "The Chinese Communist Party has never wavered from its policy of supporting Generalissimo Chiang Kai-shek, the policy of continuing cooperation between the Kuomintang and the Communist Party."[64]

There is evidence, however, that when they spoke or wrote more informally high Communist officials were less restrained in their comments on Chiang. In September, 1943, for instance, Ho Lung, the commander of the Eighth Route Army is reported to have said to foreigners in Yenan: "Chiang Kai-shek and Wang Ching-wei have now identical ideologies; the only difference between them is that Chiang is betting that the Japanese will be beaten, while Wang has backed the wrong horse."[65] In October,

[62] Robert E. Sherwood, *Roosevelt and Hopkins* (New York, 1948), pp. 902–3.

[63] Lin Tsu-han, *Annual Report of the Shensi-Kangsu-Ninghsia Border Region Government for the Year 1943*, pp. 40–41.

[64] Mao Tse-tung, "China Needs Democracy and Unity" (June 12, 1944), *Political Affairs* (New York), No. 1, January, 1945, p. 28.

[65] Band, *Two Years with the Chinese Communists*, p. 227. Wang Ching-wei died in Japan in 1944.

in an article on the recently concluded Eleventh Kuomintang Plenum written for the Yenan *Liberation Daily,* Mao made no attempt (according to a recent text of this article) to exclude Chiang from his withering criticism of the Kuomintang.[66] A year later Mao wrote of Chiang's anniversary address of October 10, 1944:

> The further Chiang goes, the more his position defies all sanity; his stubborn resistance to the political reforms demanded by the Chinese people and his passionate antagonism toward the Chinese Communists are evidence that he plans to avail himself of any pretext to launch the civil war which he has long been preparing.[67]

Chiang's speech of March 1, 1945 (one of the two which Avarin cited more or less approvingly in his April article), drew from Yenan an even sharper rebuke. According to the text of a bulletin of the New China News Agency dated March 2, this speech "reflects in detail the standpoint and plan of the most reactionary clique in the Kuomintang." [68] The bulletin goes on to attack sharply Chiang's "personal dictatorship." [69]

It is apparent then that Moscow and Yenan, in their official attitudes toward Chiang during the last year of the war, gave widely differing appraisals of his role in China. The Chinese Communists, to judge from the foregoing statements, had abandoned all pretense of supporting Chiang by the end of 1944; the Soviet Union, by contrast, refrained from an outright attack until the end of the war—and even longer.

Moscow's attitude toward the Chinese Communists during the last years of the war is not clearly indicated in Soviet press

[66] Mao Tse-tung, "On the Eleventh Kuomintang Plenum and the Second Session of the Third National Political Council" (October 5, 1943); text in Mao, *Proizvedeniia,* IV, 253–78 *passim* (English ed., IV, 131–47 *passim*).

[67] Mao Tse-tung, "Chiang Kai-shek Anniversary Speech" (October 11, 1944); text in Mao, *Proizvedeniia,* IV, 420 (English ed., IV, 224).

[68] "A Refutation of Chiang Kai-shek's March First Speech" (March 2, 1945), *Political Affairs* (New York), No. 6, June, 1945, p. 551.

[69] *Ibid.,* p. 553. See also Chou En-lai's letter of March 9, 1945 to Ambassador Hurley, in which he sharply attacks Chiang's March 1 speech; *United States Relations with China,* pp. 84–86. Additional Chinese Communist statements which were sharply critical of Chiang at the end of 1944 and early in 1945 may be found in the English-language pamphlet *Kuomintang-Communist Negotiations* issued in Yenan in 1945 by the New China News Agency.

commentaries. Some students of Soviet Far Eastern policy have argued that the attacks on the Kuomintang were dictated by a desire to enhance the Communists' prestige in China.[70] It is doubtless true that Soviet criticism did have this effect in some circles, but it is not easily demonstrated that the desire to achieve this end was a consideration of any consequence in Soviet policy. In the first place, it should be noted that Soviet criticism of Chungking was less severe than that which was appearing at this time in many liberal periodicals in England and the United States. In the second place, corruption and defeatism in Chungking were not contrasted, in Soviet commentaries, with virtue in Yenan, a contrast Soviet writers would not have failed to make if their intent had been primarily to enhance the Communists' stature. The Soviet press in fact gave little more attention to the Communists during these years than it had earlier in the war. *Pravda* made no substantive reference to the Communists until early in 1945.[71] The present writer has found no articles in Soviet publications until after the war which were directly concerned with developments in the Border areas, despite the fact that one or more Soviet correspondents, according to foreign observers, were accredited to Yenan from at least 1942 on,[72] and despite the fact that such articles began to appear elsewhere in the foreign press following the visit to Yenan of a team of six American and British correspondents in the summer of 1944.[73] Where mention

[70] E.g., Dallin, *Soviet Russia and the Far East,* pp. 217 ff.; Cheng Tien-fong, *History of Sino-Russian Relations,* p. 240.

[71] On January 31, 1945, *Pravda* carried a brief dispatch from Chungking giving Chou En-lai's views on recent Kuomintang-Communist negotiations.

[72] See Band, *Two Years with the Chinese Communists,* p. 262, and Stein, *The Challenge of Red China,* p. 437. The presence in Yenan of Soviet correspondents who were apparently in continuous residence there throughout most of the war raises several questions: Why were their dispatches, if filed, kept out of the Soviet press? Were they, in fact, *bona fide* war correspondents, or were they perhaps sent to Yenan to maintain liaison between Moscow and the Chinese Communists? The present writer has seen no materials which would shed light on their activities, nor is he familiar with any speculation on this subject by other students of Chinese Communism. It is perhaps worth noting that a Chinese correspondent from Chungking who claims to have spent three years with the Chinese Communists during the Sino-Japanese war, and who surely would have made the most of any suspected links between the Communists and Moscow, refers neither to these Soviet correspondents nor to any other Russians in Yenan in his recent account of this period; Wan Yah-Kang, *Rise of Communism in China.*

[73] See, for instance, New York *Times,* August 6, 1944, p. 19, September 25,

was made of the Chinese Communists, as in Avarin's article in *Voina i rabochii klass* in April, 1945, it was only in order to present their proposals for the solution of the internal political crisis.[74] Perhaps the most significant indication of Moscow's official attitude of ignoring the Chinese Communists during this period was the omission of any reference whatsoever in the Soviet press to the important Seventh Party Congress, the first full congress held since 1928, which met in Yenan in April and May, 1945. By contrast, a meeting of the French Communist Party two months later received extensive coverage.[75]

One need not, of course, imagine that in publicly ignoring the Chinese Communists Moscow was showing its displeasure with any of Yenan's policies. One reason, noted above, why the Russian press had refrained during 1939–41 from giving extensive coverage to Communist activities in China may have been Moscow's desire not to antagonize Chungking and thus jeopardize the united front against Japan. To some extent this consideration would have continued to carry weight in Moscow during the war years, although by then Chinese resistance was doubtless playing a less important role in the calculations of Soviet policy makers.

There was perhaps another reason why Moscow refrained from paying outward attention to Chinese Communist activity as long as the war lasted. Within the wartime Big Three coalition the United States had tacitly assumed a special responsibility with respect to China. Since the alliance with the United States against Germany was the cornerstone of Soviet foreign policy during the war, the Russians would not have wished to strain the coalition by appearing to show too great an interest in

1944, p. 9, and October 6, 1944, p. 12. These correspondents—among them Gunther Stein (covering for the *Christian Science Monitor* and the Associated Press), Harrison Forman (New York *Herald Tribune* and the United Press), Israel Epstein (*Allied Labor News*, also the New York *Times* and *Time* magazine), and Maurice Votaw (Reuters)—were the first foreign journalists during the war, apart from the Tass correspondents mentioned above, to gain Chungking's permission to visit Yenan. They left Chungking in May, 1944, and spent most of the summer in the Border areas.

[74] Avarin, "Kuda idet Kitai?" *Voina i rabochii klass*, No. 8, April 15, 1945, p. 20; see also Krainov, "Nekotorye fakty o polozhenii v Kitae," *Izvestiia*, February 18, 1945, p. 4, and Evgenev, "O polozhenii v Kitae," *Bol'shevik*, Nos. 11–12, June, 1945, pp. 70–71.

[75] *Pravda*, June 28–30, July 1–2, 1945.

China's internal affairs. Had Russia been a belligerent in the Far East, the situation would of course have been different. It would then have been entirely appropriate for the Russians to discuss the role of the Chinese Communists as a military force of some consequence on their own right flank, and Soviet policy toward Yenan would perhaps have been more clearly revealed. During the spring and early summer of 1945, after the Russians had agreed to attack the Japanese in Manchuria but before this was known outside a very small circle of high Allied officials, Moscow would not, of course, have wished to draw attention to its plans in the Far East by suddenly expressing an interest in the Chinese Communists. By the same logic, Moscow may also have decided after Yalta not to establish close contact with Yenan (or maintain it if ties already existed) for fear this liaison might be inadvertently revealed to the Japanese and cause them to wonder about Soviet intentions.

There is, in short, little evidence to go on in defining Soviet policy toward the Chinese Communists during the final months of the war. It should not, however, be assumed that the Russians had no policy. Certainly Chinese Communism in its purely revolutionary capacity held little interest for the Russians at this juncture. In this respect Communism in China served a different purpose in postwar Soviet strategy than Communism in Eastern Europe. But the potentialities of Chinese Communism do appear, in retrospect, to have entered into long-range Soviet plans and objectives in Asia. In order to understand what role Moscow assigned the Chinese Communists we need at this point to determine, in so far as this is possible, what these Soviet plans and objectives were.

SOVIET OBJECTIVES IN THE FAR EAST AND COALITION IN CHINA

It is not possible to determine, from available Soviet documentation, at what juncture during the war Moscow began to give seriour attention to its postwar objectives in the Far East. Averell Harriman, the wartime American Ambassador to the Soviet Union, has testified that Stalin told him as early as August, 1942, of Russia's intention in due course to enter the war in the Far

East.[76] The same promise was made to Patrick Hurley in a conversation with Stalin, in November, 1942.[77] A year later, during the Moscow Conference of Foreign Ministers of the United States, Russia, and Great Britain, Stalin told Cordell Hull that the Soviet Union planned to enter the Pacific war following the conclusion of the war in Europe. According to Hull, this commitment was made without any strings attached.[78]

At Teheran, late in November, 1943, Stalin for the first time gave some indication of the concessions the Soviet Union would expect to gain in the Far East in return for its entry into the war against Japan. Although nothing was put in writing at this time, Stalin apparently discussed Soviet objectives freely with Roosevelt and Churchill. At this juncture these included the return of all of Sakhalin and the Kurile Islands to Russia, in order to provide adequate protection for Vladivostok, and permanent access to some ice-free port on the Pacific Ocean.[79] According to Robert Sherwood, it was Roosevelt who suggested that Dairen might be used for this purpose, as a "free port" under an international guarantee. The President, Sherwood believed, had discussed this matter with Chiang Kai-shek at Cairo a few days earlier and Chiang had indicated he would have no objection, provided Chinese sovereignty were maintained.[80]

During the fourteen months following the Teheran Conference the Russians formulated their requirements in the Far East more precisely and finally received assurance that they would be granted in the secret agreement at Yalta which set forth the terms for Soviet entry into the war against Japan.[81] In addition to

[76] *Military Situation in the Far East,* p. 3329.

[77] *Ibid.,* p. 2836. Hurley at this time was in Moscow on a special mission for the President, prior to his appointment as Personal Representative of the President (and later Ambassador) to Chungking; in the latter capacity he visited Moscow twice again before the end of the war.

[78] *Memoirs of Cordell Hull* (New York, 1948), II, 1310.

[79] Feis, *The China Tangle,* pp. 112–13.

[80] Robert E. Sherwood, *Roosevelt and Hopkins* (New York, 1948), p. 792.

[81] According to Harriman, the aims of the Soviet Union in the Far East which Stalin made known to him on December 14, 1944, were identical with those eventually presented to the Yalta Conference; *Congressional Record* (Washington, D.C., 1951), Vol. 97, Part 14, p. A5411. For a discussion of the negotiations concerning Soviet Far Eastern objectives prior to Yalta, see Beloff, *Soviet Policy in the Far East,* pp. 22 ff., and Feis, *The China Tangle,* pp. 232–33. See also *Foreign Relations of the United States: The Conferences at Malta and Yalta, 1945,* pp. 378–79, 768–70, and 894–97.

guaranteeing the internationalization of Dairen and Soviet acquisition (from Japan) of the southern part of Sakhalin and the Kurile Islands, the Yalta agreement provided for maintenance of the status quo in Outer Mongolia, joint Soviet-Chinese operation of the Chinese Eastern and South Manchurian Railways, and restoration of Russia's lease on Port Arthur as a naval base. With respect to Dairen and the joint operation of the railways, the agreement stated that the "preeminent interests of the Soviet Union" would be safeguarded. In return for these extensive concessions Russia agreed to enter the Pacific war within "two or three months" after the surrender of Germany.[82] The agreement went on to state that the provisions respecting Outer Mongolia, the ports, and the railways would require the concurrence of Chiang Kai-shek, which President Roosevelt would undertake to secure. Somewhat incongruously, the following paragraph asserted that the Soviet claims would "unquestionably" be fulfilled after Japan's defeat, presumably whether Chiang's concurrence was obtained or not. The final paragraph proclaimed Russia's readiness to conclude an alliance with Chungking "in order to render assistance to China with its armed forces for the purpose of liberating China from the Japanese yoke." [83]

The Yalta agreement, although it gave the Russians few advantages in the Far East they had not at one time or another enjoyed, must be considered a particular success for Soviet diplomacy. It confirmed Soviet ascendancy in Outer Mongolia, which the Chinese government had persistently refused to recognize in the past.[84] It gave Russia security along her eastern frontier, the lack of which had been a cause of perennial concern to Soviet

[82] Three months was the interval used from the outset in planning circles. In his talks with Harry Hopkins late in May, 1945, Stalin is reported to have named the precise date Soviet troops would enter Manchuria—August 8. The attack actually began at dawn on August 9. See the State Department memorandum on Hopkins's Moscow visit quoted in *The Forrestal Diaries* (New York, 1951), p. 67.

[83] The Yalta agreement was made public a year after its conclusion—on February 11, 1946; an English text may be found, *inter alia,* in *United States Relations with China,* pp. 113–14.

[84] It is interesting to note that Mao, when questioned about Outer Mongolia in 1944, is reported to have said: "I hope and have no doubt that they [the Outer Mongolians] will join China the moment the National Government lives up to the promises of the founder of the Republic" (reference is made here especially to Sun Yat-sen's promise of autonomy to all national minorities in China). See Stein, *The Challenge of Red China,* p. 443.

leaders during the interwar years. It also provided Russia with a warm water port on the Pacific, a traditional goal of Russian foreign policy. In a general way the Yalta agreement restored to Russia the prestige lost forty years earlier at the Treaty of Portsmouth, a consideration that appears to have carried more than a little weight with Soviet leaders.

Chungking was not immediately informed of the terms of the Yalta agreement, allegedly for reasons of security. All the principals at Yalta agreed that, inasmuch as secrets were known to be poorly kept in Chungking, it was wiser not to inform Chiang at this juncture concerning Russia's intention to enter the war against Japan. In consequence, there was no convenient way to consult promptly with the Chungking government concerning related decisions at Yalta which affected Chinese territories and interests. It was left to Stalin to choose the moment when Chungking might safely be informed of these decisions.[85]

So long as the situation in China remained more or less as it was, Moscow could rely on pressure from Washington and London to silence any objections Chiang Kai-shek might raise to the Yalta arrangements. The real peril to Soviet aims in the Far East, as they were defined at Yalta, lay in the possibility of a fresh outbreak of civil war between the Communists and the Kuomintang. Leaders in the Kremlin perhaps reasoned along these lines after Yalta: no matter how discreetly the Soviet Union might behave in any clash between the Communists and the Nationalists, it could not avoid Chungking's charges of complicity because of its ideological identification with Yenan. An embattled Kuomintang, angered by this suspected perfidy on the part of a presumed ally, could be expected in due time to denounce the Yalta agreement, which favored Russia, as a flagrant violation of Chinese sovereignty. This could be counted a certainty if fighting broke out in China before the conclusion of the Sino-Soviet pact provided for in the agreement. Chiang, moreover, might have the tacit approval of Washington, and perhaps London, in his defiance. Under these not impossible circumstances Moscow obviously could not count on its claims in the Far East, in Manchuria especially, being "unquestionably" fulfilled.

[85] See Robert E. Sherwood, *Roosevelt and Hopkins,* p. 866, and Feis, *The China Tangle,* p. 247.

Should the Communists rise and succeed, Moscow could of course be confident of securing its objectives in Manchuria without having to negotiate with Chungking. But the risks entailed in promoting this course were grave. In the first place, Communist strength, on paper, was far less than the Kuomintang's.[86] And even if Communist morale were higher—a factor difficult to judge—Chungking still held a great strategic advantage in its control of the industrial and communications centers of the country not occupied by the Japanese. Foreign reports of Kuomintang weakness and Communist strength in China were doubtless gratifying to Moscow (and at the proper time would make excellent propaganda copy), but until the Russians could observe the Chinese Communists at close hand, they appear not to have accepted these reports as reliable intelligence. In the meantime direct military assistance to the Communists, in order to alter the balance of power in China in favor of Yenan, was of course out of the question so long as the war with Japan continued and so long as Moscow wished to preserve the wartime alliance with the United States.

If nothing was to be gained then by favoring a local Communist uprising in China and if the danger of inadvertently unleashing a civil war was to be averted at all costs, the policy for the Russians was clearly indicated: to urge greater collaboration between the Communists and the Kuomintang for the remainder of the war and to recommend that immediate preparations be made for establishing a coalition government as soon as the war was over. After Yalta these objectives were emphasized increasingly in Soviet pronouncements. For instance, in the same article in April, 1945, in which he attacked the Chungking leadership sharply, Avarin concluded with the fervent hope that China would be able to find a way to resolve its internal problems. He wrote:

[86] Official Chinese sources placed Nationalist armed strength at the end of 1944 at approximately 5,000,000; *China Handbook, 1937–1945* (rev. ed., 1947), pp. 286, 764. An American observer gave the combined strength of the Eighth Route and New Fourth Armies as 570,000 at approximately the same time; Forman, *Report from Red China,* p. 126. The Yenan radio estimated a force of 900,000 in April, 1945, and Mao, in his address to the Seventh Party Congress at about the same time, placed the figure at 910,000, plus 2,200,000 militiamen; Mao, *Proizvedeniia,* IV, 474 (English ed., IV, 253–54).

It is difficult to say at present whether or not this hope will be realized. One thing, however, is clear: without the adoption of urgent measures to democratize the political life of the country and to achieve national unity, China cannot occupy the place in the general family of democratic nations to which it aspires.[87]

In June, a commentator declared in *Bol'shevik* that China must have a "postwar national democratic front, strengthened by the wartime coalition of all democratic parties, groups, and organizations; only thus . . . can China become a strong, independent, and democratic power." [88] Stalin, in the meantime, had made substantially the same observations in April and May, 1945, to Ambassador Hurley and Harry Hopkins.[89]

There was of course nothing novel in Moscow's attitude in so far as openly proclaimed policies were concerned. Until 1941, when the threat to the Soviet Union from Japan subsided, the alliance between the Communists and the Kuomintang, we have seen, was an important factor in Russia's Far Eastern policy. But even after the removal of the Japanese threat, Soviet spokesmen had continued to pay lip-service to wartime and postwar unity in China. Thus Stalin, for instance, in May, 1943, observed that one of the happy consequences of the dissolution of the Comintern was the impetus it had given to the unification of all progressive forces in China looking toward the reconstruction of the country after the war.[90] What had changed after Yalta was that a unified China was now even more indispensable to Soviet policy than it had been in the past.

After Yalta the Chinese Communists also placed increasing emphasis on the urgent need for unity in China. The Seventh Party Congress in April and May, 1945, by which time the Chinese Communists presumably knew of the Yalta agreement,[91]

[87] Avarin, "Kuda idet Kitai?", *Voina i rabochii klass,* No. 8, April 15, 1945, p. 19.

[88] Evgenev, "O polozhenii v Kitae," *Bol'shevik,* Nos. 11–12, June, 1945, p. 73.

[89] *United States Relations with China,* pp. 94–96; Robert E. Sherwood, *Roosevelt and Hopkins,* pp. 902–3.

[90] "Otvet tov. I. V. Stalina na vopros glavnogo korrespondenta angliiskogo agentsva Reiter," *Kommunisticheskii internatsional,* Nos. 5–6, May-June, 1943, p. 11; see also Astafev, "Kitai vo vtoroi polovine 1941 goda," *Mirovoe khoziaistvo i mirovaia politika,* Nos. 1–2, January-February, 1942, pp. 71–81.

[91] Ambassador Hurley claims to have learned of the Yalta agreement from the Chinese Communists as early as mid-February, 1945; the Communists, he implied,

devoted most of its attention to this question and to the related problem of establishing a coalition government in Chungking. In his keynote report to the congress on April 24 (the report was entitled "On Coalition Government") Mao said:

How should we act in the present circumstances? Beyond a doubt what China urgently needs is the establishment of a provisional, democratic coalition government—including representatives of all parties and groups as well as non-partisan leaders—in order that democratic reforms may be initiated, the present crisis overcome, all anti-Japanese forces in the country mobilized and united for the ultimate defeat of the Japanese aggressor in collaboration with our allies, and the Chinese people given the chance of escaping from the claws of the Japanese. After this the National Assembly must be summoned, on a broad democratic basis, to establish a permanent democratic government which will also be of a coalition character and will include on an even broader basis representatives of different parties and organizations and non-partisan leaders.[92]

During the last months of the war there was, of course, some inconsistency in Soviet and, especially, in Chinese Communist policy. In the first place, Moscow and Yenan claimed to be seeking to establish a coalition in China which would avert civil war and provide a basis for a peaceful era of reconstruction after the

---

had learned of it from the Russians. See *Military Situation in the Far East,* p. 2836. While Hurley's claim appears very dubious to the present writer, in view of the Russians' evident precautions to keep their plans secret until preparations for the Manchurian campaign were more advanced, by early May, when Chungking had some knowledge of Russian intentions, it is reasonable to think that Yenan had this knowledge too.

[92] Mao, *Proizvedeniia,* IV, 459–60 (English ed., IV, 244). As in Moscow, the objective of a continuing collaboration with the Kuomintang represented no new departure in Chinese Communist policy, in so far as official pronouncements were concerned. This goal had been consistently reasserted in bulletins issuing from Yenan, especially from mid-1943 on. See, for instance, the statement of the Chinese Communists on July 9, 1943, on the occasion of the sixth anniversary of Lukouch'iao; "For Unity in China's War of Resistance," *Communist* (New York), No. 1, January, 1944, pp. 25–30. Mao's interview with a team of foreign correspondents in June, 1944, also referred to "the policy of continuing cooperation between the Kuomintang and the Communist Party"; Mao Tse-tung, "China Needs Democracy and Unity," *Political Affairs* (formerly *Communist*), No. 1, January, 1945, p. 28. As early as October, 1944, Chou En-lai spoke of collaboration with the Kuomintang in the specific terms of a coalition government, to be established on a temporary basis even before the end of the war; Chou En-lai, "The Tide Must be Turned in China" (October 10, 1944), *Political Affairs,* No. 6, June, 1945, p. 545. See also Chiang Kai-shek, *Soviet Russia in China,* pp. 122–23.

defeat of Japan. At the same time, during the spring of 1945, both the Russians and the Chinese Communists—the latter in particular—were greatly increasing their attacks on the Chungking government, thereby jeopardizing the prospect of bringing about the alliance they allegedly desired.[93]

As far as the first aspect of this policy was concerned—unity during the war and coalition government following it—Moscow, as we have seen, probably sought these objectives in order to guarantee the fulfillment of the Yalta promises. The Chinese Communists, once they sensed the Russians' attitude, followed Moscow's lead, presumably out of deference to Soviet leadership in matters of world strategy. Even if these policies—more moderate than those Mao himself would perhaps have devised were he completely free to choose his course—were objectionable in Yenan, Mao doubtless reasoned that deference to Soviet policies at this juncture would go a long way toward assuring Soviet support of his own policies at some even more critical period in the future. The Chinese Communists, in any case, had no reason to dread a unified China. Should such a China emerge (contrary, probably, to Mao's expectations), and should a coalition government actually be established in which Yenan was represented, the Communists' prestige in China would undoubtedly be enhanced. If, on the other hand, a coalition failed to materialize, the Communists could at least take some credit for having urged it so strongly and blame the Kuomintang for its failure.

It need not be assumed, however, that in advancing the idea of a coalition government either Russians or Chinese Communists anticipated any major shift in Yenan's long-range objectives in the event that a coalition should be established. Even if concessions should prove necessary—such as some reduction in the size of the Red Army[94]—the Communists' ultimate goals might

[93] The Chinese Communists appear to have recognized this ambivalence more candidly than the Russians, though they were perhaps unaware of the inconsistency in their policy. A news dispatch from Yenan at the end of the Seventh Party Congress early in June stated: "The Chinese Communist Party frankly criticizes the mistakes of the Kuomintang and points publicly to the danger of civil war, while also doing its best to form a coalition government"; New China News Agency broadcast, June 13, 1945, quoted in Brandt, etc., *Documentary History*, p. 293.

[94] According to a Yugoslav source, Stalin is alleged to have told a Yugoslav

well remain constant. In the last months of the war, the Russians did not indicate their attitude clearly in this matter, perhaps from discretion, or from uncertainty over the Communists' ability to achieve their long-range objectives in the foreseeable future. The Chinese Communists, however, left no room for doubt as to the final goal. In the course of his long report to the Seventh Party Congress in April, 1945, Mao said:

We Communists never conceal our political objectives. Our future or ultimate program has as its goal the elevation of China to a still higher level, the level of socialism and Communism. This is definite and is beyond any doubt whatsoever.[95]

The Party Constitution adopted at the close of the congress six weeks later asserted:

In the future stage of the Chinese revolution, after the complete victory of the national and democratic revolution in China, the task of the CCP will be to struggle, by necessary steps, according to the requirements of China's social and economic development and the will of her people, for the realization of socialism and Communism in China.[96]

The second aspect of Soviet and Chinese Communist policy after Yalta—the mounting criticism of the Chungking government (and, in the Chinese Communist press, of Chiang Kai-shek)—must be related, in this writer's view, to an apparent

delegation in 1948 that shortly after the war he had urged the Chinese Communists "to seek a *modus vivendi* with Chiang Kai-shek . . . and dissolve their army"; Vladimir Dedijer, *Tito* (New York, 1953), p. 322.

[95] Mao, *Proizvedeniia,* IV, 507 (English ed., IV, 274).

[96] "Constitution of the Chinese Communist Party" (June 11, 1945); text in Brandt, etc., *Documentary History,* pp. 422–23. It is also interesting to note, as a measure of the underlying orthodoxy of the Chinese Communists, Mao's views in 1945 on the relative contribution of peasants and workers to the revolutionary movement. In his report to the Seventh Congress he said: "At the present stage it is the peasantry which is the main force struggling for democracy in China. . . . When I put the matter this way, however, this does not mean that I undervalue the important part played in political, economic and cultural affairs by the remaining ninety million Chinese; still less does it mean that I underrate the role of the working class, which is of course the most politically conscious of all classes and, in consequence of this, the most qualified to provide the entire leadership for all revolutionary movements. There should be no doubts whatsoever on this point." This translation, made from the 1953 Russian text in Mao, *Proizvedeniia,* IV, 540 (English ed., IV, 295), is essentially the same as the English text published in 1945; see Mao Tse-tung, *Fight for a New China,* p. 58.

change in world Communist strategy in the early spring of 1945. The change is reflected most clearly in an article written by the French Communist Jacques Duclos for the April issue of *Cahiers du Communisme.* The article concerned what Duclos felt to be a serious deviation within the American Communist movement, then under the leadership of Earl Browder.

In 1944, motivated by the successful wartime collaboration between the United States and Russia—especially as exemplified at Teheran—Browder had effected the dissolution of the Communist Party of the United States and had reorganized it into the Communist Political Association, which, it was intended, would be a less militant organization. Duclos's article sharply attacked this strategy. Great power collaboration, Duclos argued, had been misinterpreted by Browder and had been made the justification, quite indefensibly, for the liquidation of the political independence of the "working class" in the United States as expressed through the Communist Party. The Duclos article initiated a major review of policies within the American Communist movement, during the course of which Browder was repudiated and the Communist Party as such restored in July, 1945.[97]

While the debate over Browder's revisionism was going on—and presumably as a direct consequence of the course it was taking—the attitude of American Communists shifted radically with respect to support of the administration's policies. The shift was particularly evident in the new Communist view of American policy toward China. At the end of February, 1945, *New Masses* had praised the State Department's "forthright progressive policy" in China.[98] In a speech in New York on March 13, Browder had said that the State Department "finds Yenan's policies closer to our [i.e., the American] understanding [of the situation in China] . . . than are the policies of Chungking." The sentiment, according to Browder, was reciprocal. "The Chi-

[97] A translation of Duclos's article together with various statements on the Browder issue by American Communist leaders may be found in William Z. Foster, Jacques Duclos, Eugene Dennis, and John Williamson, *Marxism-Leninism versus Revisionism* (New York, 1945); see also the texts of speeches made at a Party conference on June 18–20, 1945, in *Political Affairs,* No. 7, July, 1945.

[98] *New Masses* (New York), February 27, 1945, p. 18.

nese Communists," he said, "trust Americans." [99] As late as April 17, 1945, *New Masses* praised the recent "remarkable" speech by Secretary of State Stettinius in Chicago in which he called for "a sense of proportion" and "mutual trust" in international relations.[100]

Ten days later, when Party headquarters in New York had had time to absorb the import of the Duclos article, an entirely different note was sounded in the American Communist press. On April 28, Frederick V. Field, the chief writer on Far Eastern affairs in Communist Party publications of this period, sharply attacked Ambassador Hurley for allegedly having withdrawn American support from the truce negotiations between the Chinese Communists and the Kuomintang and for now seeking a "strong man," in the person of Chiang Kai-shek, to resolve China's problems.[101] Henceforth Communist writers in the United States persistently attacked American policy in China and excoriated the Kuomintang, although, like writers in Yenan and Moscow, they continued to make appeals for Chinese unity and coalition government.[102]

Although the Duclos article was directed at shortcomings in the Communist movement in the United States and had its greatest impact there, it also appears to have given the signal to Communist parties everywhere to revise their wartime policies. As the war in Europe drew to a close and the wartime collaboration between the Soviet Union and the Western Allies crumbled rapidly during the weeks after Yalta, it was doubtless apparent in Moscow that a reappraisal of the role of the Communist parties abroad was urgently needed. Anti-Fascist alliances and united fronts, which had been entirely appropriate to the wartime

[99] Earl Browder, *Why America Is Interested in the Chinese Communists* (New York, 1945), p. 11; see also William Z. Foster, *History of the Communist Party of the United States* (New York, 1952), pp. 419–20.

[100] *New Masses,* April 17, 1945, p. 4.

[101] *Daily Worker* (New York), April 28, 1945, p. 9.

[102] E.g., John Stuart, "Crisis in [American] Foreign Policy," *New Masses,* May 29, 1945, pp. 3–12, and the editorials in *New Masses* on June 12, 1945, pp. 12–13, and June 19, 1945, p. 6. See also the resolutions passed by the National Committee of the Communist Political Association on June 20 ("The Present Situation and Next Tasks," *Political Affairs,* July, 1945, pp. 579–90), and by the National Convention of the newly reconstituted Communist Party of the United States on July 28 (text in William Z. Foster, etc., *Marxism-Leninism,* pp. 90 ff.).

policy of coalition, no longer served a specific purpose in Communist strategy and must make way for the revival of more traditional forms of revolutionary activity. Governments which were fundamentally hostile to the spread of Communism, whatever their attitude toward Germany and Japan, could no longer receive Communist support. Duclos was a logical spokesman for Moscow in these matters. He was not only one of the leaders of the French Communist Party, probably the strongest Communist Party in Europe (outside Russia and Yugoslavia) at the end of the war, but also one of the most respected figures in the world-wide Communist movement. The Russian leadership, being unable for reasons of diplomacy to provide guidance at this juncture, may well have delegated to Duclos the task of imparting this important message to Communists throughout the world.

The more aggressive attitude toward the Chungking government revealed in both Soviet and Chinese Communist commentaries during the spring of 1945 probably reflects this reappraisal of world Communist strategy. If this surmise is correct, the ambivalence which appeared in Soviet and Chinese Communist policy toward the end of the war is perhaps more understandable: it derived from the fact that Moscow and Yenan were executing a general shift in world Communist strategy, a shift which tended to discourage the continuation of wartime alliances, while at the same time they were trying to shape a policy suited to specific circumstances in China, circumstances which required continued collaboration with Chungking. These dual requirements led to certain inconsistencies, of course, but has consistency ever been adjudged a distinguishing mark of Communist behavior?

As far as the Chinese Communists are concerned, there is perhaps one additional consideration to bear in mind in interpreting their increasingly aggressive policy toward the Kuomintang during the final months of the war. Even if they had not guessed it earlier, the Chinese Communists doubtless learned after Yalta that the United States did not plan to land American troops in China in any great numbers, prior to the invasion of Japan.[103]

[103] This decision was made by the Joint Chiefs of Staff at least by early October, 1944; see Feis, *The China Tangle*, pp. 195–96. There appears to have been no

So long as this latter event remained scheduled for some indefinite date in the future—as it apparently did through the spring of 1945[104]—the Chungking government in its dealings with Yenan could not look forward for some months to the powerful protection which a China-based American task force would provide. The Communists therefore had before them a comfortable period of time during which they were free to harass the Kuomintang and build up their own strength vis à vis Chungking without appearing to jeopardize the Allied war effort in the Far East and also without serious risk of antagonizing the United States. This they proceeded to do during the spring and early summer of 1945 in a vigorous campaign of psychological warfare against Chungking.

The abrupt collapse of Japan in August, 1945, changed the Communists' timetable by bringing American troops into China many months, perhaps even a year, ahead of schedule. Despite this new turn of events, the Communists' more aggressive policy toward Chungking had by this time yielded sufficient gains, in Yenan's judgment, to warrant its continuation. The new policy was to be modified in the months after the war only to the extent necessary to lend a show of sincerity to the Communists' truce negotiations with the Kuomintang.

The "pact of friendship and alliance" between China and the USSR, for which the Yalta agreement had made provision, was not concluded until August 14, 1945, after negotiations lasting five or six weeks.[105] It consisted of a general statement of mutual

specific mention of this decision during the military discussions at Yalta, but the course of these discussions must clearly have revealed to the Russians that the Americans planned no large-scale attack on the Chinese mainland; see *Foreign Relations of the United States: The Conferences at Malta and Yalta, 1945*, pp. 650–54, 757–60 and 834–39. Presumably the Russians found some way to pass this information on to the Chinese Communists.

[104] As late as Potsdam, in July, 1945, the invasion of Japan was apparently not anticipated until two months after the Soviet attack on Manchuria, scheduled for early August; see Harriman's testimony in *Military Situation in the Far East*, pp. 3338–39. At Yalta, in January, 1945, it had been predicted that the war in the Pacific would last another eighteen months at least, that is, until the autumn of 1946; *ibid.*, p. 3332, and John R. Deane, *The Strange Alliance* (New York, 1947), pp. 274–75.

[105] The Chinese were informed officially of the provisions of the Yalta agreement early in June, although they appear to have suspected a month earlier what

respect for the independence and territorial integrity of the signatories and a pledge of mutual assistance in the struggle against Japan, plus numerous separate protocols and exchanges concerning Sino-Soviet relations in Manchuria and Outer Mongolia, both during and after the war.[106] Ambassador Hurley, for one, had placed great reliance on this pact as a means of paving the way for more fruitful discussions between the Chinese Communists and Chungking, discussions which he had personally sponsored during the last months of the war. Early in July, more than a month before the pact was signed, he had reported from Chungking:

> We are convinced that the influence of the Soviet will control the action of the Chinese Communist Party. The Chinese Communists do not believe that Stalin has agreed or will agree to support the National Government of China under the leadership of Chiang Kai-shek. The Chinese Communists still fully expect the Soviets to support the Chinese Communists against the National Government. Nothing short of the Soviet's public commitment will change the Chinese Communists' opinion on the subject.[107]

It is easy, with the benefit of hindsight, to ridicule Hurley's view of the Chinese Communists' attitude in the summer of 1945. At the time, however, it is very doubtful if any foreign observers in China were sufficiently informed as to the true character of current Soviet-Chinese Communist relations to predict with certainty how Yenan would in fact react to the proposed Sino-Soviet treaty. Taken at face value, certain provisions of the accord, when it was announced, did appear to work to the disadvantage of the Communists. According to Article V, for instance, each signatory agreed to the principle of "non-interference in the internal affairs of the other contracting party," [108]

most of these provisions were; see Feis, *The China Tangle,* pp. 304 ff. Direct negotiations did not begin until early July when T. V. Soong arrived in Moscow; *Pravda,* July 5, 1945, p. 1. The discussions were interrupted by the departure of high Soviet officials for the Potsdam Conference later in the month and were resumed only on August 7 when a full Chinese delegation reached Moscow; see *Pravda,* August 8, 1945, p. 1.

[106] A text of the pact and accompanying protocols, etc., may be found in *United States Relations with China,* pp. 585–96.

[107] *Ibid.,* p. 90.

[108] *Ibid.,* pp. 585 ff.

a commitment on Moscow's part which might be construed to preclude Soviet support of the Communists in any form. Molotov also stated, in one of the exchanges of notes relating to the pact, that the Soviet Union would provide China with military supplies and render it moral support in the struggle against Japan, "such support and aid to be entirely given to the National Government as the central government of China." [109]

On an assumption that Yenan was counting on receiving Soviet support in its conflict with Chungking, Hurley's conclusions were entirely logical. This assumption, however, now appears to have been incorrect when judged in the light of subsequent developments in China and of later evidence on Moscow's relations with Yenan. The Chinese Communists appear, in retrospect, to have had no illusions about securing material support from the Soviet Union—at least about securing it prior to the end of the war against Japan. They also appear to have been fully cognizant of the aims of Russian policy toward China after Yalta, and at the Seventh Party Congress and subsequently they gave every indication of supporting this policy in its broad outline. There was therefore nothing in the Sino-Soviet pact which need have surprised Yenan. Even if nothing was then known specifically of the negotiations leading to the alliance of August 14, the probability of a Sino-Soviet accord could presumably have been foreseen. In any case, when the provisions of the pact were announced, Yenan gave the treaty its immediate and unqualified endorsement.[110]

In Moscow the Soviet press appeared slightly on the defensive in acclaiming the pact and devoted an unusual amount of space to the refutation of hostile comment in the foreign press, both

[109] *Ibid.*, p. 587.

[110] See the editorial, for instance. in *Emancipation Daily* (Yenan), August 29, 1945; translation at Hoover Library, Stanford University. The conclusion of the pact was announced in Moscow and Chungking on August 15, but its provisions were not made public until August 27. American observers in Yenan at the time the news of the Sino-Soviet accord was received, on August 15, had the impression that some of the Communists there were bewildered by the announcement; Feis, *The China Tangle,* p. 358. It was perhaps natural for rank-and-file Party members, who would have been most familiar with the anti-Chungking aspects of Communist policy, to be disappointed by the Sino-Soviet pact. This need not suggest, however, that there was either bewilderment or disillusion among Party leaders.

enemy and Allied. *Pravda,* for instance, in its only editorial comment on the treaty (apart from an article which appeared on the day the treaty was published and which merely summarized its contents),[111] went to some length to deny the charges of a Japanese newspaper that the treaty gave Russia major concessions while the benefits to China were "nominal" and that in consequence "the Chinese question in the future becomes even more complex." This was clearly an effort, *Pravda* argued, to sow discord among the Allies.[112] On September 1, *New Times* also devoted much of its editorial comment to an attack on hostile comment abroad:

> The circles which specialize in stirring up suspicion against the Soviet Union have for a long time talked nonsensically about "Soviet claims in the Far East," claims which they themselves have invented. Now these people are trying to put a cheerful face on the matter and pretend to be surprised at the "modesty" of the Soviet claims. They cannot bring themselves to acknowledge the self-evident fact that the Soviet Union's entire foreign policy is based on the principle of unqualified respect for the national sovereignty of its neighbors and of all peace-loving countries, both large and small.[113]

As events turned out, the Sino-Soviet pact had no great significance for Soviet Far Eastern policy after the war. This was perhaps inevitable. Despite some provisions relating to Sino-Soviet relations after Japan's defeat, the treaty was basically a wartime military alliance, the need for which no longer existed by the time it was concluded. The only political condition under which it could have remained operative after the war—a coalition regime in China—never materialized. The alliance, moreover, was not one which Moscow would have made on its own initiative, but rather constituted one part of a bargain which was extremely profitable for the Soviet Union. Moscow could well afford to carry out its share of this bargain to the letter. No wonder that within one year after the signing of the Sino-Soviet pact

[111] "Vazhnyi etap v razvitii sovetsko-kitaiskikh otnoshenii" (An Important Stage in the Development of Sino-Soviet Relations), *Pravda,* August 27, 1945, p. 1.

[112] "Mezhdunarodnoe obozrenie" (International Review), *Pravda,* September 2, 1945, p. 4.

[113] "Sovetskii Soiuz i Kitai" (The Soviet Union and China), *Novoe vremia,* No. 7 (17), September 1, 1945, p. 1.

a comprehensive survey of China published in Moscow made only passing reference to it,[114] and some later accounts have ignored the pact altogether.[115]

[114] Maslennikov, *Kitai,* p. 257.

[115] E.g., *Krizis kolonial'noi sistemy.* Two recent volumes which discuss the pact in a certain amount of detail treat it as an exclusively military alliance and make no reference either to Molotov's supplementary pledge to render aid solely to the national government or to the noninterference clause in Article V, except as this applied to Sinkiang; *Mezhdunarodnye otnosheniia na Dal'nem Vostoke,* pp. 614–17, and Efimov, *Ocherki po novoi i noveishei istorii Kitaia,* pp. 202–4. One account in 1950 prefaced its brief analysis of the pact with this rather apologetic comment: "An important characteristic of Soviet foreign policy is that, if the Soviet Union concludes an agreement with a nation dependent on imperialism and temporarily under the control of foreign hirelings or agents of imperialism, the contents of the agreement never go against the interests of the people of that nation." E. M. Zhukov, *Sovetskii soiuz v bor'be za demokraticheskoe reshenie poslevoennkyh problem Dal'nego Vostoka* (The Soviet Union in the Struggle for a Democratic Resolution of Postwar Problems in the Far East) (Moscow, 1950), p. 25.

5

RUSSIA, CHINA, AND THE UNITED STATES AFTER THE WAR, 1945–1946

The end of the war in the Far East brought no easement to the political crisis in China. It merely released with a new fury antagonisms which, though not wholly concealed during the war, had at least been kept in check. The alignment which eventually emerged—Communists with Soviet backing versus Nationalists with American backing—seems, in hindsight, an obvious one, but in the summer of 1945 this alignment was not at all obvious. In the United States, for instance, many felt that we should not intervene in China in a purely domestic political struggle and should, as a matter of principle, avoid committing ourselves to one side or to the other. Others, impressed by reports of potential Communist strength in China and by predictions of future Communist success, hoped to assure the Communists' future good will toward the United States by persuading the government to refrain from any actions which might later be interpreted as hostile. It may be said that, at the time of the Japanese surrender, a comparatively small number of officials in Washington favored all-out aid to the Chungking government.

At the same time, it need not be imagined that the Russians, any more than the Americans, had firmly laid down their future policy toward China. We must avoid any tendency to assume, merely because so little is known of the procedures by which Soviet policy is made or of the uncertainties which doubtless plague policy makers in Moscow as they do elsewhere, that the Soviet leaders are endowed with special foresight and are able to predict with a certainty the consequences of their behavior in any given set of circumstances.[1] As far as the Chinese Communists were concerned, at the end of the war Soviet leaders were still publicly disclaiming any ties with them and the Soviet press continued to ignore them as a factor of any consequence within China. That there was perhaps some design in this treatment of the Communists does not in any way lessen the contrast between the Russians' reticence at the end of the war and the attitude which they were to express openly one year later. In short, it could not be taken for granted at the time of the Japanese capitulation, on the basis of the evidence then available, that the Russians would undeniably assist the Chinese Communists to capture Manchuria, let alone all of China. Nor can it be asserted even now, on the basis of all the accumulated evidence available, that support of the Communists, which later became a factor of such major importance in China, was a principal feature of Soviet policy at the time the war ended.

Developments in China during the year following the end of the war constitute one of the most baffling chapters in the recent history of the Far East. It will require many years of painstaking scholarship to set the record of this period straight. This task has been partially carried out in so far as American policy is concerned.[2] To a lesser extent, the same is true with respect to Chi-

[1] An instance of this tendency to credit Soviet foreign policy makers with superhuman (and usually diabolic) foresight may be found in a passage in Fitzgerald, *Revolution in China*, pp. 93 ff. If we may look ahead, the Russians, according to this account, were somewhat distrustful of Mao because of his suspected unorthodoxy. They nonetheless preferred a Communist regime in Manchuria to a Nationalist one and so encouraged the Communists to consolidate themselves north of the Great Wall and, to assist them, allowed captured Japanese equipment to fall into their hands. In this way they established Yenan's indebtedness to Moscow. Kuomintang troops, in the meantime, were allowed to occupy the main cities of Manchuria, following some initial delays. In doing so, however—and this was allegedly part of the Soviet strategy—the Kuomintang so overextended itself that it was left vulnerable to Communist attack. With Yenan's eventual victory thus assured, Fitzgerald concludes, Communist dependence on the Soviet Union for some years to come was guaranteed by a systematic stripping of Manchurian industrial potential.

There are numerous objections to this analysis, but the principal one for present purposes is Fitzgerald's assumption that the Russians, presumably through intuition, knew so well what course events in Manchuria would take that they were able to outline, long in advance, a relatively inflexible policy and to follow it without hesitation.

[2] The official record of American policy in China after the war is, of course, the State Department's *United States Relations with China.* Herbert Feis, in *The*

nese Nationalist policy.[3] Soviet and Chinese Communist policies during this period, on the other hand, are still obscure and have not been greatly clarified by the numerous accounts of the post-war era published recently in Moscow or in Peking. Attempts by Western students to interpret these policies reveal the great dearth of information which chronically hampers investigation of Soviet motives and which seems to be particularly frustrating for these critical twelve months.[4] It was during this period that Soviet policy toward the Chinese Communists evolved from an outwardly ambiguous attitude in August, 1945, into a clearly defined commitment to their support by the summer of 1946.

THE RUSSIANS IN MANCHURIA: PHASE ONE AUGUST, 1945–DECEMBER, 1945

When the Japanese government announced its tentative acceptance of the Potsdam ultimatum on August 10, 1945, the

China Tangle, gives an exhaustive account of American policy up to the instructing of General Marshall in December, 1945. This will in all likelihood remain the definitive study of the subject for some years. There have also been at least three congressional investigations which probed deeply, if unsystematically, into American policy in China during 1945 and 1946. The records of these hearings have been published as: *State Department Employee Loyalty Investigation, Military Situation in the Far East,* and *Institute of Pacific Relations.*

[3] There has been no such public review of Chinese Nationalist policy as there has been of American policy. Chinese officials, however, made frequent public statements during 1945 and 1946 which revealed Chungking's (later Nanking's) position on various issues at the time. The most comprehensive statement of Nationalist policy with respect to the Russians in the postwar period that this writer has seen was contained in the remarks made by the Chinese delegate to the United Nations, Tingfu F. Tsiang, before the First Committee on November 25, 1949; *Summary Records of the First Committee,* pp. 340 ff. (also published separately by the Chinese Delegation to the United Nations under the title *China Presents Her Case to the United Nations*). See also *China Handbook, 1937–1945* (rev. ed., 1947), pp. 737–64; *China Handbook, 1950,* pp. 331–32; Chiang Kai-shek, *Soviet Russia in China,* pp. 127–93; and Cheng Tien-fong, *History of Sino-Russian Relations,* chaps. XXI and XXII.

[4] A systematic survey of Soviet policy in China following the war may be found in Beloff, *Soviet Policy in the Far East, 1944–1951,* chap. II. Other substantial treatments of Soviet postwar policy may be found in North, *Moscow and Chinese Communists* (this treatment, however, is considerably less detailed than North's treatment of Soviet-Chinese Communist relations prior to the Second World War); Dallin, *Soviet Russia and the Far East,* 1948; Wu, *China and the Soviet Union*; and Jones, *Manchuria since 1931.* An interesting, if somewhat impassioned, account of Soviet policy by an American correspondent who visited Manchuria during the Russian occupation is Moorad, *Lost Peace in China.*

Russian advance into Manchuria was twenty-four hours old. The Soviet press published the news of Japan's readiness to capitulate,[5] and on August 15 all Moscow papers announced the unconditional surrender of Japan proclaimed the day before. On August 16, however, the Soviet Chief of Staff, General A. E. Antonov, announced that the capitulation was only a "general declaration," that no cease-fire order had been issued to Japanese forces in the field and that inasmuch as Japanese resistance was continuing in Manchuria the Soviet advance would proceed.[6] On August 19, *Pravda*'s "Observer" asserted that, "while the capitulation has been announced, it is not yet a real capitulation."[7]

In the meantime Soviet troops were advancing rapidly through Manchuria along three fronts, apparently meeting little resistance. On August 17, the Soviet field commander in the Far East, Marshal Vasilevskii, ordered all units of the Kwantung Army to lay down their arms by noon on August 20.[8] On the latter date Changchun, Mukden, Harbin, Kirin, and all of the principal cities in northern Manchuria were reported in Russian hands; Port Arthur and Dairen were occupied by August 22. On August 23, at ten o'clock in the evening (Moscow time), Stalin announced the completion of the Manchurian campaign—two weeks and some hours after the fighting had begun.[9]

Much less is known of the timetable of the Chinese Communist advance into Manchuria from the south. On August 10, Chu Teh launched a general offensive of the Eighth Route Army along the entire northern front, which at this time extended from the Shantung peninsula through Hopeh, south of Peiping, and

[5] The Soviet announcement took the form of a dispatch from Tokyo giving the text of a note delivered by Foreign Minister Togo personally to the Soviet Ambassador Jacob Malik on August 10; *Pravda*, August 11, 1945, p. 4.

[6] *Pravda*, August 16, 1945, p. 1.

[7] "Mezhdunarodnoe obozrenie" (International Survey), *Pravda*, August 19, 1945, p. 4.

[8] *Pravda*, August 17, 1945, p. 1.

[9] *Pravda*, August 24, 1945, p. 1; Stalin also announced at this time the approaching conclusion of the campaigns in South Sakhalin, the Kurile Islands, and North Korea. Later Soviet sources claim that there was intermittent fighting in Manchuria for another fortnight before the last Japanese resistance collapsed; *Mezhdunarodnye otnosheniia na Dal'nem Vostoke*, p. 613.

into the province of Chahar.[10] The Communists apparently encountered little opposition. Chefoo, on the Shantung peninsula, was taken on August 24. Kalgan, the capital of Chahar province, was reported to have been occupied by Chinese Communist and Outer Mongolian troops on August 30.[11] Recent Soviet accounts note the Communist's occupation of Cheng-te, the capital of Jehol, at about the same time.[12]

There are unfortunately no reports of the first contact made between Russian and Chinese Communist forces, which presumably occurred in late August or early September, 1945.[13] Of the numerous "eyewitness" accounts of the Russian campaign published in the Soviet press in August and September, none made any mention of Communist or guerrilla forces. In fact, to judge from later Soviet accounts, a joint occupation of Manchuria by Russian and Chinese Communist troops may not have been intended initially.[14] By September 10, however, according to an

[10] *Mezhdunarodnye otnosheniia na Dal'nem Vostoke,* p. 611. The northern front was never well defined, even during the course of the war, due to the activities of Communist guerrillas behind the Japanese lines who were sometimes directly in contact with, and sometimes isolated from, the main forces of the Eighth Route Army. This army, officially designated as the Eighteenth Army Group of the Chinese National Army under Chiang Kai-shek, maintained itself in wide areas throughout north China; the New Fourth Army, disbanded by Chiang after the South Anhwei incident of January, 1941, but immediately reconstituted by the Chinese Communists, was active in central and eastern China. A detailed study of the position and strength of Chinese Communist forces in the early part of 1945 may be found in *The Chinese Communist Movement,* Vol. III, Part 7.

[11] New York *Times,* August 31, 1945, p. 5. Outer Mongolia declared war on Japan on August 10, and its forces advanced on the right flank of the Soviet forces into Chahar and Jehol. One American observer has reported that Chinese Communist troops reached Kalgan on August 23 but were compelled by Soviet-Mongol forces to quit the city a few days later; Moorad, *Lost Peace in China,* pp. 114–15. This evidence is in conflict with Tillman Durdin's report from Kalgan late in October which stated that the Communists had at that time been in control of the city for two months and had made it into a "second Yenan"; New York *Times,* October 31, 1945. See also Chiang's claim that a "Soviet-Mongolian Military Mission" was sent to Kalgan soon after its seizure to train and equip Communist troops; Chiang Kai-shek, *Soviet Russia in China,* p. 144.

[12] E.g., *Mezhdunarodnye otnosheniia na Dal'nem Vostoke,* p. 611.

[13] On August 27, Stalin informed Harriman in Moscow that the Red Army had as yet encountered no Communist forces; *United States Relations with China,* p. 119.

[14] E.g., *Mezhdunarodnye otnosheniia na Dal'nem Vostoke,* p. 611. This account emphasizes the indirect support given to Communist operations in North China by the Soviet campaign in Manchuria, but does not indicate that the Eighth Route Army attack extended beyond Jehol.

American military report from Mukden, some Eighth Route Army troops were in evidence in that city.[15] In early October, there were circumstantial reports of an active transfer of men and material from Communist-held Chefoo in the Shantung peninsula to Russian-held ports in southern Manchuria.[16] The Chinese Communists, however, did not officially acknowledge that the Eighth Route Army was in Manchuria until some time later.[17]

One issue aggravated more than any other the already tense internal situation in China after the Japanese capitulation. That was the question of disarming the Japanese troops in North China. The basic document for the surrender was General Order No. 1, drafted in Washington and issued on August 15, 1945, by General MacArthur, the Supreme Commander of the Allied Powers (SCAP). It provided for the Japanese in Manchuria to surrender to the Russians, and for those elsewhere in China to surrender to Chiang Kai-shek or his designated commanders. It was expressly stipulated in General Order No. 1 that no other forces in China were authorized to accept the surrender of Japanese troops.[18]

The Chinese Communists took vigorous exception to their complete exclusion from the surrender arrangements in areas which they felt were within their zone of operations. Even before General Order No. 1 had been issued, Chu Teh, in announcing a general attack northwards, had instructed his commanders to prepare to receive the surrender of Japanese troops in their respective areas.[19] On August 12, Chiang Kai-shek countermanded Chu's order and commanded the Eighth Army to stand fast until instructions were received from Chungking.[20] On the following

[15] Feis, *The China Tangle,* p. 382 *n*; this report was dated September 24, 1945. See also Cheng Tien-fong, *History of Sino-Russian Relations,* p. 275.

[16] Moorad, *Lost Peace in China,* p. 91.

[17] As late as October 29, 1945, a Communist spokesman in Chungking told H. R. Lieberman of the New York *Times* that the Russians did not allow the Communists to send military units into Manchuria but that some Communists were allowed in as "civilians"; New York *Times,* October 30, 1945, p. 1.

[18] General MacArthur made special efforts to stress to Japanese Imperial Headquarters the importance the American government attached to having all surrenders in China proper made to authorized Nationalist commanders; Feis, *The China Tangle,* p. 341.

[19] New York *Times,* August 12, 1945, p. 10; see also Smedley, *The Great Road,* pp. 417–18.

[20] New York *Times,* August 13, 1945, p. 1.

day, in one of its most scathing attacks on Chiang Kai-shek over the previous decade, Yenan rejected the Generalissimo's counterorder. Twice on this occasion Chiang was referred to as a "Fascist chieftain" and the reason for his counterorder was said to be his plan to use the Japanese troops in North China for an assault on the Communists. "The Chinese Communist Party," the Yenan radio asserted in an English-language broadcast, "has for eight years tasted the bitterness of attacks on two fronts by the Japanese and Chiang Kai-shek." [21] Chu Teh, meanwhile, formally rejected Chiang's counterorder as "contrary to the national interest" and commanded his troops to continue their advance.[22]

The publication of General Order No. 1 on August 15 did not cause the Chinese Communists to modify their position. On August 16, Chu asserted the right of the Communists "to accept the surrender of the Japanese and puppet armies surrounded by our armies, take over their arms, materials and resources and be responsible for carrying out all provisions of the Allied terms of surrender." [23] In the following weeks the Communists, reiterating this position, went on disarming Japanese troops wherever they found them.[24]

The Russians gave no outward indications of supporting the Chinese Communists in these first efforts of the latter to assert

[21] *Ibid.*, August 14, 1945, p. 10. Unusually full press coverage of Chinese Communist pronouncements during the summer and autumn of 1945 was made possible through the monitoring service of the United States Federal Communications Commission.

[22] *Ibid.*, August 15, 1945, p. 6.

[23] *Ibid.*, August 17, 1945, p. 5. According to Feis, Chu Teh sent the text of this statement to the American, British, and Soviet Embassies in Chungking, presumably as a formal protest against General Order No. 1. The American reply, transmitted by General Wedemeyer, reaffirmed the order and stated that the USSR, as well as England, concurred in it; Feis, *The China Tangle*, pp. 358–59. Cf. Smedley, *The Great Road*, pp. 421–22.

[24] For subsequent statements of the Communist position on the disarmament of Japanese troops in North China, see the New York *Times*, August 20, 1945, p. 1; the statement of the Central Committee of the Chinese Communist Party on August 25, 1945, printed in *Political Affairs* (New York), No. 10, October, 1945, p. 960; and the communiqué of October 11, 1945, summarizing the recent talks between Mao and Chiang Kai-shek, printed in *United States Relations with China*, p. 581. For Chiang Kai-shek's view of the Communists' insubordination in the matter of disarming Japanese troops, see Chiang Kai-shek, *Soviet Russia in China*, pp. 129–31.

their authority in North China. General Order No. 1 went unopposed in Moscow, in so far as its provisions affected the Chinese Communists,[25] and no reference was made in the Soviet press to the Communists' persistent demands for the right to receive the surrender of Japanese forces in their own zone of operations. Only in December, four months after the end of the war, did the Soviet press refer to this situation in a way which might be construed as giving guarded approval to Yenan's position. Discussing the claim that American troops were stationed in North China solely to disarm the Japanese, one of the *Pravda*'s staff writers remarked:

> It may perhaps be asserted that the armed forces of those Chinese who showed themselves able to check the Japanese attack during the war have proved themselves incomparably more qualified [than the U.S. Marines] to deal with the problem of disarming and evacuating the enemy forces after Japan's capitulation.[26]

The likelihood that the Communists, after the Japanese surrender, would ignore Chiang's orders and continue their operations in North China must of course have been anticipated in Chungking and Washington, although the urgency of measures to meet this situation was perhaps not appreciated due to the expected longer duration of the war. It should be recalled that as late as the Potsdam Conference, at the end of July, 1945, most Allied military leaders were still thinking in terms of a war which would last at least into the early part of 1946. The possibility of an earlier Japanese capitulation, however, was acknowledged in Washington with the successful testing of an atomic bomb on July 16, and shortly thereafter special directives were drafted for field commanders in the Far East, to take effect

[25] On August 16, 1945, the day following the publication of General Order No. 1, Stalin asked Truman that the order be amended on two points: to allow the Russians to accept the surrender of Japanese forces in the Kurile Islands and to allow them to occupy the northern half of Hokkaido. Only the first of these proposals was accepted by the United States; see Harry S. Truman, *Year of Decisions* (Garden City, N. Y., 1955), p. 441.

[26] N. Sokolovskii, "K polozheniiu v Kitae posle kapituliatsii Iaponii" (Toward the Situation in China after the Capitulation of Japan), *Pravda*, December 19, 1945, p. 4. The American Communist press, in contrast to the Russian, supported from the outset Yenan's claim to the right to participate in the Japanese surrender. See, for instance, Frederick V. Field, "Avert Civil War in China!" *Political Affairs*, No. 9, September, 1945, pp. 843–50.

if the war should end abruptly. On August 10, General Wedemeyer was authorized, in the event of Japanese capitulation, to transport Chiang's troops to key points in North China and to assist them in recovering control over Japanese-occupied areas.[27] In accordance with these instructions, during the weeks immediately following the surrender three Chinese armies were flown by American planes from Central China to Shanghai, Nanking, Peiping, and other critical sectors along the North China coast. During succeeding months many more Chinese troops were transported northward by ship. According to official American sources, by the end of 1945 a total of between 400,000 and 500,000 Nationalist troops had been redeployed with American assistance. In addition, during the autumn of 1945 more than 50,000 U.S. Marines were landed in North China to assist the Chinese government forces.[28]

The assistance rendered to Chiang Kai-shek in his attempt to recover North China and the use of American troops in this effort, which may not have been anticipated in Moscow or in Yenan, undoubtedly hampered the efforts of the Chinese Communists to effect a quick consolidation of their strength north of the Great Wall. The Russians may not have given a great deal of thought to this operation before launching their own attack from the north, but once the attack had begun, and especially after they had made contact with advance Chinese Communist troops, they probably attached increasing importance to the Communists' making good their position on the Russian flank. The Russians did not, however, protest American assistance to the national government until late in the autumn. There are

[27] For a discussion of this directive, see Feis, *The China Tangle*, pp. 334–38. In a press interview on August 20, 1945, Wedemeyer explained his understanding of this directive as follows: "The United States government is still supporting the Central Government of China and I am still authorized to redispose Chinese forces with a view to facilitating their rehabilitation and redeployment and the deportation of the Japanese and also with a view to the preservation of order in connection therewith"; New York *Times*, August 31, 1945, p. 5. Later Soviet sources appear to have interpreted this statement as an open threat on Wedemeyer's part to intervene in the civil war against the Chinese Communists; see Iurev, *Istoricheskaia pobeda kitaiskogo naroda nad Amerikanskim imperializmom i gomindanovskoi reaktsiei*, p. 5.

[28] *United States Relations with China*, pp. 311–12, citing Department of Army figures.

several possible reasons for their silence. In the first place, they may have felt that it would be indelicate immediately to attack American assistance to the recognized government of China at a time when their own position in Manchuria was at least diplomatically precarious, in terms of the recently concluded Sino-Soviet pact. They may also have felt that it was advantageous to win American good will by refraining from any overt criticism of American policies in China, in order to secure the "good offices" of the United States in the negotiations between the Chinese Communists and the Kuomintang which were held in Chungking from the end of August to early October, 1945. It is also possible that the Russians were aware of the firm commitment in Washington at this time not to intervene in the internal affairs of China, beyond providing assistance to the national government in the recovery of Japanese-occupied territory in North China.[29] If so, the Russians would have had little reason to fear the temporary presence of Marines in North China and would probably not have been unduly concerned over the transfer of some government troops northward.

The Chinese Communists, although more directly affected than the Russians by American policies in North China, also refrained from attacking these policies during September, presumably in deference to Moscow's apparent attitude in this matter.[30] On

[29] The instruction to General Wedemeyer on August 10 strongly cautioned against any assistance to Chiang which would violate the basic principle of non-interference in Chinese affairs. On November 10, 1945, following his return from a brief visit to Washington, Wedemeyer outlined American policy at this time in a blunt memorandum to Chiang Kai-shek. In this he referred to "the President's instruction that the United States positively should not participate in China's military clashes nor could any facilities be furnished for the Central Government's action against rebellious military elements within Chinese territory." The memorandum continued: "[The Joint Chiefs of Staff] declared plainly American military aid to China will cease immediately if evidence compels the United States Government to believe that any Chinese troops receiving such aid are using it to support any government which the United States cannot accept, to conduct civil war or for aggressive or coercive purposes" (*Military Situation in the Far East,* p. 555).

[30] The Communist press in the United States, however, which had begun to denounce American policy in China as early as May, 1945, continued to do so without interruption after the war ended; e.g., Frederick V. Field, "Dynamite in China," *New Masses* (New York), August 28, 1945, pp. 3–4; editorial in *ibid.*, September 28, 1945, pp. 16–17; Frederick V. Field, "Avert Civil War in China!" *Political Affairs,* No. 9, September, 1945, pp. 844–45.

October 5, however, Chu Teh is reported to have lodged an official protest with the American Embassy in Chungking against American interference in China's internal affairs.[31] On October 20, a United Press dispatch from Peiping reported that Eighth Route Army posters in evidence there accused the United States of "interfering in Chinese internal politics." [32] Later in the same month Wang Ping-nan, then a Communist representative at Chungking, told officials of the American Embassy that the Communists resented "American intervention" in China, both through the presence of Marines and through the ferrying of Nationalist troops by the United States Air Force.[33] On November 5, 1945, the Yenan radio and press charged that American troops were "actively collaborating with the Kuomintang Army in attacks on the Eighth Route Army in liberated areas." [34]

When the Soviet press began finally to take critical notice of American policies in China, it was more circumspect than were the official organs in Yenan. Scattered references to the "imperialist" policy of the United States and to demands for the withdrawal of the Marines appeared in Moscow newspapers after the middle of October, but through November these continued to be merely items in Tass dispatches from the United States quoting liberal sources of American public opinion.[35] It was not until December 1 that the Soviet press carried a signed article in which recent American policy in China was openly attacked. Commenting on Ambassador Hurley's resignation as Ambassador to China and on his public statement of November 27 explaining his resignation, one of *Pravda*'s staff writers remarked:

The thoughtful observer must conclude that the resignation and statement by the Republican Hurley is a clever maneuver in behalf of the

[31] Smedley, *The Great Road,* p. 427.

[32] New York *Times,* October 20, 1945, p. 6.

[33] *United States Relations with China,* p. 109.

[34] New York *Times,* November 6, 1945, p. 1; see also *ibid.,* November 12, p. 1.

[35] E.g., *Pravda,* October 17, 1945, p. 4, quoting a speech on October 10 by Congressman Mike Mansfield, in which he asked for the withdrawal of U.S. troops from China; *Pravda,* November 21, 1945, p. 4, quoting an article in the New York *Herald Tribune* in which China was described as an American "protectorate"; *Pravda,* November 30, 1945, p. 4, reporting Congressman Hugh DeLacy's bill in Congress to withdraw all American troops from China.

most unrestrained imperialist circles in the United States, seeking, under the pretext of criticizing the "professional diplomats" and of "correcting" American policy, not only to bolster the imperialist policies of these circles but also to link these policies to the American leadership.

The author suggested that, inasmuch as Secretary of State Byrnes had only a few days earlier spoken of Hurley as his "close friend" and had offered him a free hand in China if he would return, the Ambassador's resignation would probably have little effect on the course of American policy.[36] On December 19, the article in *Pravda* by Sokolovskii questioned the alleged need of "powerful American forces in North China with planes, tanks, and naval vessels" simply to assist the national government in disarming and evacuating the Japanese.[37]

These more forthright attacks on American policy in China must be related, in this writer's view, to the searching appraisal of United States objectives in China which was going on at this time in Washington and which was inevitably reflected in the American and the world press. The dilemma of American policy in China, as Wedemeyer had repeatedly observed in his dispatches to Washington, was that it was becoming virtually impossible to provide adequate assistance to Chiang Kai-shek, in his efforts to evacuate the Japanese from North China, and at the same time to keep clear of the growing conflict there between Nationalist and Chinese Communist troops. The decision which had to be reached in Washington was whether more or less assistance should be offered to the embattled Kuomintang. If more assistance were to be provided, especially in the form of increased military aid in North China, the United States ran the risk of involving the Marines in major clashes with the Communists.[38] If, on the other hand, aid was to be substantially curtailed, there was the risk that North China and possibly all Man-

[36] B. Iakovlev, "K otstavke Kherli" (Toward Hurley's Resignation), *Pravda*, December 1, 1945, p. 4.

[37] Sokolovskii, "K polozheniiu v Kitae," *Pravda*, December 19, 1945, p. 4.

[38] Isolated incidents involving Marine and Chinese Communist detachments north of Peiping were reported by foreign observers from the end of October on; see New York *Times*, October 25, 1945, p. 4; November 8, 1945, p. 7; and November 17, 1945, p. 1.

churia, with Russian connivance, would go to the Communists by default.[39]

Since Moscow, we may assume, desired to see limits set to American activity in North China, or at least wanted some assurance against its being increased, the attacks on American policy at this juncture may be considered as one aspect of a broad program to mobilize liberal opinion throughout the world against further American "intervention" in support of Chungking. Soviet comment would also have the effect of reminding American leaders of the Soviet interest in North China, of Russia's favorable geographical situation with respect to the area and of the relative ease with which Moscow could intervene, if it chose, to offset any small-scale American assistance to Chiang Kai-shek.[40]

While the Russians sought in their official pronouncements to restrain American interference in North China, Soviet actions in Manchuria were creating an entirely new situation further north. Here the Chungking government had been at the mercy of the Soviet occupation authorities from the outset. Chinese sovereignty over Manchuria was of course never denied explicitly. It had, in fact, been explicitly and repeatedly recognized by the Russians during the war, at Teheran, Yalta, and Potsdam, and it was specifically reaffirmed in the Sino-Soviet agreements of August 14, 1945. In his letter to the Chinese Foreign Minister which accompanied the treaty Molotov declared:

[39] Asked by the War Department on November 19, 1945, if he believed that the Nationalists could exert their authority in North China without further American aid, Wedemeyer answered categorically that in his view they could not; see the discussion of this reply in Feis, *The China Tangle*, pp. 399 ff.

[40] Whether or not Soviet strategems had any effect on the course of American policy, the instructions given General Marshall in mid-December, 1945, as he set out for China as the President's personal representative, indicated very little change in U.S. objectives. The Marines were to remain in China for the time being; the United States would continue to assist the national government in the evacuation and repatriation of Japanese troops; and above all, American personnel must avoid any deliberate intervention in Chinese internal conflicts. The most significant alteration in American policy was that General Marshall was given greater authority than either Hurley or Wedemeyer had had before him to make on-the-spot decisions on certain matters, such as the transportation of Nationalist troops, which he felt might affect his mediation of the internal political crisis. For a detailed discussion of the debates in Washington leading to the preparation of Marshall's instruction of December 14, 1945, and of President Truman's policy statement on China the next day, see *ibid.*, chaps. 35–37.

> In the course of conversations regarding Dairen and Port Arthur and regarding the joint operation of the Chinese Changchun Railway, the Government of the U.S.S.R. regarded the Three Eastern Provinces [Manchuria] as part of China and reaffirmed its respect for China's full sovereignty over the Three Eastern Provinces and recognized their territorial and administrative integrity.[41]

In view of this firm commitment on the part of the Soviet government, the persistent efforts of the Russians to obstruct the recovery of Manchuria by the Chinese government only two months later take on particular significance as an indication of the shift in Soviet policy in China once the war was over.

From the viewpoint of the Chinese Nationalists, one of the principal shortcomings of the August agreements, it will be recalled, was that they were written too much with an eye to regulating Sino-Soviet relations during the war against Japan and said almost nothing about Sino-Soviet relations following the end of hostilities. The special agreement on the occupation of Manchuria, for instance, as its title suggests,[42] related only to the conduct of wartime military operations, which had virtually ceased at the time the agreement came into effect. No effort was made to spell out the meaning or the duration of "present joint military operations," after which, as stated in the agreement, "the Chinese Government will assume full authority in the direction of public affairs." In particular, no reference was made in this agreement, or in any of the other agreements signed on August 14, 1945, to the withdrawal of Soviet troops from Manchuria.

According to Chinese Nationalist sources, Stalin had indicated to T. V. Soong, during the negotiations in July, 1945, that the Soviet withdrawal from Manchuria would begin within three weeks after the capitulation of Japan. Stalin did not wish to include this in the special agreement on Manchuria but assured Soong orally that the evacuation would certainly be completed within three months, perhaps within two.[43] On September 30 it

[41] *United States Relations with China*, p. 587.

[42] "Agreement Regarding Relations between the Chinese Administration and the Commander-in-Chief of the Soviet Forces after the Entry of Soviet Troops into the Three Eastern Provinces of China during the Present Joint Military Operations against Japan"; text in *ibid.*, pp. 592–93.

[43] *China Handbook, 1950*, p. 331. See also T. F. Tsiang's testimony before the First Committee of the Fourth General Assembly in December, 1949; *Summary*

was in fact announced in Moscow that the withdrawal of Soviet troops from Manchuria had already begun and would be completed by the end of November;[44] this was well within the maximum time limit which Stalin had indicated in July. Little is known of Soviet troop movements in Manchuria during the two months following this announcement. Then, on November 30, 1945, a Tass dispatch from Chungking announced that the Soviet Union had agreed to retain troops in Manchuria "for a certain time" at the request of the national government.[45]

Time has tended to obscure rather than clarify the authenticity of this request. Chinese Nationalist sources do not now acknowledge it and suggest that the request for the delay came from Moscow, not Chungking, although Chungking agreed to it.[46] At the time, however, it was reported on good authority that Chungking had asked the Russians to delay their departure, first until early January and later until February 1, 1946, in order to gain more time to prepare for the occupation of Manchuria by loyal troops, and that Moscow had agreed.[47] This has always been the explanation given by the Russians.

There is, of course, some inconsistency in the Russians' acceding to a request which, if we can credit later Soviet accounts, they knew all along was a device on the part of the Chungking government to extend its influence in Manchuria at the expense

---

Records of the First Committee, p. 341. According to T. V. Soong's version of this conversation, reported at the time to Ambassador Harriman, Stalin indicated he would be willing to put the promise in writing; Feis, *The China Tangle,* p. 321. As far as is known this was never done.

[44] *Pravda,* September 30, 1945, p. 4; see also Chiang Kai-shek, *Soviet Russia in China,* p. 142.

[45] *Pravda,* November 30, 1945, p. 4.

[46] E.g., *China Handbook, 1950,* p. 331.

[47] See the summary of an article which appeared in *Ta Kung Pao* at the end of November, 1945, reporting an agreed postponement of the withdrawal date to January 1, 1946; New York *Times,* November 28, 1945, p. 1. The State Department also reported Chungking's request for a delay in the Russians' departure from December 3, 1945, to January 3, 1946, and the Soviet acceptance of this request; New York *Times,* December 2, 1945, p. 35. See also the official communiqué of December 27, 1945, following the Foreign Ministers Conference in Moscow, in which Molotov stated that the Soviet withdrawal had been postponed to February 1, 1946, "at the request of the Chinese government." The February 1 deadline was also referred to by the Chinese Foreign Minister, Wang Shih-chieh, in a statement to the press on March 5, 1946; New York *Times,* March 6, 1946, p. 2.

of the Communists.[48] As a matter of fact, the Russians doubtless welcomed an excuse for prolonging the occupation of Manchuria. If not invited to do so, they would perhaps have extended it on their own initiative, in order to allow the Chinese Communists more time to consolidate their position there and in order to gain more time to complete the stripping of the Manchurian industries. As for facilitating the entry of additional Nationalist troops into Manchuria—the ostensible reason for extending the occupation—the Russians presumably felt confident that they could in one way or another limit the numbers and movements of these troops so that they would cause no serious embarrassment either to themselves or to the Chinese Communists.

The Soviet decision in December, 1945, to keep troops in Manchuria for the time being was doubtless linked to the continued presence of American Marines in North China. Commenting in *Pravda* of December 19 on the use of Manchuria by the Japanese as a base on the continent and referring to the extended border between the Soviet Union and Manchuria, Sokolovskii remarked: "There is a much greater justification for the retention of Soviet troops in Manchuria for a shorter or longer [*tot ili inoi*] period of time than there is for the retention of any foreign troops whatever in North China." It is perhaps significant that Sokolovskii made no reference to any definite deadline for the evacuation, although by this time the January deadline, at least, had presumably been agreed upon.

The Soviet policy of obstructing the entry of Chiang Kai-shek's troops into Manchuria, which amounted to a temporary denial of the entire area to the Chinese government, was not immediately apparent either to Chungking or to Western observers. On August 27, 1945, Stalin had told Harriman in Moscow, in what the American Ambassador apparently took to be good faith, that he expected Chungking to send troops to Manchuria in the near future to relieve the Russians of their occupation responsibilities.[49] These troops were not immediately dis-

[48] See, for instance, V. N. Nikiforov, "Ianvarskoe soglashenie 1946 g. i amerikanskii imperializm" (The January Agreement of 1946 and American Imperialism), *Uchenye zapiski* Tikhookeanskogo instituta, III (1949), 88.

[49] *United States Relations with China,* p. 119.

patched, as a result of lack of transportation facilities and because the national government was more concerned during the first weeks after Japan's surrender with the recovery of North China from the Communists. Early in October, however, the first civil administration team flew from Peiping to Changchun, the Manchurian capital, to establish a provisional Manchurian government. Soviet officials are reported to have been cooperative at the outset of this mission.[50]

Chungking's efforts to land troops in Manchuria at about the same time, however, were completely frustrated. On October 6, in reply to a note from the Chinese Foreign Minister dated October 1 requesting permission to land Chinese troops in Dairen, the Soviet Ambassador in Chungking stated that, inasmuch as Dairen was a "commercial port" under the terms of the Sino-Soviet treaty, it could not be used for the transit of troops of any power.[51] Later in the same month, when it had become apparent that no agreement could be worked out on the Chinese use of Dairen, General Malinovskii, the Russian commander in Manchuria, suggested that the Soviet government would have no objection to landings made elsewhere in Manchuria, for example, at Yingkow or Hulutao. Accordingly, on October 27 the Chinese expedition was transported on American vessels of the Seventh Amphibian Force to Hulutao, which was found to be already in Chinese Communist hands following an abrupt Soviet withdrawal. After a week or so of futile negotiations between the Russians and the Chinese government on the use of Hulutao, the Chinese troops, on November 7, were carried to Yingkow, which was also discovered to be in the hands of the

[50] See Moorad, *Lost Peace in China*, pp. 147–48, and Feis, *The China Tangle*, p. 387. This mission, numbering approximately 750 Chinese officials, was headed by General Hsiung Shih-hui and included Chiang's son, Chiang Ching-kuo.

[51] *Summary Records of the First Committee*, pp. 341–42. The exchanges between the Chinese government and the Soviet Embassy over Dairen, and subsequently over other Manchurian ports where Nationalist troops attempted to land, were not made public at the time. The Russian version of these exchanges, substantially the same as T. F. Tsiang's version, cited above, was given in *Pravda* only on November 30, 1945. The fullest account of the Chinese efforts to land troops in Manchuria during October and early November, 1945, which this writer has seen is in Feis, *The China Tangle*, pp. 383–86; this account is based on the reports of American diplomatic observers in Chungking and Moscow. See also Chiang Kai-shek, *Soviet Russia in China*, pp. 142–43, and Cheng Tien-fong, *History of Sino-Russian Relations*, p. 276.

Chinese Communists, despite Soviet assurances (according to one source) that a five-day "safe landing" period here was to begin on November 5.[52] Since the Communists stated peremptorily that they would resist any efforts to land troops and the Russians refused to render any assistance to Chungking in this matter, on the grounds that their troops had already been withdrawn from the area in accordance with a plan "announced well in advance to the Chinese," [53] the Chinese government had no recourse but to land its troops at Chinwangtao, a port just south of the Manchurian border which had been occupied by American Marines early in October.[54] From here, on about November 11, the Chinese Nationalists began their arduous land campaign to recover Manchuria, four or five weeks behind schedule.

After the Soviet evacuation of Hulutao and Yingkow and the occupation of these ports by the Chinese Communists, the Russians gradually altered their policies concerning the entry of Kuomintang troops into Manchuria. On November 13, it was reported from Chungking that the Russians had agreed to the national government's flying 1,500 troops a day to Changchun.[55] An impasse developed immediately in the execution of this plan, apparently due to the proximity of Chinese Communist troops to the airfield at Changchun, and the scheduled flights did not begin as planned. In fact, on November 16, the government mission at Changchun under Hsiung Shih-hui was ordered to withdraw as the result, it was explained a few days later, of a breakdown in Soviet-Chinese negotiations over Manchuria.[56] The

[52] This information was given to the American Embassy by a Chinese official about November 10; Feis, *The China Tangle,* p. 386. According to T. F. Tsiang, the Soviet Embassy in Chungking had sent notes to the Foreign Office on November 1 and November 3 reporting that a number of Manchurian ports were in the hands of troops "of unknown origin and allegiance"; *Summary Records of the First Committee,* p. 342.

[53] *Pravda,* November 30, 1945, p. 4. This dispatch also noted that the Soviet government, for the same reasons, had been unable to satisfy another Chinese request to assist in the transportation of troops on the Peiping-Mukden Railroad.

[54] This had been the port recommended by American naval commanders as early as October 19, when it seemed unlikely that the Russians would ease their policies. It should be noted that, although these American commanders cooperated fully with Chungking in the matter of ferrying troops to Manchuria, they took no part, as far as is known, in the negotiations between Kuomintang, Chinese Communist, and Russian officials.

[55] New York *Times,* November 14, 1945, p. 1. Cf. Cheng Tien-fong, *History of Sino-Russian Relations,* p. 276.

[56] New York *Times,* November 17, 1945, p. 2, and November 22, 1945, p. 10.

breakdown, however, was a temporary one, for on November 27, a two-point agreement between the Russians and the Chinese, following two weeks of negotiations, was authoritatively reported by a Nationalist source. According to this agreement, the Russians were to order the Chinese Communists out of Changchun and Mukden and the Hsiung mission, withdrawn from Changchun ten days earlier, was to return. The same source indicated that the withdrawal of the Communists from Changchun was already completed and that their withdrawal from Mukden was proceeding rapidly.[57] In the meantime, late in November, Stalin agreed to receive the emissary whom Chiang Kai-shek had for some weeks been trying to send to Moscow, presumably to review with Soviet leaders the entire scope of Sino-Soviet relations in Manchuria.[58]

Outwardly, the Chinese Communists were matching the Russians in their more cooperative attitude toward Manchurian problems at this time. On November 25, for instance, two days before the first reports of the two-point Sino-Soviet agreement on Manchuria, Chinese Communist spokesmen in Chungking were quoted as saying that the Soviet Union was "very friendly" toward Chiang Kai-shek's government and was holding key cities and railway points in Manchuria until the arrival of government troops.[59] On November 28, Chu Teh told several American correspondents in Yenan that the Communists had no objection "in principle" to the movement of Kuomintang troops into Manchuria; the only issue was the transit of these troops, without prior agreement, through areas which had been "liberated" by the Eighth Route Army.[60]

[57] *Ibid.*, November 28, 1945, p. 1.

[58] Feis, *The China Tangle*, p. 388. According to Chiang Kai-shek, it was Stalin who invited a Chinese representative to Moscow and not Chiang who asked that his representative be received. The emissary, Chiang's son, Chiang Ching-kuo, reached Moscow on December 30, 1945, according to *Pravda*, and remained until January 5, 1946. No record of Chiang Ching-kuo's talks with Stalin and other Soviet officials was disclosed at the time, but Chiang Kai-shek now asserts that Stalin's "real purpose" in inviting his son to the Soviet capital was to arrange for a meeting of the two leaders either in Moscow or at some suitable point on the Sino-Soviet frontier. This invitation, Chiang says, was declined; Chiang Kai-shek, *Soviet Russia in China*, pp. 147–48.

[59] New York *Times*, November 26, 1945, p. 2.

[60] Struggle for Peace and Democracy in the Northeast. See also Tillman Durdin's account of this interview in the New York *Times*, December 2, 1945, p. 34.

These milder policies in Moscow and Yenan, respecting the entry of Kuomintang troops into Manchuria, continued into December, 1945. On December 6, for instance, the Kuomintang Army newspaper reported that agreement had been reached on the occupation by Nationalist forces of Dairen and Harbin, supplementing the earlier agreement on Changchun and Mukden.[61] The Nationalists' advance into South Manchuria, in the meantime, had been quickened. In fact, the rapidity of this advance, in contrast to the slow progress made both earlier and later, suggests that Communist resistance had probably been eased by design. By the end of the first week in December, Kuomintang troops, having already occupied Hulutao and most of the important railway junctions in South Manchuria, had reached the outskirts of Mukden. By the middle of the month Chiang's troops were reported advancing northward along the Changchun Railway beyond Mukden. There was also only a mild official demurrer on the part of the Chinese Communists, and none at all by the Russians, when the State Department announced on December 18, 1945, that General Wedemeyer was henceforth authorized to transport Chinese troops on American vessels directly to Manchurian ports—a decision which, if announced one month earlier, would have been the occasion for a torrent of protest in the Communist press. The *Emancipation Daily* in Yenan commented on this decision with studied restraint:

The problem of whether the sending of troops to North China and Manchuria is still necessary and whether American help shall be needed for this purpose should first be submitted to the Political Consultative Conference[62] for discussion. Otherwise the movement would be contravening President Truman's statement [on December 15] that United States support will not extend to United States military intervention to influence the course of Chinese internal strife.[63]

[61] New York *Times,* December 7, 1945, p. 1.

[62] The Political Consultative Conference was proposed during the talks between Chiang Kai-shek and Mao Tse-tung in September, 1945, as a congress of representatives of all parties to prepare for the establishment of a unified, democratic government in China. It opened, after numerous delays, on January 10, 1946.

[63] New York *Times,* December 23, 1945, p. 14. At the time of the State Department announcement on December 18, the only port in Manchuria occupied by Kuomintang forces with adequate facilities to accommodate the proposed ferrying service was Hulutao. Landings were reported there on December 25.

While there was undoubtedly some artifice in allowing Chungking to overextend itself in Manchuria, thereby leaving its troops vulnerable to a Communist attack at some time in the future,[64] the principal consideration in the more moderate policies described above was probably political rather than military. Like the attacks on American "intervention" which were appearing in the Soviet press at this juncture, these milder policies toward Chungking can be linked to the discussions then going on in Washington over the nature of the future American commitment in China. It was not enough simply to cry "intervention." If the United States Marines were to be withdrawn from China, or at least not substantially increased in numbers, the Russians needed to give the impression, as quickly and as forcefully as they could, that Chinese sovereignty in Manchuria was in no way threatened by their own or Chinese Communist activities. This was in all likelihood the reason for the more cooperative attitude toward Chungking displayed in Moscow and in Yenan in late November and in December, 1945.

The Russians continued to question the need for American Marines in China during the Foreign Ministers Conference in Moscow, held from December 14 to December 26, 1948. According to Secretary Byrnes's subsequent account of this conference, Molotov repeatedly questioned him about the motives for stationing the Marines in North China and appeared not to believe the Secretary's assertions that they were there solely to disarm the Japanese and would be withdrawn as soon as this task was completed. Molotov proposed a simultaneous withdrawal of both American and Soviet troops, at some date to be fixed by agreement, but Byrnes rejected this proposal on the grounds that the tasks and responsibilities of the Americans in North China were entirely different from those of the Russians in Manchuria.[65]

The communiqué released at the close of the conference included no definite commitment on the part of the United States

[64] General Wedemeyer had repeatedly warned Chungking of this danger and had urged, first of all, a consolidation of Nationalist strength below the Great Wall before it attempted to recover Manchuria; see the summary of Wedemeyer's reports to Washington on November 14 and November 20, 1945, in *United States Relations with China,* pp. 131–32.

[65] James F. Byrnes, *Speaking Frankly* (New York, 1947), pp. 226–27.

to withdraw its troops by any given date, although Molotov and Byrnes stated that they were "in complete accord as to the desirability of the withdrawal of Soviet and American forces in China at the earliest practicable moment consistent with the discharge of their obligations and responsibilities." [66] Molotov indicated independently, it has been noted, that the Soviet evacuation would be completed by February 1, 1946.

By the end of 1945 it must have seemed clear to most intelligent observers in China, even to those who had previously argued that the Chinese Communists were free of Soviet control, that for allegedly independent "agrarian reformers" the Communists were displaying a surprising deference to Russian policies in Manchuria. There is, of course, little direct evidence of ties between the Russians and the Chinese Communists during the autumn of 1945, and what evidence there is cannot easily be verified.[67] The Russians understandably made no reference in their public statements to the activities of the Communists in Manchuria, and spokesmen from Yenan, on the few occasions when they allowed themselves to be drawn into a discussion of Soviet-Communist relations, denied that Yenan's policies were in any way influenced by Moscow.[68] Stalin, in the meantime, is reported

[66] *Ibid.*, p. 228.

[67] The Chinese Nationalists have been the most insistent in claims of Soviet aid to Chinese Communists in Manchuria after the war. Following the final breakdown in negotiations with the Communists early in 1947, they periodically exhibited arms and other materials captured from the Communists which allegedly proved their charges; see *Summary Records of the First Committee,* pp. 340 ff. Eyewitness accounts of the Soviet occupation by non-Chinese observers are very scarce prior to the visit of a team of correspondents to Mukden and Changchun early in 1946 and reveal almost nothing of Soviet-Chinese Communist relations; see, for instance, the report of a French consul, recently returned from Mukden, in the *Christian Science Monitor* (Boston), October 12, 1945, p. 7, and the report by Stephan Andrews in the New York *Times,* November 27, 1945, p. 2. A team of American observers from the Office of Strategic Services which had flown to Mukden shortly after the end of the war was apparently requested by Soviet authorities to leave on October 5; New York *Times,* March 9, 1946, p. 2. According to American military observers in Chungking and Yenan, there were reports of a regular liaison between the Russians and the Chinese Communists by November, 1945. It was also reported that Soviet representatives flew to Yenan, either at this time or later, to discuss with Chinese Communist leaders the coordination of Russian and Chinese Communist military operations in Manchuria. Many of these reports, however, were acknowledged to be based on rumor; see Feis, *The China Tangle,* pp. 377–78.

[68] Chu Teh is reported to have told American correspondents in Yenan at the end of November that the Chinese Communists had no contact whatever with

to have made somewhat disparaging remarks about the Chinese Communists in a conversation with Byrnes during the Foreign Ministers Conference in December.[69]

If direct evidence of Soviet-Chinese Communist ties in the autumn of 1945 is lacking, indirect evidence of a cordial and even intimate relationship between Moscow and Yenan is impressive. In the first place, Eighth Route Army forces, despite Yenan's assertions to the contrary, were known to have been in Manchuria, in something other than a "civilian" capacity, from early September on. While they may, of course, have originally entered Manchuria from the south ahead of the Russians, they could not have remained there, especially in the key positions they occupied, without the Russians' express approval. In Changchun the Communists were reported on good authority to have taken over the civil administration of the city by early November, while the Russians were still in occupation, and to have held it until the two-point agreement was signed between the Russian and Chinese governments on November 27, 1945.[70] It is, moreover, suggestive of the influence the Russians had over the Communists that in accordance with the November 27 agreement—in which Yenan took no part—Eighth Route Army forces promptly withdrew from Changchun and other designated areas early in December, presumably on Russian orders. The Communists apparently did not reenter the Manchurian capital until they had wrested it from the small Nationalist garrison left there when the Russians evacuated the city in April, 1946.

Above all, the Russians' denial of South Manchuria to Nationalist forces in October and early November, in direct viola-

---

the Russians, either in Yenan or in Manchuria; Smedley, *The Great Road,* p. 433. See also, the view on this subject expressed by Wang Ping-nan to the American Embassy in Chungking early in December, 1945; *United States Relations with China,* p. 111.

[69] Byrnes reports that Stalin laughed when he was told of Mao's claim of a Communist force of 600,000 in the Tientsin area. He subsequently asserted—to use Byrnes's phrasing—"that all Chinese were boasters who exaggerated the forces of their opponents as well as their own"; James F. Byrnes, *Speaking Frankly,* p. 228.

[70] See Moorad, *Lost Peace in China,* pp. 147–48, and Feis, *The China Tangle,* p. 387.

tion of the Sino-Soviet pact of August, 1945, seems, in retrospect, to be the clearest indication that coordination between Moscow and Yenan was neither casual nor completely unplanned. Whatever the origin of the Russians' decision in this matter—whether it was part of their early postwar strategy in Manchuria or resulted from negotiations with the Communists—Yenan gained an incalculable advantage from their action. It can be argued that the entire course of events in Manchuria from this time on was determined by the opportunity the Communists had gained during these four or five weeks to consolidate their position in Manchuria under Russian protection. It is also safe to say that a month or two earlier only the most pessimistic observers in Washington, and perhaps also in Chungking, would have predicted this behavior on the part of the Russians.

Although the Russians probably had no precise plan for Manchuria at the time of the Japanese collapse, by the end of October they could look forward with some confidence to a friendly regime which would be firmly entrenched there by the time of their evacuation (which until mid-November was apparently still scheduled for completion by December 1, 1945). Toward the end of November, however, these calculations were upset by the possibility that a major policy change in Washington would greatly extend the American commitment in North China and would perhaps enable Chungking to carry out the occupation of Manchuria despite Moscow's steps to forestall it. This would have been a serious, perhaps an irreparable, setback for the Chinese Communists. It would also have been a blow to Soviet security objectives in the Far East. Accordingly, it may be argued, the Russians managed to prolong their occupation, conveniently using as a pretext Chungking's request for a delay in the Soviet withdrawal. At the same time Moscow affected a more cooperative attitude toward Chungking and, it would appear, advised the Chinese Communists to do likewise. These policies would allow Moscow and Yenan to temporize until the nature of the new American commitment in China could be appraised, perhaps during the forthcoming Conference of Foreign Ministers in Moscow.

TOYING WITH UNITY IN CHINA AFTER THE WAR AUGUST, 1945–DECEMBER, 1945

While the Russians were consolidating their position in Manchuria and assisting the Chinese Communists to reinforce theirs, negotiations for a more viable settlement between the Kuomintang and the Communists were proceeding in Chungking. A satisfactory outcome of these negotiations, Moscow may well have reasoned in the early autumn of 1945, might affect the future position of the Communists in China more profoundly than could the military operations which were then going on in Manchuria and North China. If, as a result of these military operations, the Communists gained control of North China and Manchuria, they would have a rich and protected base in which to develop their strength, but they might still be confined to this northern section of China by a joint American-Kuomintang effort. If, on the other hand, as the result of the parleys in Chungking, the Communists succeeded in entering a coalition government with the Kuomintang on terms acceptable to them, there was a prospect of their eventually winning control over all of China by boring from within. In the months following the war, neither the Russians nor the Chinese Communists ignored this larger prospect, although the greater emphasis they seem to have placed on immediate objectives in Manchuria often cut across their efforts to achieve long-range objectives within China proper.

During the closing months of the war, as we have seen, there was no fundamental difference in the public pronouncements of the Russians and the Chinese Communists on the questions of unity and coalition government in China. The capitulation of Japan in August, 1945, did not change the official support for these objectives in Moscow and Yenan. On September 1, for instance, an editorial in *Novoe vremia* read:

It is no secret that the progressive development of China up to now has been hindered in no small degree by discord between the Kuomintang and the Chinese Communist Party. Abroad there are many dubious well-wishers who from time to time shout loudly of the inevitability of civil war in China. There can be no doubt that such a war would be a catastrophe for the country, which now more than ever needs peace and order to liquidate the devastating results of long Japanese occupation. Any real friend of China awaits the strengthening of cooperation between all progressive and democratic forces among the Chinese people, which through their continued efforts are alone able to guarantee national unity.[71]

The Chinese Communists, it has been noted, had adopted a very belligerent attitude toward Chungking in the middle of August, over the issue of disarming Japanese troops in North China, but by the end of the month they were matching the Russians in their publicly expressed support of Chinese unity. A statement by the Central Committee dated August 25, 1945, proclaimed the Communists' "willingness to reach an agreement with the Kuomintang and other democratic parties and groups in order to solve various urgent problems that have arisen, to establish lasting solidarity and unity, and to fulfill the Three Peoples' Principles of Sun Yat-sen." [72] Three days later, following repeated invitations from Chiang Kai-shek, Mao left for six week of negotiations in Chungking escorted by Ambassador Hurley.[73] Mao's departure was accompanied by an immediate softening in the tone of the Yenan press toward the Chungking government.[74]

The new round of negotiations between the Communists and the Kuomintang opened more auspiciously than had previous ones.[75] It was probably the first time Mao had negotiated directly

[71] "Sovetskii Soiuz i Kitai" (The Soviet Union and China), *Novoe vremia,* No. 7 (17), September 1, 1945, pp. 1–2.

[72] "Deklaratsiia TsK Kitaiskoi kommunisticheskoi partii" (Declaration of the CC of the Chinese Communist Party), *Pravda,* August 31, 1945, p. 4.

[73] Hurley had flown to Yenan a day or two earlier expressly to bring Mao to Chungking. Michael Lindsay, who was still in Yenan at this time, states that Mao's visit took place only after long discussion among the Chinese Communist leaders. He claims some responsibility for persuading Mao to make this visit for its effect on world opinion; see his chapter in Taylor Cole and John N. Hallowell, eds., *Post-War Governments of the Far East,* (Gainsville, Fla., 1947), pp. 543–64.

[74] See New York *Times,* August 29, 1945, p. 7.

[75] While negotiations between Chinese Communist and Kuomintang representatives had been more or less continuous since the autumn of 1943, it is possible to distinguish three previous rounds of high-level talks prior to the Mao-Chiang meetings in September, 1945. All of these occurred during the period of Hurley's mission to China, first as Special Representative of the President and later as

with Kuomintang representatives outside of Yenan, and it appears to have been his first formal encounter with Chiang Kai-shek, although it is likely that they had met informally during the Kuomintang-Communist alliance of 1926–27.[76] He appears to have been cordially received in Chungking by government officials. He dined and had several private conferences with Chiang during the first days of his visit.

Although the meetings in Chungking were held in secrecy, much of the press, both local and foreign, commented favorably and hopefully on the probable outcome of the negotiations. In Moscow, the army paper *Krasnaia zvezda* called the "collaboration of the two main parties in China" the prerequisite for peace.[77] A Tass dispatch from Khabarovsk stated that the Soviet Union "is watching the negotiations between Chiang Kai-shek and Mao Tse-tung with interest and concern. . . . It is imperative that China take the road to unity without delay." [78] On September 22, Mao held a press conference in which, in prepared replies to questions put to him several days earlier, he expressed his confidence that the negotiations would lead to a satisfactory agreement.[79] On September 28, the Moscow radio announced that "unity in China has been established" and that the negotiations had led to the achievement of a "complete central unified government." [80] The fact that this announcement was both premature and inaccurate—Nationalist sources denied the following day that any such agreement had been reached [81]—is perhaps less significant than the fact that it was made. It seems clearly to indicate Moscow's officially hopeful attitude toward the talks at this stage.[82]

Ambassador. The first high-level talks were held in November and early December, 1944; the second in late January and early February, 1945; the third—and least satisfactory—during the early part of the summer of 1945, before the Sino-Soviet pact had been concluded.

[76] As noted earlier, reports that Mao visited Nanking in August, 1937, have never, so far as this writer is aware, been verified. Chiang Kai-shek, in his recent book, makes no reference to a previous meeting with Mao.

[77] New York *Times*, September 1, 1945, p. 4.

[78] *Ibid.*, September 1, 1945, p. 4.

[79] *Ibid.*, September 23, 1945, p. 7.

[80] *Ibid.*, September 29, p. 4.

[81] *Ibid.*, September 30, p. 32.

[82] The Communist press in the United States was considerably less optimistic than Moscow concerning the course of the negotiations in Chungking; see, for instance, the editorial in *New Masses*, September 18, 1945, pp. 16–17.

The official communiqué, issued on October 11 to sum up the six weeks of conversations between the Communists and the Nationalists, dealt chiefly in generalities.[83] It was agreed that "peace, democracy, solidarity and unity should form the basis of the nation's concerted efforts"; that the normal civil liberties should be guaranteed and that all political parties should be legalized; that agencies other than the police and the courts should be prohibited from making arrests and imposing punishment and that political prisoners should be released; and that constitutional government should be inaugurated. There was also agreement on several of the preliminary steps to be taken to achieve this end, the most important of which was the early convocation of a Political Consultation (later called Consultative) Conference with representatives of all parties and of non-partisan groups. In addition, there was a semblance of agreement on the troublesome issue of the reorganization of the armed forces: the Communists agreed, in the later stages of the negotiations, to reduce their forces to twenty divisions (their earlier request had been for forty-eight), or approximately one fifth of the proposed peacetime Chinese army. On the question of local government in the Communist-held areas there was little accord. The Communists sought to have their "popularly elected" officials reappointed by Chungking. Chiang, however, refused to do this until Chungking's authority had first been established within these areas. It was finally agreed that outstanding differences would be presented to the forthcoming Political Consultation Conference.

This communiqué was a great deal more optimistic concerning the chances for peace in China than the political situation warranted. In the first place, by October 11 Kuomintang-Communist relations in North China and Manchuria had so far deteriorated that any serious thought of implementing the Chiang-Mao agreements was out of the question. But the agreements themselves were illusory. In stressing the points on which there had been a limited accord, the communiqué obscured the almost complete impasse on the one crucial issue of the day—the question of au-

[83] The text of this statement is in *United States Relations with China,* pp. 577–81.

thority in the areas under Communist control.[84] That a joint statement was made at all under these circumstances was, perhaps, because neither side wished to appear uncooperative in finding a peaceful solution to the crisis. Perhaps, too, the communiqué was a gesture of courtesy to Ambassador Hurley, who had been instrumental in arranging the talks and who retained to the end a conviction that a significant agreement could eventually be reached.[85]

The Soviet press—rather surprisingly in view of its earlier interest in the Chungking negotiations—made no mention of the October 11 communiqué. In fact, for several months after these talks ended Moscow gave little further attention to the question of unity in China.[86] Perhaps this was because the Soviet leaders felt that their position had been made sufficiently clear in past statements and that since no change had occurred in their attitude, it was unnecessary to continue issuing appeals. They would have noted, too, that the cause of Chinese unity was being eloquently defended at this time in most of the world press without prompting from Moscow and thus may have felt that their objectives would best be served by silence. It should be mentioned in this connection, however, that the Russians were also silent on other developments in China during these months and, in particular, took no cognizance of the civil conflict which was spreading throughout North China and southern Manchuria. Had the Soviet press played up the spread of civil war in China with-

[84] It should be noted that this remained the outstanding issue during the entire course of negotiations between the Communists and the Kuomintang in 1945 and 1946, although, had this issue been resolved, another would doubtless have emerged.

[85] Hurley departed for the United States, after several delays, before the talks had been concluded and did not return. Shortly before he left Chungking he gave another of his characteristically optimistic reports to the State Department on the prospects of accord in China: "The spirit between the negotiators is good. The rapprochement between the two leading parties of China seems to be progressing and the discussion and rumors of civil war recede as the conference continues." The full text of this report is in *United States Relations with China,* pp. 105–7.

[86] An occasional article did touch on this problem, but without the sense of urgency characteristic of articles and editorials appearing in the Soviet press immediately after the war; e.g., V. Maslennikov, "Kitai na poroge novoi zhizni" (China on the Threshold of a New Life), *Mirovoe khoziaistvo i mirovaia politika,* No. 10, October, 1945, pp. 1–12. This article gave no details of the negotiations in Chungking.

out expressing due concern, this might be construed as clear evidence that the Russians were shifting from their previously announced policy of seeking a rapprochement between the Communists and the Kuomintang.

At the same time, however, it should not be imagined that a rapprochement or a coalition government in China was as important to Soviet policy by mid-autumn as it had previously been. Until Soviet objectives in Manchuria had been achieved, the Russians, it has been suggested, required a more stable political situation in China than had existed there during the later months of the war. They had therefore supported the truce talks between the Communists and the Kuomintang in September. But as the Russians made good their gains with surprising ease, the question of unity in China became less urgent for them. Henceforth, the conflict in China concerned Moscow not so much as it might affect purely Russian objectives but rather as it affected the fortunes of the Chinese Communists. Had the Chinese Communists been in danger of defeat in October, 1945, the Russians would probably have continued to press for a cessation of the civil war and for a coalition government. Since there was no such danger, at least for the present, and since the negotiations in Chungking showed so little basis of agreement between the Communists and the Kuomintang, the Russians appear to have been satisfied with alternative policies in China, both for themselves and for the Chinese Communists, which were not founded on the presumption of unity and coalition.

If this was the trend of Moscow's reasoning during October and early November, 1945, we must look for some revision of these views by early December when a possible increase in the United States' commitment in China was causing the Russians some concern. There is evidence of such revision, not in Moscow but in Yenan, at the end of November and in December, 1945. On November 29, as we have seen, Chu Teh was adopting a more friendly attitude toward the Chungking government than he had expressed in several months.[87] Several days later Liu Shao-chi told foreign correspondents in Yenan that even if the

[87] New York *Times,* December 2, 1945, p. 34; dispatch by Tillman Durdin.

current talks between the Communists and the Kuomintang should fail, the Communists would not attempt to set up a rival government in China.[88] In Chungking on December 3, the Communist representative Wang Ping-nan told officials at the American Embassy that the Communists now had decided definitely to take part in the forthcoming Political Consultative Conference, scheduled to meet early in January, 1946.[89]

President Truman's policy statement of December 15 on China gave the Chinese Communists a further opportunity to express their more conciliatory attitude with respect to the internal crisis in China. The Yenan press, quite naturally, applauded in particular that portion of Truman's statement which recommended that the "one-party government [in Chungking] . . . be broadened to include other political elements in the country," but the statement as a whole received favorable comment. It was said to be "an indication that Hurley's corrupt policy of giving armed support to the Kuomintang in a civil war with the Communists has become a thing of the past." [90] General Marshall, in the meantime, was warmly greeted by the Communists when he arrived in China several days after Truman's statement. Chou En-lai took this occasion to propose a general cease-fire during the approaching sessions of the Political Consultative Conference.[91]

While the Russians continued to remain silent on the subject of a rapprochement in China during late November and early December and while they did not, like the Chinese Communists, attempt to display a more conciliatory attitude by expressing confidence in American nonintervention,[92] it is likely that Moscow fully approved of Yenan's steps in this direction. A peaceful resolution of the civil crisis in China, or at least a show

[88] *Ibid.*, December 5, 1945, p. 5.

[89] *United States Relations with China*, p. 11.

[90] New York *Times*, December 18, 1945, p. 2.

[91] *Ibid.*, December 21, 1945, p. 1. Marshall arrived by air in Shanghai on December 20, proceeded to Nanking on the following day where he was welcomed by Chiang Kai-shek, and on December 22 flew to Chungking where he was met at the airport by T. V. Soong and Chou En-lai.

[92] It has been noted that Russian opinion, as indicated, for instance, in an editorial in *Pravda* on December 1, 1945, concerning Hurley's resignation and in Sokolovskii's article in *Pravda* on December 19, remained officially suspicious of American motives in China for some weeks after the line had changed with respect to Chungking.

of sympathy toward negotiations seeking this end, was a logical adjunct of the current Russian strategy, aimed at discouraging any enlargement of the American commitment in China by demonstrating that the situation did not warrant it. The Russians, at that time, were displaying their own brand of conciliation by acceding to the request—real or alleged—to remain longer in Manchuria.

During the Foreign Ministers Conference in Moscow, Stalin showed that he was not entirely indifferent to a rapprochement in China, although his remarks, of course, need not be taken as an indication that Soviet policy depended upon this rapprochement. He told Secretary Byrnes, as he had told other American representatives before, that the Soviet Union recognized Chiang's government, in accordance with the terms of the Sino-Soviet treaty of August, 1945. He also asserted his confidence in Marshall's ability to resolve the crisis in China, if anyone could do this. According to Byrnes, the most significant result of his conversation with Stalin, which occurred toward the end of the conference, was the Soviet approval of a statement included in the final communiqué to the effect that the three Foreign Ministers "were in agreement as to the need for a unified and democratic China under the National Government, for broad participation by democratic elements in all branches of the National Government and for a cessation of civil strife." [93]

At the end of 1945, the Kremlin appears to have been marking time in so far as its attitude toward peace and coalition in China was concerned. The support which the Russians might give to the resolution of the civil crisis in China, through their influence on the Communists, was being weighed in the light of American policies in China. If the Marshall Mission proved to be a genuine effort, in Moscow's view, to bring the Communists into a broadly based coalition government, then Moscow might still give this effort its support. If, however, Marshall, like his predecessors, failed even to find the basis for agreement between the Communists and the Kuomintang, the Russians doubtless were prepared wholly to dissociate themselves from his endeavors and

[93] See James F. Byrnes, *Speaking Frankly*, p. 228.

perhaps to charge him with intervening in China as an "agent of American imperialists." In the meantime, the Russians would keep the size of the U.S. Marine forces in China under careful scrutiny to determine whether they posed a serious threat to the military position of the Communists in North China and Manchuria or to the permanent Soviet installations then being established at Port Arthur and—as it later developed—Dairen. Should this occur, the Russians probably reasoned, they would be compelled to devise far more forthright and ambitious policies than had until this time been necessary—perhaps even including direct intervention in the civil conflict on behalf of the Chinese Communists.

THE RUSSIANS IN MANCHURIA: PHASE TWO JANUARY, 1946–MAY, 1946

The Russian withdrawal from Manchuria was not completed by February 1, 1946, as Molotov had indicated it would be during the Foreign Ministers Conference in Moscow. In fact, the deadline passed without there being any indication that the evacuation had even begun.[94] Throughout February there were persistent reports that the Soviet garrisons in Manchuria were actually being strengthened in anticipation of a long occupation.[95]

Chungking took no official cognizance of these reports and government spokesmen continued, during the first part of Febru-

[94] Toward the end of January Madame Chiang Kai-shek, presumably in an effort to hasten the evacuation, flew to Changchun to express the government's gratitude to the Russians, on the eve of their departure, for their "liberation" of Manchuria. She distributed candy to the troops and dined with Red Army generals, reportedly in an atmosphere of cordiality, but to no avail. See *Pravda*, January 25, 1946, p. 6. and New York *Times*, January 26, 1946, p. 7.

[95] On February 17, 1946, for instance, the New York *Times* carried a report from unidentified Chinese sources that telephone lines between Mukden and Changchun, which had been dismantled prior to the February 1 deadline, were being restored. The same source revealed that the Russians in Mukden were again claiming the right, which they had given up on January 15 when the first Kuomintang troops entered the city, to arrest Chinese soldiers who disobeyed local ordinances issued by the Occupation authorities. On February 24, H. R. Lieberman reported from Mukden that new Soviet troops were arriving in that city, not as replacements but allegedly as permanent additions to the garrison already located there. He reported also that, according to Chinese sources, Russian officers were sending for their families; New York *Times*, February 28, 1946, p. 13. Similar reports, all unconfirmed, may be found in New York *Times*, February 25, p. 9; February 27, p. 16; and March 5, p. 15.

ary, to parry questions by foreign correspondents concerning Soviet intentions in Manchuria. On February 18, however, the Chungking press, in what appears to have been a concerted effort, sharply attacked Russian policies in Manchuria and demanded the immediate withdrawal of Soviet troops. These demands were accompanied by widespread anti-Soviet and anti-Communist demonstrations throughout China.[96] On February 24, seven government officials, all members of the Control Yuan, joined in a protest to the Chinese Foreign Office against the Yalta agreement (the text of which had been released a fortnight earlier) and against the continued presence of the Russians in Manchuria, which allegedly was the result of that agreement.[97] This was the first public complaint against the Russians by responsible members of the Chungking government.

Moscow's response to this mounting anti-Soviet sentiment in Chungking and elsewhere in China was not long in coming. On February 24, a Tass dispatch from Manchuria, evidently seeking to justify the continued presence of Russian troops there, claimed that anti-Russian activity by former Japanese puppets had been continuing since October, 1945, and added that these puppets were "led and supported by reactionary elements in China proper." [98] On February 26, General Trotsenko, the Soviet Chief of Staff in Changchun, reminded Chinese newsmen that the Chungking government had twice requested a delay in the departure of Soviet troops from Manchuria in order to allow Nationalist troops more time to take up positions at strategic points; Trotsenko indicated that the persistent delay in the arrival of these troops was a factor in the continued presence of the Russians. A second factor, he said, was the inadequacy of Manchuria's railway system for a winter evacuation. The Soviet evacuation had nonetheless been resumed on schedule, on January 15, and the "greatest part" of the occupation forces had already left. The evacuation would be completed, the Soviet

[96] The largest of these demonstrations, in which 10,000 students were said to have taken part, was held in Chungking, on February 22, 1946. On this occasion the offices of the Communist daily in Chungking were damaged and one of the editors was wounded; see the account in New York *Times*, February 23, 1946, p. 4.

[97] *Ibid.*, February 24, 1946, p. 1.

[98] *Pravda*, February 24, 1946, p. 4.

Chief of Staff asserted, before the date of the evacuation of American forces from North China, "or, at any rate, not later than that." [99]

Although Trotsenko's final remark seemed to indicate Moscow's intention to make the Soviet withdrawal contingent on that of the American forces—which had not, at this time, been announced—the Russians gave signs early in March that their departure from Manchuria was imminent and would not depend on the withdrawal of the Marines from North China. After March 1 the Soviet Ambassador to China, Appolon Petrov, began to discuss Manchurian problems directly with government officials in Chungking. Previously these discussions, at the Russians' insistence, had been carried on at Changchun, a device which had handicapped the Chinese and which many observers considered to be an indication that the Russians had not been seriously interested in reducing tension in Manchuria.[100]

On March 8, the Russians abruptly began their withdrawal from Mukden, apparently without advance notice to Chungking, and completed it one week later.[101] No further withdrawals from major cities were reported at this time, but on March 23 Moscow announced that Soviet troops would be evacuated from all of Manchuria (except Port Arthur and Dairen) by the end of April.[102] On March 31, there was an editorial note in

[99] The Soviet and Chinese accounts of Trotsenko's press interview are substantially the same; see New York *Times*, February 27, 1946, p. 16, for the Moscow radio broadcast summarizing Trotsenko's remarks and New York *Times*, February 28, 1946, p. 13, for the Chungking version. On March 5, the Chinese Foreign Minister, Wang Shih-chieh, also said that the delay in the evacuation of Soviet troops from Manchuria had been caused in part by "technical difficulties"; *ibid.*, March 6, 1946, p. 2.

[100] According to Tillman Durdin, writing in the New York *Times* on April 8, 1946, the conduct of these discussions in Chungking after the first of March was at the insistence of the Chinese government and was not a voluntary move on Moscow's part. If this was so, the Russians at least showed their willingness to meet Chungking's desires in this matter.

[101] While there were already some Nationalist troops in Mukden when the Russians withdrew, a tense situation developed as Communist forces outside the city began to move into the outskirts on March 9 and 10. The government forces appear to have gained control, however, within a few days.

[102] *Pravda*, March 24, 1946, p. 4. In a statement on March 22, Wang Shih-chieh noted that the Soviet pledge to complete the withdrawal from Manchuria by the end of April "at the latest" was made in response to his note to the Soviet government on March 6 requesting information concerning its evacuation plans; New York *Times*, March 24, 1946, p. 1.

Pravda which referred to the April 30 deadline as a firm commitment.[103]

During April the Russian withdrawal from Manchuria proceeded in orderly fashion and with due notice of the withdrawal schedule provided to Chinese officials. On April 3, Trotsenko informed the Chinese in Changchun of the forthcoming evacuation of that city and declined an alleged request from the Chinese to leave small garrisons behind until the arrival of government troops. The reason given for the refusal was that this would have delayed the April 30 deadline to which the Russians were committed.[104] On April 7, Moscow made public the withdrawal schedule for the entire month: Changchun by April 14–15, Kirin by April 18, Harbin by April 24, and so forth.[105]

The Russians appear to have adhered closely to this schedule, although following the evacution of Changchun on April 14 little is known of Soviet or Chinese Communist troop movements since neither Nationalist nor foreign observers were present in North Manchuria.[106] The Communists were reported to be in control of Changchun by April 19, after overcoming the small garrison there,[107] and with the nearest Kuomintang army held up by Eighth Route Army troops 60 to 70 miles to the south, the entire area north of the Manchurian capital fell to the Com-

[103] "Mezhdunarodnoe obozrenie" (International Survey), *Pravda,* March 31, 1946, p. 4.

[104] *Pravda,* April 6, 1946, p. 4.

[105] New York *Times,* April 8, 1946, p. 4.

[106] During the first five or six months of the Russian occupation virtually no foreign observers—excluding Chungking officials attached to government units in Changchun, Mukden, and elsewhere—had been allowed by the Soviet authorities to visit the Russian-occupied areas of Manchuria. International attention was focused on this situation at the end of 1945 when press correspondents attached to the Nationalist forces in South Manchuria quoted a Chinese press relations officer as saying that the reason correspondents were not allowed further into Manchuria was because "the Russians regard you as enemies." *Pravda* carried an official denial of this report on January 13, 1946, and early in February a group of foreign correspondents was given permission to fly to Mukden and Changchun. Several of these correspondents were turned back from Dairen, however, on February 27; see New York *Times,* March 4, 1946, p. 8. At the time of the Russian evacuation of Changchun on April 14, five American correspondents and two military observers were there, but no foreigners, up to this time, had traveled north of Changchun.

[107] According to H. R. Lieberman's delayed dispatch from Changchun, Communist forces numbered about 50,000 and Nationalist troops about 3,000; New York *Times,* April 30, 1946, p. 10.

munists without a struggle. When the Russian evacuation was completed, reportedly on May 3, the Chungking government controlled only Mukden and sections of the Peiping-Mukden and Mukden-Changchun railways in South Manchuria.[108]

This is the bare record of the Russians' withdrawal from Manchuria, concluding an occupation which in less than eight months had done considerably more to alter the economic and political outlook for China than had fourteen years of Japanese occupation. Students of Soviet Far Eastern policy do not, as a rule, agree on the reasons why the Russians extended their occupation several months beyond the date Molotov had indicated during the Moscow Conference of Foreign Ministers in December, 1945, and why they terminated it precisely when they did. The answers to these questions seem to be directly related to Soviet political and economic objectives in China after the war, but which of these often conflicting objectives had priority in Moscow at any given stage is very difficult to determine. At this juncture we need to consider these objectives in greater detail in order to understand the Russians' behavior during the last phase of their occupation of Chinese territory.

As far as the Russians' attitude toward the Chinese Communists is concerned, there is no indication that this was significantly altered during the final months of the Soviet occupation of Manchuria. To be sure, there is no better evidence of direct Soviet assistance to the Communists during the second stage of the Russian occupation than during the first,[109] and both Russians and Chinese Communists continued to deny that a close tie

[108] Malinovskii's announcement of the completed evacuation of Manchuria, as of May 3, was not made until May 21; *Pravda,* May 22, 1946, p. 4. Informal notice of the completion of the evacuation was reportedly given to a Chinese official in Vladivostok five days earlier; New York *Times,* May 17, 1946, p. 3.

[109] The most persistent reports, at the time and subsequently, concerned the Russians' turning over to the Chinese Communists large quantities of Japanese arms, which had been surrendered to them the previous autumn, as well as considerable amounts of Russian equipment; see *Summary Records of the First Committee,* pp. 340–41, and Cheng Tien-fong, *History of Sino-Russian Relations,* pp. 274–75. While there is little reason to doubt that such transfers took place, there is also no certain proof of it known to this writer. In March, 1946, the Chinese Communists stated that all Japanese arms and ammunition they had acquired in Manchuria had come from areas which they themselves had overrun and which had not been occupied by Russian forces; see the dispatch from Shanghai by

existed between them.[110] But the indirect benefits to the Communists from the Russians' behavior cannot be doubted. In denying all of Manchuria north of Mukden to the Kuomintang (except Changchun where a closely circumscribed garrison was permitted to vegetate), the Russians gave the Communists an incalculable advantage in any future struggle with the national government. When the Soviet forces quit Manchuria, they left behind them a Communist regime that was solidly entrenched there, far more so than it had been at the time of their first scheduled departure in December, 1945. The desire to achieve this objective was probably an important consideration in the decision to prolong the occupation of Manchuria beyond the February deadline. By the same logic, the achievement of the objective by early March—as it later became apparent—was doubtless a factor in the Russians' decision to withdraw.

A. T. Steele in New York *Herald Tribune,* March 15, 1946, p. 11. George Moorad reports that a Nationalist general told him in March, 1946, of three different encounters between Nationalist and Communist forces in South Manchuria in February in which Russian instructors and Russian artillery had been used. After one of these engagements, near Yingkow, Russian corpses had allegedly been found on the battlefield. Pictures of the corpses as well as pieces of Russian equipment, according to Moorad's informant, had been sent to Chungking as evidence of direct Soviet intervention in China's civil conflict. Moorad, who appears to accept this testimony, writes: "The National government did a poor job of presenting these cases and Soviet propagandists have done a spectacular job of obscuring it"; Moorad, *Lost Peace in China,* p. 179.

[110] The most vigorous Russian denial of ties with the Chinese Communists appeared in the column by *Pravda*'s "Observer" on March 31, 1946. The denial was occasioned by the publication in a Chinese newspaper of an alleged secret agreement between Moscow and Yenan which provided, *inter alia,* for Russia's maintaining a permanent force in Manchuria and for joint Russian-Chinese Communist operation of the Chinese Eastern Railway. The "Observer" wrote that these claims were "laughable" and would be ignored except for the unmistakable intent to damage Sino-Soviet relations which they revealed in certain Chinese circles. Chou En-lai, in the meantime, made repeated denials, as he had previously, of any intimate political association between the Russian and the Chinese Communists; e.g., New York *Times,* February 2, 1946, p. 3, February 18, 1946, p. 3, and May 5, 1945, p. 32. It should be noted here that the Chinese Communists have never, as far as is known, officially acknowledged Russian assistance following the war, except in a moral and ideological sense. The statement by Mao which is generally quoted by Chinese Communists as "evidence" of the ideological, as distinct from material, debt owed the Russians occurs in his article "On the People's Democratic Dictatorship" (July 1, 1949). Writing of the indispensable "weapons" which the Russians had provided the Chinese Communists, Mao observed: "These weapons are not machine-guns, but Marxism-Leninism"; text in Brandt, etc., *Documentary History,* p. 450.

It should be noted in this connection that, as the prospects for a reconciliation between Chungking and Yenan faded, the Russians' stake in the Chinese Communists' success grew larger. They became a more vital link in Russia's chain of security in the Far East, not simply as a moderating influence in Chungking, with perhaps the chance of eventually controlling all China, but as an independent military and political force in Manchuria. They could serve the Russians best, Moscow may have felt, by creating a buffer zone between Russia proper and the portions of China still controlled by Chiang's government, which, under American influence, could be counted upon to display its latent anti-Soviet sentiments as soon as the Russian evacuation was completed. During the winter of 1946, therefore, as negotiations between the Communists and the Kuomintang became less and less promising, the Russians were perhaps more willing than at the end of 1945 to risk criticism in Chungking and elsewhere in order to settle the Communists more firmly in control of northern Manchuria.

This, it may be imagined, was the essence of Moscow's political objective in Manchuria—leaving aside the establishment of Soviet control over Port Arthur and Dairen, which, thanks to the Yalta agreement and the subsequent Sino-Soviet pact, seems never to have been in the slightest doubt.[111]

The Russians appear, at the same time, to have had two distinct economic objectives in Manchuria, neither bearing any obvious relationship to the political objective indicated above. These were, first, the systematic stripping of key Manchurian in-

[111] It was not anticipated either in Chungking or in Washington that Dairen would be subject to the control of the Russians' Port Arthur naval administration after the defeat of Japan. The Yalta agreement had said on this point only that Dairen should be internationalized and that Russia's "preeminent interests" there should be safeguarded. The "Agreement Concerning Dairen" which accompanied the Sino-Soviet pact of August 14, 1945, specifically stated that Dairen would be under Chinese administration and "shall be subject to the military supervision or control established [in Port Arthur] only in case of war with Japan." In 1947, the United States twice protested to the Soviet government on the failure to open Dairen to the commercial vessels of other nations. Moscow replied that inasmuch as the war with Japan had not ended, in the absence of any peace treaty, Dairen was still properly administered by the Port Arthur naval authority. The Soviet government saw no reason for any change in this arrangement; *United States Relations with China,* pp. 125–26.

dustries, and, second, the conclusion of an agreement with Chungking providing for the joint Sino-Soviet management of certain critical Manchurian enterprises.

According to Chinese officials in Manchuria who were interviewed by American correspondents in February, 1946, Soviet technicians had arrived in Mukden and other Manchurian cities early in September, 1945, to supervise the removal of selected machinery and other equipment from former Japanese-owned factories. The first deadline for the completion of these removals was apparently November 15, in anticipation of the original date set for the withdrawal of Soviet troops early in December. There was some let-up in the Soviet operation after November 15, according to these Chinese informants, but further removals began in December, following the postponement of the Russians' departure, and continued into 1946.[112]

The Russians did not, of course, call attention to these activities, but they did evidently, as early as October, 1945, raise the general question of "war booty" with the Chungking government. On October 17, according to Chiang Kai-shek, Moscow proposed to Chungking that all Japanese-run factories and enterprises be considered Russian spoils, that factories and enterprises run by Manchurian puppets revert to China and that the disposition of jointly managed installations be the subject of special negotiations between the two governments.[113] The proposals were given no publicity at the time and what reply the Chungking government made to them is not known. On January 21, 1946, the Russians appear to have restated, more peremptorily, their understanding of "war booty": a Soviet memorandum of this date to the Chinese Foreign Minister, according to the latter's version of it, asserted bluntly that "all Japanese enterprises in the Chinese Northeastern Provinces which had rendered services to the Japanese army were regarded by [the] Soviet Union as war booty of [the] Soviet forces." [114] The first public acknowledg-

[112] See the account in Moorad, *Lost Peace in China,* pp. 162–65.
[113] Chiang Kai-shek, *Soviet Russia in China,* p. 169.
[114] *United States Relations with China,* p. 597. The Chinese Foreign Office disclosed the contents of the Soviet memorandum in a note to the State Department dated March 5, 1946; the latter was in response to a request for information concerning Sino-Soviet negotiations in Manchuria which had been sent on February

ment of Soviet removals was given, apparently inadvertently, on February 23, 1946, when General Andrei Kovtoun-Stankevich, the Soviet commandant in Mukden, sought to explain Soviet policies in this matter to a group of foreign correspondents. "As far as Japanese military industry is concerned," he is quoted as having said, "according to the Big Three it could not be left here, and so it happens that some has been taken out." Asked whether this meant that it had been removed to the Soviet Union, he said, "Perhaps." The authority for this action, he believed, was an agreement made either at Yalta or Berlin (i.e., Potsdam).[115] Several days later the Soviet press, apparently reflecting the Kremlin's anxiety over the foreign reaction to the general's remarks, carried a Tass dispatch from Changchun stating that he had been misquoted.[116]

If a desire to proceed at a more leisurely pace with the systematic stripping of the Manchurian industries was a factor in Moscow's decision to prolong the occupation beyond February 1, it is not likely that this was the crucial factor. Correspondents arriving in Mukden early in February found the Russians' operations well advanced and heard from local residents that most of the removals had been carried out before December, 1945. Despite evidence that the Russians were devoting some attention to this matter almost to the moment of their departure,[117] it is reasonable to imagine that the original schedule of Soviet removals, which would have included all important machinery and equipment, was geared to an earlier withdrawal and was doubt-

---

9 to both the Chinese and Soviet governments. See *ibid.*, pp. 596–97, and Chiang Kai-shek, *Soviet Russia in China,* p. 170. A second note was sent to the Soviet government on March 9 and a reply was received six weeks later. The contents of this reply were not divulged, but Acting Secretary of State Dean Acheson indicated in a press interview that the note was entirely unsatisfactory; see New York *Times,* April 27, 1946, p. 5.

[115] *Ibid.,* February 28, 1946, p. 1. See also Moorad, *Lost Peace in China,* p. 167. No such agreement, of course, was made at either the Yalta or Potsdam conferences, according to records thus far available.

[116] *Pravda,* March 3, 1946, p. 4.

[117] On March 5, for instance, H. R. Lieberman of the New York *Times* reported from Changchun that technicians from the Soviet Union had recently arrived there, presumably to assist in the stripping operations; New York *Times,* March 10, 1946, p. 4.

less completed before the end of 1945. Subsequent removals were probably of secondary importance.[118]

The other major economic effort of the Russians in Manchuria, the attempt to establish joint Sino-Soviet management of critical Manchurian industries, did, in all likelihood, have a direct bearing on their extended occupation. According to recent Chinese Nationalist sources, negotiations on this matter began on November 24, 1945. At this time the Soviet economic advisor, Slatekovskii, proposed the joint Sino-Soviet operation of 154 industrial and mining establishments, comprising 80 per cent of Manchuria's heavy industry. Slatekovskii's Chinese counterpart, Chang Kia-ngau, according to these same sources, refused even to discuss this matter until all Soviet troops had been withdrawn from Manchuria.[119]

In January, 1946, the Russians continued to press for economic cooperation in Manchuria, though with some modification of their proposals. A Soviet memorandum handed to Nationalist officials in Changchun at the end of January, according to the Chinese Foreign Office, proposed turning over to China some of the enterprises which Moscow considered to be legitimate "war booty"—the Russians presumably hoped this would be taken as a gesture of magnanimity—while others, including specified coal mines, power plants, iron and steel concerns, and so forth, would

[118] The report submitted in December, 1946, by Edwin C. Pauley, President Truman's Personal Representative on Reparations, estimated that the value of the damage to the Manchurian economy during the Soviet occupation totaled $858,000,000 (U.S.); the replacement cost was estimated at $2,000,000,000. In addition, $3,000,000,000 in bullion and $500,000,000 Manchurian yuan had been confiscated and the note issue had been doubled in occupation yuan; New York *Times,* December 14, 1946, p. 1. The Russians later placed the total value of equipment removed from Manchuria as reparations at $97,000,000; *Izvestiia,* January 29, 1947.

[119] See *Summary Records of the First Committee,* p. 344; this is the statement by the Chinese Nationalist delegate to the United Nations, F. T. Tsiang, delivered to the First Committee on November 25, 1949. It is apparent, if Tsiang's information is accurate and if Chiang Kai-shek's summary of the Russian proposal of October 17, 1945, is also correct, that Slatekovskii was asking for a larger share of the Manchurian economy to be jointly operated than Moscow had originally suggested. The October proposals had included for "special negotiations" between the two governments only those enterprises formerly run jointly by the Japanese and their Manchurian puppets—presumably a smaller proportion of Manchuria's heavy industry than 80 per cent.

be jointly operated. The Chinese once again rejected these proposals.[120]

There is no record of discussions on this matter during February and early March, but on March 27, 1946, again according to Chinese Nationalist sources, the Soviet Ambassador to China presented to the Chungking government a detailed plan for joint Sino-Soviet economic cooperation. This plan envisaged a joint Sino-Soviet stock company in Manchuria, with each participant holding 50 per cent of the stock and with a Chinese chairman and a Russian vice chairman. The general managers of the concerns to be jointly operated, on the other hand, would be Russians and their assistants Chinese. After thirty years the enterprises involved would be returned to China without compensation. This plan, too, came to nothing, since the Chinese refused, as they have claimed, even to discuss the Soviet proposals until the withdrawal of Russian troops from Manchuria had been completed.[121] When this withdrawal was completed, the situation had so far deteriorated in China that the Soviet proposals had become meaningless and were dropped.

It should be remarked that the meager information available on these discussions between the Chinese and Soviet governments is exclusively from Chinese Nationalist, or pro-Nationalist, sources. There seems to be little doubt, of course, that such discussions were held and that the Soviet demands were far-reaching, but without studying the Russian version of these talks it is difficult to determine with any certainty what significance Mos-

[120] The Russian memorandum is referred to in the note of March 5, 1946, sent by the Chinese Foreign Office to the Secretary of State; *United States Relations with China*, pp. 597–98. See also Chiang Kai-shek, *Soviet Russia in China*, p. 169. On March 14, 1946, in a report to the Central Executive Committee of the Kuomintang, Chang Kia-ngau described in more detail the Russians' January proposals. The first Soviet proposals in November, 1945, Chang said, had listed 22 mines, 54 power plants, and 8 major factories to be operated jointly; in January, the Russians' plan was to extend joint operation to only 9 mines, 16 power plants, and 6 factories. See New York *Times*, March 15, 1946, p. 5. It should be noted that there is some discrepancy between Chang's evidence in March, 1946, concerning the number of installations involved in Moscow's initial plan (84), assuming that his figures included all installations listed, and F. T. Tsiang's evidence on this point (154) some years later.

[121] *Summary Records of the First Committee*, pp. 344–45. See also the discussion of the Soviet proposals in 1945–46 and the Nationalist response to them in Cheng Tien-fong, *History of Sino-Russian Relations*, pp. 279–80.

cow attached to them, and what role these efforts played in Soviet strategy. At the end of 1945 the Russians did perhaps consider it of some importance to acquire further economic concessions in Manchuria. On at least one occasion, the Chinese Nationalists have reported, a Soviet official used the threat of longer occupation as a lever to secure Chungking's compliance with Moscow's demands.[122] This may also have been a factor in the Russians' decision to ignore the February 1 deadline set for their evacuation of Manchuria.[123] But as time passed the Russians had to weigh the uncertain advantages of an economic agreement with Chungking, one which had not yet been concluded, against the possibly harmful consequences of the longer occupation which they perhaps felt was necessary in order to secure this agreement.

One of the harmful consequences of a longer occupation which the Russians may have taken into account was an increase in the number of anti-Soviet demonstrations in China proper, such as those which had occurred at Chungking and other cities in mid-February. Despite claims in the Soviet press that these demonstrations were organized by reactionary elements seeking to disrupt Sino-Soviet relations and that they did not reflect the sentiments of the average Chinese citizen, Soviet leaders must certainly have been aware of the possible repercussions of this growing hostility, especially on the political fortunes of the Chinese Communists. The safety of Russian troops in Manchuria, it is safe to assume, was not greatly jeopardized by these demonstrations, but should the continued presence of the Russians in Manchuria become the occasion for widespread protests throughout China, the Chinese Communists would undoubtedly suffer loss of support in circles which, other things being equal, could be expected to be sympathetic in any final showdown with the Kuomintang.

[122] At the end of December, 1945, Malinovskii allegedly told Chang Kia-ngau that until some agreement had been reached on the question of joint economic operations he would be unable to predict the date of the Soviet evacuation of Manchuria; *Summary Records of the First Committee,* p. 377.

[123] During February the foreign press occasionally reported rumors of Soviet demands on China and linked them to the delay in the Russian evacuation; e.g., New York *Times,* February 13, 1946, p. 11, and February 17, 1946, p. 1.

As far as the danger of American "intervention" in Manchuria was concerned in case of Soviet withdrawal, the Russians were doubtless assured by early March that this was not a serious threat to the Chinese Communists. The Russians had had several months in which to appraise the new course of American policy, following the high-level discussions in Washington at the time of Ambassador Hurley's resignation. They must have discovered that it represented little change in the United States' over-all commitment in China. Soviet observers undoubtedly noted with satisfaction, for instance, the prompt State Department disclaimer of a statement made in January, 1946, by Congressman George J. Bates (Massachusetts), then visiting Tientsin, to the effect that the Marines were acting as a "stabilizing force" in China. The Marines, a State Department spokesman asserted, had no other mission than to assist Chungking in disarming and repatriating Japanese troops and they would be withdrawn as soon as the Chungking government indicated it could accomplish this task by itself.[124] The Russians perhaps also had advance notice of Wedemeyer's scheduled departure from China at the end of March, 1946, and of Washington's intention, which Wedemeyer announced on his departure, to deactivate the China Theater by May 1.[125] As for the Marshall Mission, reports of the negotiations in Chungking received in Moscow through February could only have revealed Marshall's scrupulously neutral attitude toward the disputants. In preserving this attitude, Soviet leaders must have noted, General Marshall was giving markedly less comfort to Kuomintang leaders than had Hurley and Wedemeyer during the preceding autumn.

By early March, 1946, then, it was both expedient and safe for the Russians to terminate their occupation of Manchuria. With spring coming on, moreover, removing the "technical difficulties" which had allegedly delayed the withdrawal in February, there was no longer even a plausible pretext for remaining. Having nothing further to gain in Manchuria, except an agreement with Chungking on the joint operation of certain Manchurian enter-

[124] *Ibid.*, January 22, 1946, p. 7.

[125] According to Wedemeyer's announcement the number of American troops in China would be reduced by this date to 3,000–4,000; *ibid.*, April 2, 1946, p. 2.

prises—an agreement which, though still desirable, might be meaningless within six months or a year—and perhaps fearing an ugly outbreak of anti-Soviet and anti-Communist sentiment in China proper if they remained, the Russians prudently and promptly withdrew.

So much for the political and economic considerations which led Moscow, first, to extend its occupation of Manchuria beyond the February deadline and, eventually, to terminate the occupation in April, 1946. What, now, may be said of the apparent conflict between Moscow's political and economic objectives while the occupation lasted?

It would seem that at some juncture during the Soviet occupation a conviction must have grown in Moscow either that the Chinese Communists were likely to control Manchuria permanently or that they were not. At the time this occurred, or shortly thereafter, we would expect to find some adjustment in Soviet policies reflecting this conviction. If, for instance, the Soviet leaders felt that the Communists would not be able to hold Manchuria, then we would expect Moscow to have shown some concern over the political crisis in China and to have exhibited more interest in the negotiations in Chungking for a coalition government. After the first few weeks of the Marshall Mission the Russians did neither. If, on the other hand, Moscow felt with some confidence that the Chinese Communists could maintain their hold on Manchuria—and it seems more likely in retrospect that this was the Russians' view—it is perhaps understandable that little attention was given to the question of a coalition government, but it is then curious that the Russians showed so little inclination to modify their economic policies, which were presumably based on the assumption of a Manchuria controlled by the Kuomintang. Some falling off in the removal of industrial equipment probably did occur during the second phase of the Russian occupation, but this is readily explained, as indicated above, by the fact that the most valuable equipment had already been removed in the autumn of 1945, when the occupation was expected to end before the close of the year. Efforts to conclude an economic agreement with Chungking, in the meantime, continued without abatement up until the eve of the Russian's departure. If Chinese Nationalist sources may be credited, the final and most detailed Soviet proposals for this purpose were not presented to Chungking until March 27, several weeks after the Russian decision to withdraw from Manchuria had been made.

In this writer's view, the most likely explanation of the paradox in Soviet behavior in Manchuria is that two entirely separate and unrelated policies were being pursued. We may imagine that the policies had been conceived in response to conflicting motivations, that each had been shaped in a different section of the Soviet government and was being carried out more or less independently during the Soviet occupation. The economic policies sprang from a sense of heavy loss to the Soviet economy during the war and from a rational, if somewhat unethical, desire to make good this loss by every possible means. In this respect the stripping of Manchuria was similar to Soviet reparations policies in Europe. If there was a guiding political consideration of any consequence in this activity, it was perhaps, in the light of the war recently concluded, that the Manchurian economy should not be permitted in the foreseeable future to be capable of sustaining a possible base of operations against the Soviet Union—for the Japanese, for the Chinese, or for anyone else.

As far as political policies were concerned, the Russians had doubtless anticipated for a number of years that assistance in some form or other would be given to the Chinese Communists after the war as opportunities arose. At the outset, following the capitulation of Japan, Moscow seems to have urged upon the Communists a predominantly political effort in China proper, in the belief that both Soviet and Chinese Communist objectives would be served best through collaboration rather than through rebellion. Subsequently, as new estimates of Communist strength came to the attention of Soviet leaders, Moscow appears to have inclined increasingly toward the view that a military effort by the Communists in Manchuria was not only feasible but desirable. This new attitude did not, however, affect Soviet economic policies, probably because these policies were already in force and no one bothered to change them. If responsible Soviet officials in Moscow gave any thought to the difficulties the Communists would encounter in attempting to sustain themselves in an economy which, because of systematic stripping, had been almost entirely devastated, they probably reasoned that there would be ample time in the future to make proper adjustments.

It is specious to argue that Soviet policies in Manchuria, in the aggregate, were uneconomical, as the Pauley report suggests in its estimate of a $2,000,000,000 expenditure required to replace removals totaling less than half this sum. The primary consideration in Moscow was doubtless to assure the Soviet Union of maximum protection against all contingencies; the cost was unimportant. And who, in any case, has seriously argued that frugality, any more than foresight or consistency, is an intrinsic feature of Soviet foreign policy?

THE IDEA OF CHINESE UNITY ABANDONED JANUARY, 1946–AUGUST, 1946

This account of Soviet policy toward the Chinese Communists might fittingly have closed with the Russian withdrawal from Manchuria in April, 1946, leaving Mao's forces in undisputed control of northern Manchuria and well situated to launch their attack southward when the opportunity arose. There had not, however, been any official indication at this time that all hope for a political settlement in China had been abandoned. The indication was given, in unmistakable language, only two or three months after the Russian evacuation had been completed.

During the first five or six weeks of 1946 the more moderate policies which both the Russians and the Chinese Communists displayed at the end of 1945 continued in force. In Manchuria, Nationalist forces encountered little opposition in their advance toward Mukden and entered the city, virtually unopposed, on January 15. At the same time the garrison at Changchun was being strengthened by means of an airlift from Peiping and through the conscription, with Soviet approval, of a local militia called the Peace Preservation Corps.[126] The crucial port of Ying-

[126] Early in April, H. R. Lieberman estimated that there were 7,000 Nationalist troops in Changchun. Later, at the time of the Russian evacuation of the city, he scaled this estimate down to 3,000; see New York *Times*, April 11, 1946, p. 13, and April 30, 1946, p. 10. At the end of 1945 the garrison in Changchun had numbered only two or three hundred.

kow was also occupied by the Nationalists early in January as the Communists withdrew to the neighboring countryside.[127] Sporadic fighting was reported between Nationalist and Communist forces in southern Jehol in January, especially along the Peiping-Mukden Railroad, but this ceased as the Russians withdrew from this area at the end of the month.[128]

In Chungking, in the meantime, there were two developments during January which seemed to ease the internal crisis. The first was a cease-fire agreement on January 10, arranged by a three-man committee including General Chang Chun for the Nationalists, Chou En-lai for the Communists, and General Marshall as chairman.[129] The cease-fire was to be effective throughout China and of indefinite duration. An Executive Headquarters was to be set up in Peiping to carry out the provisions of the cease-fire. This, like the Committee of Three, was to be made up of representatives of the national government, the Chinese Communists, and the United States, the latter serving as mediator. According to the official press release announcing the cease-fire, the order "does not prejudice military movements of forces of the National Army into or within Manchuria which are for the purpose of restoring Chinese sovereignty." [130]

The second notable development was the plenary session of the Political Consultative Conference which opened on a cordial note on January 10 and continued with at least an outward display of good will throughout the rest of the month. On January 31, the texts of the resolutions agreed upon were made public.[131] The major points covered were: (*a*) the establishment of a Constitu-

[127] Yingkow was retaken by the Communists, however, later in the month and remained under Yenan's control until April 2, 1946.

[128] Eyewitness accounts of developments in Jehol during January may be found in New York *Times*, January 5, 1946, p. 5, January 21, 1946, p. 7, and January 24, 1946, p. 2. Though not actually part of Manchuria, Jehol had been administered by the Japanese as part of Manchukuo. This was the reason for the Soviet occupation of the province in the autumn of 1945.

[129] This committee, called the Committee of Three, was set up on January 7, 1946, at the suggestion of the national government.

[130] The texts of the cease-fire order, the press release concerning it, and the resolutions and memoranda relative to the establishment of the Executive Headquarters may be found in *United States Relation with China*, pp. 609–10 and pp. 627–33.

[131] Thirty-eight delegates attended the Political Consultative Conference: eight from the Kuomintang (headed by Sun Fo), seven from the Chinese Communist Party (headed by Chou En-lai), fourteen from other minor parties, and nine

tion Draft Committee to revise the existing Constitution of 1936 in accordance with certain basic principles spelled out by the Political Consultative Conference; (*b*) the convocation of a National Assembly of representatives of all parties on May 5, 1946, to enact the new constitution; (*c*) the reorganization of the present administration, prior to the meeting of the National Assembly, to provide for a State Council of forty members—half from the Kuomintang and half from Communist and other groups—which would act as the supreme organ of the government in domestic affairs;[132] (*d*) and the creation of a three-man Military Commission to consider ways of uniting all armed forces within three months into a nonpolitical national army of ninety divisions (eventually to be reduced to forty or fifty divisions). It was further agreed, in an annex to a very general resolution on national reconstruction, that in areas where control of the local government was still in dispute the status quo would be preserved pending a settlement between the disputants to be reached after the reorganization of the government.

The Chinese Communists and the Russians expressed their official satisfaction, in varying degrees, with the work of the Political Consultative Conference. Chu Teh, even before the close of the conference, told foreign correspondents in Yenan that he was confident a definitive agreement would be reached during the current discussions.[133] Chou En-lai, in numerous interviews, indicated his approval of the resolutions passed by the conference and on at least one occasion praised General Marshall for his efforts in making the conference a success.[134] In Moscow a

---

nonparty leaders. The texts of the principal resolutions, as well as of Chiang's opening and closing addresses to the conference, may be found in *China Handbook, 1937–1945* (rev. ed., 1947), pp. 742–55; see also *United States Relations with China*, pp. 610–21.

[132] Chiang Kai-shek was authorized to appoint the State Councilors, both the twenty from the Kuomintang and the additional twenty non-Kuomintang members, and he retained a veto power over all Council decisions, subject to reversal by a three-fifths vote.

[133] New York *Times*, February 1, 1946, p. 3; the interview was held on January 27. See also Smedley, *The Great Road*, p. 436.

[134] New York *Times*, February 18, 1946, p. 3. See also Agnes Smedley's account of Chu Teh's warm praise of Marshall on the occasion of the latter's visit to Yenan early in March; Smedley, *The Great Road*, p. 437. Marshall did not take part directly in the deliberations of the Political Consultative Conference but apparently made himself available to representatives of all factions for consultation; see *United States Relations with China*, p. 139.

favorable summary of the resolutions appeared in *Pravda* on February 9. A week later A. Perevertailo, who emerged after the war as one of the principal Soviet authorities on the Far East, considered that the work of the Political Consultative Conference warranted an optimistic view of the prospects for peace in China.

> The very fact [he wrote] that these extremely important decisions to democratize the country were adopted, and the statement by Generalissimo Chiang Kai-shek that he was ready to implement them, warrant the assumption that the resistance of the reactionaries will be overcome and that there will be no divergence between declarations and deeds.[135]

It should perhaps be pointed out that the Perevertailo article was the only editorial or quasi-editorial comment on the Political Consultative Conference which appeared in the Soviet press in the first weeks after its conclusion—at least in so far as this writer has discovered. The article cannot therefore be regarded as indicating a particularly decisive attitude in Moscow concerning the prospects for a peaceful settlement of China's internal problems. The appearance of this article, however, may perhaps be taken as a sign that the more kindly policy toward Chungking which had been adopted at the end of 1945 was still in effect in mid-February, 1946, at least officially. Whatever they may have thought of the real chances of peace, Soviet leaders had not yet reached a point where they felt they could ignore, let alone disparage, the efforts to achieve a political solution in China through peaceful means.

The truce in China, which accompanied the first (and only) plenary session of the Political Consultative Conference was short-lived. Ten days after the close of the session a supposedly peaceful demonstration in Chungking, held to celebrate the successes of the Political Consultative Conference, was broken up by right-wing elements in the Kuomintang. The Soviet press carried an account of this episode, thereby indicating to Russian readers for the first time since the end of the war that there was

[135] A. Perevertailo, "The Struggle for National Unity and Democracy in China," *New Times,* No. 4, February 15, 1946, p. 28; this article is a far-ranging review of Rosinger's *China's Wartime Politics.*

serious political tension in China.[136] It was during the next fortnight that anti-Soviet and anti-Communist demonstrations broke out in various parts of China, further testifying to the disintegration of the January truce. *Pravda* charged that one demonstration in Chungking had been "organized with the participation and open support of the local authorities," as indicated by the fact that the participants had been given a free meal afterwards.[137]

In Manchuria, in the meantime, fighting had been resumed in earnest. By mid-February it had reached a level of intensity comparable to that of October and November, 1945. On February 15, Yenan announced that there were 300,000 Communist troops in Manchuria and demanded joint control of the three Manchurian provinces with the national government.[138] Two days later Chou En-lai repeated this demand in Chungking and warned that there would be civil war in Manchuria if the government refused.[139]

Despite these growing indications of disunity, a three-man Military Subcommittee, made up of General Chang Chih-chung, Chou En-lai, and General Marshall, succeeded, on February 25, in reaching agreement on the basis for the reorganization of the armed forces and for the integration of the Communist troops into a national army. According to this agreement, the national government was to reduce its forces within twelve months to ninety divisions and within eighteen months to fifty divisions; the Chinese Communists during the same period were to reduce their forces to eighteen then to ten divisions. The demobilization was to begin immediately and information concerning the divisions retained by each side, up to the authorized limit, was to be submitted to the Military Subcommittee within three weeks.[140]

The Soviet press made no mention of the February 25 communiqué, although this was the most important and by far the most detailed agreement which had emerged from the Communist-Kuomintang negotiations since the end of the war. Instead, Moscow newspapers, in their modest coverage of develop-

[136] *Pravda,* February 14, 1946, p. 6; this account is substantially the same as that appearing in the New York *Times,* February 11, 1946, p. 9.
[137] *Pravda,* February 25, 1946, p. 4.
[138] New York *Times,* February 16, 1946, p. 1.
[139] *Ibid.,* February 18, 1946, p. 3.
[140] *United States Relations with China,* pp. 622–26.

ments in China, continued to focus attention on evidence of political unrest—for instance, a sequence of unsolved political assassinations in Manchuria early in March.[141] In this emphasis the Soviet press perhaps revealed, on the part of Soviet leaders, a distinct lack of interest, or at least a lack of confidence, in a peaceful resolution of the internal crisis in China.

The tension in China increased during the second plenary session of the Sixth Kuomintang Central Executive Committee, held in Chungking from March 1 to March 18. Conservative elements within the Kuomintang, who appear to have dominated the plenum from the outset, criticized sharply the government's allegedly "soft" policy toward the Russians in Manchuria and demanded an explanation of Chiang and his advisors. In the course of justifying their policies, government officials revealed for the first time the scope of the Russians' heretofore secret economic demands in Manchuria, a circumstance that undoubtedly embarrassed the Soviet leaders and further alienated them from Chungking.[142]

At the end of the plenary session, at Chiang Kai-shek's request, the Central Executive Committee finally ratified "unanimously" the resolutions of the Political Consultative Conference, which the Kuomintang plenum had primarily been called to consider. The language of the ratification, however, as well as that of an accompanying manifesto, was ambiguous enough to leave some doubt as to the future intentions of the Kuomintang.[143] Chou En-lai found little that pleased him in the Kuomintang's action. On March 18, he attacked the ratification statement as indicating an unmistakable intent on the part of the Kuomintang to perpetuate its one-party dictatorship, and he expressed himself as "amazed" that Chiang Kai-shek should have allowed the statement to pass.[144] Whether because of their dissatisfaction with the action of the Kuomintang plenum and their uncertainty concerning the future status of the resolutions which had been passed by

[141] E.g., *Pravda,* March 10, 11, and 17, 1946, p. 4.

[142] See, especially, the report by Chang Kia-ngau, summarized in the New York *Times,* March 15, 1946, p. 5.

[143] The texts of both the ratification and the manifesto are in *United States Relations with China,* pp. 634–39.

[144] New York *Times,* March 19, 1946, p. 17.

the Political Consultative Conference, or for other reasons, the Chinese Communists canceled their own plenum which had been scheduled to meet on March 31 to pass on these resolutions. This in turn led to a suspension of the work of the Constitution Draft Committee, the most important interim body of the Political Consultative Conference, which was preparing the groundwork for the National Assembly, still scheduled to open on May 5.[145]

By the end of March, therefore, a virtual stalemate had been reached in the negotiations in Chungking. Marshall's absence from China at this time—he was on a visit to the United States from March 11 to April 18—hardly eased the crisis. It is likely, however, that the rapid march of events in Manchuria, as the Russians began their evacuation, would have rendered all truce negotiations in Chungking meaningless, with or without the presence of General Marshall and with or without favorable action on the January resolutions in Chungking or Yenan.

During April the situation in China grew steadily worse. On April 1, Chiang Kai-shek told the People's Political Council, during its first meeting since the end of the war, that he would consider no political demands in Manchuria "before the complete restoration of Chinese sovereignty." [146] On April 7, the Yenan *Emancipation Daily* replied with its sharpest attack on Chiang since the end of the war. Reference was made to Chiang's alleged "lust for battle and slaughter" and to his undisguised effort to establish a personal dictatorship.[147] On April 14, Chou En-lai again asserted the right of the Communists to play a role in the government of Manchuria, as he had in mid-February. "We cannot recognize the right of government forces," Chou told foreign correspondents, "to drive the Communists out of places from which the Russians have withdrawn and where government troops have not arrived in time." [148] Chungking officials reminded

[145] See *United States Relations with China*, p. 144. Cheng Tien-fong notes that while the government submitted to the Military Subcommittee on March 26 a list of its divisions to be retained, in accordance with the agreement of February 25, the Communists never submitted theirs; *History of Sino-Russian Relations*, p. 288.

[146] A partial text of Chiang's address is given in *China Handbook, 1937–1945* (rev. ed., 1947), pp. 760–64.

[147] New York *Times*, April 9, 1946, p. 5.

[148] *Ibid.*, April 15, 1946, p. 1.

Chou in vain that only three months earlier he himself, in agreeing to the provisions of the January 10 cease-fire, had acknowledged that, while all Chinese troops, both Communist and Nationalist, should remain stationary, an exception might be made in the case of government troops moving "into and within Manchuria . . . for the purpose of restoring Chinese sovereignty."

To the Chinese Communists, agreements made as long ago as January were now obsolete and they would not be bound by them. As though to emphasize their utter disregard of the three-months old cease-fire agreement, on April 20 the Communists, having already seized Changchun, bluntly announced their intention of occupying Harbin as soon as the Russian evacuation was completed.[149] On April 22, Yenan announced, perhaps superfluously, that in view of the political situation in China no Communist delegates would be sent to the National Assembly on May 5.[150] On April 26, Chou En-lai demanded a new and "unconditional cease-fire" and stated that the Communists would engage in no further talks on Manchuria until Chiang Kai-shek had given this order to his troops. Chiang refused this demand and reasserted his position of April 1: there would be neither negotiations nor a cease-fire before the extension of government control throughout the entire Northeast.[151]

During May the situation only worsened, culminating in Chiang Kai-shek's dramatic but doubtless ill-advised departure for Mukden on May 23. To the Communists, Chiang's mission must have had the appearance of an intended triumphal entry into Manchuria, timed to coincide with their own planned withdrawal from Changchun at this time in accordance with General Marshall's most recent proposal for a settlement of the civil crisis. The Generalissimo's use of Marshall's official plane for his eleven-day visit to Manchuria, moreover, did not help to strengthen the impression of American neutrality which Marshall had conscientiously sought to preserve. In Nanking, meanwhile, negotiations

[149] *Ibid.*, April 21, 1946, p. 1.

[150] *Ibid.*, April 23, 1946, p. 11.

[151] *Ibid.*, April 27, 1946, p. 5. It is possible that the transfer of the seat of the national government during the latter part of April from Chungking to Nanking hampered communications between Communist and Kuomintang spokesmen and compounded the difficulties of negotiating.

continued as well as they could during Chiang's absence, but with little effect on developments in Manchuria.[152]

So long as the Russians remained in Manchuria, the Soviet press scrupulously ignored the fighting in China. On several occasions, it has been noted—as, for instance, during the Chiang-Mao talks in September, 1945, and following the plenary session of the Political Consultative Conference in January, 1946—certain Soviet newspapers or journals had applauded the efforts made to resolve the internal crisis through negotiation. But as the prospects for a settlement grew dim, the Russians had refrained from calling attention to the see-saw course of the conflict in North China and South Manchuria. The Soviet press was, in fact, so guarded in its references to the civil crisis in China that the average Russian reader could have gained no inkling of it at all before the end of February, 1946 (which was when the accounts of anti-Soviet and anti-Communist demonstrations first began to appear in *Pravda*), and he could have formed no accurate impression of the magnitude of the crisis until the end of April.

As the Russian occupation drew to a close, however, the Soviet press began to devote some attention to the tense situation in China. An article by K. Evgen'ev in the April issue of *Bol'shevik*, for instance (the issue did not go to press till April 30), gave an extensive review of developments in China since the end of the war and made no effort to minimize the fighting, both past and present, between Communist and Nationalist forces. The high point in bringing about better relations between the two parties was seen as the Political Consultative Conference in January. The achievements of this body, however, had been greatly weakened by Chinese reactionaries, Evgen'ev argued, especially during the Kuomintang plenum in March. Evgen'ev was somewhat noncommittal over the prospects of a negotiated settlement in China, but he stated that such a settlement was still desirable, "especially at the present time." [153]

If Evgen'ev expressed less enthusiasm for the truce negotiations

[152] For a fuller summary of developments in China and Manchuria during April and May, see *United States Relations with China*, pp. 147–55.

[153] K. Evgen'ev, "Kitai posle kapituliatsii Iaponii" (China after the Capitulation of Japan), *Bol'shevik*, Nos. 7–8, April, 1946, p. 65. This was the first article on China which had appeared in *Bol'shevik* since June, 1945.

than Perevertailo had in mid-February in *New Times*, and a good deal less enthusiasm than had been expressed in Soviet newspapers immediately after the war, he nonetheless did express some concern. We must presume that this represented at least a semiofficial view on the question of a peaceful resolution of the crisis in China and that Moscow was still unprepared, at the end of April, to speak out openly against General Marshall's efforts.

Soon after the appearance of Evgen'ev's article in *Bol'shevik*, the daily Moscow press also began to report on the crisis in China. On May 8, *Pravda* carried a summary of a recent article by John Hersey in the *New Yorker* in which he charged Chiang Kai-shek and the Kuomintang with primary responsibility for the tense situation in China.[154] On May 19, several Tass dispatches in *Pravda* reported on the progress of the fighting in North China and Manchuria. On May 25, a Tass dispatch from New York, published by *Pravda*, quoted the New York *Post* as saying that Chiang Kai-shek had ordered his local commanders to wage a "secret civil war" wherever this seemed to them necessary and without waiting for explicit instructions.

The June 1 issue of *New Times* included an article by Perevertailo which went somewhat further than Evgen'ev's article a month earlier in pointing out the seriousness of the impasse in China. The situation had reverted to that existing at the end of the war, Perevertailo felt, and he naturally placed the blame for this squarely on the Kuomintang. Matters had in fact deteriorated so far as the result of developments during April and May, Perevertailo wrote, that "the participation of the Communists in the government and the National Assembly under such conditions would be senseless and would turn into a farce hiding the real state of affairs." Perevertailo made no reference at all to the need for a resolution of the political crisis and a unified China—references which had appeared in every Soviet commentary on China since the end of the war.[155]

[154] Hersey's article appeared in the May 4 issue of the *New Yorker*, pp. 86–98. Reviewing the breakdown in Nationalist-Communist negotiations, Hersey wrote: "There appears to be little question that the main responsibility for this breakdown rests with the Generalissimo and the Kuomintang."

[155] A. Perevertailo, "The Situation in China," *New Times*, No. 11, June 1, 1946, pp. 11–17.

The United States, in the meantime, had again come under attack in the Soviet press for its policies in China. The *Bol'shevik* article at the end of April, for instance, placed considerable stress on American intervention in China as a factor influencing the course of events there.[156] On May 13, after the last Russian troops had allegedly left North Manchuria, *Pravda* noted the landing of 2,000 United States Marines at Hulutao. On May 19, *Pravda* reported an agreement between China and the United States which would give American shipping special privileges in Chinese ports. On May 22, *Pravda* carried a report that in recent fighting in Manchuria between the Kuomintang and the "people's armies" American bombardiers and pilots had been used.[157] The Perevertailo article in *New Times* on June 1 also claimed "the direct participation of American soldiers in the Civil War" and contrasted this with the orderly withdrawal of Soviet troops from Manchuria in accordance with the decision on China reached at the Moscow Conference of Foreign Ministers.[158]

Early in June, following Chiang Kai-shek's return from Mukden, General Marshall succeeded in arranging a final truce between the Communists and the Kuomintang. The cease-fire orders, issued on June 6, to take effect at noon on June 7, were to cover a fifteen-day period. At the end of this time the cease-fire was extended to June 30. During this period negotiations went on

[156] Evgen'ev, "Kitai posle kapituliatsii," *Bol'shevik,* Nos. 7–8, April, 1946, pp. 64–65. The Chinese Communists, who, like the Russians, had refrained from criticizing American policies in China since December, 1945, had resumed their attack a month before the Russians. On April 2, Yenan released the text of a recent letter from Chou En-lai to Lieutenant General Alvan G. Gillem, Jr., the new Commander in Chief of American forces in China, in which a sharp protest was made against the American ferrying of Kuomintang troops into Manchuria, allegedly for civil war operations; New York *Times,* April 3, 1946, p. 10.

[157] Inasmuch as other foreign dispatches from China at this time make no mention of such a report, it is likely that the *Pravda* dispatch refers to an incident that allegedly occurred a month earlier. On April 21, the Communists claimed that American planes strafed Red Army units near Changchun and that the body of an American pilot was found in one of the planes which was shot down. General Marshall demanded that the Communists produce evidence of this claim or retract it. When they did neither, Marshall's headquarters on April 23, following an investigation, issued a statement that the planes concerned belonged to the Nationalists but had perhaps been mistaken for American planes due to "faulty markings"; see New York *Times,* April 22, 1946, p. 1, April 23, 1946, p. 1, and April 24, 1946, p. 17.

[158] Perevertailo, "The Situation in China," *New Times,* No. 11, June 1, 1946, pp. 13–14.

constantly with Marshall acting as intermediary between the Generalissimo and Chou En-lai. Agreement was reached, apparently with no great difficulty, on two of the three items on the agenda announced at the time of the cease-fire—a general order for a "permanent" cessation of hostilities in Manchuria and a plan for the resumption of communications in North China. Some measure of agreement was also reached on the third item—a revision of the military reorganization plan of February 25, 1946, and a practical formula for putting this plan into effect. It was tentatively agreed, for instance, that the original ratio of one Communist division to fifteen Kuomintang divisions in Manchuria should be revised, in view of the altered position of forces there, to a ratio of three Communist to fifteen Kuomintang divisions.

Chiang, however, had stipulated that before any decisions could be given effect there must be agreement on all major items on the original agenda. Since, in the end, no agreement was reached on the issue of military reorganization—due largely to the failure to find a meeting of minds on the question of local government in areas to be evacuated by the Communists—the negotiations failed in their entirety. On July 1, Chiang and Mao Tse-tung both published orders to their respective field commanders to continue observance of the cease-fire agreement,[159] but, in fact, fighting was resumed within a few days and continued with growing intensity until a state of full-fledged civil war was acknowledged later in the year by both parties.

The Soviet press had taken virtually no notice of the June 6 cease-fire order[160] or of the negotiations following it. In fact, during the first fortnight of the truce period the Moscow press remained ominously silent with respect to all developments in China. During the last ten days of June, however, there began to appear in *Pravda* and in other organs what must be considered, in comparison with previous months, a virtual deluge of news

[159] The texts of both orders may be found in *United States Relations with China*, pp. 649–50.

[160] The only reference to the cease-fire which this writer has discovered in the Soviet press during June occurs in a weekly chronology of international events appearing in *New Times*, No. 12, June 15, 1946, p. 31.

dispatches from or concerning China. In this writer's opinion, the sudden interest in Chinese affairs expressed in these published dispatches signaled a definitive turn in Russia's policy toward China. The editorial comment which presently followed confirmed the change. It was the most decisive observable development in Soviet Far Eastern policy since the end of the war.

It was not simply the volume of comment on China which indicated the shift in Soviet policy—though this in itself was enough to indicate a sharp change—but the substance of this comment as well. For instance, charges of American intervention became markedly sharper than in previous months and Soviet writers now identified this intervention as the factor primarily responsible for the deepening crisis in China.[161] At the same time General Marshall, toward whom the Soviet press had maintained a scrupulously correct attitude during the first six months of 1936, came under direct attack. On June 26 and June 29, *Pravda* carried summaries of foreign news stories criticizing him. Six weeks later one of *Pravda*'s editorial writers observed:

> It is very curious to consider the "mediation" of General Marshall and Ambassador Stuart[162] who are allegedly concerned with negotiating a truce between the Kuomintang and the Communists. These American "negotiators" act according to the principle: the left hand must not know what the right hand is doing—for while the left hand "negotiates," the right painstakingly arms Chiang Kai-shek's armies.[163]

[161] E.g., V. Avarin, "Chto proiskhodit v Kitae" (What Is Happening in China), *Pravda*, July 5, 1946, p. 3; Boris Isakov, "Mezhdunarodnoe obozrenie" (International Survey), *Pravda*, July 7, 1946; A. Perevertailo, "United States Policy in China," *New Times*, No. 14, July 15, 1946, pp. 3–6; V. Avarin, "Kitaiskii narod v bor'be protiv reaktsii" (The Chinese People in the Struggle against Reaction), *Mirovoe khoziaistvo i mirovaia politika*, No. 9, September, 1946, pp. 5–17; M. Markov, "Amerikanskie voiska v Kitae" (The American Forces in China), *Pravda*, September 15, 1946, p. 4.

[162] Dr. J. Leighton Stuart, President of the Yenching University in Peiping, had been named by Truman on July 11, 1946, to succeed Patrick Hurley as American Ambassador to China. General Marshall was accredited to China as the President's Special Representative.

[163] Ia. Viktorov, "Mezhdunarodnoe obozrenie" (International Survey), *Pravda*, August 13, 1946, p. 4. The Chinese Communists had expressed official doubts concerning Marshall's efforts even earlier. On June 6, Chou En-lai said that, while "we have trusted General Marshall," the spectacle of Americans on one hand seeking peace in China and on the other providing munitions to the government for use in the civil war had disillusioned Communists about the Marshall Mission; New York *Times*, June 7, 1946, p. 8.

The clearest indication of a fundamental shift in Soviet policy, however, was in the attention now openly given to the Chinese Communists. Since the end of August, 1945, the Soviet press had given virtually no coverage either to the activities of the Chinese Communists or to important policy statements by Communist leaders.[164] Now, in mid-1946, Chinese Communism again became a proper subject for discussion. On June 27, *Pravda* carried a statement by Mao—apparently his first public statement since mid-October, 1945—protesting American aid to China and demanding the immediate withdrawal of American troops.[165] On July 11, *Pravda* summarized an important manifesto issued by the Central Committee of the Chinese Communist Party on the ninth anniversary of the Lukouch'iao incident. This manifesto exuded confidence. "Never during its past hundred years' struggle for independence and democracy," the manifesto declared, "has our people been so powerful and so filled with bright hope as now. . . . Even with foreign aid, the reactionary clique in China cannot overcome its numerous difficulties. The present fierce violence of the Chinese reactionaries does not indicate their might and vitality but the feebleness and momentary brightness of the sunset." [166] On July 19, *Pravda* carried an official statement by Chou En-lai which he apparently intended as an ultimatum to the Nationalist government: if the Kuomintang did not take immediate steps toward democratic reform, Chou warned, "all further political conversations would be in vain." The "democratic forces" in China, in the meantime, which the Russian press had often described as a vast protesting segment

[164] On August 31, 1945, *Pravda* had carried the text of a resolution passed by the Central Committee of the Chinese Communist Party on August 25, as well as a summary of Mao's statement following his arrival in Chungking with Hurley on August 29.

[165] Mao appears to have been inaccessible to foreign visitors in Yenan following his return there after the negotiations with Chiang Kai-shek in September and early October, 1945; see Smedley, *The Great Road,* p. 432 and New York *Times,* February 1, 1946, p. 2. In May, 1946, rumors circulated in Chungking that Mao was on a visit to Moscow, but these rumors were never verified; see, for instance, the Reuters dispatch on Mao's alleged visit in *ibid.,* May 13, 1946, p. 1 and the denial of this report in *ibid.,* May 14, 1946, p. 2.

[166] A full English text of this manifesto may be found in *Political Affairs* (New York), No. 10, October, 1946, pp. 915–21.

of the population, but without specifying any particular leadership, were now directly linked, in Soviet accounts, to the Chinese Communists. Avarin's long review in *Pravda* on July 5, for instance, spoke repeatedly of Yenan's direction and supervision of these forces.[167]

It is not worth while, for the purposes of this study, to explore further the extensive coverage of developments in China by the Soviet press during the summer of 1946 or to pursue this comment into the autumn of 1946 and thereafter. The negotiations between the Chinese Communists and the Kuomintang continued for some months after the Soviet press ceased to express any interest in them. They were not even interrupted after the statement by General Marshall and Ambassador Stuart in August revealing the almost hopeless impasse in China, or by the Communists' general mobilization order on August 19, following the bombing of Yenan.[168] Neither the course of these further negotiations nor other developments in China, however, resulted in any appreciable change in the pattern of Soviet comment which had emerged in the early part of the summer of 1946. If there was any change at all in Moscow's attitude after July, 1946, it was in the direction of a steadily increasing confidence that the Chinese Communists could not be beaten. Writing in the September issue of *Mirovoe khoziaistvo i mirovaia politika,* V. Avarin reflected this confidence:

It it now clear to all political observers that the democratic forces in China have grown to such an extent that no bloc of reactionaries could succeed in turning back the wheels of history. The Chinese people must of course overcome many obstacles and survive many serious tests before all China becomes a democratic country. But at the same time it is apparent that this great nation will no longer be

[167] Avarin, "Chto proiskhodit v Kitae," *Pravda,* July 5, 1946, p. 3.

[168] Chou En-lai left Nanking only on November 19, 1946, ending the discussions which had been going on continuously since early January of the same year and intermittently since the autumn of 1943. A small Chinese Communist delegation remained in Nanking until February 11, 1947, when the government formally requested its withdrawal. General Marshall was recalled, at his own request, on January 8, 1947. For a review of the negotiations during the final phase of the Marshall Mission, see *United States Relations with China,* pp. 180–229.

returned to that state of political and economic stagnation and exploitation in which it has lived so long.[169]

It is interesting, finally, to consider why the Russians' sudden concern with the situation in China, which we take to mark a turn in, or at least a more positive articulation of, Soviet policy, should have occurred at the end of June and early in July rather than at some time earlier or later. It may be argued, of course, that the complete futility of the negotiations in Nanking became apparent to the Russians only at this time and that their concern was simply the consequence of this realization. In this connection, General Marshall has testified that "the general effort of the Nationalist Government to destroy the power of the Communist regime by military action had its beginnings in June [1946]." [170] An awareness of such a decision, or even a strong suspicion of it, it could be argued, may have prompted the Russians to express themselves more openly on the situation in China.

If, on the other hand, the strongly worded article by Perevertailo in the issue of *New Times* for June 1, 1946, may be taken as a reliable indication of Soviet policy at that time, the Russians were deeply pessimistic over the possibility of a negotiated peace in China nearly a month before the Soviet press in general began to express this view and at least a week before the opening of the discussions which were to follow the June 6 cease-fire. The fact, moreover, that the Soviet press showed no interest in the June discussions, and began its critical coverage of Chinese affairs when the discussions were at their most crucial stage, in the last

[169] Avarin, "Kitaiskii narod v bor'be protiv reaktsii," *Mirovoe khoziaistvo i mirovaia politika,* No. 9, September, 1946, p. 17.

[170] *Military Situation in the Far East,* p. 659. Chiang Kai-shek, while acknowledging no general plan of attack against the Communists in June, 1946, lends some support to the thesis that this was a crucial month for the Nationalists. He writes: "The second cease-fire order [of June 6] turned out to be the beginning of the Government forces' debacle in Manchuria. If at the time Government pursuit units . . . had pressed on toward [Harbin] . . . , Communist remnants in northern Manchuria would have been liquidated and the situation throughout Manchuria stabilized. If the Chinese Communists were driven out of their foothold in northern Manchuria, Soviet Russia would have found no way to send them any more supplies and a fundamental solution of the problem of Manchuria would have been at hand. The subsequent defeat of Government troops in Manchuria in the winter of 1948 was largely due to the second cease-fire order"; from *Soviet Russia in China* (p. 168) by Chiang Kai-shek, copyright 1957 by Farrar, Straus and Cudahy, Inc. Used by permission of the publisher. See also Cheng Tien-fong, *History of Sino-Russian Relations,* p. 289.

week or ten days of June, suggests that the course of these negotiations had little effect on Soviet policy. The most that may reasonably be argued along these lines is that the Russians perhaps delayed their most important editorial statements on the crisis in China—as, for instance, Avarin's article in *Pravda* of July 5—until the formal truce period ended in June 30, in order not to give the appearance of sabotaging the negotiations.

It is interesting also to weigh the possible effect on Soviet policy of Chiang Kai-shek's rejection about this time of a second invitation to meet with Stalin. According to Chiang, this invitation—for which, it should be said, there is no other evidence except Chiang's known to the author—was tendered on May 6, discussed for some time in government and party circles, and finally rejected on the grounds that until the Soviet Union gave some indication of fulfilling its obligations under the Sino-Soviet Treaty of Friendship and Alliance there was no point to such a meeting. Chiang does not give the date of his refusal but it is likely, to judge from the account in his recent book, that his answer was made known to the Russians sometime in June.[171] It should not be imagined, of course, that Chiang's rejection of the alleged invitation angered the Russians and in itself caused a turn in Soviet policy. However, his refusal to come to Moscow at this time left the Russians free to develop a new line toward China which was indicated by other considerations. Had Chiang decided to meet with Stalin, it would have been inappropriate for the Soviet press to unleash so violent an attack on the Chungking government and on American intervention during the summer of 1946, and the turn in Russian policy—or, at least, a clear indication of this turn—would have necessarily been delayed for several months.

[171] Chiang Kai-shek, *Soviet Russia in China,* pp. 148–49. Relating his decision to China's relations with the United States at this juncture, Chiang writes: "A hidden international current was already lashing at Sino-American relations, and China was already being isolated. It was no longer possible for China and the United States to work out a joint policy toward Soviet Russia on the basis of our common interests. Consequently the only thing we could do was to disregard what attitude and policy the Western nations might or might not adopt toward us, and to be prepared, in consonance with our own independent policy, to go it alone, if necessary, in combatting Soviet aggression to the bitter end. It was on such considerations that I decided to turn down Stalin's second invitation." Used by permission of the publisher, Farrar, Straus and Cudahy, Inc.

Perhaps the most plausible explanation of Moscow's abrupt and newly expressed concern with the situation in China at the end of June is that the Russians viewed with apprehension new indications in Washington that the American government was again weighing the possibility of undertaking a greater commitment in China. On June 13 and June 14, 1946, respectively, bills had been introduced into the United States Senate and House of Representatives to provide increased military advice and assistance to the Chinese Nationalists. Hearings on these bills began almost immediately and were the subject of some discussion in the Soviet press until it became clear, by mid-July, that no final action would be taken by the Seventy-ninth Congress.[172] The Soviet press also showed concern at this time over the rumored extension of American lend-lease aid to the Nationalist government. On June 23, *Pravda* reported that a secret agreement had been reached between Washington and Nanking on the temporary continuation of lend-lease until a formal loan had been negotiated. In the ensuing weeks Russian newspapers devoted a good deal of attention to criticism of this alleged agreement in the foreign press, both in China and elsewhere.[173]

The Russians undoubtedly hoped, by calling attention to American aid to the Nationalists and by emphasizing the effect of this aid in sharpening the civil crisis in China, to mobilize public opinion both inside China and abroad against any increase in the volume of American assistance. Similar attacks on alleged

[172] See, especially, *Pravda,* June 22, 1946, p. 5, and July 14, 1946, p. 4. While these two bills failed of passage in 1946, a naval aid bill authorizing, *inter alia,* the transfer to China of 271 American naval vessels was passed by both Houses and signed by President Truman on July 16, 1946 (Public Law 512, 79th Congress). Legislation authorizing grants to China for military expenditures—up to $125,000,000—was enacted only in 1948 in the China Aid Act (Title IV, Public Law 472, 80th Congress).

[173] In a statement released on June 28, 1946, Acting Secretary of State Dean Acheson noted that a "pipeline lend-lease agreement" had recently been concluded with Chungking, authorizing expenditures up to $58,000,000; see the text of this statement in the New York *Times,* June 29, 1946, p. 8. A later State Department source indicates that this agreement was specifically intended to continue lend-lease to China beyond the official termination of the program in other countries on June 30 and that it remained in effect until the passage of the China Aid Act of 1948. The total value of lend-lease aid to China from V-J Day to June 30, 1948, according to this source, was $781,000,000; *United States Relations with China,* pp. 969–70. Cf. Cheng Tien-fong, *History of Sino-Russian Relations,* p. 296.

American intervention in November, 1945, it has been suggested, had had this goal. There was an important difference, however, in the attitude of the Russians in the autumn of 1945 and in the summer of 1946. At the end of 1945, it will be recalled, attacks on American intervention had been accompanied by a more conciliatory attitude toward the Nationalist government, both in Moscow and in Yenan, presumably in order to persuade Washington and Chungking that neither Soviet nor Chinese Communist objectives represented a threat which would warrant an increase in American aid. In the summer of 1946 no such conciliatory policies accompanied the attacks on American intervention. On the contrary, at no time since the 1920s had the Soviet press expressed such confidence in the potentialities of the Communist (thinly disguised as the "democratic") movement in China. Any limitation of American aid to the Kuomintang was presumably desirable, in Moscow's view, but it was not to be purchased by further "concessions" on the part of the Chinese Communists.

At what date, precisely, Moscow's confidence in the ultimate victory of the Chinese Communists crystallized, it is impossible to say with certainty. Some evidence exists that Soviet spokesmen were privately confident of a Communist victory by April, 1946.[174] Later Soviet sources argue that there was little doubt of the outcome even earlier than this but that the Communists went ahead with the discussions with the Kuomintang "to give the masses the possibility of satisfying themselves through their own experiences that the question of a democratic reorganization of China could not be resolved by an agreement with internal reaction and with American imperialism."[175] In any case, it was

[174] According to Marjorie Ravenholt, an American correspondent in Shanghai after the war, a Tass official there asserted in April, 1946, in response to an informal question concerning future Soviet intentions respecting the Communists, that it was not necessary for the Russians to do anything; it was "already done." She understood him to mean by this off-hand remark not only that the Russians had by this time given the Communists in Manchuria all the assistance they needed but also that the situation in China proper, even without Soviet assistance, was developing in a manner which could not fail to favor Mao's position; conversation with the author in February, 1953.

[175] *Krizis kolonial'noi sistemy,* pp. 58–59. See also V. N. Nikiforov, "Ianvarskoe soglashenie 1946 g. i Amerikanskii imperializm" (The Agreement of January, 1946, and American Imperialism), *Uchenye zapiski* Tikhookeanskogo instituta, III (1949), 112, and M. F. Iurev, *Istoricheskaia pobeda kitaiskogo naroda nad Amerikanskim imperializmom i gomindanovskoi reaktsiei,* p. 9.

not until early in the summer of 1946 that the Soviet press finally abandoned the ambiguous attitude toward events in China which it had preserved since the end of the war. From this time on readers of the Soviet press need not necessarily have inferred that Moscow would immediately underwrite the Communists' further efforts in China or support them with material aid. They could, however, safely assume that, barring unforeseen developments, the Chinese Communists could count on Moscow's political, diplomatic, and moral support in their struggle with Chiang Kai-shek's regime—a struggle which Moscow appears to have felt by this time would eventually end in a Communist victory.

CONCLUSION

If we focus our attention on the entire course of Soviet-Chinese Communist relations from 1931 to 1946, three aspects of this relationship are, I think, deserving of special notice.

First, there is no clear evidence that the Russians made any strenuous efforts during this period to intervene in the internal political affairs of the Chinese Communist Party in support of one faction over another. If Mao's leadership of the Party, which he had gained through indigenous Chinese agencies over which Moscow had little or no control, was in any way objectionable to the Russians, they had the good grace—and the good sense—to accept this leadership without public demurrer. If Wang Ming, as has been suggested, was dispatched to China in 1937 as the Comintern's special emissary, Moscow made no protest, so far as is known, when the leadership in China relegated Wang to an inferior position in the Party, a position from which he never again emerged.

Second, there is no good evidence that the Chinese Communists, for their part, ever used their independence either to evade Soviet policies which they may have found objectionable or to refute formulations in Marxism-Leninism which the Kremlin endorsed as dogma valid for Communists everywhere. All of the major turns in Soviet foreign policy during these years—as, for instance, the treaties with Germany and Japan in 1939 and 1941 and the Sino-Soviet pact of 1945—were applauded promptly and without equivocation in Yenan, regardless of the adverse effect they may have had on projects currently under consideration by the Chinese Communist leadership. As far as ideology is concerned, apart from certain expressions of national self-consciousness during the wartime *cheng-feng* era, no aspect of Maoism before 1946, either as a body of theory or as a program of action, departed in any appreciable respect from Bolshevism. For instance, some significance attaches to the fact that, although the strength of the Chinese revolution was acknowledged to be agrarian during the entire period from 1931 to 1946, Mao persistently rationalized it, in orthodox Bolshevik terms, as a fundamentally proletarian effort.

Third, there is no occasion after the Fourth Plenum of the Chinese Communist Party, held in January, 1931, when the Russians are known to have expressed their disapproval of Chinese Communist policies, as they had done frequently and caustically during the previous decade. If at times the Russians seemed to take little interest in the Chinese Communists, this was doubtless due to their preoccupation with more urgent matters elsewhere and, after 1937, to their desire not to antagonize Chungking, and later Washington, by appearing to show too great a concern with a rebellious faction in China. It cannot be demonstrated that Moscow's ostensible inattention to Chinese Communist affairs during extended periods reflected Soviet indifference.

No evidence exists, in short, to cast serious doubts on the underlying allegiance of the Chinese Communists to Moscow during these years and on Moscow's confidence in their loyalty.

We might at this juncture reconsider, in the light of the foregoing observations, the disclaimers by Stalin and Molotov in 1944 and 1945 of any special interest in Chinese Communism, disclaimers which were noted at the outset of this study. It is apparent, in the first place, that the Russian leaders greatly misrepresented Chinese Communism in asserting that it was "in no way at all" related to Russian Communism. While it was perhaps true that no intimate contact had been maintained with the Chinese Communists since the early 1930s, no informed Russian at the end of the war could have been ignorant of their fundamental and continuing orthodoxy as Marxists of the Bolshevik stamp.

It is considerably less clear, however, whether in making these assertions Stalin and Molotov sought deliberately to mislead American diplomats (to whom they made their disclaimers) concerning Soviet intentions in China. One of the principal features of Russian policy in China during the last year of the war, and especially after Yalta, it has been argued, was Soviet support of a unified program of resistance centered around Chiang Kai-shek. It has also been argued that collaboration between Chungking and Yenan, which was obviously the *sine qua non* of this policy, appears to have been a sincere objective of Soviet policy at the time in order that a civil war disastrous to other Soviet objectives, and perhaps disastrous also to the Chinese Communists, might be averted. Had Stalin and Molotov been speaking to men of their own school, they might have said, very bluntly: "The Chinese Communists are good Communists, so far as we know, but we are not supporting them; we are supporting a coalition government under Chiang Kai-shek." To Americans like Hurley, Donald Nelson, and Byrnes, who were doubtless presumed from the outset to be suspicious of Soviet motives, the Russian leaders had to speak more circumspectly. Their total disavowal of Chinese Communism, therefore, was intended merely to persuade these Americans that Soviet policy in China truly supported Chungking; only such disclaimers, they must have felt, would carry conviction.

Collaboration between the Communists and the Kuomintang does not, however, appear to have remained a primary objective of Soviet policy in China once the war was over. As the Russians realized their aims in Manchuria, with an ease that perhaps surprised them, and as they began, early in the autumn of 1945, to gain a new perspective on the role the Communists might play in China, the urgency of a rapprochement between Chungking and Yenan gradually diminished. It was therefore no longer necessary, for tactical reasons, publicly to disavow the Communists, and after September, 1945, no Soviet spokesman did so. In December, 1945, when Byrnes reminded Stalin of Molotov's statement at Potsdam that the Chinese Communists were not real Communists, it is probably significant that Stalin, according to Byrnes's account, neither confirmed nor denied this view. Instead he simply observed that the Soviet Union had signed a treaty with the Chinese which recognized the Chungking government.[1]

[1] James F. Byrnes, *Speaking Frankly* (New York, 1947), p. 228.

At the end of the war the Russians appear to have made one rather important miscalculation with respect to the Chinese Communists, if we judge their Far Eastern policy in its totality. This was in their estimate of Mao's very meager chances of success in an open conflict with the Kuomintang in the summer of 1945. It is perhaps appropriate at this point to give in full the much-quoted statement which Stalin is alleged to have made in 1948 to a Yugoslav delegation visiting in Moscow, just prior to Yugoslavia's expulsion from the Cominform:

> After the war we invited the Chinese comrades to come to Moscow and we discussed the situation in China. We told them bluntly that we considered the development of the uprising in China had no prospect and that the Chinese comrades should seek a *modus vivendi* with Chiang Kai-shek, that they should join the Chiang Kai-shek government and dissolve their army. The Chinese comrades agreed here with the views of the Soviet comrades, but went back to China and acted quite otherwise. They mustered their forces, organized their armies and now, as we see, they are beating Chiang Kai-shek's army. Now, in the case of China, we admit we were wrong.[2]

The authenticity of this statement may be challenged, of course. In the first place, the source for it was one of the ranking Yugoslav Communist leaders during the critical break with the Cominform and, a few years later (but, of course, before his break with Tito), he was perhaps not above distorting Stalin's remarks in his efforts to argue the Yugoslavs' cause more persuasively. There is also no other evidence, known to this writer, of the reported visit to Moscow after the war of "the Chinese comrades" (who, it is implied, were responsible Party leaders). It is, moreover, not to be inferred from the information thus far available on the attitudes of the Chinese Communist leaders that given explicit advice from Moscow they would have bluntly ignored it as Stalin allegedly indicates they did. Finally, the picture of Stalin acknowledging past errors of judgment respecting foreign revolutionary movements is not exactly compatible with the more widely accepted picture of Stalin asserting his infallibility in these matters. Still, in so far as his estimate of the situ-

[2] Vladimir Dedijer, *Tito* (New York, 1953), p. 322. Used by permission of the publisher, Simon and Schuster, Inc.

ation in China in 1945 is concerned, the *sense* of these remarks attributed to him may well be authentic.[3]

If the Russians did miscalculate, it cost them very little. In particular, it did not mean any appreciable forfeiture of Soviet prestige among the Chinese Communists. This became clear in the subsequent course of events in China. Soviet policy, to use the words that George Kennan applied to it in April, 1945, proved to be sufficiently "fluid" and "resilient" to adjust to circumstances that were perhaps unforeseen at the end of the war.[4] Within a year following the Japanese capitulation, the course of events in China had turned decidedly in favor of Moscow's long-range objectives. Within four years gains had been made which only the most exuberant soothsayer in Moscow could have anticipated in 1945.

[3] Agnes Smedley, who was of course extremely partial to the Chinese Communists and never critical—as far as this writer is aware—of the Soviet Union, lends some support to the view that the Russians underestimated the strength of Mao's movement at the end of the war. Commenting on this period, she writes: "There is no doubt . . . that the Soviet Union sympathized fundamentally with the Chinese Communists, though it is doubtful if they believed the Chinese Communists strong enough to come to power"; Smedley, *The Great Road,* p. 482.

[4] *United States Relations with China,* p. 97. In his telegram to the State Department on April 23, 1945, in which he questioned Hurley's interpretation of Soviet policy on the basis of the latter's recent talks with Stalin, Kennan said: "Actually I am persuaded that in the future Soviet policy respecting China will continue to be what it has been in the recent past: a fluid resilient policy aimed at the achievement of maximum power with minimum responsibility for portions of the Asiatic continent lying beyond the Soviet border."

APPENDIX: CHINESE COMMUNIST DECLARATIONS RELATING TO JAPANESE AGGRESSION AND THE FORMATION OF A UNITED ANTI-JAPANESE FRONT

STATEMENTS BETWEEN THE FIRST JAPANESE ATTACK ON MANCHURIA, SEPTEMBER 19, 1931, AND THE SEVENTH COMINTERN CONGRESS, AUGUST, 1935

September 20, 1931—Joint Declaration of the Central Committees of the Chinese and Japanese Communist Parties

The declaration is a denunciation of Japanese aggression in Manchuria. Inasmuch as the Japanese attack began only two days before, it is probable, if the date is given correctly, that the joint declaration was prepared by Chinese and Japanese representatives attached to the Comintern in Moscow rather than by the Central Committees in Shanghai and Tokyo, both operating underground at this juncture as the result of rigid police controls.

Text in *Okkupatsiia Manchzhurii i bor'ba imperialistov,* pp. 148–50.

September 25, 1931—Declaration of the Soviet Governments of Various Regions of China concerning the Japanese Seizure of Manchuria

This declaration, addressed to the "workers, peasants, soldiers, and all toilers in China," and signed by the heads of seven soviet governments, asserts that the Japanese invasion is directed primarily against the USSR; both the Kuomintang and Japanese imperialists must be destroyed.

Text in *Programmnye dokumenty kommunisticheskikh partii Vostoka,* pp. 229–31.

September 30, 1931—Declaration of the Central Committee of the Chinese Communist Party

The declaration, addressed to "the workers, peasants, soldiers, students, and toiling masses of China," was also directed equally against the Kuomintang and the Japanese invaders. Of particular note is the comment on the Kuomintang's rumored efforts to form a national united front. "The Kuomintang even resorted to the trick of threatening the imperialist countries with 'cooperation with the USSR and the Communists' in the hope that in the face of this threat the imperialists would undertake 'active resistance.'" Also: "The Kuomintang recently has begun to spread amusing, absurd, and lying rumors that in Kiangsi the Communists and the leaders of the workers-peasants' Red Army, Chu Teh and Mao Tse-tung, are ready to fight for a 'united front against the external enemy' and go over to the side of the Kuomintang. The Chinese Communist Party is the eternal enemy of the imperialists and the Kuomintang."

Text in *Okkupatsiia Manchzhurii i bor'ba imperialistov,* pp. 150–54.

November, 1931—Manifesto of the Provisional Government of the Chinese Soviet Republic to the Toiling Masses and Governments of the World

This manifesto was issued by the First Soviet Congress and announces to the world the formation of the Chinese Soviet Republic. Concerning the Japanese seizure of Manchuria, the manifesto states that this will be resisted but considers the elimination of the Kuomintang a prerequisite to victory: "only the overthrow of the Kuomintang, which has betrayed the national interest, and the establishment of the rule of the people can guarantee victory in the struggle against imperialism."

Text in *Programmnye dokumenty kommunisticheskikh partii Vostoka,* pp. 227–29.

Mid-November, 1931—Telegram from the First Soviet Congress to the Toilers of China

This telegram stresses that Japanese aggression is aimed at the USSR with the connivance of Nanking. Resistance to both the Japanese and the Kuomintang is urged to defend the USSR and save China.

Text in *Sovety v Kitae,* pp. 418–19.

December 11, 1931—Open Letter from the Central Committee of the Chinese Communist Party to All Party Members on the Present Political Situation in China

The analysis of the Japanese seizure of Manchuria in this letter is unchanged from that indicated in the foregoing declarations. There is a special emphasis placed here on the need for Party discipline. It is interesting to note that "the tearing up of pictures of Sun Yat-sen" is considered here as one of several indications that the masses are in revolt over the Manchurian crisis.[1]

Text in *Okkupatsiia Manchzhurii i bor'ba imperialistov,* pp. 154–57, and *Inprecor,* No. 5, February 4, 1932, pp. 86–87.

January 31, 1932—Appeal from the Central Committee on the Events in Shanghai

This is an appeal to all workers and military units in the Shanghai area to unite in the defense of the city, then under attack by Japanese forces.

Text in *Sovety v Kitae,* pp. 448–50.

February 14, 1932—Declaration of the Red Army to the Soldiers of the 19th Army and to All People in China

This declaration, signed by Chu Teh and very similar to the foregoing appeal, was addressed specifically to the 19th (Kuomintang) Army. This army was then under the leadership of officers who were not entirely in sympathy with Chiang Kai-shek and were presumed willing to cooperate with Communist-led forces.

Text in *Sovety v Kitae,* p. 453.

February 14, 1932—Declaration of the Central Committee of the Chinese Communist Party

This document indicates that the destruction of Kuomintang rule was still as great an objective as the defeat of the Japanese: "for a complete victory in the people's revolutionary war it is necessary to destroy the leadership of the Kuomintang militarists and to put the leadership in the hands of the people themselves."

Text in *Sovety v Kitae,* p. 451.

[1] Disparagement of Sun Yat-sen was also a feature in the Comintern line on China during this period. Pavel' Mif, for instance, wrote in 1931: "The Chinese Communist Party must expose Sun Yat-sen's reactionary utopian concepts"; from an article in *Problemy Kitaia,* Nos. 8–9, 1931, quoted in Mif, *Kitaiskaia revoliutsiia,* p. 320.

April 5, 1932—Declaration of War against Japan by the Chinese Soviet Republic

The declaration of war was signed by the Provisional Central Government of the Chinese Soviet Republic at Juichin on April 26, 1932. There is no explanation for the discrepancy between the date given in the heading of the available text and the date of the signature. The tone of this document is much like that of the preceding one: "in order to wage war actively against Japanese imperialism, it is necessary first of all to destroy the reactionary rule of the Kuomintang which is assisting the imperialists to strangle the national revolutionary movement."

Text in *Programmnye dokumenty kitaiskikh sovetov*, pp. 90–93.

April 20, 1932—Declaration of the Chinese Soviet Republic

Again the overthrow of the Kuomintang regime is stressed as "an important prerequisite for the success of the revolutionary struggle against Japanese imperialism." This document reads much like the declaration of war of April 5 and may even be another Russian translation of the same document.

Text in *Sovety v Kitae*, p. 455.

January 10, 1933—Declaration of the Provisional Government of the Chinese Soviet Republic and the Revolutionary Military Council of the Red Army

This declaration, signed by Mao and Chu Teh, was the first published Chinese Communist offer to conclude "a military alliance with any armed forces for joint resistance to Japanese aggression." The three conditions set forth by the Communists for collaboration were: (*a*) cessation of the offensive against the soviet districts, (*b*) granting of civil rights (freedom of assembly, press, etc.), and (*c*) arming of volunteer units. Although addressed, presumably, to the Kuomintang troops surrounding the soviet areas, the declaration indicated that the proposed alliance was to be directed against the Kuomintang itself as well as against the Japanese and other imperialists.[2]

Text in *Programmnye dokumenty kitaiskikh sovetov*, p. 95.

September(?), 1933—Second Declaration of the Provisional Central Government of the Chinese Soviet Republic concerning the United Front for Struggle against Japan

This document, signed by Mao Tse-tung, Chu Teh, Chang Kuo-t'ao,

[2] See pp. 64–65 above for a discussion of this declaration.

and Hsiang Ying is very similar to the declaration of January, 1933. An appeal is made to "any army or armed military unit" for "an operating military alliance" to resist the Japanese; the same three conditions are again indicated. Both the Kuomintang and Chiang Kai-shek are attacked for "their plans to partition China."

Text in *Programmnye dokumenty kitaiskikh sovetov,* pp. 93–94.

September 6, 1933—Appeal of the Central Executive Committee of the Chinese Soviet Republic to the Workers of the United States, England, Japan, France, and Germany

This appears to be a companion to the preceding document. It describes the "Second Declaration" and appeals to foreign workers to help the Chinese resistance to Japan. It is signed by Mao Tse-tung, Chu Teh, Chang Kuo-t'ao, and Hsiang Ying.

Text in *Programmnye dokumenty kitaiskikh sovetov,* pp. 96–100; *Programmnye dokumenty kommunisticheskikh partii Vostoka,* pp. 232–35; *Kommunisticheskii internatsional,* No. 28, October 1, 1933, pp. 22–24; *Inprecor,* No. 44, 1933, pp. 971–72.

December 13, 1933—Appeal of the Central Committee to the Masses on the Events at Fukien

The Fukien "people's government" is attacked here for having done no more than utter "sweet revolutionary phrases." Communists, however, are urged to ally with the Fukien government against both the Kuomintang and the Japanese. The January and September declarations are described as having appealed for resistance to both.

Text in *Inprecor,* No. 11, February 23, 1934, pp. 300–301.

January, 1934—Appeal of the Second Soviet Congress to the Northeastern People's Revolutionary Army and to the Anti-Japanese Volunteer Army

According to this appeal, signed by Mao Tse-tung as the Chairman of the Presidium of the Second Congress, the Communists, on the basis of the three conditions first announced in January, 1933, offered "an agreement with all anti-Japanese volunteer units for joint struggle against Japan and the Kuomintang." It appears that this offer was made only to units in Manchuria. Another declaration by the Second Congress addressed to "the entire population of China," while it referred to the 1933 appeals for anti-Japanese resistance, did not repeat the appeal but asked instead for a determined resistance to the sixth Kuomintang campaign against the soviet districts.

Text in *Programmnye dokumenty kitaiskikh sovetov,* pp. 100–102, and *Vtoroi s"ezd kitaiskikh sovetov,* pp. 180–82.

August 20, 1934—Declaration of the Central Committee of the Chinese Young Communist League to the Toiling Youth and Students of China

The view expressed here is once again that the destruction of the Kuomintang is a necessary preliminary to anti-Japanese resistance: "we call on the entire armed toiling youth of China to wage a ruthless struggle against the landowners, the capitalists, the Kuomintang, and the fascists. Only on these conditions can we achieve full victory in the struggle against Japanese imperialism."

Text in Alekseev, *Komsomol Kitaia,* pp. 43–47.

June 15, 1935—Declaration of the Soviet Republic on the Occupation of North China by Japan

This declaration, signed by Mao Tse-tung, Chu Teh, Chang Kuo-t'ao, Chou En-lai, Hsiang Ying, and Wang Chia-Hsiang,[3] is an appeal for unity addressed to workers, peasants, and intellectuals rather than, as previously, to military units willing to fight the Japanese. The Kuomintang and particularly Chiang Kai-shek are sharply attacked.

Text in *Inprecor,* No. 32, August 3, 1935, pp. 380–81.

June 20, 1935—Manifesto to the Manchurian People on the Events in North China

This manifesto, signed by various commanders of the "United Front Committee for War against Japan" (none of them recognized Red Army or soviet leaders), describes the united front as directed against Japanese imperialism, Manchukuo, and Chiang Kai-shek. The Kuomintang as a whole is not singled out for attack.

Text in *Communist International,* "Special Number on China," February, 1936, pp. 225–28.

August 1, 1935—Declaration of the Chinese Soviet Government and the Central Committee of the Chinese Communist Party on Resistance to Japan and Salvation of the Fatherland

This declaration, the first to be issued jointly by the Party and soviet leaderships, is the best known of all Chinese Communist statements on the question of united resistance to Japan. It appeals to all Chinese factions, including "the Kuomintang armies," to join the Red Army in

[3] Since the date given for this declaration is earlier than the meeting of the First and Fourth Armies in Nanking, in Szechwan province, it is probable that the declaration was drafted by the Chu-Mao headquarters and the signatures of other soviet and Red Army leaders, like Chang Kuo-t'ao and Hsiang Ying, simply appended to the finished document.

a common struggle against the Japanese. The only condition given for an alliance is a cessation of attack on the soviets. The first part of the declaration consists of a sharp attack on the past policies of the Kuomintang, and of Chiang Kai-shek in particular.[4]

Text in *Kommunisticheskii internatsional,* Nos. 33–34, 1935; there is an English translation in Rosinger, *China's Wartime Politics,* pp. 63–69.

STATEMENTS BETWEEN THE SEVENTH COMINTERN CONGRESS AND THE FORMATION OF THE UNITED FRONT, SEPTEMBER 22, 1937

November 25, 1935—Appeal of the Central Committee of the Communist Party of China

This is essentially the same as the declaration of August 1, 1935, but with no specific reference to the Kuomintang.

Text in *Bor'ba za edinyi natsional'nyi anti-iaponskii front,* pp. 110–11.

December 25, 1935—Resolution [of the Politburo] on the Present Political Situation and the Tasks of the Party

This resolution names Chiang Kai-shek as a "traitor to the country" and links him with the Japanese as the principal enemy of the Chinese people. It was anticipated, however, that a portion of the "national bourgeoisie" might assist the united front by maintaining a benevolent neutrality toward the anti-Japanese crusade.

Text in Mao, *Proizvedeniia,* I, 473–76; English ed., I, 328–30.

May 5, 1936—Telegram from the Military Revolutionary Committee of the Red Army to the Nanking Government

Another appeal—and apparently the first made directly to Nanking—for the termination of civil war and for the formation of a united front of all armies and other groups in China against the Japanese. A reference to Chiang indicates he was not necessarily excluded from the proposed alliance.

Text in Mao, *Proizvedeniia,* I, 476–78; English ed., I, 330–31.

August 10, 1936—Letter from Mao Tse-tung to the Leaders of the All-China Association for the Salvation of the Country

Mao invites leaders of this progressive association to send delegates to participate in the soviet government and proposes that the question of soviets in China be put to a popular vote of the entire country.

[4] See pp. 66–67 above for a discussion of the relationship between this declaration and the decisions reached at the Seventh Comintern Congress then in session in Moscow.

There are no attacks here either on the Kuomintang or on Chiang. A reference to Mao's favorable response to an anti-Japanese appeal by the Canton rebels earlier in the summer shows him to have been, unwittingly or not, in opposition to Moscow's view of these rebels as reflected in the Soviet press.[5]

Text in *Bor'ba za edinyi natsional'nyi anti-iaponskii front,* pp. 34–42.

August 25, 1936—Open Letter from the Central Committee of the Communist Party of China to the Kuomintang

This is the most conciliatory statement made by the Communists to this date. In it the Communists stated their willingness to participate in a democratic central government and to have the Red Army "submit to the orders of a unified anti-Japanese army headquarters." Chiang was still criticized for his alleged efforts to compromise with the Japanese but far less critically than before. The position he had taken in July respecting nonrecognition of Japanese puppet governments was acknowledged as "a step ahead as compared with the past; we sincerely welcome this."

Text in *Kommunisticheskii internatsional,* No. 18, December 29, 1936, pp. 79–84.

September, 1936—Resolution of the Central Committee of the Chinese Communist Party on the Question of a Democratic Republic

The Central Committee here proposed a democratic republic as the only means of resolving the political crisis in China and of uniting the country against Japan. The resolution states: "When a democratic republic is formed and a parliament established on the basis of a general election, the Red regions will immediately enter this republic as one of its component parts."

Text in Mao, *Proizvedeniia,* I, 479–80; English ed., I, 331–32.

November, 1936—Message from Red Army Commanders to All Military Units in China

This is described as an appeal to all military commanders, including Chiang Kai-shek, for a conference to establish an all-Chinese anti-Japanese army.

Referred to in *China: The March Toward Unity,* p. 13.

December 1, 1936—Circular Telegram from the Central Committee of the Chinese Communist Party and the Chinese Soviet Government

[5] Cf. A. Kantorovich, "Dymovaia zavesa ili provokatsiia?" (Smoke Screen or Provocation?), *Izvestiia,* June 10, 1936, p. 2; see also pp. 74–75 above.

to the Kuomintang, the Nanking Government, the Press, All Political Parties, and so forth.

In more forceful language than the "Open Letter" of August 25, 1936, this telegram demanded the cessation of attacks on the Red Army, immediate resistance to Japan, and the convocation of a congress on national defense. "We are glad and willing," the Communists declared, "to accept the orders of the highest military commanding council of all the anti-Japanese armies."

Text in *China: The March Toward Unity,* pp. 119–21.

December 19, 1936—Telegram from the Central Committee of the Chinese Communist Party and the Chinese Soviet Government to the Nanking and Sian Authorities

This message, drafted in the middle of the Sian crisis (after Chiang's detention by Chang Hsüeh-liang), proposed an immediate truce between Nanking and the Sian leaders and the convocation of a national peace conference to determine the disposition of Chiang Kai-shek and to discuss other matters relating to Chinese unity. The Communists were willing to attend the conference, but did not insist on it. It was proposed that the conference be held in Nanking. The telegram further stated, contrary to the earliest reaction to the crisis in Moscow, that "the Sian leaders acted with patriotic sincerity and zeal."

Text in *China: The March Toward Unity,* pp. 122–23.

December 28, 1936—Statement by Mao Tse-tung concerning Chiang Kai-shek's First Post-Sian Announcement

Although sharply critical of Chiang's statement after his release (December 25, 1936)—particularly the reference to his captors as "reactionaries"—Mao pledged Communist support to Chiang and the Kuomintang on condition that they cease their collaboration with the Japanese, terminate the civil war, and immediately enter a united anti-Japanese front including all parties.

Text in Mao, *Proizvedeniia,* I, 431–38; English ed., I, 254–57.

January 6, 1937—Telegram from the Central Committee of the Chinese Communist Party and the Chinese Soviet Government to the Kuomintang, the Nanking Government, the Military Affairs Council, Chiang Kai-shek . . . and others

The Communists expressed their frank dissatisfaction with the course of events since Chiang's release at Sian, due chiefly to pro-Japanese elements in the government. "The present situation," the telegram declared, "applies an acid test to General Chiang's political integrity." The usual appeals for a democratic government and a strong anti-Japanese military union were repeated.

Text in *China: The March Toward Unity,* pp. 124–25.

February 10, 1937—Telegram from the Chinese Communist Party to the Third Kuomintang Plenum

This telegram included the first comprehensive proposals made by the Communists for the establishment of a united front. If the Nanking government would cease its attacks on the Communists, show its determination to resist Japan, guarantee freedom of speech and assembly, liberate all political prisoners, and undertake various other reforms, the Communists would be willing to abandon the soviets as such, incorporating the former soviet areas into the Chinese republic as a Special Region under Nanking's control, and to transform the Red Army into a national-revolutionary army under a Military Council in Nanking.

Text in *Pravda,* February 18, 1937, p. 5.

Note: No declarations are available for the spring of 1937 when actual discussions between Communist and Kuomintang representatives were in progress.

August 15, 1937—The Ten Great Policies of the Chinese Communist Party for Anti-Japanese Resistance and National Salvation

This declaration was not an appeal for unity, unity having already been achieved in large measure, but stated the principal objectives to be achieved by the united front: the defeat of the Japanese throughout China, including Manchuria, the total mobilization of the nation to this end, the election of a democratic national defense government, the improvement of living conditions in China, the guarantee of civil liberties to all but traitors, and so forth.

Text in Brandt, etc., *Documentary History,* pp. 242–45.

September 22, 1937—Statement by the Chinese Communist Party on the Establishment of the United Front

This announces, on behalf of the Communists, the conclusion of an understanding with the Kuomintang "on the basis of peace, national unity and joint resistance against foreign aggression." The Communists agree immediately to abandon the soviets and change the designation of the Red Army to the National Revolutionary Army. In a subsequent statement Mao claimed that this announcement was drafted on July 4, 1937, and presented to the Kuomintang eleven days later.[6] The announcement was made public in Nanking, however, only on September 22 and was followed the next day by a parallel announcement by Chiang Kai-shek.

Text in Brandt, etc., *Documentary History,* pp. 245–47.

[6] Mao Tse-tung, "Urgent Tasks of the Chinese Revolution since the Formation of the KMT-CCP United Front"; text in Brandt, etc., *Documentary History,* p. 248.

BIBLIOGRAPHY

Abend, Hallett. My Life in China, 1926–1941. New York, 1943, 396 pp.
Akademiia nauk, Institut mirovogo khoziaistva i mirovoi politiki (Institute of World Economy and Politics), Kolonial'nye problemy (Colonial Problems). No. 3–4. Moscow, 1935. [Papers read at a conference of Soviet specialists on China at the Institute of World Economy and Politics, June-July, 1934.]
Akademiia nauk, Institut vostokovedeniia (Institute of Oriental Studies). Trudy (Transactions). Vol. I. Moscow, 1939.
—— Uchenye zapiski (Learned Transactions). Vol. II, Kitaiskii sbornik (Collection on China), and Vol. III. Moscow, 1951.
Akademiia nauk, Nauchno-issledovatel'skii institut po izucheniiu natsional'nykh i kolonial'nykh problem (Research Institute for the Study of National and Colonial Problems). Natsional'no-kolonial'nye problemy: sbornik materialov (National Colonial Problems: Collection of Materials). Vol. I. Moscow, 1937. [Articles commemorating the fifteenth anniversary of the Chinese Communist Party.]
Akademiia nauk, Tikhookeanskii institut (Pacific Ocean Institute). Uchenye zapiski (Learned Transactions). Vol. III, Kitaiskii sbornik (Collection on China). Moscow, 1949.
Note: Numerous prewar serial publications of the Soviet Academy of Sciences relating to the Chinese Communist movement have not been located.
Alekseev, A. Komsomol Kitaia (Young Communists of China). Moscow, 1935. 47 pp.
Astafev, G. China from a Semi-Colony to a People's Democracy. Bombay, 1950. [Translation of an article in *Krizis kolonial'noi sistemy*; see below.]
Avarin, V. Bor'ba kitaiskogo naroda za svoiu natsional'nuiu nezavisimost' (Struggle of the Chinese People for National Independence). Moscow, 1945. [Text of a lecture delivered on March 14, 1945.]
—— Bor'ba za Tikhii okean (Struggle for the Pacific Ocean). Mos-

cow, 1947. 467 pp. [An account, principally, of Japanese-American rivalry in the Far East.]

Bakulin, A. V. Zapiski ob ukhanskom periode kitaiskoi revoliutsii (Notes concerning the Wuhan Period of the Chinese Revolution). Moscow, 1930. 288 pp. [A study of the Wuhan coalition of 1926–27 prepared by the Research Institute on China of the Communist Academy; includes texts of some original documents.]

Band, Claire, and William Band. Two Years with the Chinese Communists. New Haven, 1947. 247 pp.

Barandov, G. V. Kitaiskaia revoliutsiia i bor'ba kitaiskoi kompartii: posobie dlia propagandistov i agitatorov (The Chinese Revolution and the Struggle of the Chinese Communist Party: Textbook for Propagandists and Agitators). Moscow, 1934. [A popular study of the Chinese revolution through 1933.]

Belden, Jack. China Shakes the World. New York, 1949. 524 pp.

Beloff, Max. The Foreign Policy of Soviet Russia, 1929–1941. 2 vols. New York, 1947–49.

—— Soviet Policy in the Far East, 1944–1951. New York, 1953. 278 pp.

Bertram, James M. First Act in China: The Story of the Sian Mutiny. New York, 1938. 284 pp.

—— Unconquered: Journal of a Year's Adventure among the Fighting Peasants of North China. New York, 1939. 340 pp.

Bisson, T. A. Japan in China. New York, 1938. 417 pp.

Blofeld, John. Red China in Perspective. London, 1951. 242 pp.

Bor'ba za edinyi natsional'nyi anti-iaponskii front v Kitae: sbornik (Struggle for a United National Anti-Japanese Front in China: Collection). Moscow, 1937. 131 pp. [Articles by Mao Tse-tung, Wang Ming, and others relating to the united front policy in China between 1933 and 1937. This volume has been translated into English *as China: The March Toward Unity;* see below.]

Brandt, Conrad, Benjamin Schwartz, and John K. Fairbank. A Documentary History of Chinese Communism. Cambridge, Mass., 1952. 552 pp.

Brieux, Jean-Jacques. La Chine: du nationalisme au communisme. Paris, 1950. 446 pp.

Carlson, Evans F. Twin Stars of China. New York, 1940. 331 pp.

Chang Kuo-t'ao. Interview with H. R. Lieberman. Hong Kong, 1952. Manuscript summary at Hoover Library, Stanford University.

—— Interview with Robert C. North. Hong Kong, November 3, 1950. Manuscript summary at Hoover Library, Stanford University.

Chassin, Lionel Max. La Conquête de la Chine par Mao Tse-tung, 1945–1949. Paris, 1952. 244 pp.

Cheng Tien-fong. A History of Sino-Russian Relations. Washington, D.C., 1957. 389 pp. [A comprehensive study by a former Chinese Ambassador to Germany; strongly pro-Nationalist.]

Ch'en Shao-yü (alias Wang Ming). Old Intrigues in New Clothing. Chungking, 1939. 31 pp. New China Information Committee, Bulletin No. 7. [Includes two articles concerning friction between the Chinese Communists and the Kuomintang during the second year of the united front.]

—— A Summary of the Conference of the [Chinese] Politburo in March, 1938. Manuscript trans. by Wen Shun-chi from *K'ang-jih min-tsu t'ung-i chan-hsien chih-man,* Vol. III, Yenan, 1943, in Hoover Library, Stanford University.

Ch'en Shao-yü (alias Wang Ming) and Kan Sing [K'ang Sheng]. Revolutionary China Today. Moscow, 1934. 126 pp. [Addresses at the XIII Plenum of the ECCI, December, 1933.]

Chiang Kai-shek. Collected Wartime Messages of Generalissimo Chiang Kai-shek, 1937–1945. 2 vols. New York, 1946.

—— Soviet Russia in China: A Summing-up at Seventy. New York, 1957. 392 pp. [Chiang's version of Communist strategy in China from 1924 to 1949; an important source of information but with few primary materials and little supporting evidence for many of his claims.]

Chiang Mayling Soong (Mme. Chiang Kai-shek). Sian: A Coup d'Etat. Shanghai, 1937. 119 pp. [Includes also Chiang Kai-shek's diary version of the Sian episode of December, 1936.]

China Handbook, 1937–1943. New York, 1943. 951 pp.

China Handbook, 1937–1945. Rev. ed. (with 1946 supplement). New York, 1947. 862 pp.

China Handbook, 1950. New York, 1950. 799 pp.

China Presents Her Case to the United Nations. New York, 1949. 79 pp. *See also* United Nations.

China: The March Toward Unity. New York, 1937. See also *Bor'ba za edinyi natsional'nyi anti-iaponskii front.*

The Chinese Communist Movement. *See* United States Government, War Department.

Chou En-lai, Yen Chien-ying, and others. China's Resistance, 1937–1939. Chungking, 1940. 71 pp. New China Information Committee, Bulletin No. 12.

Chzen-lin [Cheng-lin?]. Dva goda geroicheskoi bor'by kitaiskogo naroda (Two Years of the Heroic Struggle of the Chinese People). Moscow, 1939. 44 pp.

—— Kitaiskii narod v bor'be protiv iaponskogo agressora (The Chinese People in the Struggle against the Japanese Aggressor). Moscow, 1938. 56 pp.

Communist Plottings in the Far East. Dairen, Manchuria, 1938. [A statement by the Information and Publicity Department of the Japanese-controlled South Manchurian Railway Co.]

Compton, Boyd. Mao's China: Party Reform Documents, 1942–1944. Seattle, 1952. 278 pp. [Includes, in addition to the author's comprehensive introduction, translations of the principal documents relating to the *cheng-feng* movement of 1942–44.]

Dallin, David J. Soviet Russia and the Far East. New Haven, 1948. 398 pp.

Davies, Joseph E. Mission to Moscow. New York, 1941. 659 pp.

Deane, John R. The Strange Alliance. New York, 1947. 344 pp.

Degras, Jane, ed. Soviet Documents on Foreign Policy. 3 vols. Oxford, 1951–53.

Den Chzhun-sia [Teng Chung-hsia]. Kratkaia istoriia profsoiuznogo dvizheniia v Kitae (Short History of the Trade Union Movement in China). Moscow, 1952. 309 pp. Trans. from a Chinese edition first published in Moscow in 1930.

Dimitrov, G. The United Front. New York, 1938. 287 pp.

Documents on the Problem of the Chinese Communist Party. Chungking, 1944. [Alleged evidence of Communist subversion, presented to the Central Executive Committee of the Kuomintang. September, 1943.]

ECCI, *see* XII plenum IKKI and XIII plenum IKKI.

Economic Reconstructions [*sic*] in North China Border Regions. Yenan, 1943.

Efimov, G. Ocherki po novoi i noveishei istorii Kitaia (Studies on the Recent and Contemporary History of China). Rev. ed. Moscow, 1951. 575 pp. [A comprehensive survey of Chinese history from the seventeenth century, with particular emphasis on the period 1911–49; includes bibliography.]

Elegant, Robert S. China's Red Masters. New York, 1951. 264 pp.

Emi Siao [Emi Hsiao?]. Kitai nepobedim: ocherki (China Invincible: Studies). Moscow, 1940. 108 pp. Trans. from Chinese.

—— Mao Tsze-dun, Chzhe De (Mao Tse-tung, Chu Teh). Moscow, 1939. 108 pp. Trans. from Chinese.

Epstein, Israel. The Unfinished Revolution in China. Boston, 1947. 422 pp.

Erenburg, G. B. Grazhdanskaia voina i natsional'no-osvoboditel'noe dvizhenie v Kitae v 1928–1936 godakh (The Civil War and National Liberation Movement in China in 1928–1936). Moscow, 1951. 22 pp. [Text of a public lecture delivered by Professor Erenburg in July, 1951.]

—— Ocherki natsional'no-osvoboditel'noi bor'by kitaiskogo naroda v noveishee vremia (Studies of the National Liberation Struggle of the Chinese People in Contemporary Times). Moscow, 1951. 238 pp. [History of the Chinese revolution since the Second World War.]

—— Sovetskii Kitai (Soviet China). Moscow, 1934. 142 pp. [A popular account of the soviet movement in China.]

Ermashev, N. Svet nad Kitaem (Light on China). Moscow, 1950. 459 pp. [A popular illustrated history of China from the middle of the nineteenth century.]

Feis, Herbert. The China Tangle. Princeton, N.J., 1953. 445 pp.

Fitzgerald, Charles P. Revolution in China. New York, 1952. 290 pp.

Foreign Relations of the United States, 1931–1942. *See* United States Government, Department of State.

Foreign Relations of the United States: Conferences at Malta and Yalta, 1945. *See* United States Government, Department of State.

Forman, Harrison. Report from Red China. New York, 1945. 250 pp. [Translated into Russian in Moscow in 1948 as *V novom Kitae.*]

Friction Aids Japan: Documents concerning Instances of Friction, 1939–1940. Chungking, 1940. 70 pp. New China Information Committee, Bulletin No. 14.

Fundamental Laws of the Chinese Soviet Republic. New York, 1934. 87 pp. [Includes an introduction by Bela Kun.]

Gelder, Stuart. The Chinese Communists. London, 1946. 290 pp. [Contains numerous wartime materials from the Chinese Communist areas; translated and edited by a former British correspondent in China.]

Glushakov, P. I. Kitai: ekonomichesko-geograficheskii ocherk (China: Economic-Geographic Study). Moscow, 1940. 112 pp.

The Guerrilla Front in North China. *See* United States Government, Office of Strategic Services.

Hidaka, Noboru. The Comintern's Intrigues in Manchoukuo. Dairen, Manchuria, 1940. 64 pp. [A Japanese view.]

Hsiang Ying, Yeh T'ing, and others. The Eighth Route and New

Fourth Armies. Chungking, 1939. New China Information Committee, Bulletin No. 10.

Hsu Yung Ying. A Survey of Shensi-Kansu-Ninghsia Border Region. New York, 1945. 159 pp. [A comprehensive study of this Communist area based on materials then available; mimeographed by the Institute of Pacific Relations.]

Hu Chiao-mu. Thirty Years of the Communist Party of China. London, 1951. 97 pp. *See also* Khu Tsiao-mu.

Iashnov, E. E. Ocherki kitaiskogo krestianskogo khoziaistva (Studies of the Chinese Peasant Economy). Moscow, 1935. [Critically reviewed in *Revoliutsionnyi vostok*, No. 3, 1936, p. 331.]

Institute of Pacific Relations, Hearings, *see* United States Government, Eighty-second Congress, First and Second Sessions.

International Military Tribunal for the Far East. Judgment. 2 vols. Tokyo, 1948. [Part B, chap. VI, is concerned with Japanese aggression against the USSR.]

Iolk, E. Kitaiskaia revoliutsiia (The Chinese Revolution). Moscow, 1931.

Isaacs, Harold R. The Tragedy of the Chinese Revolution. London, 1938. 501 pp. Rev. ed. Stanford, Calif., 1951. 382 pp.

Iurev, M.F. Istoricheskaia pobeda kitaiskogo naroda nad amerikanskim imperializmom i gomindanovskoi reaktsiei: 1945–1949 gg. (The Historic Victory of the Chinese People over American Imperialism and Kuomintang Reaction: 1945–1949). Moscow, 1950. 31 pp. [Text of a public lecture delivered by Professor Iurev in July, 1950.]

Ivin, A. Bor'ba za vlast sovetov: ocherki sovetskogo dvizheniia v Kitae (Struggle for Soviet Power: Studies of the Soviet Movement in China). Moscow, 1933.

—— Krasnye partizany v Kitae (Red Partisans in China). Moscow, 1930. 62 pp.

—— Ocherki partizanskogo dvizheniia v Kitae 1927–1930 gg. (Studies of the Partisan [Soviet] Movement in China in 1927–1930). Moscow, 1930. 107 pp.

James, M., and R. Doonping. Soviet China. New York, 1932. 31 pp.

Jones, F. C. Manchuria since 1931. New York, 1949. 256 pp.

Kapitsa, M. S. Sovetsko-kitaiskie otnosheniia v 1931–1945 gg. (Sino-Soviet Relations, 1931–1945). Moscow, 1956. 141 pp.

Karmen, P. God v Kitae (A Year in China). Moscow, 1941. 160 pp. [Notes of a Soviet correspondent in China.]

Kazanin, M. I. Ocherk ekonomicheskoi geografii Kitaia (Study of the Economic Geography of China). Moscow, 1935. 226 pp.

Ke Han [Ku Yuan?]. The Shansi-Hopei-Chahar Border Region, 1937–38. Chungking, 1940. New China Information Committee, Bulletin No. 8.

—— The Shansi-Hopei-Honan Border Region, Report for 1937–1939. Chungking, 1940. New China Information Committee, Bulletin No. 15.

Khamadan, Al. Vozhdi i geroi kitaiskogo naroda (Leaders and Heroes of the Chinese People). Moscow, 1936. 40 pp. [Biographies of Mao Tse-tung, Chu Teh, and others.]

Khu Tsiao-mu [Hu Chiao-mu]. Tridtsat' let kommunisticheskoi partii Kitaia (Thirty Years of the Communist Party of China). Moscow, 1952. 103 pp. Trans. from Chinese. [Official history of the Chinese Communist Party as of 1951.]

Note: The translations used in the present study are from the Russian edition of this volume, not the English edition (see above, Hu Chiao-mu). However, references to the English edition have been added in the footnotes.

Kitai: istoriia, ekonomika, geroicheskaia bor'ba za natsional'nuiu nezavisimost' (China: History, Economics, Heroic Struggle for National Independence). Moscow, 1940. 536 pp. [A symposium of articles on China published by the Institute of Oriental Studies of the Academy of Sciences; reviewed by Owen Lattimore in *Pacific Affairs,* No. 17, 1944, p. 81.]

Kitaiskii narod pobedit! sbornik statei i dokumentov (The Chinese People Will Win! Collection of Articles and Documents). Moscow, 1938. 109 pp. Trans. from Chinese. [Articles by Mao Tse-tung, Wang Ming, and other Chinese Communist leaders after the formation of the united front.]

Kogan, A. Natsional'no-osvoboditel'naia voina geroicheskogo kitaiskogo naroda (The War of National Liberation of the Heroic Chinese People). Moscow, 1939. 143 pp.

Kolonial'nye problemy. *See* Akademiia nauk, Institut mirovogo khoziaistva i mirovoi politiki.

Kommunisticheskii internatsional pered VII vsemirnym kongressom: materialy (The Communist International on the Eve of the VII World Congress: materials). Moscow, 1935. 604 pp. [An official Comintern document.]

Krizis kolonial'noi sistemy: natsional'no-osvoboditel'naia bor'ba narodov vostochnoi Azii (Crisis of the Colonial System: The Struggle for National Liberation of the Peoples of East Asia). Moscow, 1949. 289 pp.

Kuchumov, V. Ocherki po istorii kitaiskoi revoliutsii (Studies on the History of the Chinese Revolution). Moscow, 1934. 146 pp. [A review of the Chinese revolution through 1933 by a Soviet scholar.]

Kuomintang-Communist Negotiations. Yenan, 1945. [Chinese Communist view of truce negotiations with the Kuomintang in 1944–45.]

Liakhov, N. Kitaiskii narod v bor'be za svoiu nezavisimost' (The Chinese People in the Struggle for their Independence). Moscow, 1938, 47 pp.

Li Ang. The Red Stage. 1941. [A bitter account of Chinese Communism in the early 1930's by an ex-Party member; manuscript translation by Wen Shun-chi at the Hoover Library, Stanford University].

Lin Tsu-han (alias Lin Po-ch'u). Annual Report of the Shensi-Kangsu-Ninghsia Border Region Government for the Year 1943. Yenan, 1944. 41 pp.

Liu Shao-chi. Liquidate the Menshevist Ideology within the Party. Peking, 1951. Translation of an article first published in Yenan in July, 1943.

Madiar, L. Sovetskoe dvizhenie v Kitae (Soviet Movement in China). Moscow, 1931. 37 pp.

Manuil'skii, D. Z. The Communist Parties and the Crisis of Capitalism: Report to the Eleventh Plenum of the ECCI (March, 1931). Moscow, 1931. 121 pp.

—— Doklad delegatsii VKP(b) v IKKI na XVIII s"ezde VKP(b) (Report of the CPSU Delegation in the ECCI to the XVIII Congress of the CPSU). Moscow, 1939. 46 pp.

—— Otchetnyi doklad XVII s"ezdu VKP(b) o rabote delegatsii VKP(b) v IKKI (Report to the XVII Congress of the CPSU concerning the Work of the CPSU Delegation in the ECCI). Moscow, 1934. 45 pp.

—— The Revolutionary Crisis is Maturing. New York, 1934. 48 pp. Translation of his *Otchetnyi doklad XVII s"ezdu.*

—— The Work of the Seventh Congress of the Communist International. Moscow, 1936. 90 pp. [Manuil'skii's report to the Moscow organization of the CPSU, September 14, 1935.]

Mao Tse-tung. China and the Second Imperialist World War. Chungking, 1939. 50 pp. New China Information Committee, Bulletin No. 9. [Includes several of Mao's addresses and interviews between May and October, 1939, not in the *Selected Works.*]

—— China's New Democracy. Bombay, 1944. 47 pp. [First English text of Mao's treatise written in January, 1940, generally translated

"On the New Democracy." An American edition, with an introduction by Earl Browder, was published in New York in 1945.]

—— The Chinese Revolution and the Communist Party of China. New York, 1950. 20 pp. [Text of an important article allegedly written in December, 1939, but published officially only in 1949; now available in English in several editions.]

—— The Fight for a New China. New York, 1945. 80 pp. [Text of Mao's address to the Seventh Party Congress, April, 1945; normally translated "On Coalition Government."]

—— (Mao Tsze-dun). Izbrannye proizvedeniia (Selected Works). 4 vols. Moscow, 1952–53. Trans. from the four-volume Chinese edition of 1951–52. [Includes Mao's principal works, with commentaries, through August 9, 1945. The Russian and English editions are incomplete inasmuch as the fourth volume of each covers materials only through the third volume of the Chinese edition. An earlier and shorter Chinese edition of Mao's writings was published in Shantung in 1944; see Brandt, etc., *Documentary History,* p. 511.]

Note: The translations used in the present volume are from the Russian edition of Mao's *Selected Works*—the only one available to the writer at the time most of his research was in progress; references to the English edition (*q.v.*), however, have been added in the footnotes for the benefit of readers unfamiliar with Russian.

—— The New Stage. Chungking, 1938. 76 pp. [Mao's report to the Sixth Plenum of the Central Committee of the Chinese Communist Party, November, 1938.]

—— Red China. New York, 1934. 34 pp. [Text of Mao's address to the Second Congress of Chinese Soviets, February, 1934.]

—— Selected Works. 4 vols. New York, 1954–55. *See also* Mao Tse-tung, *Izbrannye proizvedeniia.*

Note: For other works by Mao translated into English see Brandt, etc., *Documentary History*; Compton, *Mao's China*; and Steiner, *Maoism.*

Mao Tsze-dun: biograficheskii ocherk (Mao Tse-tung: A Biographical Study). Moscow, 1939. 101 pp.

Maslennikov, V. Kitai: politiko-ekonomicheskii ocherk (China: Political-Economic Study). Moscow, 1946. 264 pp.

Melnalksnis, A. Zhizn' i bor'ba krestianstva Kitaia (The Life and Struggle of the Chinese Peasantry). Moscow, 1931(?). 48 pp.

Mezhdunarodnye otnosheniia na Dal'nem Vostoke, 1870–1945 (International Relations in the Far East, 1870–1945). Moscow, 1951. 790

pp. [A comprehensive survey prepared by the Soviet Academy of Sciences.]

Mif, Pavel'. Heroic China: Fifteen Years of the Communist Party of China. New York, 1937. 96 pp. [American edition of Mif, *15 let.*]

—— Kitaiskaia revoliutsiia (The Chinese Revolution). Moscow, 1932. 321 pp. [Account of the first decade of the Chinese Communist movement by a former Comintern agent in China.]

—— 15 let geroicheskoi bor'by (15 Years of Heroic Struggle). Moscow, 1936. 118 pp. [A comprehensive review of Chinese Communist policies and politics on the fifteenth anniversary of the Party's founding.]

Mikhailov, G., and M. Stepanov. Iapono-kitaiskaia bor'ba (Sino-Japanese Struggle). Moscow, 1941.

Mikhailov, K(?). Kak zhivet i boretsia Krasnaia Armiia Kitaia (How the Chinese Red Army Lives and Fights). Leningrad, 1934. 44 pp.

Military Situation in the Far East. *See* United States Government, Eighty-second Congress, First Session.

Moorad, George. Lost Peace in China. New York, 1949. 262 pp.

Moore, Harriet L. Soviet Far Eastern Policy, 1931–1945. Princeton, N.J., 1945. 284 pp.

Motylev, V. Tikhookeanskii uzel vtoroi imperialisticheskoi voiny (Pacific Ocean Nexus of the Second Imperalist War). Moscow, 1940. 200 pp.

Natsional'no-kolonial'nye problemy. *See* Akademiia nauk, Nauchno-issledovatel'skii institut po izucheniiu natsional'nykh i kolonial'nykh problem.

Nazi-Soviet Relations, 1939–1941. *See* United States Government, Department of State.

New China Information Committee. Bulletin. Nos 1–16. Chungking, 1938–40. [Pamphlets issued by the Chinese Communist Party during the early years of the united front; only Nos. 7–16 have been located.]

Nolde, John J. Chinese Communism: A Partial Bibliography. Ithaca, N.Y., 1949.

North, Robert C. Kuomintang and Chinese Communist Elites. Stanford, Calif., 1952. 130 pp.

—— Moscow and Chinese Communists. Stanford, Calif., 1953. 306 pp.

Novaia i noveishaia istoriia Kitaia: kratkii ocherk (The Recent and Contemporary History of China: Short Study). Moscow, 1950. 265 pp. Trans. from Chinese edition of 1949. [Articles by Chinese Communist writers on various aspects of the revolution.]

Noveishaia istoriia stran zarubezhnogo Vostoka (Contemporary History of the Countries of the Non-Soviet East). 2 vols. Moscow, 1955.

Ocherki po novoi istorii Kitaia (Studies of the Recent History of China). Moscow, 1956. 175 pp. Trans. from the Chinese. [Articles by a group of Chinese historians, covering the period from the Taiping Rebellion through the establishment of the Chinese People's Republic.]

Okkupatsiia Manchzhurii i bor'ba imperialistov: sbornik statei (The Occupation of Manchuria and the Struggle among the Imperialists: Collection of Articles). Moscow, 1932. 167 pp. [Materials relating to the Comintern's and the Chinese Communists' attitude to the Manchurian Incident; edited by Pavel' Mif, G. N. Voitinskii, and others.]

Okkupatsiia Manchzhurii i bor'ba kitaiskogo naroda (The Occupation of Manchuria and the Struggle of the Chinese People). Moscow, 1937. [Three articles by N. Fedorov and G. N. Voitinskii on the situation in Manchuria.]

Otsuka, Reizo. The Red Influence in China. Tokyo, 1936. 98 pp. [Materials prepared by the Japanese delegation to the Sixth Conference of the Institute of Pacific Relations held at Yosemite in August, 1936.]

Pashkova, M. K. Molodezh' Kitaia (The Youth of China). Moscow, 1940. 62 pp.

—— V bor'be za raskreposhchenie kitaiskogo naroda: ocherki rabochego dvizheniia v Kitae 1925–39 (In the Struggle for the Liberation of the Chinese People: Studies of the Working Movement in China, 1925–39). Moscow, 1939. 144 pp.

Payne, Robert. Journey to Red China. London, 1947. 198 pp.

Peng Teh-huai [P'eng Te-huai]. Unity and the Defense of North China. Chungking, 1940. New China Information Committee, Bulletin No. 13.

Programmnye dokumenty kitaiskikh sovetov: sbornik (Program Documents of the Chinese Soviets: Collection). Moscow, 1935. 102 pp. [Translations of key Chinese soviet documents with an instructive introduction by the Russian editors.]

Programmnye dokumenty kommunisticheskikh partii Vostoka (Program Documents of the Communist Parties of the East). Moscow, 1934. 293 pp. [Includes about 100 pages of translations of Chinese Communist documents dating from the early 1920s; introduction by Pavel' Mif.]

Räte-China: Dokumente der Chinesischen Revolution (Red China:

Documents of the Chinese Revolution). Moscow, 1933. See *Sovety v Kitae.*

Resolutions and Telegrams of the Sixth Plenum, Central Committee of the Communist Party of China (November 6, 1938). Hong Kong, 1938.

Rosinger, Lawrence K. China's Crisis. New York, 1945. 259 pp.

—— China's Wartime Politics, 1937–1944. Princeton, N.J., 1945. 133 pp.

Roy, M. N. Revolution and Counterrevolution in China. Calcutta, 1946. 689 pp. [A translation of the German edition of 1930 with two chapters added in 1939 and an epilogue in 1946. Roy was a Comintern agent in China in 1926–27.]

Safarov, G. I. The Far East Ablaze. London, 1933. 47 pp. Trans. from Russian. [English edition of *Ocherki po istorii Kitaia.*]

—— Ocherki po istorii Kitaia (Studies on the History of China). Moscow, 1933.

—— Problemy natsional'no-kolonial'noi revoliutsii (Problems of the National Colonial Revolution). Moscow, 1931. 286 pp.

Schwartz, Benjamin I. Chinese Communism and the Rise of Mao. Cambridge, Mass., 1951. 258 pp.

Selle, Earl Albert. Donald of China. New York, 1948. 374 pp. [Chapter XXIII gives an excellent account of the Sian episode of December, 1936.]

VII Congress of the Communist International; Abridged Stenographic Report of Proceedings. Moscow, 1939. 604 pp. [The best summary in English of the last Comintern Congress, August, 1935].

Shin' Shi-tsai [Sheng Shih-ts'ai]. Osnovnye ocherednye zadachi pravitel'stva (Basic Pending Tasks of the Government). Urumchi, 1940. Trans. from Chinese. [Articles and speeches relating to the united front by the Governor of Sinkiang.]

Simon, Paul. Le Mouvement Communiste en Chine des Origines à nos Jours. Paris, 1939. 263 pp. [A pro-Japanese account of the situation in China in the late 1930s.]

Smedley, Agnes. Battle Hymn of China. New York, 1943. 528 pp.

—— The Great Road: The Life and Times of Chu Teh. New York, 1956. 460 pp. [Based on notes taken during interviews with Chu Teh in 1937; edited and published posthumously.]

Snow, Edgar. Red Star over China. London, 1938. 464 pp.

Note: References throughout this study are to the Modern Library edition of 1944.

Sovety v Kitae; sbornik materialov i dokumentov (The Soviets in

China: A Collection of Materials and Documents). Moscow, 1933, 522 pp. 2d ed., 1934, 524 pp. [Documents concerning the Chinese soviet movement with a comprehensive introduction by J. Johanson and O. Taube, translated from the manuscript of *Räte-China,* cited above.]

The Soviet Worker Looks at the War. London, 1943. [Translations of a selection of articles appearing in the first twelve issues of *Voina i rabochii klass,* June-November, 1943.]

Stalin, I. V. Sochineniia (Works). 13 vols. Moscow, 1946–51; English ed., 13 vols., Moscow, 1952–55. [Stalin's major statements on China are in Vol. VIII, 1948, and Vol. IX, 1949.]

State Department Employee Loyalty Investigation. *See* United States Government, Eighty-first Congress.

Stein, Gunther. The Challenge of Red China. New York, 1945. 490 pp.

Steiner, H. Arthur, ed. Maoism: A Sourcebook. Los Angeles, 1952. 142 pp. Mimeographed. (Selected writings of Mao Tse-tung.]

Strany Tikhogo okeana (Countries of the Pacific Ocean). Moscow, 1942. 564 pp. [A reference work published by the Institute of the Soviet Encyclopedia; includes a 100-page description of China plus a comprehensive bibliography.]

Strategiia i taktika Kominterna v natsional'no-kolonial'noi revoliutsii, na primere Kitaia (Strategy and Tactics of the Comintern in the National-Colonial Revolution, for instance China). Moscow, 1934. 394 pp. [Documents concerning Comintern policy in China from 1925 through 1933; prepared by the Research Institute on China of the Communist Academy, edited by Pavel' Mif and with an introduction by Kara-Murza.]

The Strategy and Tactics of World Communism. *See* United States Government, Eightieth Congress.

Strong, Anna Louise. China's New Crisis. London, 1942. 62 pp.

—— The Chinese Conquer China. Garden City, N.Y., 1949. 275 pp.

Struggle for Peace and Democracy in the Northeast. Yenan, 1947. Manuscript translation at Hoover Library, Stanford University. [Materials relating to the Communist movement in Manchuria.]

Summary Records of the First Committee. *See* United Nations.

T'ang Leang-li. Suppressing Communist-Banditry in China. Shanghai, 1934. 131 pp. [An account based on Shanghai police records.]

Taylor, George E. The Struggle for North China. New York, 1940. 250 pp.

Teng Chung-hsia. *See* Den Chzhun-sia.

XIII plenum IKKI, stenograficheskii otchet (XIII Plenum of the ECCI [December, 1933], Stenographic Report). Moscow, 1934. 597 pp.

Tien-fong Cheng. *See* Cheng Tien-fong.

Trotsky, Leon. Problems of the Chinese Revolution. New York, 1932. 432 pp.

Trudy. *See* Akademiia nauk, Institut vostokovedeniia.

Tsin' Ben-li [Ch'in Peng-li?]. Istoriia ekonomicheskoi agressii amerikanskogo imperializma v Kitae (A History of the Economic Aggression of American Imperialism in China). Moscow, 1951. 122 pp. Trans. from Chinese.

XII plenum IKKI, stenograficheskii otchet. (XII Plenum of the ECCI [August 27–September 18, 1932], Stenographic Report). 3 vols. Moscow, 1933.

Uchenye zapiski. *See* Akademiia nauk, Institut vostokovedeniia and Tikhookeanskii institut.

United Nations, General Assembly, Fourth Session. Summary Records of the First Committee. Lake Success, N.Y., September 20–December 6, 1949. [A statement by the Chinese representative at the United Nations, Tingfu F. Tsiang; also published by the Chinese Delegation to the United Nations under the title *China Presents Her Case to the United Nations.*]

United States Government, Department of State. Foreign Relations of the United States, 1931–42. Washington, D.C., 1946–57.

—— Foreign Relations of the United States: Conferences at Malta and Yalta, 1945. Washington, D.C., 1955. 1,032 pp.

—— Nazi-Soviet Relations, 1939–1941. Washington, D.C., 1948. 362 pp.

—— United States Relations with China: With Special Reference to the Period 1944–1949. Washington, D.C., 1949. 1,054 pp.

United States Government, Eightieth Congress, Second Session, House Committee on Foreign Affairs. The Strategy and Tactics of World Communism. Washington, D.C., 1949. 105 pp. House Document No. 154. [Part III is a review of Communism in China.]

United States Government, Eighty-first Congress, Second Session, Committee on Foreign Relations, Subcommittee. State Department Employee Loyalty Investigation, Hearings. Washington, D.C., March-May, 1950.

United States Government, Eighty-second Congress, First Session, Committees on Armed Services and Foreign Relations. Military Situation in the Far East, Hearings. Washington, D.C., May-June, 1951. [The so-called "MacArthur Hearings".]

United States Government, Eighty-second Congress, First and Second Sessions, Committee on the Judiciary, Subcommittee to Investigate the Administration of the Internal Security Act and Other Internal Security Laws. Institute of Pacific Relations, Hearings. Washington, D.C., July, 1951–May, 1952.

United States Government, Office of Strategic Services, Research and Analysis Branch. The Guerrilla Front in North China. Washington, D.C., 1943. Report No. 892. Declassified.

United States Government, War Department, Military Intelligence Division. The Chinese Communist Movement. 3 vols. Washington, D.C., July 5, 1945. Declassified. [Published also in *Institute of Pacific Relations, Hearings* (Part 7A, Appendix II, 1952).]

United States Relations with China. *See* United States Government, Department of State.

Vagram, V. Kak zhivut i boriutsia rabochie Kitaia (How Chinese Workers Live and Struggle). Moscow, 1931.

Van der Sprenkel, Otto, Robert Guillian, and Michael Lindsay. New China: Three Views. London, 1950. 241 pp.

Vandervelde, Emile. A travers la Révolution Chinoise: soviets et Kuomintang. Paris, 1931. 240 pp. [A view of the Chinese revolution by a non-Stalinist Belgian Marxist.]

Vishniakova, V. V sovetskikh raionakh Kitaia (In the Soviet Regions of China). Moscow, 1931.

Vladimirova, T. Bor'ba za sovety v Kitae (The Struggle for Soviets in China). Moscow, 1931. 60 pp. [A popular account of the soviets in China in their early years.]

Voitinskii, G. N. Kitai i velikie derzhavy (China and the Great Powers). Moscow, 1947. 21 pp.

Voprosy kitaiskoi revoliutsii (Questions of the Chinese Revolution). Moscow, 1927. 240 pp. [Includes important statements by Stalin and Bukharin about the Chinese revolution in 1926 and early 1927.]

Vtoroi s"ezd kitaiskikh sovetov (Second Congress of the Chinese Soviets). Moscow, 1935. 191 pp. [Principal speeches and resolutions of the Second Soviet Congress of January, 1934, with an introduction by Wang Ming.]

Wales, Nym. Inside Red China. New York, 1939. 356 pp.

—— Red Dust: Autobiographies of Chinese Communists (As Told to Nym Wales). Palo Alto, Calif., 1952. 238 pp. [Includes an introduction by Robert C. North.]

Wang Chia-hsiang, Ch'en Po-ta, and Lo Fu [alias Chang Wen-t'ien].

Communists and the Three People's Principles. Chungking, 1940. New China Information Committee, Bulletin No. 16.

Wang Ming. *See* Ch'en Shao-yü.

Wan Yah-Kang. The Rise of Communism in China, 1920–1950. Hong Kong, 1952. 77 pp. Trans. from Chinese. [A hostile survey of Chinese Communism by a former war correspondent accredited to Yenan.]

Wei, Henry. China and Soviet Russia. New York, 1956. 379 pp.

Who Threatens China's Unity? Bombay, 1943. [Selected wartime articles translated from the Soviet press.]

Wilbur, C. Martin, and Julie Lien-ying How. Documents on Communism, Nationalism, and Soviet Advisors in China, 1918–1927. New York, 1956. 617 pp. [Based on papers seized in the 1927 raid on the Soviet Consulate in Peking.]

Wu, Aitchen K. China and the Soviet Union. New York, 1950. 434 pp.

Yakhontoff, Victor A. The Chinese Soviets. New York, 1934. 296 pp. [An account drawn chiefly from Russian materials then available.]

PERIODICALS

The following Soviet and Comintern periodicals have been examined for the period 1931–56. Unless otherwise indicated all issues were located, except for scattered gaps in some items during the early years of the Second World War.

Bibliograficheskii biulleten' zhurnal'nyk statei po zarubezhnomu i sovetskomu Vostoku (Bibliographic Bulletin of Periodical Articles on the Soviet and Non-Soviet East). [Published by the Research Association for the Study of National and Colonial Problems of the Communist Academy; dates and frequency unknown. Only scattered issues have been located.]

Bloknot propagandista (Propagandist's Notebook). See *Propagandist i agitator RKKA.*

Bol'shevik (Bolshevik). [Organ of the Central Committee of the CPSU, 1924–52; semimonthly. Renamed *Kommunist* in November, 1952.]

Bor'ba klassov (Struggle of the Classes). [Organ, first, of the Society of Historical Marxists of the Communist Academy, and, later, of the Institute of History of the Academy of Sciences, 1931–36; monthly. Renamed *Istoricheskii zhurnal* in 1936 and *Voprosy istorii* in 1945.]

Communist International. [English language edition of *Kommunisticheskii internatsional.* Called British edition, 1919–35, and American edition, 1935–39.]

Communist International. [Published in New York during 1940 and edited by Earl Browder; monthly. Not a translation of *Kommunisticheskii internatsional.*]

Inprecor. See *International Press Correspondence.*

International Press Correspondence. [Semiofficial organ of the Comintern, 1922–41; weekly. Published first in Vienna and Berlin and from 1933 to 1941 in London; renamed *World News and Views* in July, 1938.]

Istoricheskii zhurnal (Historical Journal). See *Bor'ba klassov.*

Izvestiia (News). [Organ of the Soviets of Workers' Deputies; daily. Consulted irregularly, 1931–46.]

Kommunist (Communist). See *Bol'shevik.*

Kommunisticheskii internatsional (Communist International). [Organ of the Executive Committee of the Communist International, 1919–43; weekly, later biweekly. The English, French, and German editions sometimes vary slightly from the Russian.]

Krasnaia nov' (Red Virgin Soil). [Literary journal, after 1934 organ of the Union of Soviet Writers, 1921–42; bimonthly, later monthly.]

Krasnyi internatsional profsoiuzov (Red International of Trade Unions, 1921–36; monthly.]

Mirovoe khoziaistvo i mirovaia politika (World Economy and World Politics). [Published by the Institute of World Economy and Politics of the Communist Academy, later the Academy of Sciences, 1926–45; monthly. Renamed *Voprosy ekonomiki* in 1945.]

New Times. [English edition of *Novoe vremia;* from June, 1945.]

Novoe vremia (New Times). See *Voina i rabochii klass.*

Partiinaia zhizn' (Party Life). See *Propagandist i agitator RKKA.*

Partiinoe stroitel'stvo (Party Construction). [Publication of the Central Committee of the CPSU, 1929–41; biweekly.]

Pravda (Truth). [Organ of the Central Committee of the CPSU; daily.]

Problemy Kitaia (Problems of China). [Published by the Research Institute on China, Institute of World Economy and Politics of the Communist Academy, irregular. Ceased publication about 1935; only scattered issues have been located.]

Propagandist i agitator RKKA (Red Army Propagandist and Agitator). [Official agitational organ of the Red Army, 1926(?)–46; bimonthly.

Called also *Bloknot propagandista* and *Propagandist RKKA;* combined with *Partiinoe stroitel'stvo* in 1946 to become *Partiinaia zhizn'*.]

Revoliutsiia i natsional'nosti (Revolution and the Nationalities). [Published by the Soviet of Nationality, 1930–37; monthly.]

Revoliutsionnyi vostok (The Revolutionary East). [Organ of the Research Institute for the Study of National and Colonial Problems of the Communist Academy, 1927–37; quarterly.]

Tikhii okean (Pacific Ocean). [Published by the Pacific Ocean Section of the Institute of World Economy and Politics of the Communist Academy, 1934–38; quarterly.]

Vlast' sovetov (Rule of the Soviets). [Organ of the Central Executive Committee of the Congress of Soviets, 1922–38; weekly.]

Voina i rabochii klass (War and the Working Class). [Perodical designed chiefly to fill the gap left by the termination of *Kommunisticheskii internatsional* in June, 1943; renamed *Novoe vremia* in June, 1945, published in English, French, German, and other editions.]

Voprosy ekonomiki (Questions of Economics). See *Mirovoe khoziaistvo i mirovaia politika.*

Voprosy istorii (Question of History). See *Bor'ba klassov.*

World News and Views. See *International Press Correspondence.*

INDEX